Augusta Jane Evans

Altars of Sacrifice

Second Edition

Augusta Jane Evans

Altars of Sacrifice
Second Edition

ISBN/EAN: 9783743358140

Manufactured in Europe, USA, Canada, Australia, Japa

Cover: Foto ©ninafisch / pixelio.de

Manufactured and distributed by brebook publishing software (www.brebook.com)

Augusta Jane Evans

Altars of Sacrifice

OR,

ALTARS OF SACRIFICE.

BY THE AUTHOR OF "BEULAH."

"We have all to be laid upon an altar; we have all, as it were, to be subjected to the action of fire."—MELVILL.

SECOND EDITION.

RICHMOND:
WEST & JOHNSTON, 145 MAIN STREET.
1864.

Evans & Cogswell, Printers,
Columbia, S. C.

TO THE
ARMY OF THE SOUTHERN CONFEDERACY,
WHO HAVE DELIVERED THE SOUTH FROM DESPOTISM, AND WHO HAVE WON FOR GENERATIONS YET UNBORN THE PRECIOUS GUERDON OF CONSTITUTIONAL REPUBLICAN LIBERTY:

TO THIS VAST LEGION OF HONOR,
WHETHER LIMPING ON CRUTCHES THROUGH
THE LAND THEY HAVE SAVED AND IMMORTALIZED,
OR SURVIVING UNINJURED TO SHARE THE BLESSINGS THEIR
UNEXAMPLED HEROISM BOUGHT, OR SLEEPING DREAMLESSLY IN NAMELESS
MARTYR-GRAVES ON HALLOWED BATTLE-FIELDS WHOSE
HISTORIC MEMORY SHALL PERISH ONLY WITH
THE REMNANTS OF OUR LANGUAGE,
THESE PAGES ARE
GRATEFULLY AND REVERENTLY DEDICATED
BY ONE WHO, ALTHOUGH DEBARRED FROM THE
DANGERS AND DEATHLESS GLORY OF THE "TENTED FIELD,"
WOULD FAIN OFFER A WOMAN'S INADEQUATE TRIBUTE TO THE NOBLE
PATRIOTISM AND SUBLIME SELF-ABNEGATION OF HER
DEAR AND DEVOTED COUNTRYMEN.

MACARIA.

CHAPTER I.

The town-clock was on the last stroke of twelve, the solitary candle measured but two inches from its socket, and, as the summer wind rushed through the half-closed shutters, the melted tallow dripped slowly into the brightly-burnished brazen candlestick. The flickering light fell upon grim battalions of figures marshalled on the long blue-lined pages of a ledger, and flashed fitfully on the face of the accountant as he bent over his work. In these latter days of physical degeneration, such athletic frames as his are rarely seen among the youth of our land. Sixteen years growth had given him unusual height and remarkable breadth of chest, and it was difficult to realize that the stature of manhood had been attained by a mere boy in years. A gray suit (evidently home-made), of rather coarse texture, bespoke poverty; and, owing to the oppressive heat of the atmosphere, the coat was thrown partially off. He wore no vest, and the loosely-tied black ribbon suffered the snowy white collar to fall away from the throat and expose its well-turned outline. The head was large, but faultlessly proportioned, and the thick black hair, cut short and clinging to the temples, added to its massiveness. The lofty forehead, white and smooth; the somewhat heavy brows, matching the hue of the hair; the straight, finely-formed nose, with its delicate but clearly-defined nostril, and full firm lips, unshaded by mustache, combined to render the face one of uncommon beauty. Yet, as he sat absorbed by his figures, there was nothing prepossessing or winning in his appearance; for though you could not carp at the moulding of his features, you involuntarily shrank from the prematurely grave, nay, austere expression which seemed habitual to them. He looked just what he was—youthful in months and years, but old in trials, sorrows, and labors; and to one who analyzed his countenance, the conviction was inevitable that his will was gigantic, his ambition unbounded, his intellect wonderfully acute and powerful. It is always sad to remark in young faces the absence of that beaming enthusiasm which only a joyous heart imparts, and though in this instance there was nothing dark or sinister, you could not fail to be awed by the cold, dauntless resolution which said so plainly, "I struggle, and shall conquer. I shall mount, though the world defy me." Although he had labored since dawn, there was no drooping of the muscular frame, no symptom of fatigue, save in the absolute colorlessness of his face. Firm, as some brazen monument on its pedestal he sat and worked on, one hand wielding the pen, the other holding down the leaves which fluttered, now and then, as the breeze passed over them.

"Russell, do you know it is midnight?"

He frowned, and answered without looking up—

"Yes."

"How much longer will you sit up?"

"Till I finish my work."

The speaker stood on the threshold, leaning against the door-facing, and, after waiting a few moments, softly crossed the room and put her hand on the back of his chair. She was two years his junior, and though evidently the victim of recent and severe illness, even in her feebleness she was singularly like him. Her presence seemed to annoy him, for he turned round and said hastily:

"Electra, go to bed. I told you good-night three hours ago."

She stood still, but silent.

"What do you want?"

"Nothing."

He wrote on for some ten minutes longer, then closed the ledger and put it aside. The candle had burned low; he took a fresh one from the drawer of the table, and, after lighting it, drew a Latin dictionary near to him, opened a worn copy of Horace, and began to study. Quiet as his own shadow stood the fragile girl behind his chair, but as she watched him a heavy sigh escaped her. Once more he looked up with a finger still in the dictionary, and asked impatiently:

"Why on earth don't you go to sleep?"

"I can't sleep; I have tried my best."

"Are you sick again, my poor little cousin?"

He stretched out his arm and drew her close to him.

"No; but I know you are up, hard at work, and it keeps me awake. If you would only let me help you."

"But you can't help me; I have told you so time and again. You only interrupt and hinder me."

She colored, and bit her lip; then answered, sorrowfully:

"If I thought I should be weak and sickly all my life, I would rather die at once and burden you and Auntie no longer."

"Electra, who told you that you burdened me?"

"Oh, Russell! don't I know how hard you have to work; and how difficult it is for you to get even bread and clothes. Don't I see how Auntie labors day after day, and month after month? You are good and kind, but does that prevent my feeling the truth, that you are working for me too? If I could only help you in some way." She knelt down by his chair and leaned her head on his knee, holding his hands between both hers.

"Electra, you do help me; all day long when I am at the store your face haunts me, strengthens me: I feel that I am striving to give you comforts, and when at night you meet me at the gate, I am repaid for all I have done. You must put this idea out of your head, little one; it is altogether a mistake. Do you hear what I say? Get up and go to sleep like a good child, or you will have another wretched headache to-morrow, and can't bring me my lunch."

He lifted her from the floor and kissed her hastily. She raised her arms as if to wind them about his neck, but his grave face gave her no encouragement; and turning away she retired to her room, with hot tears rolling over her cheeks. Russell had scarcely read half a dozen lines after his cousin's departure when a soft hand swept back the locks of hair on his forehead and wiped away the heavy drops that moistened them.

"My son, you promised me you would not sit up late to-night."

"Well, Mother, I have almost finished. Remember the nights are very short now, and twelve o'clock comes early."

"The better reason that you should not be up so late. My son, I am afraid you will ruin your health by this unremitting application."

"Why—look at me. I am as strong as an Athlete of old." He shook his limbs and smiled, proud of his great physical strength.

"True, Russell; but, robust as you are, you can not stand such toil without detriment. Put up your books."

"Not yet; I have more laid out, and you know I invariably finish all I set apart to do. But, Mother, your hand is hot; you are not well."

He raised the thin hand and pressed it to his lips.

"A mere headache, nothing more. Mr. Clark was here to-day; he is very impatient about the rent; I told him we were doing all we could, and thought that by September we should be able to pay the whole. He spoke of going to see you, which I urged him not to do, as you were exerting yourself to the utmost."

She scanned his face while she spoke, and noted the compression of his mouth. He knew she watched him, and answered with a forced smile:

"Yes, he came to the store this morning. I told him we had been very unfortunate this year in losing our only servant; and that sickness had forced us to incur more expense than usual. However, I drew fifty dollars and paid him all I could. True, I anticipated my dues, but Mr. Watson gave me permission. So for the present you need not worry about rent."

"What is the amount of that grocery-bill you would not let me see last week?"

"My dear mother, do not trouble yourself with these little matters; the grocery-bill will very soon be paid. I have arranged with Mr. Hill to keep his books at night, and, therefore, you may be easy. Trust all to me, Mother; only take care of your dear self, and I ask no more."

"Oh, Russell! my son, my son!"

She had drawn a chair near him, and now laid her head on his shoulder, while tears dropped on his hand. He had not seen her so unnerved for years; and as he looked down on her grief-stained, yet resigned face, his countenance underwent a marvellous change; and, folding his arms about her, he kissed her pale, thin cheek repeatedly.

"Mother, it is not like you to repine in this way; you who have suffered and endured so much must not despond, when, after a long, starless night, the day begins to dawn."

"I fear 'it dawns in clouds and heralds only storms.' For myself I care not, but for you, Russell—my pride, my only hope, my brave boy! it is for you that I suffer. I have been thinking to-night that this is a doomed place for you, and that if we could only save money enough to go to California, you might take the position you merit; for there none would know of the blight which fell upon you: none could look on your brow and dream it seemed sullied. Here you have such bitter prejudice to combat; such gross injustice heaped upon you."

He lifted his mother's head from his bosom and rose, with a haughty, defiant smile on his lip.

"Not so; I will stay here and live down their hate. Mark me, Mother, I will live it down, so surely as I am Russell Aubrey, the despised son of a ——. Let them taunt and sneer! let them rake up the smouldering ashes of the miserable Past to fling in my face and blind me; let them, and welcome! I will gather up these same ashes, dry and bitter, and hide them with sacred zeal in a golden urn; and I will wreathe it with chaplets that never die. Aye! the Phœnix lies now in dust, but one day the name of Aubrey will rise in more than pristine glory; and mine be the hand to resurrect its ancient splendor. '*Mens cujusque is est quisque!*' Menzikoff, who ruled the councils of the Kremlin in its palmiest days, once sold pies for a living in the streets of Moscow. '*Miens cujusque is est quisque!*' I will vow no man thanks; none shall point to me and say, 'He was drowning in the black, seething gulf of social prejudice, and I held out a finger, and clinging to it he lived.' Not so! dollar for dollar, service for service, I will pay as I rise. I scorn to ask favors; I am glad none are tendered me. I have a grim satisfaction in knowing that I owe no human being a kindness, save you, my precious mother. Go to California! not I! not I! In this state will I work and conquer; here, right here, I will plant my feet upon the necks of those that now strive to grind me to the dust. I swore it over my father's coffin! I tell you, Mother, I will trample out the stigma, for, thank God! 'there is no free-trade measure which will ever lower the price of brains.'"

"Hush, Russell; you must subdue your fierce temper; you must! you must! remember it was this ungovernable rage which brought disgrace upon your young, innocent head. Oh! it grieves me, my son, to see how bitter you have grown; it wrings my heart to hear you challenge Fate, as you so often do. Once you were gentle and forgiving; now scorn and defiance rule you."

"I am not fierce; I am not in a rage. Lay your hand on my temples—here on my wrist; count the pulse, slow and steady, Mother, as your own. I am not vindictive; am no Indian to bear about a secret revenge, ready to consummate it at the first propitious moment. If I should meet the judge and jury who doomed my father to the gallows, I think I would serve them if they needed aid. But I am proud; I inherited my nature; I writhe, yes, Mother, writhe under the treatment I constantly receive. I defy Fate? Well, suppose I do: she has done her worst. I have no quarrel with her for the past; but I will conquer her in the future. I am not bitter; would I not give my life for you? Are you not dearer to me than my own soul? Take back your words, they hurt me; don't tell me that I grieve you, Mother."

His voice faltered an instant, and he put his arms tenderly round the drooping form.

"We have troubles enough, my son, without dwelling upon what is past and irremediable. So long as you seem cheerful, I am content. I know that God will not lay more on me than I can bear: 'as my day, so shall my strength be.' Thy will be done, oh! my God."

There was a brief pause, and Russell Aubrey passed his hand over his eyes and dashed off a tear. His mother watched him, and said cautiously:

"Have you noticed that my eyes are rapidly growing worse?"

"Yes, Mother; I have been anxious for some weeks."

"You know it all, then?"

"Yes, Mother."

"I shall not murmur; I have become resigned at last; though for many weeks I have wrestled for strength, for patience. It was so exceedingly bitter to know that the time drew near when I should see you no more; to feel that I should stretch out my hands to you, and lean on you, and yet look no longer on the dear face of my child, my boy, my all. But my prayers were heard; the sting has passed away, and I am resigned. I am glad we have spoken of it; now my mind is calmer, and I can sleep. Good-night, my son."

She pressed the customary good-night kiss on his lips, and left him. He closed the dictionary, leaned his elbow on the table, and rested his head on his hand. His piercing black eyes were fixed gloomily on the floor, and now and then his broad chest heaved as dark and painful thoughts crowded up.

Mrs. Aubrey was the only daughter of wealthy and ambitious parents, who refused to sanction her marriage with the object of her choice, and threatened to disinherit her if she persisted in her obstinate course. Mr. Aubrey was poor, but honest, highly cultivated, and, in every sense of that much-abused word, a gentleman. His poverty was not to be forgiven, however, and when the daughter left her father's roof, and wedded the man whom her parents detested, the die was cast; she was banished for ever from a home of affluence, and found that she had indeed forfeited her fortune. For this she was prepared, and bore it bravely; but ere long severer trials came upon her. Unfortunately, her husband's temper was fierce and ungovernable; and pecuniary embarrassments rarely have the effect of sweetening such. He removed to an inland town and embarked in mercantile pursuits; but misfortune followed him, and reverses came thick and fast. One miserable day, when from early morning everything had gone wrong, an importunate creditor, of wealth and great influence in the community, chafed at Mr. Aubrey's tardiness in repaying some trifling sum, proceeded to taunt and insult him most unwisely. Stung to madness, the wretched man resented the insults; a struggle ensued, and at its close Mr. Aubrey stood over the corpse of the creditor. There was no mode of escape, and the arm of the law consigned him to prison. During the tedious weeks that elapsed before the trial, his devoted wife strove to cheer and encourage him by every effort which one human being can make for another. Russell was about eleven years of age, and, boy though he was, realized most fully the horrors of his parent's situation. The days of the trial came at last; but he had surrendered himself to the demon Rage—had taken the life of a fellow-creature; what could legal skill accomplish? The affair produced great and continued excitement; the murdered man had been exceedingly popular, and the sympathies of the citizens were enlisted in behalf of his family. Although clearly a case of manslaughter only, the violent prejudice of the community and the exertions of influential friends so biassed the jury that, to the astonishment of the counsel on both sides, the cry of "blood for blood" went out from that crowded court-room, and, in defiance of precedent, Mr. Aubrey was unjustly sentenced to be hung. When the verdict was pronounced Russell placed his insensible mother on a couch, from which it seemed probable she would never rise. But there is an astonishing amount of endurance in even a feeble woman's frame, and after a time she went about her house once more, doing her duty to her child and learning to "suffer and grow strong." Fate had ordained, however, that Russell's father should not die upon the gallows; and soon after the verdict was pronounced, when all Mrs. Aubrey's efforts to procure a pardon had proved unavailing, the proud and desperate man, in the solitude of his cell, with no eye but Jehovah's to witness the awful deed, the consummation of his woes, took his own life—with the aid of a lancet launched his guilty soul into eternity. On the floor of the cell was found a blurred sheet, sprinkled with blood, directed to his wife, bidding her farewell, and committing her and her boy to the care of an outraged and insulted God. Such was the legacy of shame which Russell inherited; was it any marvel that at sixteen that boy had lived ages of sorrow? Mrs. Aubrey found her husband's financial affairs so involved that she relinquished the hope of retaining the little she possessed, and retired to a small cottage on the outskirts of the town, where she endeavored to support herself and the two dependent on her by taking in sewing.

Electra Grey was the orphan child of Mr. Aubrey's only sister, who dying in poverty bequeathed the infant to her brother. He had loved her as well as his own Russell; and his wife, who cradled her in her arms and taught her to walk by clinging to her finger, would almost as soon have parted with her son as the little Electra. For five years the widow had toiled by midnight-lamps to feed these two; now oppressed nature rebelled, the long overtaxed eyes refused to perform their office; filmy cataracts stole over them, veiling their sadness and their unshed tears—blindness was creeping on. At his father's death Russell was forced to quit school, and with some difficulty he succeeded in obtaining a situation in a large dry-goods store, where his labors were onerous in the extreme and his wages a mere pittance. To domineer over those whom adverse fortune places under their control is by no means uncommon among ignorant and selfish men, whose industry has acquired independence, and though Russell's employer, Mr. Watson, shrank from committing a gross wrong, and prided himself on his scrupulous honesty, still his narrow mind and penurious habits strangled every generous impulse, and, without being absolutely cruel or unprincipled, he contrived to gall the boy's proud spirit and render his position one of almost purgatorial severity.

The machinery of human will is occult and complicated; very few rigidly analyze their actions and discern the motives that impel them, and if any one had told Jacob Watson that Envy was the secret spring which prompted his unfriendly course toward his young clerk he would probably have indignantly denied the accusation. The blessing of an education had been withheld from him; he grew up illiterate and devoid of refinement; fortune favored him, he amassed wealth, and determined that his children should enjoy every advantage which money could command. His eldest son was just Russell's age, had been sent to various schools from his infancy, was indolent, self-indulgent, and thoroughly dissipated. Having been a second time expelled from school for most disgraceful misdemeanors, he lounged away his time about the store, or passed it still more disreputably with reckless companions.

The daily contrast presented by Cecil and Russell irritated the father, and hence his settled dislike of the latter. The faithful discharge of duty on the part of the clerk afforded no plausible occasion for invective; he felt that he was narrowly watched, and resolved to give no ground for fault-finding; yet during the long summer days, when the intense heat prevented customers from thronging the store, and there was nothing to be done, when Russell, knowing that the books were written up and the counters free from goods, took his Latin grammar and improved every leisure half-hour, he was not ignorant of the fact that an angry scowl darkened his employer's visage, and understood why he was constantly interrupted to perform most unnecessary labors. But in the same proportion that obstacles thickened his energy and resolution doubled; and herein one human soul differs from another, in strength of will which furnishes powers of endurance. What the day denied he reclaimed from night, and succeeded in acquiring a tolerable knowledge of Greek, besides reading several Latin books. Finding that his small salary was inadequate, now that his mother's failing sight prevented her from accomplishing the usual amount of sewing, he solicited and obtained permission to keep an additional set of books for the grocer who furnished his family with provisions, though by this arrangement few hours remained for necessary sleep. The protracted illness and death of an aged and faithful servant, together with Electra's tedious sickness, bringing the extra expense of medical aid, had prevented the prompt payment of rent due for the three-roomed cottage, and Russell was compelled to ask for a portion of his salary in advance. His mother little dreamed of the struggle which took place in his heart ere he could force himself to make the request, and he carefully concealed from her the fact that, at the moment of receiving the money, he laid in Mr. Watson's hand, by way of pawn, the only article of any value which he possessed—the watch his father had always worn, and which the coroner took from the vest-pocket of the dead, dabbled with blood. The gold chain had been sold long before, and the son wore it attached to a simple black ribbon. His employer received the watch, locked it in the iron safe, and Russell fastened a small weight to the ribbon, and kept it around his neck that his mother might not suspect the truth. It chanced that Cecil stood near at the time; he saw the watch deposited in the safe, whistled a tune, fingered his own gold repeater, and walked away.

Such was Russell Aubrey's history; such his situation at the beginning of his seventeenth year. Have I a reader whose fond father lavishes on him princely advantages, whose shelves are filled with valuable but unread volumes, whose pockets are supplied with more than necessary money, and who yet saunters through the precious season of youth, failing utterly to appreciate his privileges? Let him look into that little room where Russell sits, pale, wearied, but unbending, pondering his dark future, planning to protect his mother from want and racking his brain for some feasible method of procuring such books as he absolutely needs; books which his eager hungry eyes linger on as he passes the bookstore every morning going to his work. Oh, young reader! if such I have, look at him struggling with adversity as a strong swimmer with the murderous waves that lash him, and, contrasting your own fortunate position, shake off the inertia that clings to you tenaciously as Sinbad's burden, and go to work earnestly and bravely, thanking God for the aids he has given you.

"Disappointment's dry and bitter root,
Envy's harsh berries, and the choking pool
Of the world's scorn, are the right mother-milk
To the tough hearts that pioneer their kind."

CHAPTER II.

"Irene, your father will be displeased if he sees you in that plight."

"Pray, what is wrong about me now? You seem to glory in finding fault. What is the matter with my 'plight,' as you call it?"

"You know very well your father can't bear to see you carrying your own satchel and basket to school. He ordered Martha to take them every morning and evening, but she says you will not let her carry them. It is just sheer obstinacy in you."

"There it is again! because I don't choose to be petted like a baby or made a wax-doll of, it is set down to obstinacy, as if I had the temper of a heathen. See here, Aunt Margaret, I am tired of having Martha tramping eternally at my heels as though I were a two-year-old child. There is no reason in her walking after me when I am strong enough to carry my own books, and I don't intend she shall do it any longer."

"But, Irene, your father is too proud to have you trudging along the road like any other beggar, with your books in one arm and a basket swinging on the other. Just suppose the Carters or the Harrisses should meet you? Dear me! they would hardly believe you belonged to a wealthy, aristocratic family like the Huntingdons. Child, I never carried my own dinner to school in my life."

"And I expect that is exactly the reason why you are for ever complaining, and scarcely see one well day in the three hundred and sixty-five. As to what people think, I don't care a cent; as to whether my ancestors did or did not carry their lunch in their own aristocratic hands is a matter of no consequence whatever. I despise all this ridiculous nonsense about aristocracy of family, and I mean to do as I please. I thought that really well-bred persons of high standing and birth could afford to be silent on the subject, and that only *parvenus*—coarse, vulgar people with a little money—put on those kinds of airs, and pretended to be shocked at what they had been accustomed to in early life."

"I do not see where you get such plebeian ideas; you positively make me ashamed of you sometimes, when fashionable, genteel persons come to the house. There is such a want of refinement in your notions. You are anything but a Huntingdon."

"I am what God made me, Aunt Margaret. If the Huntingdons stand high, it is because they won distinction by their own efforts; I don't want the stepping-stones of my dead ancestry; people must judge me for myself, not from what my grandmother was."

Irene Huntingdon stood on the marble steps of her palatial home, and talked with the maiden aunt who governed her father's household. The girl was about fourteen, tall for her age, straight, finely-formed, slender. The broad straw hat shaded, but by no means concealed, her features, and as she looked up at her aunt the sunshine fell upon a face of extraordinary beauty, such as is rarely seen save in the idealized heads of the old masters. Her hair was of an uncommon shade, neither auburn nor brown, but between gold and bronze; and as the sun shone on it the rippling waves flashed until their burnished glory seemed a very aureola. It was thick and curling; she wore it parted on her pale, polished forehead, and it hung around her like a gilded veil. The face was an oval; you might measure it by all the rules of art and no imperfection could be found, unless the height of the brow were considered out of proportion. The nose was delicate and clearly cut, and in outline resembled that in the antique medals of Olympias, the wife of Philip of Macedonia. The upper lip was short, and curved like a bow; the lower, thin, firm, and straight. Her eyes were strangely, marvellously beautiful; they were larger than usual, and of that rare shade of purplish blue which borders the white velvet petals of a clematis. When the eyes were uplifted, as on this occasion, long curling lashes of the bronze hue of her hair rested against her brow. Save the scarlet lines which marked her lips, her face was of that clear colorlessness which can be likened only to the purest ivory. Though there was an utter absence of the rosy hue of health, the transparency of the complexion seemed characteristic of her type, and precluded all thought of disease. People are powerfully attracted by beauty, either of form, color, or a combination of both; and it frequently happens that something of pain mingles with the sensation of pleasure thus excited. Now, whether it be that this arises from a vague apprehension engendered by the evanescent nature of all sublunary things, or from the inability of earthly types to satisfy the divine ideal which the soul enshrines, I shall not here attempt to decide; but those who examined Irene's countenance were fully conscious of this complex emotion, and strangers who passed her in the street felt intuitively that a noble, unsullied soul looked out at them from the deep, calm, thoughtful eyes. Miss Margaret muttered something inaudible in reply to her last remark, and Irene walked on to school. Her father's residence was about a mile from the town, but the winding road rendered the walk somewhat longer; and on one side of this road stood the small house occupied by Mrs. Aubrey. As Irene approached it she saw Electra Grey coming from the opposite direction, and at the cottage-gate they met. Both paused; Irene held out her hand cordially—

"Good-morning. I have not seen you for a fortnight. I thought you were coming to school again as soon as you were strong enough?"

"No; I am not going back to school."

"Why?"

"Because Auntie can't afford to send me any longer. You know her eyes are growing worse every day, and she is not able to take in sewing as she used to do. I am sorry; but it can't be helped."

"How do you know it can't be helped? Russell told me he thought she had cataracts on her eyes, and they can be removed."

"Perhaps so, if we had the means of consulting that celebrated physician in New Orleans. Money removes a great many things, Irie, but unfortunately we have n't it."

"The trip would not cost much; suppose you speak to Russell about it."

"Much or little, it will require more than we can possibly spare. Everything is so high we can barely live as it is. But I must go in, my aunt is waiting for me."

"Where have you been so early, Electra? I hope you will not think me impertinent in asking such a question."

"I carried this waiter full of bouquets to Mr. Carter's. There is to be a grand dinner-party there to-day, and Auntie promised as many flowers as she could furnish. However, bouquets pay poorly. Irie, wait one minute; I have a little border of mignonette all my own, and I should like to give you a spray."

She hurried into the garden, and returning with a few delicate sprigs, fastened one in her friend's belt and the remainder in the ribbon on her hat.

"Thank you, Electra; who told you that I love mignonette so well? It will not do for you to stay away from school; I miss you in my class, and, besides, you are losing too much time. Something should be done, Electra. Good-by."

They shook hands, and Irene walked on.

"Something should be done," she repeated, looking down fixedly yet vacantly at the sandy road. Soon the brick walls of the Academy rose grim and uninviting, and taking her place at the desk she applied herself to her books. When school was dismissed in the afternoon, instead of returning home as usual, she walked down the principal street, entered Mr. Watson's store, and put her books on the counter. It happened that the proprietor stood near the front-door, and he came forward instantly to wait upon her.

"Ah, Miss Irene! happy to see you. What shall I have the pleasure of showing you?"

"Russell Aubrey, if you please."

The merchant stared, and she added:

"I want some kid gauntlets, but Russell can get them for me."

The young clerk stood at the desk in the rear of the store, with his back toward the counter; and Mr. Watson called out:

"Here, Aubrey, some kid gauntlets for this young lady."

He laid down his pen, and taking a box of gloves from the shelves placed it on the counter before her. He had not noticed her particularly, and when she pushed back her hat and looked up at him he started slightly.

"Good-evening, Miss Huntingdon. What number do you wish?"

Perhaps it was from the heat of the day, or

from stooping over his desk, or perhaps it was from something else, but his cheek was flushed, and gradually it grew pale again.

"Russell, I want to speak to you about Electra. She ought to be at school, you know."

"Yes."

"But she says your mother can't afford the expense."

"Just now she can not; next year things will be better."

"What is the tuition for her?"

"Five dollars a month."

"Is that all?"

He selected a delicate fawn-colored pair of gloves and laid them before her, while a faint smile passed over his face.

"Russell, has anything happened?"

"What do you mean?"

"What is troubling you so?"

"Nothing more than usual. Do those gloves suit you?"

"Yes, they will fit me, I believe." She looked at him very intently.

He met her gaze steadily, and for an instant his face brightened; then she said abruptly:

"Your mother's eyes are worse?"

"Yes, much worse."

"Have you consulted Dr. Arnold about them?"

"He says he can do nothing for her."

"How much would it cost to take her to New Orleans and have that celebrated oculist examine them?"

"More than we can afford just now; at least two hundred dollars."

"Oh, Russell! that is not much. Would not Mr. Watson lend you that little?"

"I shall not ask him."

"Not even to restore your mother's sight?"

"Not to buy my own life. Besides, the experiment is a doubtful one."

"Still it is worth making."

"Yes, under different circumstances it certainly would be."

"Have you talked to Mr. Campbell about it?"

"No, because it is useless to discuss the matter."

"It would be dangerous to go to New Orleans now, I suppose?"

"October or November would be better."

Again she looked at him very earnestly, then stretched out her little hand.

"Good-by, Russell; I wish I could do something to help you, to make you less sorrowful."

He held the slight waxen fingers, and his mouth trembled as he answered:

"Thank you, Miss Huntingdon. I am not sorrowful, but my path in life is not quite so flowery as yours."

"I wish you would not call me 'Miss Huntingdon,' in that stiff, far-off way, as if we were not friends. Or maybe it is a hint that you desire me to address you as Mr. Aubrey. It sounds strange, unnatural, to say anything but Russell."

She gathered up her books, took the gloves, and went slowly homeward, and Russell returned to his desk with a light in his eyes which, for the remainder of the day, nothing could quench. As Irene ascended the long hill on which Mr. Huntingdon's residence stood she saw her father's buggy at the door, and as she approached the steps he came out, drawing on his gloves.

"You are late, Irene. What kept you?"

"I have been shopping a little. Are you going to ride? Take me with you."

"Going to dine at Mr. Carter's."

"Why, the sun is almost down now. What time will you come home? I want to ask you something."

"Not till long after you are asleep."

He took his seat in the buggy, and the spirited horse dashed down the avenue. A servant came forward to take her hat and satchel and inform her that her dinner had waited some time. Miss Margaret sat crocheting at the front-window of the dining-room, and Irene ate her dinner in silence. As she rose and approached her aunt the door swung open and a youth entered, apparently about Russell's age, though really one year older.

"Irene, I am tired to death waiting for you. What a provoking girl you are! The horses have been saddled at least one hour and a half. Do get on your riding-dress. I am out of all patience."

He rapped his boot heavily with his whip by way of emphasis, and looked hurriedly at his watch.

"I did not promise to ride with you this evening, Hugh," answered his cousin, seating herself on the window-sill and running her fingers lightly over the bars of a beautiful cage, where her canary pecked playfully at the fair hand.

"Oh, nonsense! Suppose you did n't promise; I waited for you, and told Grace Harriss and Charlie that we would meet them at the upper bend of the river, just above the Factory. Charlie's new horse has just arrived from Vermont—Green Mountain Boy he calls him—and we have a bet of a half-dozen pairs of gloves that he can't beat my Eclipse. Do come along! Aunt Margaret, make her come."

"I should like to see anybody make her do what she is not in the humor for," said his aunt, looking over her glasses at the lithe, graceful figure on the window-sill.

"Hugh, I would rather stay at home, for I am tired, but I will go to oblige you."

Miss Margaret lifted her eyebrows, and as his cousin left the room Hugh Seymour exclaimed:

"Is n't she the greatest beauty in the United States?"

"She will be a belle when she is grown; just such a one as your mother was, only she lacks her gayety of disposition. She is full of strange notions, Hugh; you don't know the half of her character—her own father does not. Frequently I am puzzled to understand her myself."

"Oh! she will come out of all that. She is curious about some things now, but she will outgrow it."

"I am afraid she will not, for it is as much a part of her as the color of her hair or the shape of her nose. She has always been queer."

Irene appeared at the door with a small silver *porte-monnaie* in her hand. She counted the contents, put it into her pocket, and, gathering up the folds of her habit, led the way to the front door. Hugh adjusted the reins, and laying one hand on his she sprang lightly to her saddle, then stroked her horse's silky mane and said:

"Erebus can leave Green Mountain Boy so far behind that Charlie would find it no easy matter to count the plumes in my hat. Are you ready?"

The beautiful jetty creature, as if conscious of her praise, tossed his head and sprang off in a canter, but, wheeling round, she called to the groom who stood watching them:

"Unchain Paragon!"

Five minutes later the cousins were galloping on, with a superb greyhound following close at Erebus' heels, and leaping up now and then in obedience to the motion of Irene's hand. The road ran through a hilly country, now clad in stern ancestral pines, and now skirted with oak and hickory, and about a mile beyond the town it made a sharp angle and took the river bank. The sun had set, but the western sky was still aglow; and near the bank, where the current was not perceptible, the changing tints of the clouds were clearly mirrored, but in the middle of the stream a ledge of rock impeded its course and the water broke over with a dull roar, churning itself into foam and spray as it dashed from shelf to shelf of the stony barrier. Just opposite the Fall Irene checked her horse and paused to admire the beauty of the scene; but in another moment the quick tramp of hoofs fell on her ear, and Hugh's young friends joined them. Green Mountain Boy was flecked with foam, and as Irene measured his perfections at one hasty glance, she patted her favorite's head and challenged Charlie for a trial of speed.

"No; Charlie and I must have the race. Miss Grace, you and Irene can take care of yourselves for a few minutes. We will wait for you on the edge of town, at the graveyard. Now, Charlie, I am ready."

They took their places in front, and were soon out of sight, as the road followed the curves of the river. Erebus plunged violently at first, not being accustomed to lag behind Eclipse, but by much persuasion and frequent kind touches on his head, Irene managed to reconcile him to the temporary disgrace.

Grace looked at his antics rather fearfully, and observed that no amount of money could tempt her to mount him.

"Why not?"

"He will break your neck yet."

"He is very spirited, but as gentle as Paragon. Come, Grace, it is getting late; they will be waiting for us. Quicken your sober, meek little brownie."

"So Electra is not coming back to school. It is a great pity she can't have an education."

"Who told you anything about her?"

"Oh, everybody knows how poor her aunt is; and now, to mend matters, she is going blind. I would go to see Electra occasionally if the family had not been so disgraced. I like her, but no genteel person recognizes Mrs. Aubrey, even in the street."

"That is very unjust. She is one of the most refined, elegant women I have ever seen. She ought not to be blamed for her husband's misfortune. Poverty is no crime."

If she had been treated to a Hindostanee proverb Grace could not have looked more stupidly surprised.

"Why, Irene! Mrs. Aubrey wears a bit-calico to church."

"Well, suppose she does? Is people's worth to be determined only by the cost or the quality of their clothes? If I were to give your cook a silk dress exactly like that one your uncle sent you from Paris, and provide her with shawl and bonnet to match, would she be your equal, do you think? I imagine you would not thank me or anybody else who insinuated that Mrs. Harriss' negro cook was quite as genteel and elegant as Miss Grace herself, because she wore exactly the same kind of clothes. I tell you, Grace, it is all humbug! this everlasting talk about fashion, and dress, and gentility! Pshaw! I am sick of it. When our forefathers were fighting for freedom, for a national existence, I wonder whether their wives measured each other's respectability or gentility by their lace collars or the number of flounces on their dresses? Grace Harriss, your great-grandmother, and mine, and probably everybody's else, spun the cotton, and wove the cloth, and cut and made their homespun dresses, and were thankful to get them. And these women who had not even bit-calicoes were the mothers and wives and sisters and daughters of men who established the most glorious government on the face of the broad earth! The way the women of America have degenerated is a crying shame. I tell you, I would blush to look my great-grandmother in the face."

Grace shrugged her shoulders in expressive silence, and, soon after, they reached the spot where the boys were waiting to join them.

"Eclipse made good his name!" cried Hugh, triumphantly, while Charlie bit his lip with chagrin.

"Never mind, Charlie; Erebus can distance Eclipse any day."

"Not so easily," muttered Hugh.

"I will prove it the next time we ride. Now for a canter as far as Grace's door."

On they went, through the main street of the town: Erebus ahead, Paragon at his heels, then all the others. The wind blew Irene's veil over her eyes, she endeavored to put it back, and in the effort dropped her whip. It was dusk; they were near one of the crossings, and a tall, well-known form stooped, found the whip, and handed it up. Erebus shied, but the hand touched Irene's as it inserted the silver handle in the slender fingers.

"Thank you, Russell; thank you very much."

He bowed formally, drew his straw hat over his brow, and walked on with two heavy account-books under his arm.

"I can't endure that boy," said Hugh, at the distance of half a square, flourishing his whip energetically as he spoke.

"Nor I," chimed in Charlie.

"Why not? I have known him a long time, and I like him very much."

"He is so confoundedly proud and saintly."

"That exists entirely in your imagination, Hugh. You don't know half his good qualities," returned Irene, a little quickly.

"Bah!—" began her cousin; but here their companions bade them good-night, and, as if disinclined to continue the subject, Irene kept in advance till they reached home. Tea was waiting; Miss Margaret and Hugh talked of various things; Irene sat silent, balancing her spoon on the edge of her cup. Finally, tired of listening, she glided to the front-door and seated herself on the steps. Paragon followed, and laid down at her feet. Everything was quiet, save the distant roar of the river as it foamed over its rocky bed; below, hanging on the bank of the stream, lay the town. From her elevated position she could trace the winding of the streets by the long rows of lamps, and now and then a faint hum rose on the breeze as it swept up the hill and lost itself in the forest behind the house. Very soon Hugh came out, cigar in hand, and threw himself down beside her.

"What is the matter, Irie?"

"Nothing."

"What are you moping here for?"

"I am not moping at all; I am waiting for Father."

"He will not be here for three hours yet. Don't you know that Mr. Carter's dinners always end in card-parties? He is famous for whist and euchre, and doubtless his dinners pay him well. What do you want with Uncle?"

"Hugh, do throw away your cigar. It is ridiculous to see a boy of your age puffing away in that style. Betting and smoking seem to be the only things you have learned at Yale. By the way, when do you go back?"

"Are you getting tired of me? I go back in ten days. Irene, do you know that I am not coming home next vacation? I have promised a party of merry fellows to spend it with them in Canada. Then the next summer I go to Europe for two years at least. Are you listening? Do you understand that it will be four years before I see you again?"

"Yes, I understand."

"I dare say the time will seem longer to me than to you."

"I hope, when you do come back, we shall not be disappointed in you."

He took her hand, but she withdrew her fingers.

"Irene, you belong to me, and you know it."

"No! I belong to God and myself."

She rose, and, retreating to the library, opened her books and began to study. The night passed very slowly: she looked at the clock again and again. Finally the house became quiet, and at last the crush of wheels on the gravel-walk announced her father's return. He came into the library for a cigar, and, without noticing her, drew his chair to the open window. She approached and put her hand on his shoulder.

"Irene! what is the matter, child?"

"Nothing, sir; only I want to ask you something."

"Well, Queen, what is it?"

He drew her tenderly to his knee and passed his hand over her floating hair.

Leonard Huntingdon was forty years old; tall, spare, with an erect and martial carriage. He had been trained at West Point, and perhaps early education contributed somewhat to the air of unbending haughtiness which many found repulsive. His black hair was slightly sprinkled with gray and his features were still decidedly handsome, though the expression of mouth and eyes was, ordinarily, by no means winning. He could seem very fascinating, but rarely deigned to be so; and an intimate acquaintance was not necessary to teach people that he was proud, obstinate, and thoroughly selfish, loving only Hugh, Irene, and himself. She was his only child; her mother had died during her infancy, and on this beautiful idol he lavished all the tenderness of which his nature was capable. His tastes were cultivated, his house was elegant and complete, and furnished magnificently; every luxury that money could yield him he possessed, yet there were times when he seemed moody and cynical, and no one could surmise the cause of his gloom. To-night there was no shadow on his face, however; doubtless the sparkle of the wine-cup still shone in his piercing blue eye, and the girl looked up at him fearing no denial.

"Father, I wish, please, you would give me two hundred dollars."

"What would you do with it, Queen?"

"I do not want it for myself; I should like to have that much to enable a poor woman to recover her sight. She has cataracts on her eyes, and there is a physician in New Orleans who can relieve her. She is poor, and it will cost about two hundred dollars. Father, won't you give me the money?"

He took the cigar from his lips, shook off the ashes, and asked indifferently:

"What is the woman's name? Has she no husband to take care of her?"

"Mrs. Aubrey; she—"

"What!—"

The cigar fell from his fingers, he put her from his knee, and rose instantly. His swarthy cheek glowed, and she wondered at the expression of his eyes, so different from anything she had ever seen there before.

"Father, do you know her?"

"What do you know of her? What business is it of yours, whether she goes blind or not? Is it possible Margaret allows you to visit at that house? Answer me, what do you know about her?"

"I know that she is a very gentle, unfortunate woman; that she has many bitter trials; that she works hard to support her family; that she is noble and—"

"Who gave you permission to visit that house?"

"No permission was necessary. I go there because I love her and Electra, and because I like Russell. Why should n't I go there, sir? Is poverty disgrace?"

"Irene, mark me. You are to visit that house no more in future; keep away from the whole family. I will have no such association. Never let me hear their names again. Go to bed."

"Give me one good reason, and I will obey you."

"Reason! My will, my command, is sufficient reason. What do you mean by catechising me in this way? Implicit obedience is your duty."

The calm, holy eyes looked wonderingly into his; and as he marked the startled expression of the girl's pure face his own eyes drooped.

"Father, has Mrs. Aubrey ever injured you?"

No answer.

"If she has not, you are very unjust to her; if she has, remember she is a woman, bowed down with many sorrows, and it is unmanly to hoard up old differences. Father, please give me that money."

"I will bury my last dollar in the Red Sea first! Now are you answered?"

She put her hand over her eyes, as if to shut out some painful vision; and he saw the slight form shudder. In perfect silence she took her books and went up to her room. Mr. Huntingdon reseated himself as the door closed behind her, and the lamp-light showed a sinister smile writhing over his dark features. In the busy hours of day, in the rush and din of active life, men can drown remorseful whispers and shut their eyes to the panorama which Memory strives to place before them; but there come still hours, solemn and inexorable, when struggles are useless and the phantom recollections of early years crowd up like bannered armies. He sat there, staring out into the starry night, and seeing by the shimmer of the setting moon only the graceful form and lovely face of Amy Aubrey, as she had appeared to him in other days. Could he forget the hour when she wrenched her cold fingers from his clasp, and, in defiance of her father's wishes, vowed she would never be his wife? No; revenge was sweet, very sweet; his heart had swelled with exultation when the verdict of death upon the gallows was pronounced upon the husband of her choice; and now, her poverty, her humiliation, her blindness gave him deep, unutterable joy. This history of the Past was a sealed volume to his daughter, but she was now for the first time conscious that her father regarded the widow and her son with unconquerable hatred; and with strange, foreboding dread she looked into the Future, knowing that forgiveness was no part of his nature; that insult or injury was never forgotten.

CHAPTER III.

Whether the general rule of implicit obedience to parental injunction admitted of no exceptions, was a problem which Irene readily solved; and on Saturday, as soon as her father and cousin had started to the plantation (twenty-five miles distant), she put on her hat and walked to town. Wholly absorbed in philanthropic schemes, she hurried along the sidewalk, ran up a flight of steps, and knocked at a door on which was written, in large gilt letters, "Dr. Arnold."

"Ah, Beauty! come in. Sit down, and tell me what brought you to town so early."

He was probably a man of fifty; gruff in appearance, and unmistakably a bachelor. His thick hair was grizzled; so was the heavy beard; and shaggy gray eyebrows slowly unbent as he took his visitor's little hands and looked kindly down into her grave face. From her infancy he had petted and fondled her, and she stood as little in awe of him as of Paragon.

"Doctor, are you busy this morning?"

"I am never too busy to attend to you, little one. What is it?"

"Of course you know that Mrs. Aubrey is almost blind."

"Of course I do, having been her physician."

"Those cataracts can be removed, however."

"Perhaps they can, and perhaps they can't."

"But the probabilities are that a good oculist can relieve her."

"I rather think so."

"Two hundred dollars would defray all the expenses of a trip to New Orleans for this purpose. but she is too poor to afford it."

"Decidedly too poor."

His gray eyes twinkled promisingly, but he would not anticipate her.

"Dr. Arnold, don't you think you could spare that small sum without much inconvenience?"

"Really! is that what you trudged into town for?"

"Yes, just that, and nothing else. If I had had the money I should not have applied to you."

"Pshaw! your father could buy me a dozen times."

"At any rate, I have not the necessary amount at my disposal just now, and I came to ask you to lend it to me."

"For how long, Beauty?"

"Till I am of age—perhaps not so long. I will pay you the interest."

"You will climb Popocatapetl, won't you? Hush, child."

He went into the adjoining room, but soon returned and resumed his seat on the sofa by her side.

"Irene, did you first apply to your father? I don't relish the idea of being a *dernier ressort*."

"What difference can it make to you whether I did or did not? That I come to you at all is sufficient proof of my faith in your generosity."

Hiram Arnold was an acute and practised physiognomist, but the pale, quiet face perplexed him.

"Do you want the money now?"

"Yes, if you please; but before you give it to me I ought to tell you that I want the matter kept secret. No one is to know anything about it—not even my father."

"Irene, is it right to inveigle me into schemes with which you are ashamed to have your own father acquainted?"

"You know the whole truth, therefore you are not inveigled; and moreover, Doctor, I am not ashamed of anything I do."

She looked so unembarrassed that for a moment he felt puzzled.

"I knew Mrs. Aubrey before her marriage." He bent forward to watch the effect of his words, but if she really knew or suspected aught of the past, there was not the slightest intimation of it. Putting back her hair, she looked up and answered:

"That should increase your willingness to aid her in her misfortunes."

"Hold out your hand: fifty, one hundred, a hundred and fifty, two hundred. There, will that do?"

"Thank you! thank you! You will not need it soon, I hope?"

"Not until you are ready to pay me."

"Dr. Arnold, you have given me a great deal of pleasure—more than I can express. I—"

"Don't try to express it, Queen. You have given me infinitely more, I assure you."

Her splendid eyes were lifted toward him, and with some sudden impulse she touched her lips to the hand he had placed on her shoulder. Something like a tremor crossed the doctor's habitually stern mouth as he looked at the marvellous beauty of the girl's countenance, and he kissed her slender fingers as reverently as though he touched something consecrated.

"Irene, shall I take you home in my buggy?"

"No, thank you, I would rather walk. Oh! Doctor, I am so much obliged to you."

She drew her hat over her face and went down the steps. Dr. Arnold walked slowly across the office-floor with his hands behind him; the grim face was placid now, the dark furrows on his brow were not half so deep, and as he paused and closed a ponderous volume lying on the table, a smile suddenly flitted over his features, as one sees a sunbeam struggle through rifts in low rain-clouds. He put the book in the case and locked the glass door. The "Augustinian Theory of Evil" was contained in the volume, which seemed by no means to have satisfied him.

"All a maze worse than that of Crete! I will follow that girl; she shall be my Ariadne in this Egyptian darkness. Pshaw! if His Highness of Hippo were right, what would become of the world? All social organizations are based (and firmly too) on man's faith in man; establish the universal depravity, devilishness of the human race, and lo! what supports the mighty social fabric? Machiavelism? If that queer little untrained freethinker, Irene, is not pure and sinless, then there are neither seraphim nor cherubim in high Heaven! Cyrus, bring out my buggy."

In answer to Irene's knock, Electra opened the cottage-door and ushered her into the small room which served as both kitchen and dining-room. Everything was scrupulously neat, not a spot on the bare polished floor, not a speck to dim the purity of the snowy dimity curtains, and on the table in the centre stood a vase filled with fresh fragrant flowers. In a low chair before the open window sat the widow, netting a blue and white nubia. She glanced round as Irene entered.

"Who is it, Electra?"

"Miss Irene, Aunt."

"Sit down, Miss Irene; how are you to-day?"

She spoke rapidly, and for a moment seemed confused, then resumed her work. Irene watched her pale, delicate fingers, and the long auburn lashes drooping over the colorless cheeks, and, when she looked up for an instant, the visitor saw that the mild, meek brown eyes were sadly blurred. If ever Resignation enthroned itself on a woman's brow, one might have bowed before Amy Aubrey's sweet, placid, subdued face. No Daniel was needed to interpret the lines which sorrow had printed around her patient, tremulous mouth.

"Mrs. Aubrey, I am sorry to hear your eyes are no better."

"Thank you for your kind sympathy. My sight grows more dim every day."

"I should think netting would be injurious to you now."

"It is purely mechanical; I use my eyes very little. Electra arranges the colors for me, and I find it easy work."

Irene knelt down before her, and, folding one of the hands in both hers, said eagerly:

"You shan't suffer much longer; these veils shall be taken off. Here is the money to enable you to go to New Orleans and consult that physician. As soon as the weather turns cooler you must start."

"Miss Irene, I can not tax your generosity so heavily; I have no claim on your goodness. Indeed I—"

"Please don't refuse the money! You will distress me very much if you do. Why should you hesitate? if it makes me happy and benefits you, why will you decline it? Do you think if my eyes were in the condition of yours that I would not thank you to relieve me?"

The widow had risen hastily and covered her face with her hands, while an unwonted flush dyed her cheeks. She trembled, and Irene saw tears stealing through the fingers.

"Mrs. Aubrey, don't you think it is your duty to recover your sight if possible?"

"Yes, if I could command the means."

"You have the means—you must employ them. There, I will not take back the money; it is yours."

"Don't refuse it, Auntie; you will wound Irie," pleaded Electra.

How little they understood or appreciated the struggle in that gentle sufferer's heart; how impossible for them to realize the humiliation she endured in accepting such a gift from the child of Leonard Huntingdon?

With a faltering voice she asked:

"Did your father send me this money?"

"No."

It was the first time she had ever alluded to him, and Irene saw that some painful memory linked itself with her father. What could it be? There was silence for a few seconds; then Mrs. Aubrey took the hands from her face and said: "Irene, I will accept your generous offer. If my sight is restored, I can repay you some day; if not, I am not too proud to be under this great obligation to you. Oh, Irene! I can't tell you how much I thank you; my heart is too full for words." She threw her arm round the girl's waist and strained her to her bosom, and hot tears fell fast on the waves of golden hair. A moment after, Irene threw a tiny envelope into Electra's lap, and without another word glided out of the room. The orphan broke the seal, and as she opened a sheet of note-paper a ten-dollar bill slipped out.

"Electra, come to school Monday. The enclosed will pay your tuition for two months longer. Please don't hesitate to accept it, if you really love

"Your friend,

"IRENE."

Mrs. Aubrey sat with her face in her hands, listening to the mournful, solemn voice that stole up from the mouldering, dusty crypts of by-gone years; and putting the note in her pocket, Electra leaned her head against the window and thanked God for the gift of a true friend. Thinking of the group she had just left, Irene approached the gate and saw that Russell stood holding it open for her to pass. Looking up she stopped, for the expression of his face frightened and pained her.

"Russell, what is the matter? oh! tell me."

A scornful, defiant smile distorted his bloodless lips, but he made no answer. She took his hand; it was cold, and the fingers were clenched.

"Russell, are you ill?"

She shuddered at the glare in his black eyes.

"I am not ill."

"Won't you tell your friend what ails you?"

"I have no friend but my mother!"

"Oh, Russell, Russell!"

Her head drooped, and the glittering hair swept as a veil between them. The low, flute-like, pleading voice stirred his heart, and the blood surged over his pallid forehead.

"I have been injured and insulted. Just now I doubt all people and all things, even the justice and mercy of God."

"Russell, 'shall not the righteous Judge of all the earth do right?'"

"Shall the rich and the unprincipled eternally trample upon the poor and the unfortunate?"

"Who has injured you?"

"A meek-looking man, who passes for a Christian, who turns pale at the sound of a violin, who exhorts to missionary labors, and talks often about widows and orphans. Such a man, knowing the circumstances that surround me—my poverty, my mother's affliction—on bare and most unwarrantable suspicion turns me out of my situation as clerk, and endeavors to brand my name with infamy. To-day I stand disgraced in the eyes of the community, thanks to the vile slanders of that pillar of the church, Jacob Watson. Four hours ago I went to my work quietly, hopefully; but now another spirit has entered and possessed me. Irene, I am desperate. Do you wonder? It seems to me ages have rolled over me since my mother kissed me this morning; there is a hissing serpent in my heart which I have no power to expel. I could bear it myself, but my mother! my noble, patient, suffering mother! I must go in and add a yet heavier burden to those already crushing out her life.

Pleasant tidings, these I bring her: that her son is disgraced, branded as a rogue!"

There was no moisture in the keen eye, no tremor in the metallic ring of his voice, no relaxation of the curled lip.

"Can't you prove your innocence? Was it money?"

"No, it was a watch; my watch, which I gave up as security for drawing a portion of my salary in advance. It was locked up in the iron safe; this morning it was missing, and they accuse me of having stolen it."

He took off his hat as if it oppressed him, and tossed back his hair.

"What will you do, Russell?"

"I don't know yet."

"Oh! if I could only help you."

She clasped her hands over her heart, and for the first time since her infancy tears rushed down her cheeks. It was painful to see that quiet girl so moved, and Russell hastily took the folded hands in his and bent his face close to hers.

"Irene, the only comfort I have is that you are my friend. Don't let them influence you against me. No matter what you may hear, believe in me. Oh, Irene, Irene! believe in me always!"

He held her hands in a clasp so tight that it pained her, then suddenly dropped them and left her. As a pantomime all this passed before Electra's eyes; not a word reached her, but she knew that something unusual had occurred to bring her cousin home at that hour, and felt that now he was but the avant-courier of a new sorrow. She glanced toward her aunt's bowed form, then smothered a groan, and sat waiting for the blow to fall upon her. Why spring to meet it? He went to his own room first, and five, ten, fifteen minutes rolled on. She listened to the faint sound of his steps, and knew that he paced up and down the floor; five minutes more of crushing suspense, and he came along the passage and stood at the door. She looked at him, pale, erect, and firm, and shuddered in thinking of the struggle which that calm exterior had cost him. Mrs. Aubrey recognized the step, and looked round in surprise.

"Electra, I certainly hear Russell coming."

He drew near and touched her cheek with his lips, saying tenderly:

"How is my mother?"

"Russell, what brings you home so early?"

"That is rather a cold welcome, Mother, but I am not astonished. Can you bear to hear something unpleasant? Here, put your hands in mine; now listen to me. You know I drew fifty dollars of my salary in advance, to pay Clark. At that time I gave my watch to Mr. Watson by way of pawn, he seemed so reluctant to let me have the money; you understand, Mother, why I did not mention it at the time. He locked it up in the iron safe, to which no one has access except him and myself. Late yesterday I locked the safe as usual, but do not remember whether the watch was still there or not; this morning Mr. Watson missed it; we searched safe, desk, store, could find it nowhere, nor the twenty-dollar gold piece deposited at the same time. No other money was missing, though the safe contained nearly a thousand dollars. The end of it all is that I am accused as the thief, and expelled in disgrace for—"

A low, plaintive cry escaped the widow's lips, and her head sank heavily on the boy's shoulder. Passing his arm fondly around her, he kissed her white face, and continued in the same hushed, passionless tone, like one speaking under his breath, and stilling some devouring rage:

"Mother, I need not assure you of my innocence. You know that I never could be guilty of what is imputed to me; but, not having it in my power to prove my innocence, I shall have to suffer the disgrace for a season. Only for a season, I trust, Mother, for in time the truth must be discovered. I have been turned out of my situation, and, though they have no proof of my guilt, they will try to brand me with the disgrace. But they can't crush me; so long as there remains a drop of blood in my veins, I will scorn their slanders and their hatred. Don't cry, Mother; your tears hurt me more than all my wrongs. If you will only be brave, and put entire confidence in me, I shall bear all this infinitely better. Look at the bitter truth, face to face; we have nothing more to lose. Poor, afflicted, disgraced, there is nothing else on earth to fear; but there is everything to hope for: wealth, name, fame, influence. This is my comfort; it is a grim philosophy, born of Despair. I go forward from to-day like a man who comes out of some fiery furnace, and, blackened and scorched though he be, looks into the future without apprehension, feeling assured that it can hold no trials comparable to those already past. Herein I am strong; but you should have another and far brighter hope to rest upon; it is just such ordeals as this for which religion promises you strength and consolation. Mother, I have seen you supported by Christian faith in a darker hour than this. Take courage; all will be well some day."

For a few moments deep silence reigned in the little kitchen, and only the Infinite eye pierced the heart of the long-tried sufferer. When she raised her head from the boy's bosom the face, though tear-stained, was serene, and, pressing her lips twice to his, she said slowly:

"'Beloved, think it not strange concerning the fiery trial which is to try you; as though some strange thing happened unto you. For whom the Lord loveth he chasteneth, and scourgeth every son whom he receiveth.' I will wait patiently, my son, hoping for proofs which shall convince the world of your innocence. I wish I could take the whole burden on my shoulders, and relieve you, my dear boy."

"You have, Mother; it ceases to crush me, now that you are yourself once more." He spoke with difficulty, however, as if something stifled him, and, rising, hastily poured out and drank a glass of water.

"And now, Russell, sit down and let me tell you a little that is pleasant and sunshiny. There is still a bright spot left to look upon."

Stealing her hand into his, the mother informed him of all that had occurred during Irene's visit, and concluded by laying the money in his palm.

Electra sat opposite, watching the change that came over the face she loved best on earth. Her large, eager, midnight eyes noted the quick flush and glad light which overspread his features; the deep joy that kindled in his tortured soul; and unconsciously she clutched her fingers till the nails grew purple, as though striving to strangle some hideous object thrusting itself before her. Her breathing became labored and painful, her gaze more concentrated and searching, and when her cousin exclaimed, "Oh, Mother! she is an angel! I have always known it. She is unlike everybody else!" Electra's heart seemed to stand still; and from that moment a sombre curtain fell between the girl's eyes and God's sunshine. She rose, and a silent yet terrible struggle took place in her passionate soul. Justice and Jealousy wrestled briefly; she would be just, though every star fell from her sky, and with a quick, uncertain step she reached Russell, thrust Irene's note into his fingers, and fled into solitude.

An hour later Russell knocked at the door of an office, which bore on a square tin plate these words, "Robert Campbell, Attorney-at-Law." The door was only partially closed, and as he entered an elderly man looked up from a desk covered with loose papers and open volumes, from which he was evidently making extracts. The thin hair hung over his forehead as if restless fingers had ploughed carelessly through it, and, as he kept one finger on a half-copied paragraph, the cold blue eye said very plainly, "This is a busy time with me; despatch your errand at once."

"Good-morning, Mr. Campbell; are you particularly engaged?"

"How-d'y-do, Aubrey. I am generally engaged; confoundedly busy this morning. What do you want?"

His pen resumed its work, but he turned his head as if to listen.

"I will call again when you are at leisure," said Russell, turning away.

"That will be—next month—next year; in fine, postponing your visit indefinitely. Sit down—somewhere—well—clear those books into a corner, and let's hear your business. I am at your service for ten minutes—talk fast."

He put his pen behind his ear, crossed his arms on the desk, and looked expectant.

"I came here to ask whether you wished to employ any one in your office."

"And what the deuce do you suppose I want with an office-lad like yourself? To put the very books I need at the bottom of a pile tall as the Tower of Babel, and tear up my briefs to kindle the fire or light your cigar? No, thank you, Aubrey; I tried that experiment to my perfect satisfaction a few months ago. Is that all?"

"That is all, sir."

The boy rose, but the bitter look that crossed his face as he glanced at the well-filled book-shelves arrested the lawyer's attention, and he added:

"Why did you leave Watson, young man? It is a bad plan to change about in this style."

"I was expelled from my situation on a foul and most unjust accusation. I am seeking employment from necessity."

"Expelled is a dark word, Aubrey; it will hardly act as a passport to future situations. Expelled clerks are not in demand."

"Still, I must state the truth unreservedly."

"Let's hear the whole business; sit down."

Without hesitation he narrated all the circumstances, once or twice pausing to still the tempest of passion that flashed from his eyes. While he spoke Mr. Campbell's keen eyes searched him from head to foot, and at the conclusion he asked sharply:

"Where is the watch, do you suppose?"

"Heaven only knows. I have a suspicion, but no right to utter it, since I might thereby inflict a wrong equal to that from which I now suffer."

"It is a dark piece of business as it stands."

"Yes, but time will clear it up."

"See here, Aubrey; I have noticed you two or three times in the court-house listening to some of my harangues. I knew your father, and I should like to help you. It seems to me you might make better use of your talents than you are doing. And yet, if you rise it will be over greater obstacles than most men surmount. Do you understand me?"

"I do; for I am too painfully aware of the prejudice against which I have to contend. But if I live, I shall lift myself out of this pool where malice and hate have thrust me."

"What do you propose to do?"

"Work at the plough or before the anvil, if nothing else can be done to support my mother and cousin; and, as soon as I possibly can, study law. This is my plan, and for two years I have been pursuing my Latin and Greek with an eye to accomplishing the scheme."

"I see Fate has thumped none of your original obstinacy out of you. Aubrey, suppose I shut my eyes to the watch transaction, and take you into my office?"

"If so, I shall do my duty faithfully. But you said you did not need any one here, and though I am anxious to find work I do not expect or desire to be taken in from charity. I intend to earn my wages, sir, and from your own account I should judge you had very little use for an assistant."

"Humph! a bountiful share of pride along with prodigious obstinacy. Though I am a lawyer, I told you the truth; I have no earthly use for such assistants as I have been plagued with for several years. In the main, office-boys are a nuisance, comparable only to the locusts of Egypt; I washed my hands of the whole tribe months since. Now I have a negro to attend to my office, make fires, etc., and if I could only get an intelligent, ambitious, honorable, trustworthy young man, he would be a help to me. I had despaired of finding such, but, on the whole, I rather like you; believe you can suit me exactly if you will, and I am disposed to give you a trial. Sit down here and copy this paragraph; let me see what sort of hieroglyphics I shall have to decipher if I make you my copyist."

Russell silently complied, and after a careful examination it seemed the chirography was satisfactory.

"Look there, Aubrey, does that array frighten you?"

He pointed to the opposite side of the room, where legal documents of every shape and size were piled knee-deep for several yards.

"They look formidable, sir, but nothing would afford me more pleasure than to fathom their mysteries."

"And what security can you give me that the instant my back is turned you will not quit my work and go off to my books yonder, which I notice you have been eying very greedily."

"No security, sir, but the promise of an honest soul to do its work faithfully and untiringly. Mr. Campbell, I understand my position thoroughly; I know only too well that I have everything to make—an honorable name, an unblemished reputation—and, relying only on myself, I expect to help myself. If you really need an assistant, and think me trustworthy, I will be very glad to serve you, and shall merit your confidence. I come to you under adverse circumstances, with a tarnished character, and of course you feel some hesitancy in employing me. I have concealed nothing; you are acquainted with all the facts, and must decide accordingly."

There was nothing pleading in his tone or mien, but a proud, desperate calmness unusual in one of his age. When a truly honest, noble soul meets an equal, barriers of position and age melt like snow-flakes in sunshine, all extraneous circumstances fall away, and, divested of pomp or rags, as the case may be, the full, undimmed majesty of spirit greets spirit, and clear-eyed Sympathy, soaring above the dross and dust of worldly conventionalities, knits them in bonds lasting as time. Looking into the resolute yet melancholy face before him, the lawyer forgot the poverty and disgrace clinging to his name, and leaning forward grasped his hand.

"Aubrey, you and I can work peaceably together; I value your candor, I like your resolution. Come to me on Monday, and in the matter of salary you shall find me liberal enough. I think you told me you had a cousin as well as your mother to support; I shall not forget it. Now, good-morning, and leave me, unless you desire to accumulate work for yourself."

People called Mr. Campbell "miserly," "egotistic," and "selfish." These are harsh adjectives, and the public frequently applies them with culpable haste and uncharitableness, for there is an astonishing proclivity in human nature to detract, to carp, to spy out, and magnify faults. If at all prone to generous deeds, Mr. Campbell certainly failed to placard them in public places; he had never given any large amount to any particular church, institution, or society, but the few who knew him well indignantly denied the charge of penuriousness preferred by the community. A most unsafe criterion is public estimation; it canonizes many an arch-hypocrite and martyrs many a saint.

CHAPTER IV.

From early childhood Irene had experienced a sensation of loneliness. Doubtless the loss of her mother enhanced this feeling, but the peculiarity of her mental organization would have necessitated it even under happier auspices. Her intellect was of the masculine order, acute and logical, rather deficient in the imaginative faculties, but keenly analytical. It is an old predicate that women are deductionists—that womanly intuitions are swift and infallible. In richly-endowed female minds it not unfrequently happens that tedious, reflective processes are ignored; but Irene was a patient rather than brilliant thinker, and with singular perseverance searched every nook and cranny, and sifted every phase of the subject presented for investigation. Her conclusions were never hasty, and consequently rarely unsound. From the time her baby-fingers first grasped a primer she became a student; dolls and toys such as constitute the happiness of most children had never possessed any attraction for her, and before she was eight years old she made the library her favorite resort. She would climb upon the morocco-covered table where stood two globes, one celestial, the other terrestrial, and spend hours in deciphering the strange, heathenish figures twined among the stars. When weary of studying the index of the thermometer and barometer, and wondering why the quicksilver varied with sunshine and shower, she would throw herself down on the floor and fall asleep over the quaint pictures in an old English encyclopedia, numbering thirty volumes. She haunted this room, and grew up among books centuries old. Thus until her tenth year there was no authority exerted over her, and the strong, reflective tendency of her mind rapidly developed itself. This was an abnormal condition, and indisputably an unfortunate training, and perhaps in after years it might have been better had she spent the season of careless, thoughtless childhood in childish sports and childhood's wonted ways, for anxious inquiry and tedious investigations come soon enough with maturity.

She was not an enthusiastic, impulsive nature, fitful in moodiness or ecstacy, inclined to passionate demonstrations of any kind; but from infancy evinced a calm, equable temperament, uniformly generous and unselfish, but most thoroughly firm, nay obstinate, in any matter involving principle or conflicting with her opinions of propriety. How she obtained these notions of right and wrong in minor details, was a subject of some mystery. They were not the result of education in the ordinary acceptation of that term, for they had never been instilled by anybody; and, like a wood-flower in some secluded spot, she lived, grew, and expanded her nature, without any influences to bias or color her views. In her promiscuous reading she was quite as apt to imbibe poisonous as healthy sentiments; and knowing that she had been blessed with few religious instructions, her father often wondered at the rigidness of her code for self-regulation. Miss Margaret considered her "a strange little thing," and rarely interfered with her plans in any respect, while her father seemed to take it for granted that she required no looking after. He knew that her beauty was extraordinary; he was proud of the fact; and having provided her with a good music-master, and sent her to the best school in the county, he left her to employ her leisure as inclination prompted. Occasionally her will conflicted with his, and more than once he found it impossible to make her yield assent to his wishes. To the outward observances of obedience and respect she submitted, but whenever these differences occurred he felt that in the end she was unconquered. Inconsistent as it may appear, though fretted for the time by her firmness, he loved her the more for her "wilfulness," as he termed it; and despotic and exacting though he certainly was in many respects, he stood somewhat in awe of his purehearted, calm-eyed child. His ward and nephew, Hugh Seymour, had resided with him for several years, and it was well known that Mr. Huntingdon had pledged his daughter's hand to his sister's son. The age of infant betrothals has passed away, consequently this rare instance gave rise to a deal of gossiping comment. How the matter became public he never knew; probably Sparrowgrass's "carrier-pigeon" migrated southward, for it is now no uncommon thing to find one in our cities and country towns; and at all events Mr. Huntingdon soon found that his private domestic affairs were made an ordinary topic of conversation in social circles. Irene had never been officially apprised of her destiny, but surmised very accurately the true state of the case. Between the two cousins there existed not the slightest congeniality of taste or disposition; not a sympathetic link, save the tie of relationship. On her part there was a moderate share of cousinly affection; on his, as much love and tenderness as his selfish nature was capable of feeling. They rarely quarrelled as most children do, for when (as frequently happened) he flew into a rage and tried to tyrannize, she scorned to retort in any way, and generally locked him out of the library. What she thought of her father's intentions concerning herself, no one knew; she never alluded to the subject, and if in a frolicsome mood Hugh broached it, she invariably cut the discussion short. When he went to college in a distant state she felt infinitely relieved, and during his vacations secluded herself as much as possible. Yet the girl's heart was warm and clinging; she loved her father devotedly, and loved most intensely Electra Grey, whom she had first met at school. They were nearly the same age, class-mates, and firm friends. That she was beautiful, Irene of course knew quite as well as her father or any one else; how could she avoid knowing it? From her cradle she had been called "Queen" and "Beauty;" all her acquaintances flattered her—strangers commented on her loveliness; she no more doubted it than the fact of her existence; and often stopped before the large parlor mirrors and admired her own image, just as she would have examined and admired and enjoyed one of the elegant azaleas or pelargoniums in the greenhouse. I repeat it, she prized and enjoyed her loveliness, but she was not vain. She was no more spoiled by adulation than a meek and snowy camellia, or one of those immense golden-eyed pansies which astonish and delight visitors at the hothouses on Long Island. God conferred marvellous beauty on her, and she was grateful for the gift—but to the miserable weaknesses of vanity she was a stranger. In the midst of books and flowers she was happy, and seemed to desire no companions but Erebus and Paragon. She rode every day when the weather permitted, and the jetty horse, with its graceful young rider, followed by the slender, silky greyhound, was a familiar spectacle in the vicinity of her home. She knew every hill and valley within ten miles of the town; could tell where the richest, rarest honeysuckles grew, where the yellow jasmine clambered in greatest profusion, and always found the earliest sprays of graybeard that powdered the forest. Often Mr. Huntingdon had ordered his horse and gone out in the dusky twilight to search for her, fearing that some disaster had overtaken his darling, and at such times met Erebus laden with her favorite flowers. These were the things she loved; and thus, independent of society, yet conscious of her isolation, she grew up what nature intended her to be.

As totally different in character as appearance was Electra Grey. Rather smaller and much thinner than Irene, with shining purplish black hair, large, sad, searching black eyes, from which there was no escape, a pale olive complexion, and full crimson lips that rarely smiled. The forehead was broad and prominent, and rendered very peculiar by the remarkable width between the finely-arched brows. The serene purity characteristic of Irene's features was entirely wanting in this face, which would have seemed Jewish in its contour but for the Grecian nose; and the melancholy yet fascinating eyes haunted the beholder with their restless, wistful, far-reaching expression. Electra was a dreamer, richly gifted; dissatisfied because she could never attain that unreal world which her busy brain kept constantly before her. The child of Genius is rarely, if ever, a happy one—

"Heaven lies about us in our infancy."

If so, its recollections cling tenaciously to those who, like Electra, seek continually for the airy castles of an ideal realm. Her vivid imagination shaped and painted, but, as too often happens, her eager blood and bone fingers could not grasp the glories. The thousand cares, hardships, and rough handlings of Reality struck cold and jarring on her sensitive, highly-strung nature. She did not complain; murmuring words had never crossed her lips in the hearing of any who knew her; she loved her aunt too well to speak of sorrow or disappointment. Fourteen years had taught her an unusual amount of stoicism, but sealed lips can not sepulchre grief, and trials have a language which will not be repressed when the mouth is at rest. She looked not gloomy, nor yet quite unhappy, but like one who sees obstacles mountain-high loom between her and the destined goal, and asks only permission to press on. Hers was a passionate nature; fierce blood beat in her veins, and would not always be bound by icy fetters. There was no serene plateau of feeling where she could repose; she enjoyed keenly, rapturously, and suffered acutely, fearfully. Unfortunately for her, she had only Himalayan solitudes, sublime in their dazzling height, or valleys of Tophet, appalling with flame and phantom. She knew wherein she was gifted, she saw whither her narrow pathway led, and panted to set her little feet in the direction of the towering steeps crowned with the Temple of Art. To be an artist; to put on canvas the grand and imperishable images that crowded her brain, and almost maddened her because she could not give them tangible form—this was the day-dream spanning her life like a bow of promise, but fading slowly as years thickened o'er her head and no helping hand cleared the choked path. "Poverty! poverty!" Many a night she buried her face under the pillow and hissed the word through closed teeth, fearful of disturbing the aunt who slumbered at her side. Poverty! poverty! What an intolerable chain it binds around aspiring souls! And yet the world's great thinkers have felt this iron in their flesh, and, bursting the galling bonds, have carved their way to eminence, to immortality. It is a lamentable and significant truth that, with a few honorable, noble exceptions, wealth is the Cannæ of American intellect. Poverty is a rigid school, and the sessions are long and bitter; but the men and women who graduate therein come forth with physical frames capable of enduring all hardships, with hearts habituated to disappointment and fortified against the rebuffs of fortune, with intellects trained by patient, laborious, unbending application. The tenderly-nurtured child of wealth and luxury very naturally and reasonably shrinks from difficulties; but increase the obstacles in the path of a son or daughter of penury, inured to trial, and in the same ratio you strengthen his or her ability and determination to surmount them.

Electra's love of drawing had early displayed itself; first, in strange, weird figures on her slate, then in her copy-book, on every slip of paper which she could lay her hands upon; and, finally, for want of more suitable material, she scrawled all over the walls of the little bedroom, to the great horror of her aunt, who spread a coat of whitewash over the child's frescoes, and begged her to be guilty of no such conduct in future, as Mr. Clark might with great justice sue for damages. In utter humiliation Electra retreated to the garden, and here, after a shower had left the sandy walks white and smooth, she would sharpen a bit of pine, and draw figures and faces of all conceivable and inconceivable shapes. Chancing to find her thus engaged one Sunday afternoon, Russell supplied her with a package of drawing-paper and pencils. So long as these lasted she was perfectly happy, but unluckily their straitened circumstances admitted of no such expenditure, and before many weeks she was again without materials. She would not tell Russell that she had exhausted his package, and passed sleepless nights trying to devise some method by which she could aid herself. It was positive torture for her to sit in school and see the drawing-master go round, giving lessons on this side and that, skipping over her every time, because her aunt could not afford the extra three dollars. How longingly the eyes followed the master's form—how hungrily they dwelt upon the sketches he leaned over to examine and retouch! Frequently during drawing-hour she would sit with her head bent down pretending to study, but the pages of the book were generally blistered with tears which no eye but the Father's looked upon. There was, however, one enjoyment which nothing could steal from her: the town contained two book-stores, and here she was wont to linger over the numerous engravings and occasional oil-paintings they boasted. The proprietors and clerks seemed rather pleased than otherwise by the silent homage she paid their pictures, and, except to tender her a seat, no one ever interfered with her examinations. One engraving interested her particularly: it represented St. John on Patmos, writing Revelations. She went as usual one Saturday morning for another look at it, but a different design hung in its place; she glanced around, and, surmising the object of her search, the proprietor told her it had been sold the day before. An expression of sorrow crossed her face, as though she had sustained an irreparable loss, and, drawing her bonnet down, she went slowly homeward. Amid all these yearnings and aspirations she turned constantly to Russell with a worshipping love that knew no bounds. She loved her meek, affectionate aunt as well as most natures love their mothers, and did all in her power to lighten her labors, but her affection for Russell bordered on adoration. In a character so exacting and passionate as hers there is necessarily much of jealousy, and thus it came to pass that, on the day of Irene's visit to the cottage, the horrible suspicion took possession of her that he loved Irene better than herself. True, she was very young, but childish hearts feel as keenly as those of maturer years; and Electra endured more agony during that day than in all of her past life. Had Irene been other than she was, in every respect, she would probably have hated her cordially; as matters stood, she buried the suspicion deep in her own heart, and kept as much out of everybody's way as possible. Days and weeks passed very wearily; she busied herself with her text-books, and, when the lessons had been recited, drew all over the margins—here a hand, there an entire arm, now and then a face, sad-eyed as Fate.

Mrs. Aubrey's eyes became so blurred that finally she could not leave the house without having some one to guide her, and, as cold weather had now arrived, preparations were made for her journey. Mr. Hill, who was going to New Orleans, kindly offered to take charge of her, and the day of departure was fixed. Electra packed the little trunk, saw it deposited on the top of the stage, in the dawn of an October morning saw her aunt comfortably seated beside Mr. Hill, and in another moment all had vanished. In the afternoon of that day, on returning from school, Electra went to the bureau, and, unlocking a drawer, took out a small paper box. It contained a miniature of her father, set in a handsome gold frame. She knew it had been her mother's most valued trinket; her aunt had carefully kept it for her, and as often as the temptation assailed her she had resisted; but now the longing for money triumphed over every other feeling. Having touched the spring, she took a knife and cautiously removed the bit of ivory beneath the glass, then deposited the two last in the box, put the gold frame in her pocket, and went out to a jewelry-store. As several persons had preceded her, she leaned against the counter, and, while waiting, watched with some curiosity the movements of one of the goldsmiths, who, with a glass over one eye, was engaged in repairing watches. Some had been taken from their cases, others were untouched; and as her eyes passed swiftly over the latter, they were suddenly riveted to a massive gold one lying somewhat apart. A half-smothered exclamation caused the workman to turn round and look at her; but in an instant she calmed herself, and, thinking it a mere outbreak of impatience, he resumed his employment. Just then one of the proprietors approached, and said politely, "I am sorry we have kept you waiting, Miss. What can I do for you?"

"What is this worth?"

She laid the locket down on the counter and looked up at him with eyes that sparkled very joyously, he thought. He examined it a moment, and said rather drily:

"It is worth little or nothing to us, though you may prize it."

"If I were to buy another just like it, would you charge me 'little or nothing?'"

He smiled good-humoredly.

"Buying and selling are different things, don't you know that? Come, tell me what you want to sell this for?"

"Because I want some money."

"You are Mrs. Aubrey's niece, I believe?"

"Yes, sir."

"Well, how do I know, in the first place, that it belongs to you? Jewellers have to be very particular about what they buy."

She crimsoned, and drew herself proudly away from the counter, then smiled, and held out her hand for the locket.

"It is mine; it held my father's miniature, but I took it out because I want a paint-box, and thought I could sell this case for enough to buy one. It was my mother's once; here are her initials on the back—H. G., Harriet Grey. But of course you don't know whether I am telling the truth; I will bring my cousin with me; he can prove it. Sir, are you so particular about everything you buy?"

"We try to be."

Again her eyes sparkled; she bowed, and left the store.

Once in the street, she hurried to Mr. Campbell's office, ran up the steps, and rapped loudly at the door.

"Come in!" thundered the lawyer.

She stopped on the threshold, glanced round, and said timidly:

"I want to see Russell, if you please."

"Russell is at the post-office. Have you any particular spite at my door, that you belabor it in that style? or do you suppose I am as deaf as a gate-post?"

"I beg your pardon; I did not mean to startle you, sir. I was not thinking of either you or your door."

She sprang down the steps to wait on the sidewalk for her cousin, and met him at the entrance.

"Oh, Russell! I have found your watch."

A ray of light seemed to leap from his eyes as he seized her hand.

"Where?"

"At Mr. Brown's jewelry-store."

"Thank God!"

He went up the stairway, delivered the letters, and came back, accompanied by Mr. Campbell.

"This is my cousin, Electra Grey, Mr. Campbell."

"So I inferred from the unceremonious assault she made on my door just now. However, shake hands, little lady; it seems there is some reason for your haste. Let's hear about this precious watch business."

She simply told what she had seen. Presently Russell said:

"But how did you happen there, Electra?"

"Your good angel sent me, I suppose;—" and she added, in a whisper, "I will tell you some other time."

On re-entering the store she walked at once to the workman's corner and pointed out the watch.

"Yes, it is mine. I would know it among a thousand."

"How can you identify it, Aubrey?"

He immediately gave the number, and name of the manufacturer, and described the interior tracery, not omitting the quantity of jewels. Mr. Campbell turned to the proprietor (the same gentleman with whom Electra had conversed), and briefly recapitulated the circumstances which had occurred in connection with the watch. Mr. Brown listened attentively, then requested Russell to point out the particular one that resembled his. He did so, and on examination the number, date, name, and all the marks corresponded so exactly that no doubt remained on the jeweller's mind.

"Young man, you say you were accused of stealing your own watch?"

"Yes."

"Then I will try to clear your name. This watch was brought here several weeks since, while I was absent. I am very guarded in such matters, and require my young men here to take a certificate of the name and place of residence of all strangers who offer articles for sale or exchange. I once very innocently bought some stolen property, and it taught me a lesson. This watch was sold for ninety dollars by a man named Rufus Turner, who lives in New Orleans, No. 240 —— street. I will write to him at once, and find out, if possible, how it came into his possession. I rather think he had some horses here for sale."

"Did he wear green glasses?" inquired Russell of the young man who had purchased the watch.

"Yes, and had one arm in a sling."

"I saw such a man here about the time my watch was missing."

After some directions from Mr. Campbell concerning the proper course to be pursued, Electra drew out her locket, saying—

"Now, Russell, is not this locket mine?"

"Yes; but where is the miniature? What are you going to do with it?"

"The miniature is at home, but I want to sell the frame, and Mr. Brown does not know but that it is another watch case?"

"If it is necessary, I will swear that it belongs lawfully to you; but what do you want to sell it for? I should think you would prize it too highly to be willing to part with it."

"I do prize the miniature, and would not part with it for any consideration; but I want something far more than a gold case to keep it in."

"Tell me what you want, and I will get it for you," whispered her cousin.

"No; I am going to sell this frame."

"And I am going to buy it from you," said the kind-hearted merchant, taking it from her hand and weighing it.

Russell and Mr. Campbell left the store, and soon after Mr. Brown paid Electra several dollars for the locket.

In half an hour she had purchased a small box of paints, a supply of drawing-paper and pencils, and returned home, happier and prouder than many an empress whose jewels have equalled those of the Begums of Oude. She had cleared Russell's character, and her hands were pressed over her heart to still its rapturous throbbing. Happy as an uncaged bird, she arranged the tea-table and sat down to wait for him. He came at last, later than usual, and then she had her reward; he took her in his arms and kissed her. Yet, while his lip rested on hers, Irene's image rose before her, and he felt her shiver as she clung to him. He was her idol, and the bare suggestion of his loving another better chilled the blood in her veins. He spoke little of the watch, appeared to miss his mother, and soon went to his room and began to study. How ignorant he was of what passed in his cousin's heart; how little he suspected the intensity of her feelings! Constantly occupied during the day, he rarely thought of her away from home; and though always kind and considerate, he failed to understand her nature, or fully appreciate her affection for him. Many days elapsed before Mr. Turner's answer arrived. He stated that he had won the watch from Cecil Watson at a horse-race, where both were betting; and proved the correctness of his assertion by reference to several persons who were present, and who resided in the town. Russell had suspected Cecil from the moment of its disappearance, and now, provided with both letter and watch, and accompanied by Mr. Brown, he repaired to Mr. Watson's store. Russell had been insulted, his nature was stern, and now he exulted in the power of disgracing the son of the man who had wronged him. There was no flush on his face, but a cold, triumphant glitter in his eyes as he approached his former employer, and laid watch and letter before him.

"What business have you here?" growled the merchant, trembling before the expression of the boy's countenance.

"My business is to clear my character which you have slandered, and to fix the disgrace you intended for me on your own son. I bring you the proofs of his, not my villany."

"Come into the back room; I will see Brown another time," said Mr. Watson, growing paler each moment.

"No, sir; you were not so secret in your dealings with me. Here where you insulted me you shall hear the whole truth. Read that. I suppose the twenty-dollar gold piece followed the watch."

The unfortunate father perused the letter slowly, and smothered a groan. Russell watched him with a keen joy which he might have blushed to acknowledge had he analyzed his feelings. Writhing under his empaling eye, Mr. Watson said:

"Have you applied to the witnesses referred to?"

"Yes; they are ready to swear that they saw Cecil bet Turner the watch."

"You did not tell them the circumstances, did you?"

"No."

"Well, it is an unfortunate affair; I want it dropped as quietly as possible. It will never do to have it known far and wide."

"Aha! you can feel the sting now. But, remember you took care to circulate the slander on my name. I heard of it. You did not spare me, you did not spare my mother; and, Jacob Watson, neither will I spare you. You never believed me guilty, but you hated me, and gloried in an opportunity of injuring me. Do you suppose I shall shield your unprincipled son for your sake? You showed me no mercy; you may expect as little. The story of the watch shall make its way wherever we—"

He paused suddenly, for the image of his gentle, forgiving mother rose before him, and he knew that she would be grieved at the spirit he evinced. There was an awkward silence, broken by Mr. Watson.

"If I retract all that I have said against you, and avow your innocence, will it satisfy you? Will you be silent about Cecil?"

"No!" rose peremptorily to his lips, but he checked it; and the patient teaching of years, his mother's precepts and his mother's prayers brought forth their first fruit—golden Charity.

"You merit no forbearance at my hands, and I came here intending to show you none; but, on reflection, I will not follow your example. Clear my name before the public, and I leave the whole affair with you. There has never been any love between us, because you were always despotic and ungenerous, but I am sorry for you now, for you have taught me how heavy is the burden you have to bear in future. Good-morning."

Afraid to trust himself, he turned away and joined Mr. Campbell in the office.

In the afternoon of the same day came a letter from Mr. Hill containing sad news. The oculist had operated on Mrs. Aubrey's eyes, but violent inflammation had ensued; he had done all that scientific skill could prompt, but feared she would be hopelessly blind. At the close of the letter Mr. Hill stated that he would bring her home the following week. One November evening, just before dark, while Russell was cutting wood for the kitchen-fire, the stage stopped at the cottage-gate, and he hurried forward to receive his mother in his arms. It was a melancholy reunion; for a moment the poor sufferer's fortitude forsook her, and she wept. But his caresses soothed her, and she followed Electra into the house while he brought in the trunk. When shawl and bonnet had been removed, and Electra placed her in the rocking-chair, the light fell on face and figure, and the cousins started at the change that had taken place. She was so ghastly pale, so very much reduced. She told them all that had occurred during the tedious weeks of absence; how much she regretted having gone since the trip proved so unsuccessful; how much more she deplored the affliction on their account than her own; and then from that hour no allusion was ever made to it.

CHAPTER V.

Weeks and months slipped away, and total darkness came down on the widow. She groped with some difficulty from room to room, and Electra was compelled to remain at home and watch over her. Russell had become a great favorite with his crusty employer, and, when the labors of the office were ended, brought home such books as he needed, and spent his evenings in study. His powers of application and endurance were extraordinary, and his progress was in the same ratio. As he became more and more absorbed in these pursuits his reserve and taciturnity increased, and his habitually hasty step and abstracted expression of countenance told of a strong nature straining its powers to the utmost to attain some distant, glimmering goal. His employer was particularly impressed by the fact that he never volunteered a remark on any subject, and rarely opened his lips except to ask some necessary information in connection with his business. Sometimes the silence of the office was unbroken for hours, save by the dull scratching of pens, or an impatient exclamation from Mr. Campbell. Respectful in deportment, attentive to his duties, never presuming upon kindness, constantly at work from morning until night, yet with an unmistakable sorrow printed on his face—a sorrow never obtruded on any one, never alluded to—he won first the rigid scrutiny of the lawyer, then his deepest, most abiding affection. Naturally cold and undemonstrative in manner, Mr. Campbell gave little evidence of feeling of any kind, yet the piercing blue eye lost its keenness when resting on the tall, stalwart form of the clerk, and once or twice the wrinkled hand sought his broad shoulder almost caressingly. He had not married; had neither mother nor sisters to keep his nature loving and gentle; and, though he occasionally visited his brother, who was a minister in the same town, he was held in awe by the members of that brother's family. He comprehended Russell's character, and quietly facilitated his progress. There was no sycophancy on the part of the young man; no patronage on that of the employer.

One afternoon Irene tapped lightly at the cottage-door, and entered the kitchen. Mrs. Aubrey sat in a low chair close to the fireplace, engaged in knitting; her smooth, neat calico dress and spotless linen collar told that careful hands tended her, and the soft auburn hair brushed over her temples showed broad bands of gray as the evening sun shone on it. She turned her brown, sightless eyes toward the door, and asked in a low voice:

"Who is it?"

"It is only me, Mrs. Aubrey."

Irene bent down, laid her two hands on the widow's, and kissed her forehead.

"I am glad to hear your voice, Irene; it has been a long time since you were here."

"Yes, a good many weeks, I know; but I could not come."

"Are you well? Your hands and face are cold."

"Yes, thank you, very well. I am always cold, I believe. Hugh says I am. Here are some flowers from the greenhouse. I brought them because they are so fragrant; and here, too, are a few oranges from the same place. Hush! don't thank me, if you please. I wish I could come here oftener. I always feel better after being with you; but I can't always come when I want to do so."

"Why not, Irene?"

"Oh, because of various things. Between school and music, and riding and reading, I have very little time; and, besides, father wants me with him when he is at home. I play chess with him, and sometimes we are three or four days finishing one game. Somehow, Mrs. Aubrey, though I don't mean to be idle, it seems to me that I do very little. Everybody ought to be of some use in this world, but I feel like a bunch of mistletoe growing on somebody else, and doing nothing. I don't intend to sit down and hold my hands all my life, but what can I do? Tell me how to begin."

She lifted a large tortoise-colored cat from a small stool and drew it near the hearth, just at the widow's feet, seating herself and removing her hat.

"That is more easily asked than answered; you are a great heiress, Irene, and in all human probability will never be obliged to do anything. For what is generally denominated work, you will have no occasion; but all who wish to be really happy should be employed in some way. You will not have to labor for your food and clothes like my Russell and Electra; but you will have it in your power to do a vast deal more good. In cultivating your mind, do not forget your heart; it is naturally full of very generous, noble impulses; but all human beings have faults; what yours may be you know best, and you should constantly strive to correct them. Read your Bible, dear child; not now and then, but daily and prayerfully. Oh, Irene! I have had some bitter, bitter sorrows, and frequently I thought that they would crush out my life. In those times of trial, if I had not had my Bible and my God I believe I should have lost my reason. But I read and was comforted. His promises sustained me; and in looking back I see many places which should be called *Jehovah-Jireh*, for the Lord saw and provided. Your Bible will teach you your duty much better than I possibly can. You owe your father a great deal; his hopes and joys centre in you, and through life he will look to you for his happiness. When you are grown, society, too, will claim you; you will be sought after and flattered; and, Irene, under these circumstances—with your remarkable beauty and wealth—you will find it a difficult matter to avoid being spoiled. Your influence will be very great, and a fearful responsibility must attend its employment. Let it be for good. Try to keep your heart free from all selfish or ignoble feelings; pray to God for guidance, that you may be enabled through His grace to keep yourself 'unspotted from the world;' those words contain the whole: '*unspotted from the world.*' You have not been spoiled thus far by luxury and life-long petting, and I hope and believe that you never will be; but remember, we must be continually on the watch against temptation. Irene, have I spoken too plainly?"

"No; I thank you for your candor. I want you to advise me just as you would Electra. I don't read my Bible as often as I ought, but there are so many things in it which I do not understand that I hardly ever open it now. I have nobody to explain the difficulties."

"It is very clear on the subject of our duty; God left not the shadow of mystery in his laws for the government of the heart and regulation of the life. He commands us to receive certain rules, to practice certain principles, and to abstain from certain sinful things, all of which are specified, and not to be mistaken by even the most obtuse. Melvill has said, in one of his beautiful and comforting sermons: 'God breathed himself into the compositions of prophets and apostles and evangelists, and there, as in the mystic recesses of an everlasting sanctuary, he still resides, ready to disclose himself to the humble and to be evoked by the prayerful. But in regard to every other book, however fraught it may be with the maxims of piety, however pregnant with momentous truth, there is nothing of this shrining himself of Deity in the depths of its meaning. Men may be instructed by its pages, and draw from them hope and consolation, but never will they find there the burning Shekinah which proclaims the actual presence of God; never hear a voice as from the solitudes of an oracle pronouncing the words of immortality.'"

"How then does it happen, Mrs. Aubrey, that different churches teach such conflicting doctrines? Why are there so many denominations? If the teachings of the Bible are so plain, how can such various creeds arise?"

"Because poor human nature is so full of foibles; because charity, the fundamental doctrine of Christ, is almost lost sight of by those churches; it has dwindled into a mere speck, in comparison with the trifles which they have magnified to usurp its place. Instead of one great Christian church holding the doctrines of the New Testament, practising the true spirit of the Saviour, and in genuine charity allowing its members to judge for themselves in the minor questions relating to religion—such for instance as the mode of baptism, the privilege of believing presbyters and bishops equal in dignity or otherwise, as the case may be, the necessity of ministers wearing surplices or the contrary, as individual taste dictates—we have various denominations, all erected to promulgate some particular dogma, to magnify and exalt as all-important some trifling difference in the form of church-government. Once established, the members of each sect apply themselves to the aggrandizement of their peculiar church; and thus it comes to pass that instead of one vast brotherhood, united against sin and infidelity, they are disgracefully wrangling about sectarian matters of no consequence whatever. In all this there is much totally antagonistic to the principles inculcated by our Saviour, who expressly denounced the short-sighted bigotry of those who magnified external observances and non-essentials at the expense of the genuine spirit of their religion. I wish most earnestly that these denominational barriers and distinctions could be swept away, that the names of Methodist and Episcopal, Presbyterian and Baptist could be obliterated, and that all the members were gathered harmoniously into one world-wide pale, the Protestant Church of our Lord Jesus Christ."

"Mrs. Aubrey, do you belong to any church?"

"Yes, Irene, because Christ founded a church, and I think every man and woman should belong to some religious organization. Moreover, unless a member of some one of the denominations, you can not commune; and, as the sacrament particularly established by our Saviour, all ought to be able to partake of it. I think it a matter of little consequence which of the evangelical sects one selects. Do not imagine that I believe people can only be saved by entrance into some church; I think no such thing; the church is a valuable instrument, but God who established it can work without it. Still, it is very reasonable to suppose that regular attendance on divine service fosters piety, and keeps the subject of our duty more constantly before us."

She had finished her knitting, and sat with her thin hands folded in her lap—the meek face more than usually serene, the sightless eyes directed toward her visitor. Sunshine flecked the bare boards under the window, flashed on the tin vessels ranged on the shelves, and lingered like a halo around Irene's head. Her hair swept on the floor, and the cat played now and then with the golden rings so softly as not to attract notice, as though conscious the new toy was precious. The countenances of the group contrasted vividly: the sweet resignation of the blind sufferer, the marble purity of Irene's face, and, just in the rear, Electra's broad, pale brow and restless, troubled, midnight eyes. The latter had been drawing at the table in the middle of the room, and now sat leaning on her hand, watching the two at the fire. Presently Irene approached and began to examine the drawings, which were fragmentary, except one or two heads, and a sketch taken from the bank opposite the Falls. After some moments passed in looked over them, Irene addressed the quiet little figure.

"Have you been to Mr. Clifton's studio?"

"No; who is he?"

"An artist from New York. His health is poor, and he is spending the winter South.

Have n't you heard of him? Everybody is having portraits taken. He is painting nine now—father would make me sit again, though he has a likeness which was painted four years ago. I am going down to-morrow for my last sitting, and should like very much for you to go with me. Perhaps Mr. Clifton can give you some valuable hints. Will you go?"

"With great pleasure."

"Then I will call for you a little before ten o'clock. Here are some crayons I bought for you a week ago. Good-by."

She left the room as quietly as she had entered, and found Paragon waiting for her at the door. He gambolled before her all the way—now darting off, and as suddenly returning, to throw himself at her feet and wonder why she failed to caress him as usual. Other thoughts engaged her now; she could see nothing but the form of the widow, and to-day she realized more than ever before how much she needed a mother. Low, sweet, gentle tones rarely fell upon her ear, and, except her father and Dr. Arnold, no one had ever attempted to caress her. She wearied of the fourteen years of isolation, and now on entering her fifteenth looked about her for at least one congenial spirit. She knew of none but Electra and Mrs. Aubrey who in any degree sympathized with her, and from these she was debarred by parental interdict. Miss Margaret, seconded by Mr. Huntingdon, now constantly prescribed a course of conduct detestable to the girl, who plainly perceived that as she grew older these differences increased. Was it her duty to submit unhesitatingly to their dictation? Did the command of filial obedience embrace all such matters, or was it modified—limited by the right of individual conscience? This consultation was long and patient, and the conclusion unalterable. She would do what she believed to be proper, whatever she thought her duty, at all hazards. She had no one to guide her, and must rely only on God and her own heart.

The following day Miss Margaret accompanied her to the studio. As the carriage approached the cottage-gate Irene directed the driver to stop.

"For what?" asked her aunt.

"Electra Grey is going with me; I promised to call for her. She has an extraordinary talent for drawing, and I want to introduce her to Mr. Clifton. Open the door, Andrew."

"Irene, are you deranged? Your father never would forgive you if he knew you associated with those people. I can't think of allowing that girl to enter this carriage. Drive on. I must really speak to Leonard about your obstinacy in visiting at that—"

"Stop, Andrew! If you don't choose to ride with Electra, Aunt Margaret, you may go on alone, for either she shall ride or I will walk with her."

Andrew opened the door, and she was stepping out, when Electra appeared in the walk and immediately joined her. Miss Margaret was thoroughly aroused and indignant, but thought it best to submit for the time, and when Irene introduced her friend she took no notice of her whatever, except by drawing herself up in one corner and lowering her veil. The girls talked during the remainder of the ride, and when they reached Mr. Clifton's door ran up the steps together, totally unmindful of the august lady's ill-humor.

The artist was standing before an easel which held Irene's unfinished portrait, and as he turned to greet his visitors Electra saw that, though thin and pale, his face was one of rare beauty and benevolence. His brown curling hair hung loosely about his shoulders, and an uncommonly long beard of the same silky texture descended almost to his waist. He shook hands with Irene, and looked inquiringly at her companion.

"Mr. Clifton, this is Miss Electra Grey, whose drawings I mentioned to you last week. I wish, if you please, you would examine some of them when you have leisure."

Electra looked for an instant into his large, clear gray eyes as he took her drawings, and said he would be glad to assist her, and knew that henceforth the tangled path would be smoothed and widened. She stood at the back of his chair during the hour's sitting, and with peculiar interest watched the strokes of his brush as the portrait grew under his practised hand. When Irene rose, the orphan moved away and began to scrutinize the numerous pictures scattered about the room. A great joy filled her heart and illumined her face, and she waited for the words of encouragement that she felt assured would be spoken. The artist looked over her sketches slowly, carefully, and his eye went back to her brilliant countenance, as if to read there answers to ciphers which perplexed him. But yet more baffling cryptography met him in the deep, flashing, appealing eyes, on the crimson, quivering lips, on the low, full brow, with its widely-separated black arches. Evidently the face possessed far more attraction than the drawings, and he made her sit down beside him, and passed his hand over her head and temples, as a professed phrenologist might preparatory to rendering a chart.

"Your sketches are very rough, very crude, but they also display great power of thought; some of them singular beauty of conception; and I see from your countenance that you are dissatisfied because the execution falls so far short of the conception. Let me talk to you candidly: you have uncommon talent, but the most exalted genius can not dispense with laborious study. Michael Angelo studied anatomy for twelve years; you will require long and earnest application before you can possibly accomplish anything of importance. The study of

Art is no mere pastime, as some people suppose; an artist's life is an arduous one at best. I have been told something of your history; you are very poor, and wish to make painting a profession. Think well before you decide this matter; remember that long, tedious months must elapse before you can hope to execute even an ordinary portrait. You must acquaint yourself with the anatomy of the human system before you undertake anything. I thought I had finished my course seven years ago, but I went to Italy and soon saw that I had only begun to learn my profession. Think well of all this."

"I have thought of it; I am willing to work any number of years; I have decided, and I am not be frightened from my purpose. I am poor, I can barely buy the necessary materials, much less the books, but I will be an artist yet. I have decided, sir; it is no new whim; it has been a bright dream to me all my life, and I am determined to realize it."

"Amen; so let it be, then. I shall remain here some weeks longer; come to me every day at ten o'clock, and I will instruct you. You shall have such books as you need, and with perseverance you have nothing to fear."

He went into the adjoining room and returned with a small volume. As he gave it to her, with some directions concerning the contents, she caught his hand to her lips, saying hastily:

"My guardian angel certainly brought you here to spend the winter. Oh, sir! I will prove my gratitude for your goodness by showing that I am not unworthy of it. I thank you from the very depths of my glad heart."

As she released his hand and left the studio he found two bright drops on his fingers—drops called forth by the most intense joy she had ever known. Having some commission from her aunt, she did not re-enter the carriage, and, after thanking Irene for her kindness, walked away. The ride home was very silent; Miss Margaret sat stiff and icy, looking quite insulted, while her niece was too much engrossed by other reflections to notice her. The latter spent the remainder of the morning in writing to Hugh and correcting her French exercises, and when summoned to dinner she entered the room expecting a storm. A glance sufficed to show her that Miss Margaret had not yet spoken to her father, though it was evident from her countenance that she was about to make what she considered an important revelation. The meal passed, however, without any allusion to the subject, and, knowing what she had to expect, Irene immediately withdrew to the library to give her aunt an opportunity of unburdening her mind. The struggle must come some time, and she longed to have it over as soon as possible. She threw up the sash, seated herself on the broad cedar window-sill, and began to work out a sum in algebra.

Nearly a half-hour passed; the slamming of the dining-room door was like the first line of foam curling and whitening the sea when the tempest sweeps forward; her father stamped into the library, and the storm broke over her.

"Irene! did n't I positively order you to keep away from that Aubrey family? What do you mean by setting me at defiance in this way, you wilful, spoiled, hard headed piece? Do you suppose I intend to put up with your obstinacy all my life, and let you walk roughshod over me and my commands? You have queened it long enough, my lady. If I don't rein you up, you will turn your aunt and me out of the house next, and invite that precious Aubrey crew to take possession. Your confounded stubbornness will ruin you yet. You deserve a good whipping, Miss; I can hardly keep my hands off of you."

He did not; rough hands seized her shoulders, jerked her from the window-sill, and shook her violently. Down fell book, slate, and pencil with a crash; down swept the heavy hair, blinding her. She put it back, folded her hands behind her as if for support, and, looking up at him, said in a low, steady, yet grieved tone:

"I am very sorry you are angry with me, Father."

"Devilish sorry, I dare say! Don't be hypocritical! Did n't I tell you to keep away from those people? Don't stand there like a block of stone; answer me!"

"Yes, sir; but I did not promise to do so. I am not hypocritical, Father."

"You did not promise, indeed! What do I care for promises? It was your duty to obey me."

"I don't think it was, Father, when you refused to give me any reason for avoiding Mrs. Aubrey or her family. They are unfortunate, but honorable people; and, being very poor and afflicted, I felt sorry for them. I can't see how my going there occasionally harms you, or me, or anybody else. I know very well that you dislike them, but you never told me why, and I can not imagine any good reason for it. Father, if I love them, why should not I associate with them?"

"Because I say you shan't! you tormenting, headstrong little imp!"

"My Father, that is no reason."

"Reason! I will put you where you will have no occasion for reasons. Oh! I can match you, you perverse little wretch! I am going to send you to a boarding-school, do you hear that? send you where you will have no Aubreys to abet your obstinacy and disobedience; where that temper of yours can be curbed. How will you relish getting up before day, kindling your own fire, if you have any, making your own bed, and living on bread and water? I will take you to New York, and keep you there till you are grown and learn common sense. Now get out of my sight!"

With a stamp of rage he pointed to the door. Hitherto she had stood quite still, but now an expression of anguish passed swiftly over her face, and she put out her hands appealingly—

"Father! my Father! don't send me away!! Please let me stay at home."

"Not if I live long enough to take you. Just as certainly as the sun shines in heaven, you will go as soon as your clothes can be made. Your aunt will have you ready in a week. Don't open your mouth to me! I don't want to hear another word from you. Take yourself off."

She picked up her slate and book and left the room. Her hat hung on the rack in the hall, and, taking it down, she passed out through the rear piazza. Paragon leaped and whined at sight of her; she unchained him, and, leaving the yard, turned into a narrow zigzag path leading in an opposite direction from the front of the house. The building stood on quite a hill, one side of which sloped down to the brink of a creek that emptied itself into the river a mile above the town. This declivity was thickly wooded, and, on the opposite side of the stream, a dense swamp stretched away. Cypress, pine, beech, magnolias, towered far as the eye could reach, and now, in the gathering gloom of evening, looked sombre and solemn. This was a favorite haunt of Irene's; she knew every nook of the forest and bend of the creek as well as the shy rabbits that flitted away at her approach; and on this occasion she sought a rude seat formed by the interlacing of two wild grape-vines. At her feet the channel ran deep and strong, and the rocky bed was distinctly seen; but a few yards off the stream widened into a small lake, and there, on its dark, still surface masses of water-lilies spread out their broad, green, glossy leaves. It was a lonely place; even in the day owls hooted one to another; and strange, harsh cries were heard from birds that never forsook the swamp. It was April, early April, and from the hill-side, fringed with honeysuckles of varied hue, and festooned with yellow jasmine that clambered in wild luxuriance over tree and shrub, the southern breeze wafted spicy, intoxicating aromas. Redbuds lifted their rosy limbs against dark, polished magnolias, and here and there masses of snow told where the dogwoods grew. Clusters of violets embroidered the hill-side, and crimson woodbine trailed over the ground, catching at every drooping bough, and climbing stealthily, anxious, like all weak natures, to hang on something sturdy. Irene usually revelled amid this wealth of floral beauty, but now she could not enjoy it. She looked at her favorites, and understood what was meant by the words—

"I see them all so excellently fair,
I see, not feel, how beautiful they are."

The first great grief of her life had fallen on her; heretofore all had been so serene, so flowery, that she could not easily understand or endure the crushing weight on her heart. Reared in seclusion, the thought of being sent from her beautiful, luxurious home, and thrust among utter strangers, startled and filled her with dread. She was astonished, pained, and mortified by her father's harsh language; and, loving him very sincerely, she shrank from the long separation he threatened; yet, amid all these complex emotions, she felt not the slightest regret for the course she had pursued; under similar circumstances she would again act just as she had done. Then came the remembrance that she might meet her unfortunate friends no more. Mrs. Aubrey was evidently declining rapidly, and what would become of Electra and Russell? They might move away; they, too, might die; nay, she might never come back to the home of her birth; death's harvest was in all seasons, and, looking upon the lakelet, she shuddered and moaned. The snowy water-lilies glanced up at her, and seemed to say, as they trembled unceasingly in the current far below the surface, "Bend! bend!" A passage in Dante, which she had read the week before, crossed her mind now, as she noted the constant swaying of the fragile flowers, so impotent to resist that under-current sweeping their roots:

"———No other plant,
Covered with leaves, or hardened in its stalk,
There lives, not bending to the water's sway."

He had selected reeds as a type of Patience, but the pale, pure, quivering lilies were to her a far more impressive symbol of Resignation. An aged gnarled cypress towered above her, and from the knotted limbs drooped long funeral wreaths of gray moss, fluttering mournfully in the evening wind, like badges of crape in houses of death. From amid this sombre drapery came the lonely hoot of an owl, and, with a strange sensation of desolation, Irene fell on her knees and committed herself to the care of the Great Shepherd. Darkness closed around, but as she prayed the silver rays of the evening-star peered down through the trembling streamers of moss and gleamed on the upturned face. She broke one of the lilies, and, fastening it among her curls, followed Paragon up the hill-side.

The week which succeeded was wretched to the girl, for her father's *surveillance* prevented her from visiting the cottage, even to say adieu to its inmates; and no alternative presented itself but to leave for them (in the hands of Nellie, her devoted nurse) a note containing a few parting words and assurances of unfading friendship and remembrance. The day of departure dawned rainy, gloomy, and the wind sobbed and wailed down the avenue as Irene stood at her window looking out on the lawn where her life had been passed. Although Nellie was weeping bitterly at her side, she had not shed a tear; but the face was full of grief, and her little hands were clasped tightly as the faithful nurse pressed them affectionately in her palms. Disengaging herself, Irene took an umbrella and went to the stable for a last look at Erebus. This tried her sorely; and her lip was unsteady when she left him and sought Paragon. The latter, little suspecting the true state of affairs, gambolled and whined as joyously as ever at her approach; and, when the crowned head went down moaningly on his silky neck, he barked and frisked in recognition of the caress. The breakfast-bell summoned her away, and, a half-hour after, she saw the lofty columns of the old house fade from view, and knew that many months, perhaps years, must elapse before the ancestral trees of the long avenue would wave again over the head of their young mistress. Her father sat beside her, moody and silent, and, when the brick wall and arched iron gate vanished from her sight, she sank back in one corner, and, covering her face with her hands, smothered a groan and fought desperately with her voiceless anguish.

CHAPTER VI.

Youth is hopeful, beautifully hopeful, and fresh pure hearts rebound from sorrow with wonderful elasticity. When clouds lower and the way seems dark and tangled, Hope flies forward, pioneer-like, to clear away all obstacles. Huge barriers frowned between Electra and the heights she strained every nerve to reach, but never for an instant did she doubt the success of the struggle. Like Orpheus seeking Eurydice, to look back was fearful and hazardous; and, fixing her eyes steadily on the future, she allowed herself no haunting foreboding.

"Cry, faint not! climb the summit's slope
Beyond the furthest flights of hope,
Wrapt in dense cloud from base to cope."

What human powers can endure and accomplish is to be measured only by the necessity which goads, and all herculean trophies are won by desperate needs. The laws which govern our moral and intellectual natures are as rigid and inevitable in their operation as those whose workings we constantly trace in the physical world—of which truth the history of nations and memoirs of great men furnish innumerable exemplifications. Consequently it is both unjust and illogical to judge of the probability of this or that event or series of events, or the naturalness of this or that character, whether in authenticated history or fictitious works, without a thorough acquaintance with all antecedents and the various relations surrounding the actor. Reader, as you walk side by side with these whose lives I am narrating, bear this in mind—the silver-winged pigeons that flash in and out of the venerable trees shading the old homestead, and coo and flutter amid the rainbow-spray of the fountain, would droop, shiver, and die on bald, awful Alpine pinnacles, where in the fierce howl and scourging of tempests eaglets wheel in triumph, and scream defiantly; and tender pet lambs, coaxed into flowery, luxuriant meadows, would soon make their graves in the murderous snow over which young chamois bleat and skip in wild glee, fearless as the everlasting hills.

Day after day Electra toiled over her work; the delicate frame learned its destiny, sighed at its future, but grew strong; and complaining nerves, catching some of her iron resolve, endured patiently—became finally thoroughly inured to their arduous duties. Her aunt constantly claimed her attention for the various little offices so grateful to an invalid, but by an extraordinary alchemy she contrived to convert every interruption into an occasion of profit. If lending her arm to support the drooping form in a short walk around the little garden, she would describe the varying tints of sky, as the clouds shifted their gorgeous curtains of purple and scarlet and gold, until thoroughly familiarized with the varied chameleon hues and strange, grotesque outlines traced by every rift. Nature was a vast storehouse of matchless, unapproachable beauty to that eager, thirsty soul—a boundless studio, filled with wonderful creations, open to her at all times—in the rosy, opaline flush of morning, the blazing splendor of full-orbed noon, the silver-gray of twilight, peopled with dusky phantoms, weird and shifting as Fata-Morgana—the still sublimity, the solemn, sacred witchery of star-crowned, immemorial Night. She answered the first hoarse call of thunder by stationing herself at the window to watch the stormy panorama sweep over the heavens; and not Ruysdael, nor Vandervelde, nor Turner ever gazed with more intense delight on the hurrying masses of vapor than that fragile girl, as she stood with the forked lightning glaring luridly over her upturned, enraptured face. Favored ones of fortune lean against marble pillars in royal museums to study the imperishable works of earth's grandest old artists; but she lived in a cosmopolitan temple whose skyey frescos were fresh from the hands of Jehovah himself. The rapidity of her progress astonished Mr. Clifton. He questioned her concerning the processes she employed in some of her curious combinations, but the fragmentary, abstracted nature of her conversation during the hours of instruction gave him little satisfactory information. His interest in her increased, until finally it became absorbing, and he gave her all the time that she could spare from home. The eagerness with which she listened to his directions, the facility with which she applied his rules, fully repaid him; and from day to day he postponed his return to the North, reluctant to leave his indefatigable pupil. Now and then the time of departure was fixed, but ere it arrived he wavered and procrastinated.

Electra knew that his stay had been prolonged beyond his original intention, and she dreaded the hour when she should be deprived of his aid and advice. Though their acquaintance had been so short, a strangely strong feeling had grown up in her heart toward him; a feeling of clinging tenderness, blended with earnest, undying gratitude. She knew that he understood her character and appreciated her struggles, and it soothed her fierce, proud heart, in some degree, to receive from him those tokens of constant remembrance which she so yearned to have from Russell. She felt, too, that she was not regarded as a stranger by the artist; she could see his sad eyes brighten at her entrance, and detect the tremor in his hand and voice when he spoke of going home. His health had improved, and the heat of summer had come; why did he linger? His evenings were often spent at the cottage, and even Mrs. Aubrey learned to smile at the sound of his step.

One morning, as Electra finished her lesson and rose to go, he said slowly, as if watching the effect of his words:

"This is the last hour I can give you. In two days I return to New York. Letters of importance came this morning; I have waited here too long already."

"Are you in earnest this time?"

"I am; it is absolutely necessary that I should return home."

"Mr. Clifton, what shall I do without you?"

"Suppose you had never seen me?"

"Then I should not have had to lose you. Oh, sir! I need you very much."

"Electra, child, you will conquer your difficulties without assistance from any one. You have nothing to fear."

"Yes, I know I shall conquer at last, but the way would be so much easier if you were only with me. I shall miss you more than I can tell you."

He passed his hand over her short shining hair, and mused for a moment as if laying conflicting emotions in the balance. She heard his deep, labored breathing, and saw the working of the muscles in his pale face; when he spoke, his voice was husky:

"You are right; you need me, and I want you always with me; we must not be parted. Electra, I say we shall not. Come to me, put your hands in mine—promise me that you will be my child, my pupil; I will take you to my mother, and we need never be separated. You require aid, such as can not be had here; in New York you shall have all that you want. Will you come with me?"

He held her hands in a vice-like grasp, and looked pleadingly into her astonished countenance. A mist gathered before her, and she closed her eyes.

"Electra, will you come?"

"Give me ten minutes to think," she answered shiveringly. He turned away and walked up and down the floor, taking care to conceal his face. She sat down before a table and dropped her forehead in her palms. What slight things often shape human destiny; how little people realize the consequences of seemingly trivial words, looks, or actions! The day before Electra would unhesitatingly have declined this proposition: but only that morning, as she passed Russell's door before breakfast, she saw him with Irene's farewell note in his hand; saw him press his lips hastily to the signature. Her jealous heart was on fire; the consciousness of his love for another rendered her reckless and indescribably miserable. In this mood she reflected: Mr. Clifton seemed to have become warmly attached to her, and could help her to attain the eminence she had in view; she was poor, why not accept his generous offer? Russell would not miss her—would not care whether she left him or remained. If she were far away, at least she would not be tormented by his coldness and indifference. The future (barring her ambitious dreams) was dim, joyless; she had to earn a support, she scorned to be dependent on her cousin, fame lured her on. Yes, she would go. Mr. Clifton took out his watch and paused beside her:

"Ten minutes have passed; Electra, will you come?"

She raised her bloodless face, stamped with stern resolve, and ere the words were pronounced he read his answer in the defiant gleam of her eyes, in the hard, curved lines of the mouth.

"Mr. Clifton, I can not go with you just now, for at present I can not, ought not, to leave my aunt. Helpless as she is, it would be cruel, ungrateful, to desert her; but things can not continue this way much longer, and I promise you that as soon as I can I will go to you. I want to be with you; I want somebody to care for me, and I know you will be a kind friend always. Most gratefully will I accept your generous offer so soon as I feel that I can do so."

He stooped and touched her forehead with his lips.

"My dear Electra, I will shield you from trials and difficulties; I will prize you above everything on earth; I know you are making a great sacrifice to be with me; I know how hard it is for you to leave home and relatives. But, my child, your aunt has only a short time to live; she is failing very fast, and your duty to her will not keep you here long. You are right to remain with her, but when she needs you no more I shall expect you to come to me in New York. Meantime, I shall write to you frequently, and supply you with such books and materials as you require. My pupil, I long to have you in my own home.

"Remember, no matter what happens, you have promised yourself to me."

"I shall not forget;" but he saw her shudder.

"Shall I speak to your aunt about this matter before I go?"

"No, it would only distress her; leave it all with me. It is late, and I must go. Good-by, sir."

He promised to see her again before his departure, and she walked home with her head bowed and a sharp continual pain gnawing at her heart.

In the calm, peaceful years of ordinary childhood the soul matures slowly; but a volcanic nature like Electra's, subjected to galling trials, rapidly hardens, and answers every stroke with the metallic ring of age. Keen susceptibility to joy or pain taught her early what less impressive characters are years in learning, and it was lamentably true that, while yet a mere girl, she suffered as acutely as a woman. The battle of life must be fought, and if one begins skirmishing in the cradle tactics are soon learned and the conflict ends more speedily. But Electra had also conned another lesson: to lock her troubles in her own heart, voicing no complaint, and when she sought her aunt, and read aloud the favorite chapters in the Bible, or led her up and down the garden-walk, talking of various things, telling of the growth of pet plants, there was no indication whatever of any unusual strife or extraordinary occurrence. Russell knew that a change had come over his cousin, but was too constantly engaged, too entirely absorbed by his studies, to ask or analyze the cause. She never watched at the gate for him now, never sprang with outstretched arms to meet him, never hung over the back of his chair and caressed his hands as formerly. When not waiting upon her aunt she was as intent on her books as he, and, though invariably kind and unselfish in her conduct toward him, she was evidently constrained in his presence. As the summer wore on Mrs. Aubrey's health failed rapidly, and she was confined to her couch. There, in a low chair close to the pillow, sat Electra reading, talking, exerting herself to the utmost to cheer the widow. She filled the thin fingers with dewy roses, and expatiated on the glories of the outer world, while the thoughts of the invalid wandered to the approaching shores of another realm, and she thanked God that, though thick folds of darkness shrouded earth, the veil dropped from her soul and the spiritual vision grew clear and piercing. If faith and resignation could be taught like music or arithmetic, then had Electra learned the grandest truths of Christianity; but it is a mournful fact that the bloody seal of Experience must stamp the lesson ere deep thinkers or strong natures receive it, and as she watched that precious life fade, like the purple light of summer in evening skies, the only feeling she knew was that of grief for the impending loss —undefined apprehension of coming isolation. If Mrs. Aubrey could have seen the countenance which bent over her pillow, her serene soul would have been painfully disturbed. She felt hot tears fall on her hands and cheeks, and knew that the lips which pressed hers often trembled; but this seemed natural enough under the circumstances, and she sank quietly down to the edge of the tomb ignorant of the sorrows that racked the girl's heart. One morning when Mr. Campbell, the pastor, had spent some time in the sick-room praying with the sufferer, and administering the sacrament of the Lord's Supper, Electra followed him to the door, leaving Russell with his mother. The gentle pastor took her hand kindly, and looked at her with filling eyes.

"You think my aunt is worse?"

"Yes, my child. I think that very soon she will be with her God. She will scarcely survive till night—"

She turned abruptly from him, and threw herself down across the foot of the bed, burying her face in her arms. Russell sat with his mother's hands in his, while she turned her brown eyes toward him and exhorted him to commit himself and his future to the hands of a merciful God. She told him how the promises of the Saviour had supported and cheered her in times of great need, and implored him to dedicate his energies, his talents, his life, to the service of his Maker. Electra was not forgotten; she advised her to go to a cousin of her mother residing in Virginia. Long before she had written to this lady, informing her of her own feebleness and of the girl's helpless condition; and a kind answer had been returned, cordially inviting the orphan to share her home, to become an inmate of her house. Russell could take her to these relatives as soon as possible. To all this no reply was made, and, a few moments later, when Russell kissed her tenderly and raised her pillow, she said faintly—

"If I could look upon your face once more, my son, it would not be hard to die. Let me see you in heaven, my dear, dear boy." These were the last words, and soon after a stupor fell upon her. Hour after hour passed; Mrs. Campbell came and sat beside the bed, and the three remained silent, now and then lifting bowed heads to look at the sleeper. Not a sound broke the stillness save the occasional chirp of a cricket, and a shy mouse crept twice across the floor, wondering at the silence, fixing its twinkling bright eyes on the motionless figures. The autumn day died slowly as the widow, and when the clock dirged out the sunset hour Russell rose, and, putting back the window-curtains, stooped and laid his face close to his mother's. Life is at best a struggle, and such perfect repose as greeted him is found only when the marble hands of Death transfer the soul to its guardian angel. No pulsation stirred the folds over the heart, or the soft bands of hair on the blue-veined temples; the still mouth had breathed its last sigh, and the meek brown eyes had opened in Eternity. The long, fierce ordeal had ended, the flames died out, and from smouldering ashes the purified spirit that had toiled and fainted not, that had been faithful to the end, patiently bearing many crosses, heard the voice of the Great Shepherd, and soared joyfully to the pearly gates of the Everlasting Home. The day bore her away on its wings, and as Russell touched the icy cheek a despairing cry rolled through the silent cottage—

"Oh, Mother! my own precious dead mother!"

Falling on his knees, he laid his head on her pillow, and when kind friendly hands bore her into the adjoining room, he knelt there still, unconscious of what passed, knowing only that the keenest of many blows had fallen, that the last and bitterest vial of sorrows had been emptied.

Night folded her starry curtains around the earth; darkness settled on river and hill and valley. It was late September; autumn winds rose, eager for their work of death, and rushed rudely through the forests, shaking the sturdy primeval monarchs in token of their mission and mastery, and shivering leaves rustled down before them, drifting into tiny grave-like hillocks. Gradually the stars caught the contagious gloom, and shrank behind the cloud-skirts sweeping the cold sky. It was a solemn, melancholy night, full of dreary phantoms, presaging a dark, dismal morrow. Amy Aubrey's still form reposed on the draped table in the kitchen, and the fitful candle-light showed only a dim, rigid outline of white linen. Mr. Campbell and his wife sat together in the next room, and the two young mourners were left in the silence of the kitchen. Russell sat at the open window, near the table; his head leaned on his hand, tearless, mute, still as his mother. At the opposite window stood Electra, pressing her face against the frame, looking out into the moaning, struggling night, striving to read the mystic characters dimly traced on the ash-gray hurrying clouds as the reckless winds parted their wan folds. The stony face of her merciless destiny seemed to frown down at her cold, grim, Sphinx-like. Hitherto she had walked with loved ones; now a vast sepulchre yawned to receive them; a tomb of clay for the quiet sleeper, one of perhaps final separation for Russell, and over this last hideous chasm Hope hovered with drooping wings. To leave him was like inurning her heart and all the joy she had ever known; and then, to crown her agony, a thousand Furies hissed "Irene will come back, and loving her he will forget that you toil among strangers."

She crushed her fingers against each other and stifled a groan, while the chilling voice of Destiny added, "Trample out this weakness; your path and his here separate widely; you are nothing to him, go to work earnestly, and cease repining." She shrank away from the window and approached her cousin. For two hours he had not changed his position—as far as she knew, had not moved a muscle. She sat down at his feet and crossed her arms over his knees; he took no notice of her.

"Oh, Russell! say something to me, or I shall die."

It was the last wail she ever suffered to escape her in his presence. He raised his head and put his hand on her forehead, but the trembling lips refused their office, and as she looked up at him tears rolled slowly down and fell on her cheek. She would have given worlds to mingle her tears with his, but no moisture came to her burning eyes; and there these two, so soon to separate, passed the remaining hours of that long, wretched night of watching. The stormy day lifted her pale, mournful face at last, and with it came the dreary patter and sobbing of autumn rain, making it doubly harrowing to commit the precious form to its long, last resting-place. Electra stood up beside her cousin and folded her arms together.

"Russell, I am not going to that cousin in Virginia. I could owe my bread and clothes to you, but not to her. She has children, and I do not intend to live on her charity. I know you and I must part; the sooner the better. I would not be willing to burden you a day longer. I am going to fit myself to work profitably. Mr. Clifton offered me a home in his house, said his mother was lonely, and would be rejoiced to have me; that letter which I received last week contained one from her, also urging me to come; and, Russell, I am going to New York to study with him as long as I need instruction. I did not tell aunt of this, because I knew it would grieve her to think that I would be thrown with strangers; and having fully determined to take this step, thought it best not to distress her by any allusion to it. You know it is my own affair, and I can decide it better than any one else."

His eyes were fixed on the shrouded table, and he answered without looking at her:

"No, Electra, you must go to Mrs. Harden; she seems anxious to have you; and as for being dependent on charity, you never shall be, so long as I live. You will merely reside under her roof, and shall not cost her a cent; leave this with me."

"I can not leave it with anybody; I must depend upon myself. I have thought a great deal about it, and my resolution is not to be shaken. You have been very kind to me, Russell, all my life; and only God knows how I love and thank you. But I will not accept your hard earnings in future; I should be miserable unless at work, and I tell you I must and will go to Mr. Clifton."

He looked at her now, surprised and pained.

"What is the matter with you, Electra? Have I not sorrows enough, that you must try to add another by your obstinacy? What would she. think of you?"

He rose, and laid his hand on the pure, smooth brow of the dead.

"There is nothing new the matter with me. I have determined to go; nobody has any right to control me, and it is worse than useless for you to oppose me. We have but little time to spend together; do not let us quarrel here in *her* presence. Let there be peace between us in these last hours. Oh, Russell! it is hard enough to part, even in love and kindness; do not add painful contention."

"So you prefer utter strangers to your relatives and friends?"

"Ties of blood are not the strongest; strangers step in to aid where relatives sometimes stand aloof and watch a fatal struggle. Remember Irene; who is nearer to you, she or your grandfather? Such a friend Mr. Clifton is to me, and go to him I will at all hazards. Drop the subject, if you please."

He looked at her an instant, then turned once more to his mother's face, and his cousin left them together.

The day was so inclement that only Mr. and Mrs. Campbell and Russell's employer attended the funeral. These few followed the gentle sleeper, and laid her down to rest till the star of Eternity dawns; and the storm chanted a long, thrilling requiem as the wet mound rose above the coffin.

Back to a deserted home, whence the crown of joy has been borne. What a hideous rack stands at the hearth-stone whereon merciless Memory stretches the bereaved ones! In hours such as this we cry out fiercely, "The sun of our life has gone down in starless, everlasting night; earth has no more glory, no more bloom or fragrance for us; the voices of gleeful children, the carol of summer birds, take the mournful measure of a dirge. We hug this great grief to our hearts; we hold our darling dead continually before us, and refuse to be glad again." We forget that Prometheus has passed from the world. Time bears precious healing on its broad pinions; folds its arms compassionately about us as a pitying father; softly binds up the jagged wounds, drugs memory, and though the poisonous sting is occasionally thrust forth, she soon relapses into stupor. So, in the infinite mercy of our God, close at the heels of Azrael follow the winged hours laden, like Sisters of Charity, with balm for the people.

The kind-hearted pastor and his wife urged the orphans to remove to their house for a few days at least, until the future could be mapped; but they preferred to meet and battle at once with the spectre which they knew stood waiting in the desolate cottage. At midnight a heavy sleep fell on Russell, who had thrown himself upon his mother's couch; and, softly spreading a shawl over him, Electra sat down by the dying fire on the kitchen-hearth and looked her future in the face. A few days sufficed to prepare for her journey; and a gentleman from New York, who had met her cousin in Mr. Campbell's office, consented to take charge of her and commit her to Mr. Clifton's hands. The scanty furniture was sent to an auction-room, and a piece of board nailed to the gate-post announced that the cottage was for rent. Russell decided to take his meals at a boarding-house, and occupy a small room over the office, which Mr. Campbell had placed at his disposal. On the same day the cousins bade adieu to the only spot they had called "home" for many years, and as Russell locked the door and joined Electra his melancholy face expressed, far better than words could have done, the pain it cost him to quit the house where his idolized mother had lived, suffered, and died. Mr. Colton was waiting for Electra at the hotel, whither the stage had been driven for passengers; and as she drew near and saw her trunk among others piled on top, she stopped and grasped Russell's hand between both hers. A livid paleness settled on her face, while her wild black eyes fastened on his features. She might never see him again; he was far dearer to her than her life; how could she bear to leave him, to put hundreds of miles between that face and her own? An icy hand clutched her heart as she gazed into his deep, sad, beautiful eyes. His feeling for her was a steady, serene affection, such as brothers have for dear young sisters, and to give her up now filled him with genuine, earnest sorrow.

"Electra, it is very hard to tell you goodby. You are all I have left, and I shall be desolate indeed when you are away. But the separation will not be long, I trust; in a few years we shall be able to have another home; and where my home is, yours must always be. Toil stretches before me like a sandy desert, but I shall cross it safely; and then, Electra, my dear cousin, we shall be parted no more. I should feel far better satisfied if you were with Mrs. Harden, but you determined otherwise, and, as you told me a few days ago, I have no right to control you. Write to me often, and believe that I shall do all that a brother could for you. Mr. Colton is waiting; good-by, darling."

He bent down to kiss her, and the strained, tortured look that greeted him he never forgot. She put her arms around his neck, and clung to him like a shivering weed driven by rough winds against a stone wall. He removed her clasping arms, and led her to Mr. Colton; but as the latter offered to assist her into the stage she drew back, that Russell might perform that office. While he almost lifted her to a seat, her fingers refused to release his, and he was forced to disengage them. Other passengers entered, and the door was closed. Russell stood near the window, and said gently, pitying her suffering:

"Electra, won't you say good-by?"

She leaned out till her cheek touched his, and in a hoarse tone uttered the fluttering words:

"Oh, Russell! Russell! good-by! May God have mercy on me!"

And the stage rolled swiftly on; men laughed, talked, and smoked; an October sun filled the sky with glory, and gilded the trees on the road-side; flame-colored leaves flashed in the air as the wind tossed them before it; the deep, continual thunder of the foaming falls rose soothingly from the river banks, and a wretched human thing pressed her bloodless face against the morocco lining of the coach and stared down, mute and tearless, into the wide grave of her all—

"Fresh as the first beam glittering on a sail,
That brings our friends up from the under world;
Sad as the last which reddens over one
That sinks with all we love below the verge,
So sad, so fresh, the days that are no more."

CHAPTER VII.

As tall tyrannous weeds and rank unshorn grass close over and crush out slender, pure, odorous floweretts on a hill-side, so the defects of Irene's character swiftly strengthened and developed in the new atmosphere in which she found herself. All the fostering stimulus of a hot-bed seemed applied to them, and her nobler impulses were in imminent danger of being entirely subdued. Diogenes Teufelsdröckh's "Crim Tartary Enclosure of a High Seminary" is but the prototype of hundreds, scattered up and down through Christendom; and the associations which surrounded Irene were well calculated to destroy the native purity and unselfishness of her nature. The school was on an extensive scale, thoroughly fashionable, and thither pupils were sent from every section of the United States. As regarded educational advantages, the institution was unexceptionable; the professors were considered unsurpassed in their several departments, and every provision was made for thorough tuition. But what a Babel reigned outside of the recitation-room. One hundred and forty girls to spend their recesses in envy, ridicule, malice, and detraction. The homely squad banded in implacable hatred against those whom nature had cast in moulds of beauty; the indolent and obtuse ever on the alert to decry the successful efforts of their superiors; the simply-clad children of parents in straitened circumstances feeding their discontent by gazing with undisguised envy at the richly-apparelled darlings of fortune; and the favored ones sneering at these unfortunates, pluming themselves on wealth, beauty,

intellect, as the case might be—growing more arrogant and insufferable day by day. A wretched climate this for a fresh, untainted soul; and it is surprising how really fond parents, anxious to promote the improvement of their daughters in every respect, hasten to place them where poisonous vapors wreathe and curl about them. The principals of such institutions are doubtless often conscientious, and strive to discharge their duty faithfully; but the evils of human nature are obstinate, difficult to subdue under even the most favorable auspices; and where such a mass of untrained souls are turned into an enclosure, to amuse themselves at one another's expense, mischief is sure to follow. Anxious to shake off the loneliness which so heavily oppressed her, Irene at first mingled freely among her companions; but she soon became disgusted with the conduct and opinions of the majority, and endeavored to find quiet in her own room. Maria Ashley, who shared the apartment, was the spoiled child of a Louisiana planter, and her views of life and duty were too utterly antagonistic to Irene's to allow of any pleasure in each other's society. To cheat the professors by ingenious stratagems, and to out-dress her companions, seemed the sum total of the girl's aspirations; and gradually, in lieu of the indifference she evinced toward her roommate, a positive hatred made itself apparent in numberless trifles. Feeling her own superiority, Irene held herself more and more aloof; her self-complacency grew amazingly, the graceful figure took a haughty, unbending posture, and a coldly contemptuous smile throned itself on her lip. The inevitable consequence was, that she became a target for the school. Thus the months crept away; her father wrote rarely, and Miss Margaret's letters contained no allusion to the family that had caused her banishment. Finally she wrote to Dr. Arnold, inquiring concerning Mrs. Aubrey, but no reply reached her. Early in winter a new pupil, a "day scholar," joined her class; she resided in New York, and very soon a strong friendship sprang up between them. Louisa Young was about Irene's age, very pretty, very gentle and winning in her manners. She was the daughter of an affluent merchant, and was blessed in the possession of parents who strove to rear their children as Christian parents should. Louisa's attachments were very warm and lasting, and ere long she insisted that her friend should visit her. Weary of the school, the latter gladly availed herself of the invitation, and one Friday afternoon she accompanied Louisa home. The mansion was almost palatial, and as Irene entered the splendidly-furnished parlors her own Southern home rose vividly before her.

"Mother, this is Miss Huntingdon."

Mrs. Young received her cordially, and as she held the gloved hand, and kindly expressed her pleasure at meeting her daughter's friend, the girl's heart gave a quick bound of joy.

"Come up stairs and put away your bonnet."

In Louisa's beautiful room the two sat talking of various things till the tea-bell rang. Mr. Young's greeting was scarcely less friendly than his wife's, and as they seated themselves at the table the stranger felt at home for the first time in New York.

"Where is Brother?" asked Louisa, glancing at the vacant seat opposite her own.

"He has not come home yet; I wonder what keeps him? There he is now, in the hall," answered the mother.

A moment after he entered and took his seat. He was tall, rather handsome, and looked about thirty. His sister presented her friend, and with a hasty bow he fastened his eyes on her face. Probably he was unconscious of the steadiness of his gaze, but Irene became restless under his fixed, earnest eye, and, perceiving her embarrassment, Mrs. Young said—

"Harvey, where have you been? Dr. Melville called here for you at four o'clock; said you had made some engagement with him."

"Yes, Mother; we have been visiting together this afternoon."

Withdrawing his eyes, he seemed to fall into a reverie, and took no part in the conversation that ensued. As the party adjourned to the sitting-room he paused on the rug and leaned his elbow on the mantle. Louisa lingered, and drew near. He passed his arm around her shoulders and looked affectionately down at her.

"Well, what is it?"

"Come into the sitting-room and help me entertain Irene, instead of going off to your stupid study; do, Harvey."

"A very reasonable request, truly! I must quit my work to talk to one of your schoolmates; nonsense! How old is she?"

"Fifteen. Is not she a beauty?"

"Yes."

"Oh, Harvey! you are so cold! I thought you would admire Irene prodigiously; and now you say 'yes' just exactly as if I had asked you whether it was snowing out of doors."

"Which is certainly the fact; the first flakes fell as I reached home."

He stepped to the window and looked out, saying carelessly—

"Go to your friend, and when you are at a loss for conversation, bring her to my study to see those sketches of Palmyra and Baalbec."

He passed on to his work and she to the sitting-room. The study was simply the library, handsomely fitted up with choice old books in richly-carved rosewood cases, and antique busts peering down from the tops of each. Crimson damask curtains swept from the ceiling to the carpet, and a luxurious armchair sat before the glowing coal-fire. The table was covered with books and loose sheets of paper were scattered around, as if the occupant had been suddenly called from his labor. The gas burned brightly; all things beckoned back to work. He sat down, glanced over the half-written sheets, numbered the pages, laid them away in the drawer, and opened a volume of St. Chrysostom. As the light fell on his countenance it was very apparent that he had been a student for years; that his mind was habituated to patient, laborious investigation. Gravity, utterly free from sorrow or sternness, marked his face; he might have passed all his days in that quiet room, for any impress which the cares or joys of outdoor life had left on his features; a strong, clear intellect; a lofty, earnest soul; a calm, unruffled heart, that knew not half its own unsounded abysses. He read industriously for some time, occasionally pausing to annotate; and once or twice he raised his head and listened, fancying footsteps in the hall. Finally he pushed the book away, took a turn across the floor, and resumed his seat. He could not rivet his attention on St. Chrysostom, and, folding his arms over his chest, he studied the red coals instead. Soon after, unmistakable steps fell on his ear, and a light tap at the door was followed by the entrance of the two girls. Irene came very reluctantly, fearful of intruding; but he rose, and placed a chair for her close to his own, assuring her that he was glad to see her there. Louisa found the portfolio, and, bringing it to the table, began to exhibit its treasures. The two leaned over it, and as Irene sat resting her cheek on her hand, the beauty of her face and figure was clearly revealed. Harvey remained silent, watching the changing expression of the visitor's countenance; and once he put out his hand to touch the hair floating over the back and arms of her chair. Gradually his still heart stirred, his brow flushed, and a new light burned in the deep clear eyes.

"Louisa, where did you get these?"

"Brother brought them home when he came from the East."

Irene lifted her eyes to his and said:

"Did you visit all these places? Did you go to that crumbling Temple of the Sun?"

He told her of his visit to the Old World, of its mournful ruins, its decaying glories: of the lessons he learned there; the sad but precious memories he brought back; and as he talked time passed unheeded—she forgot her embarrassment; they were strangers no longer. The clock struck ten; Louisa rose at once.

"Thank you, Harvey, for giving us so much of your time. Father and Mother will be waiting for you."

"Yes, I will join you at once."

She led the way back to the sitting-room, and a few moments afterward, to Irene's great surprise, the student came in, and sitting down before the table, opened the Bible and read a chapter. Then all knelt and he prayed. There was a strange spell on the visitor; in all this there was something so unexpected. It was the first time she had ever knelt around the family altar, and, as she rose, that sitting-room seemed suddenly converted into a temple of worship. Mutual " good-nights " were exchanged, and as Irene turned toward the young minister he held out his hand. She gave him hers, and he pressed it gently, saying:

"I trust this is the first of many pleasant evenings which we shall spend together."

"Thank you, sir. I hope so too, for I have not been as happy since I left home."

He smiled, and she walked on. His mother looked up as the door closed behind her, and exclaimed:

"What a wonderfully beautiful face she has! Louisa often rhapsodized about her, and now I am not at all surprised at her enthusiasm."

"Yes, such perfection of features as hers is seen but once in a lifetime. I have travelled over the greater part of the world; I have looked upon all types of beauty, from the Andalusians whom Murillo immortalized, to the far-famed Circassians of Kabarda, but never before have I found such a marvel of loveliness as that girl. In Venice I spent a morning studying one of Titian's faces, which somewhat resembles hers; there is an approximation to the same golden hair—forming a nimbus, as it were—the same contour of features, but Titian's picture lacked her pure, unsearchable, indescribable eyes. Have you noticed what a rare, anomalous color her hair is? There never was but one other head like it; the threads of fine gold in that celebrated lock of her own hair which Lucretia Borgia gave Cardinal Bembo, match Irene Huntingdon's exactly. Well and truly has it been said of that glittering relic in the Ambrozian Library, 'If ever hair was golden, it is this of Lucretia Borgia's; it is not red, it is not yellow, it is not auburn; it is golden, and nothing else.' I examined it curiously, and wondered whether the world could furnish a parallel; consequently, when that girl's head flashed before me I was startled. Stranger still than her beauty is the fact that it has not spoiled her thus far."

He folded his arms over his chest as if crushing out something.

His mother laughed.

"Why, Harvey! What a riddle you are. Take care, my son; that child would never do for a minister's wife."

"Of course not; who ever dreamed that she would? Good-night, Mother; I shall not be at home to breakfast; do not wait for me; I am going to Long Island with Dr. Melville."

He bent down to receive her customary kiss, and went to his own room.

"Louisa, how came your brother to be a minister?" asked Irene, when they had reached their apartment.

"When he was a boy he said he intended to preach, and father never dissuaded him. I was quite young when he went to the East, and since his return he has been so engrossed by his theological studies that we are rarely together. Harvey is a singular man—so silent, so equable, so cold in his manner, and yet he has a warm heart. He has declined two calls since his ordination; Dr. Melville's health is very poor, and Harvey frequently fills his pulpit. Sometimes he talks of going West, where ministers are scarce; thinks he could do more good there, but mother will not consent for him to leave us. I am afraid, though, he will go—he is so determined when he once makes up his mind. He is a dear, good brother; I know you will like him when you know him well; everybody loves Harvey."

The inclemency of the weather confined the girls to the house the following day. Harvey was absent at breakfast, and at dinner the chair opposite Irene's was still vacant. The afternoon wore away, and at dusk Louisa opened the piano and began to play Thalberg's " Home, sweet home." Irene sat on a sofa near the window, and as she listened visions of the South rose before her, till she realized—

"That a sorrow's crown of sorrow is remembering happier things."

She longed inexpressibly for her own home, for her father, for the suffering friends of the cottage, and, as she thought of his many trials, Russell's image was more distinct than all. She closed her eyes, and felt again his tight clasp of her hands; his passionate, pleading words sounded once more, "Oh, Irene! believe in me! believe in me always!" It seemed to her so unnatural, so cruel that they should be separated. Then came the memory of Mrs. Aubrey's words of counsel: "Pray constantly; keep yourself unspotted from the world." What would the blind woman think if she knew all the proud, scornful, harsh feelings which were now in her heart? A sensation of deep contrition and humiliation came upon her; she knew she was fast losing the best impulses of her nature, and experienced keen regret that she had yielded to the evil associations and temptations of the school. How could she hope to grow better under such circumstances? What would become of her? The snow drifted against the panes, making fairy fretwork, and through the feathery flakes the gas-light at the corner burned steadily on. " So ought the light of conscience to burn," thought she; "so ought I to do my duty, no matter how I am situated. That light is all the more necessary because it is stormy and dark."

Somebody took a seat near her, and, though

the room was dim, she knew the tall form and the touch of his hand.

"Good-evening, Miss Irene; we have had a gloomy day. How have you and Louisa spent it?"

"Not very profitably I dare say, though it has not appeared at all gloomy to me. Have you been out in the snow?"

"Yes; my work has been sad. I buried a mother and child this afternoon, and have just come from a house of orphanage and grief. It is a difficult matter to realize how many aching hearts there are in this great city. Our mahogany doors shut out the wail that hourly goes up to God from the thousand sufferers in our midst."

Just then a servant lighted the chandelier, and she saw that he looked graver than ever. Louisa came up and put her arms around his neck, but he did not return the caress; said a few kind words, and rising, slowly paced the floor. As his eye fell on the piano he paused, saying, "Come, Louisa, sing that song for me."

She sat down and began, "Comfort ye my people;" and gradually the sadness melted from his features. As Irene listened to the solemn strains she found it difficult to control her feelings, and by degrees her head sank until it touched the arm of the sofa. The minister watched the effect of the music, and, resuming his seat, said gently:

"It is genuine philosophy to extract comfort and aid from every possible source. There is a vast amount of strength needed to combat the evils and trials which necessarily occur in even the sunniest, happiest lives; and I find that sometimes I derive far more from a song than a lengthy sermon. We are curious bits of mechanism, and frequently music effects what learned disputation or earnest exhortation could not accomplish. I remember once, when I was a child, I had given my mother a great deal of trouble by my obstinacy. She had entreated me, reasoned with me, and finally punished me, but all to no purpose; my wickedness had not been conquered. I was bitter and rebellious, and continued so all day. That evening she sat down to the piano and sang a hymn for my father. The instant the strains fell on my ear I felt softened, crept down stairs to the parlor-door, and before she had finished was crying heartily, begging her forgiveness. When a sublime air is made the vehicle of a noble sentiment there is no computing the amount of good it accomplishes, if properly directed. During my visit to London I went to hear a very celebrated divine. I had just lost a dear friend, the companion who travelled with me to Jerusalem and Meroe, and I went to church full of sorrow. The sermon was able, but had no more effect in comforting me than if I had not listened to it. He preached from that text of Job treating of the resurrection, and at the conclusion the very words of his text, 'I know that my Redeemer liveth,' were sung by the choir. When the organ rolled its solemn tones under the dim arched roof, and I heard the voices of the choir swelling deep and full—

'Throb through the ribbed stone,'

then, and not till then, I appreciated the grand words to which I had listened. The organ spoke to my soul as man could not, and I left the church calmed and comforted. All things are capable of yielding benefit, if properly applied, though it is a lamentable truth that gross abuse has involved many possible sources of good in disrepute; and it is our duty to extract elevating influences from all departments. Such an alchemy is especially the privilege of a Christian."

As he talked she lifted her beautiful eyes and looked steadily at him, and he thought that, of all the lovely things he had ever seen, that face was the most peerless. She drew closer to him, and said earnestly:

"Then you ought to be happy, Mr. Young."

"That implies a doubt that I am."

"You do not seem to me a very happy man."

"There you mistake me. I presume there are few happier persons."

"Countenance is not a faithful index, then; you look so exceedingly grave."

"Do you suppose that gravity of face is incompatible with sunshine in the heart?"

"I think it reasonable that the sunshine should sparkle in the eyes and gleam over the features. But, sir, I should like, if you please, to talk to you a little about other things. May I?"

"Certainly; speak on, and speak freely; you may trust me, I think."

He smiled encouragingly as he spoke, and without a moment's thought she laid her delicate hand in his.

"Mr. Young, I want somebody to advise me. Very often I am at a loss about my duty, and, having no one to consult, either do nothing at all, or that which I should not. If it will not trouble you too much, I should like to bring my difficulties to you sometimes, and get you to direct me. If you will only talk frankly to me, as you do to Louisa, oh! I will be very grateful."

He folded his hands softly over the white, fluttering fingers.

"Louisa is my sister, and therefore I do not hesitate to tell her unwelcome truths. But you happen to be a perfect stranger, and might not relish my counsel."

"Try me."

"How old are you? Pardon my inquisitiveness."

"Fifteen."

"An age when young ladies prefer flattery to truth. Have you no brother?"

"I am an only child."

".You would like a brother, however?"

"Yes, sir, above all things."

"Take care; you express yourself strongly. If you can fancy me for a brother, consider me such. One thing I can promise—you will have a guardian sleepless as Ladon, and untiring in his efforts to aid you as if he were in truth a Briareus. If you are not afraid of espionage, make me your brother. What say you?"

"I am not afraid, sir. I believe I need watching."

"Ah, that you do!" he exclaimed, with unusual emphasis.

"He can be very stern, Irene, gentle as he looks," suggested Louisa.

"If he never found fault with me I should not need his friendship."

When Monday morning came, and she was obliged to return to school, Irene reluctantly bade farewell to the new friends. She knew that, in conformity to the unalterable regulation of Crim Tartary, she could only leave the institution once a month, and the prospect of this long interval between her visits was by no means cheering. Harvey assisted her into the carriage.

"I shall send you some books in a day or two, and if you are troubled about anything before I see you again, write me a note by Louisa. I would call to see you occasionally if you were boarding anywhere else. Good-morning, Miss Irene; do not forget that I am your brother so long as you stay in New York, or need one."

The books were not forgotten; they arrived the ensuing week, and his selection satisfied her that he perfectly understood what kind of aid she required. Her visit made a lasting impression on her mind, and the Sabbath spent in Louisa's home often recurred to her in after years, as the memory of some green, sunny isle of rest haunts the dreams of weary, tempest-lashed mariners in a roaring sea. Maria Ashley was a sore trial of patience, and occasionally, after a fruitless struggle to rise above the temptations presented almost hourly, Irene looked longingly toward Louisa's fireside, as one turns to the last source of support. Finally she took refuge in silence, and, except when compelled to do so, rarely commented upon anything that occurred. The days were always busy, and when the text-books were finished she had recourse to those supplied by her new friends. At the close of the next month, instead of accompanying Louisa home, Irene was suffering with severe cold, and too much indisposed to quit the house. This was a grievous disappointment, but she bore it bravely and went on with her studies. What a dreary isolation in the midst of numbers of her own age. It was a thraldom that galled her; and more than once she implored her father's permission to return home. His replies were positive denials, and after a time she ceased to expect release until the prescribed course should be ended. Thus another month dragged itself away. On Friday morning Louisa was absent. Irene felt anxious and distressed; perhaps she was ill; something must have happened. As the day-pupils were dismissed she started back to her own room, heart-sick because of this second disappointment. "After all," thought she, "I may as well accustom myself to being alone. Of course I can't have the Youngs always. I must learn to depend on myself." She put away the bonnet and cloak laid out in readiness for departure, and sat down to write to her Aunt Margaret. A few minutes after a servant knocked at the door and informed her that a gentleman wished to see her in the parlor.

CHAPTER VIII.

"I am so glad to see you, Mr. Young. Louisa is not sick, I hope?"

"I came for you in Louisa's place; she is not well enough to quit her room. Did you suppose that I intended leaving you here for another month?"

"I was rather afraid you had forgotten me; the prospect was gloomy ten minutes ago. It seems a long time since I was with you."

She stood close to him, looking gladly into his face, unconscious of the effect of her words.

"You sent me no note all this time; why not?"

"I was afraid of troubling you; and, besides, I would rather tell you what I want you to know."

"Miss Irene, the carriage is at the door. I am a patient man, and can wait half an hour if you have any preparation to make."

In much less time she joined him, equipped for the ride, and took her place beside him in the carriage. As they reached his father's door, and he assisted her out, she saw him look at her very searchingly.

"It is time that you had a little fresh air. You are not quite yourself. Louisa is in her room; run up to her."

She found her friend suffering with sore throat, and was startled at the appearance of her flushed cheeks. Mrs. Young sat beside her, and after most cordial greetings the latter resigned her seat and left them, enjoining upon her daughter the necessity of remaining quiet.

"Mother was almost afraid for you to come, but I teased and coaxed for permission; told her that even if I had scarlet-fever, you had already had it, and would run no risk. Harvey says it is not scarlet-fever at all, and he persuaded mother to let him go after you. He always has things his own way, though he brings it about so quietly that nobody would ever suspect him of being self-willed. Harvey is a good friend of yours, Irene."

"I am very glad to hear it; he is certainly very kind to me. But recollect you are not to talk much; let me talk to you."

Mrs. Young sent up tea for both, and about nine o'clock Mr. Young and his son both entered. Louisa had fallen asleep holding Irene's hand, and her father cautiously felt the pulse and examined the countenance. The fever had abated, and, bending down, Harvey said softly:

"Can't you release your hand without waking her?"

"I am afraid not; have prayer without me to-night."

After the gentlemen withdrew, Mrs. Young and Irene watched the sleeper till midnight, when she awoke. The following morning found her much better, and Irene and the mother spent the day in her room. Late in the afternoon the minister came in and talked to his sister for some moments, then turned to his mother.

"Mother, I am going to take this visitor of yours down to the library; Louisa has monopolized her long enough. Come, Miss Irene, you shall join them again at tea."

He led the way, and she followed him very willingly. Placing her in a chair before the fire, he drew another to the rug, and seating himself, said just as if speaking to Louisa:

"What have you been doing these two months? What is it that clouds your face, my little sister?"

"Ah, sir! I am so weary of that school. You don't know what a relief it is to come here."

"It is rather natural that you should feel homesick. It is a fierce ordeal for a child like you to be thrust so far from home."

"I am not homesick now, I believe. I have in some degree become accustomed to the separation from my father; but I am growing so different from what I used to be; so different from what I expected. It grieves me to know that I am changing for the worse; but, somehow, I can't help it. I make good resolutions in the morning before I leave my room, and by noon I manage to break all of them. The girls try me, and I lose my patience. When I am at home nothing of this kind troubles me. I know you will think me very weak, and I dare say I am; still I try much harder than you think I do."

"If you never yielded to temptation you would be more than mortal. We are all prone to err; and, Miss Irene, did it never occur to you that, though you may be overcome by the evil prompting, yet the struggle to resist strengthened you? So long as life lasts this conflict will be waged; though you have not always succeeded thus far, earnest prayer and faithful resolve will enable you to conquer. Look to a merciful and watchful God for assistance; 'divine knowledge took the measure of every human necessity, and divine love and power gathered into salvation a more than adequate provision.' Louisa has told me the nature of the trials that beset you, and that you still strive to rise superior to them ought to encourage you. The books which I sent were calculated to aid you in your efforts to be gentle, forgiving, and charitable under adverse circumstances. I use the word charity in its broad, deep, true significance. Of all charities mere money-giving is the least; sympathy, kind words, gentle judgments, a friendly pressure of weary hands, an encouraging smile, will frequently outweigh a mint of coins. Bear this in mind: selfishness is the real root of all the evil in the world; people are too isolated, too much wrapped up in their individual rights, interests, or enjoyments. I, Me, Mine, is the God of the age. There are many noble exceptions; philanthropic associations abound in our cities, and individual instances of generous self-denial now and then flash out upon us. But we ought to live more for others than we do. Instead of the narrow limits which restrict so many, the whole family of the human race should possess our cordial sympathy. In proportion as we interest ourselves in promoting the good and happiness of others our natures become elevated, enlarged; our capacities for enjoyment are developed and increased. The happiest man I ever knew was a missionary in Syria. He had abandoned home, friends, and country; but, in laboring for the weal of strangers, enjoyed a peace, a serenity, a deep gladness, such as not the wealth of the Rothschilds could purchase. Do not misapprehend me. All can not be missionaries in the ordinary acceptation of that term. I believe that very few are really called to spend their lives under inclement skies, in dreary by-corners of the earth, amid hostile tribes. But true missionary work lies at every man's door, at every woman's; and, my little sister, yours waits for you, staring at you daily. 'Do the work that lies nearest to thee.' Let me give you the rule of a profound thinker, who might have accomplished incalculable good had he walked the narrow winding path which he stood afar off and pointed out to others: 'Know what thou canst work at, and work at it like a Hercules;' and, amid the holy hills of Jerusalem, the voice of Inspiration proclaimed: 'Whatsoever thy hand findeth to do, do it with thy might'"

His low voice fell soothingly on her ear; new energy kindled, new strength was infused, as she listened, and she said hastily:

"It would be an easy matter to do all this, if I had somebody like you always near to direct me."

"Then there would be no glory in conquering. Every soul has trials which must be borne without any assistance, save that which the Father mercifully bestows. Remember the sublime words of Isaiah: 'I have trodden the wine-press alone; and of the people there was none with me. And I looked, and there was none to help, and I wondered that there was none to uphold; therefore mine own arm brought salvation unto me.' Miss Irene, you, too, must '*tread the wine-press alone.*'"

She held her breath and looked up at him: the solemn emphasis of his words startled her; they fell upon her weighty as prophecy, adumbrating weary years of ceaseless struggling. The fire-light glowed on her sculptured features, and he saw an expression of vague dread in her glance.

"Miss Irene, yours is not a clinging, dependent disposition; if I have rightly understood your character, you have never been accustomed to lean upon others. After relying on yourself so long, why yield to mistrust now? With years should grow the power, the determination, to do the work you find laid out for you."

"It is precisely because I know how very poorly I have managed myself thus far, that I have no confidence in my own powers for future emergencies. Either I have lived alone too long, or else not long enough: I rather think the last. If they had only suffered me to act as I wished, I should have been so much better at home. Oh, sir! I am not the girl I was eight months ago. I knew how it would be when they sent me here."

Resting her chin in her hands she gazed sadly into the grate, and saw, amid glowing coals, the walls of the vine-clad cottage, the gentle face of the blind woman groping her way, the melancholy eyes of one inexpressibly dear to her.

"We can not always live secluded, and at some period of your life you would have been forced to enter the world and combat its troubles, even had you never seen New York. It is comparatively easy for anchorites to preserve a passionless, equable temperament; but to ignore the very circumstances and relations of social existence in which God intended that we should be purified and ennobled by trial, is both sinful and cowardly."

Taking a small volume from the table, he read impressively:

"What are we set on earth for? Say, to toil;
Nor seek to leave thy tending of the vines,
For all the heat o' the day, till it declines,
And death's mild curfew shall from work assoil.
God did anoint thee with his odorous oil,
To wrestle, not to reign . . . . . so others shall
Take patience, labor, to their heart and hand,
From thy hand, and thy heart. and thy brave cheer,
And God's grace fructify through thee to all."

"Some portentous cloud seems lowering over your future. What is it? You ought to be a gleeful girl, full of happy hopes."

She sank farther back in her chair to escape his searching gaze, and drooped her face lower.

"Yes, yes: I know I ought, but one can't always shut their eyes."

"Shut their eyes to what?"

"Various coming troubles, Mr. Young."

His lip curled slightly, and, replacing the book on the table, he said, as if speaking rather to himself than to her:

"'The heart knoweth his own bitterness, and a stranger doth not intermeddle with his joy.'"

"You are not a stranger, sir."

"I see you are disposed to consider me such. I thought I was your brother. But no matter; after a time all will be well."

She looked puzzled; and, as the tea-bell summoned them, he merely added:

"I do not wonder. You are a shy child; but you will soon learn to understand me; you will come to me with all your sorrows."

During the remainder of this visit she saw him no more. Louisa recovered rapidly, and when she asked for her brother on Sabbath evening, Mrs. Young said he was to preach twice that day. Monday morning arrived, and Irene returned to school with a heavy heart, fearing that she had wounded him; but a few days after Louisa brought her a book and brief note of kind words. About this time she noticed in her letters from home allusions to her own future lot, which increased her uneasiness. It was very palpable that her father expected her to accede to his wishes regarding a union with her cousin; and she knew only too well how fierce was the contest before her. Hugh wrote kindly, affectionately; and if she could have divested her mind of this apprehension, his letters would have comforted her. Thus situated, she turned to her books with redoubled zest, and her naturally fine intellect was taxed to the utmost. Her well-earned pre-eminence in her classes increased the jealousy, the dislike, and censoriousness of her less studious companions. Months passed; and though she preserved a calm, impenetrable exterior, taking no heed of sneers and constant persecution, yet the worm gnawed its slow way, and the plague-spot spread in that whilom pure spirit. One Saturday morning she sat quite alone in her small room; the week had been specially painful, and, wearied in soul, the girl laid her head down on her folded arms and thought of her home in the far South. The spicy fragrance of orange and magnolia came to her, and Erebus and Paragon haunted her recollection. Oh! for one ride through the old pine-woods. Oh! for one look at the water-lilies bending over the creek. Only one wretched year had passed—how could she endure those which were to come. A loud rap startled her from this painful reverie, and, ere she could utter the stereotyped "come in," Louisa sprang to her side.

"I have come for you, Irene; have obtained permission from Dr. ——— for you to accompany us to the Academy of Design. Put on your bonnet; Harvey is waiting in the reception-room. We shall have a charming day."

"Ah, Louisa! you are all very kind to recollect me so constantly. It will give me great pleasure to go."

When they joined the minister Irene fancied he received her coldly, and as they walked on he took no part in the conversation. The annual exhibition had just opened; the rooms were thronged with visitors, and the hushed tones swelled to a monotonous hum. Some stood in groups, expatiating eagerly on certain pictures; others occupied the seats and leisurely scanned now the paintings, now the crowd. Furnished with a catalogue, the girls moved slowly on, while Mr. Young pointed out the prominent beauties or defects of the works exhibited. They made the circuit of the room, and began a second tour, when their attention was attracted by a girl who stood in one corner, with her hands clasped behind her. She was gazing very intently on an Ecce-Homo, and, though her face was turned toward the wall, the posture bespoke most unusual interest. She was dressed in black, and, having removed her straw hat, the rippling jetty hair, cut short like a boy's, glistened in the mellow light. Irene looked at her an instant, and held her breath; she had seen only one other head which resembled that—she knew the purplish waving hair. "What is the matter?" asked the minister, noting the change in her countenance. She made no answer, but leaned forward to catch a glimpse of the face. Just then the black figure moved slightly; she saw the profile, the beautiful straight nose, the arched brow, the clear olive cheek; and gliding up to her she exclaimed:

"Electra! Electra Grey!"

The orphan turned, and they were locked in a tight embrace.

"Oh, Irie! I am so glad to see you. I have been here so long, and looked for you so often, that I had almost despaired. Whenever I walk down Broadway, whenever I go out any where, I look at every face, peep into every bonnet, hoping to find you. Oh! I am so glad."

Joy flushed the cheeks and fired the deep eyes, and people turned from the canvas on the walls to gaze upon two faces surpassing in beauty aught that the Academy contained.

"But what are you doing in New York, Electra? Is Russell with you? How long have you been here?"

"Since October last. Russell is at home; no, he has no home now. When my aunt died we separated; I came on to study under Mr. Clifton's care. Have you not heard of our loss?"

"I have been able to hear nothing of you. I wrote to Dr. Arnold, inquiring after you, but he probably never received my letter."

"And your father?" queried Electra proudly.

"Father told me nothing."

"Is the grave not deep enough for his hate?"

"What do you mean?"

"You don't probably know all that I do; but this is no place to discuss such matters; some time we will talk of it. Do come and see me soon—soon. I must go now, I promised."

"Where do you live; I will go home with you now."

"I am not going home immediately. Mr. Clifton's house is No. 85 West —— street. Come this afternoon."

With a long, warm pressure of hands they parted, and Irene stood looking after the graceful figure till it glided out of sight.

"In the name of wonder, who is that? You two have been the 'observed of all observers,'" ejaculated the impulsive Louisa.

"That is my old school-mate and friend of whom I once spoke to you. I had no idea that she was in New York. She is a poor orphan."

"Are you ready to return home? This episode has evidently driven pictures out of your head for to-day," said Mr. Young, who had endeavored to screen her from observation.

"Yes, quite ready to go, though I have enjoyed the morning very much indeed, thanks to your kindness."

Soon after they reached home Louisa was called into the parlor to see a young friend; and as Mrs. Young was absent, Irene found it rather lonely up stairs. She thought of a new volume of travels which she had noticed on the hall-table as they entered, and started down to get it. About half-way of the flight of steps she caught her foot in the carpeting, where one of the rods chanced to be loose, and, despite her efforts to grasp the railing, fell to the floor of the hall, crushing one arm under her. The library-door was thrown open instantly, and the minister came out. She lay motionless, and he bent over her.

"Irene! where are you hurt? Speak to me."

He raised her in his arms and placed her on the sofa in the sitting-room. The motion produced great pain, and she groaned and shut her eyes. A crystal vase containing some exquisite perfume stood on his mother's work-table, and, pouring a portion of the contents in his palm, he bathed her forehead. Acute suffering distorted her features, and his face grew pallid as her own while he watched her. Taking her hand, he repeated:

"Irene, my darling! tell me how you are hurt?"

She looked at him, and said with some difficulty:

"My ankle pains me very much, and I believe my arm is broken. I can't move it."

"Thank God you were not killed."

He kissed her, then turned away and despatched a servant for a physician. He summoned Louisa, and inquired fruitlessly for his mother; no one knew whither she had gone; it would not do to wait for her." He stood by the sofa and prepared the necessary bandages, while his sister could only cry over and caress the sufferer. When the physician came the white dimpled arm was bared, and he discovered that the bone was broken. The setting was extremely painful, but she lay with closed eyes and firmly compressed lips, uttering no sound, giving no token of the torture, save in the wrinkling of her forehead. They bound the arm tightly, and then the doctor said that the ankle was badly strained and swollen, but there was, luckily, no fracture. He gave minute directions to the minister and withdrew, praising the patient's remarkable fortitude. Louisa would talk, and her brother sent her off to prepare a room for her friend.

"I think I had better go back to the Institute, Mr. Young. It will be a long time before I can walk again, and I wish you would have me carried back. Dr. —— will be so uneasy, and will prefer my returning, as Father left me in his charge." She tried to rise, but sank back on the pillow.

"Hush! hush! You will stay where you are, little cripple. I am only thankful you happened to be here."

He smoothed the folds of hair from her temples, and for the first time played with the curls he had so often before been tempted to touch. She looked so slight, so childish, with her head nestled against the pillow, that he forgot she was almost sixteen, forgot everything but the beauty of the pale face, and bent over her with an expression of the tenderest love. She was suffering too much to notice his countenance, and only felt that he was very kind and gentle. Mrs. Young came in very soon, and heard with the deepest solicitude of what had occurred. Irene again requested to be taken to the school, fearing that she would cause too much trouble during her long confinement to the house. But Mrs. Young stopped her arguments with kisses, and would listen to no such arrangement; she would trust to no one but herself to nurse "the bruised Southern lily." Having seen that all was in readiness, she insisted on carrying her guest to the room adjoining Louisa's and opening into her own. Mr. Young had gone to Boston the day before, and, turning to her son, she said:

"Harvey, as your father is away, you must take Irene up stairs; I am not strong enough. Be careful that you do not hurt her."

She led the way, and bending down, he whispered:

"My little sister, put this uninjured arm around my neck; there—now I shall carry you as easily as if you were in a cradle."

He held her firmly, and as he bore her up the steps the white face lay on his bosom and the golden hair floated against his cheek. If she had looked at him then, she would have seen more than he intended that any one should know; for, young and free from vanity though she was, it was impossible to mistake the expression of the eyes riveted upon her. She never knew how his great heart throbbed, nor suspected that he turned his lips to the streaming curls. As he consigned her to his mother's care she held out her hand and thanked him for his great kindness, little dreaming of the emotions with which he held her fingers. He very considerately offered to go at once to the principal of the school and acquaint him with all that had occurred; and, ere long, when an anodyne had been administered, she fell asleep, and found temporary relief. Mrs. Young wrote immediately to Mr. Huntingdon, and explained the circumstances which had made his daughter her guest for some weeks at least, assuring him that he need indulge no apprehension whatever on her account, as she would nurse her as tenderly as a mother could. Stupefied by the opiate, Irene took little notice of what passed, except when roused by the pain consequent upon dressing the ankle. Louisa went to school as usual, but her mother rarely left their guest; and after Mr. Young's return he treated her with all the affectionate consideration of a parent. Several days after the occurrence of the accident Irene turned toward the minister, who stood talking to his mother.

"Your constant kindness emboldens me to ask a favor of you, which I think you will scarcely deny me. I am very anxious to see the friend whom I so unexpectedly met at the Academy of Design; and if she knew the circumstances that prevent my leaving the house, I am very sure she would come to me. Here is a card containing her address; will you spare me the time to bring her here to-day? I shall be very much obliged to you."

"I think you ought to keep perfectly quiet, and see no company for a few days. Can't you wait patiently?"

"It will do me no harm to see her. I feel as if I could not wait."

"Very well. I will go after her as soon as I have fulfilled a previous engagement. What is her name?"

"Electra Grey. Did you notice her face?"

"Yes; but why do you ask?"

"Because I think she resembles your mother."

"She resembles far more an old portrait hanging in my room. I remarked it as soon as I saw her."

He seemed lost in thought, and immediately after left the room. An hour later Irene's listening ear detected the opening and closing of the hall-door.

"There is Electra on the steps; I hear her voice. Will you please open the door?"

Mrs. Young laid down her work and rose to comply, but Harvey ushered the stranger in and then retired.

The lady of the house looked at the newcomer, and a startled expression came instantly into her countenance. She made a step forward and paused irresolute.

"Mrs. Young, allow me to introduce my friend, Miss Electra Grey." Electra bowed, and Mrs. Young exclaimed:

"Grey! Grey! Electra Grey; and so like Robert? Oh! it must be so. Child, who are you? Where are your parents?"

She approached, and put her hand on the girl's shoulders, while a hopeful light kindled in her eyes.

"I am an orphan, Madam, from the South. My father died before my birth—my mother immediately after."

"Was your father's name Robert? Where was he from?"

"His name was Enoch R. Grey. I don't know what his middle name was. He came originally from Pennsylvania, I believe."

"Oh! I knew that I could not be mistaken! My brother's child! Robert's child!"

She threw her arms around the astonished girl and strained her to her heart.

"There must be some mistake, Madam. I never heard that I had relatives in New York."

"Oh, child! call me Aunt; I am your father's sister. We called him by his middle name, Robert, and for eighteen years have heard nothing of him. Sit down here, and let me tell you the circumstances. Your father was the youngest of three children, and in his youth gave us great distress by his wildness; he ran away from college and went to sea. After an absence of three years he returned, almost a wreck of his former self. My mother had died during his long voyage to the South Sea islands, and father, who believed him to have been the remote cause of her death (for her health failed soon after he left), upbraided him most harshly and unwisely. His reproaches drove poor Robert to desperation, and, without giving us any clew, he left home as suddenly as before. Whither he went we never knew. Father was so incensed that he entirely disinherited him; but at his death, when the estate was divided, my Brother William and I decided that we would take only what we considered our proportion, and we set apart one-third for Robert. We advertised for several years, but could hear nothing of him; and at the end of the fifth year William divided that remaining third. We knew that he must have died, and I have passed many a sleepless night weeping over his wretched lot, mourning that no kind words reached him from us—that no monumental stone marked his unknown grave. Oh, my dear child! I am so glad to find you out. But where have you been all this time? Where did Robert die?"

She held the orphan's hand, and made no attempt to conceal the tears that rolled over her cheeks. Electra gave her a detailed account of her life from the time when she was taken to her uncle, Mr. Aubrey, at the age of four months, till the death of her aunt and her removal to New York.

"And Robert's child has been in want, while we knew not of her existence! Oh, Electra! you shall have no more sorrow that we can shield you from. I loved your father very devotedly, and I shall love his orphan quite as dearly. Come to me; let me be your mother. Let me repair the wrong of by-gone years."

She folded her arms around the graceful young form and sobbed aloud, while Irene found it difficult to repress her own tears of sympathy and joy that her friend had found such relatives. Of the three, Electra was calmest. Though glad to meet with her father's family, she knew better than they that this circumstance could make little alteration in her life, and therefore, when Mrs. Young left the room to acquaint her husband and son with the discovery she had made, Electra sat down beside her friend's sofa just as she would have done two hours before.

"I am so glad for your sake that you are to come and live here. Until you know them all as well as I do, you can not properly appreciate your good fortune," said Irene, raising herself on her elbow.

"Yes, I am very glad to meet my aunt," returned Electra evasively, and then she added earnestly:

"But I rather think that I am gladder still to see you again. Oh, Irene! it seems an age since I came to this city. We have both changed a good deal; you look graver than when we parted that spring morning that you took me to see the painter. I owe even this acquaintance to your kindness."

"Tell me of all that happened after I left home. You know that I have heard nothing."

The orphan narrated the circumstances connected with her aunt's last illness and death; the wretchedness that came upon her and Russell; the necessity of their separation.

"And where is Russell now?"

"At home—that is, still with Mr. Campbell, who has proved a kind friend. Russell writes once a week; he seems tolerably cheerful, and speaks confidently of his future as a lawyer. He studies very hard, and I know that he will succeed."

"Your cousin is very ambitious. I wish he could have had a good education."

"It will be all the same in the end. He will educate himself thoroughly; he needs nobody's assistance," answered Electra with a proud smile.

"When you write to him again don't forget to tender him my remembrances and best wishes."

"Thank you."

A slight change came over the orphan's countenance, and her companion noted without understanding it.

"Electra, you spoke of my father the other day in a way that puzzled me, and I wish, if you please, you would tell me what you meant."

"I don't know that I ought to talk about things that should have been buried before you were born. But you probably know something of what happened. We found out after you left why you were so suddenly sent off to boarding-school, and you can have no idea how much my poor aunt was distressed at the thought of having caused your banishment. Irene, your father hated her, and of course you know it; but do you know why?"

"No; I never could imagine any adequate cause."

"Well I can tell you. Before Aunt Amy's marriage your father loved her, and to please her parents she accepted him. She was miserable, because she was very much attached to my uncle, and asked Mr. Huntingdon to release her from the engagement. He declined, and, finding that her parents sided with him, she left home and married against their wishes. They adopted a distant relative, and never gave her a cent. Your father never forgave her. He had great influence with the governor, and she went to him and entreated him to aid her in procuring a pardon for her husband. He repulsed her cruelly, and used his influence against my uncle. She afterward saw a letter which he wrote to the governor, urging him to withhold a pardon. Oh, Irene! if you could have seen Russell when he found out all this. Now you have the key to his hatred; now you understand why he wrote you nothing concerning us. Not even Aunt Amy's coffin could shut in his hate."

She rose, and, walking to the window, pressed her face against the panes to cool her burning cheeks.

Irene had put her hand over her eyes, and a fearful panorama of coming years rolled before her in that brief moment. She saw with miserable distinctness the parallelism between Mrs. Aubrey's father and her own, and, sick at heart, she moaned, contemplating her lot. A feeling of remorseful compassion touched the orphan as she heard the smothered sound, and, resuming her seat, she said gently:

"Do not be distressed, Irene; 'let the dead past bury its dead;' it is all over now, and no more harm can come of it. I shall be sorry that I told you if you let it trouble you."

Irene knew too well that it was not over; that it was but the beginning of harm to her; but she repressed her emotion, and changed the subject by inquiring how Electra progressed with her painting.

"Even better than I hoped. Mr. Clifton is an admirable master, and does all that he can to aid me. I shall succeed, Irene! I know, I feel that I shall, and it is a great joy to me."

"I am very glad to hear it; but now you will have no need to labor, as you once expected to do. You are looking much better than I ever saw you, and have grown taller. You are nearly sixteen, I believe?"

"Yes, sixteen. I am three months your senior. Irene, I must go home now, for they will wonder what has become of me. I will see you again soon."

She was detained by her aunt, and presented to the remainder of the family, and it was arranged that Mr. and Mrs. Young should visit her the ensuing day. While they talked over the tea-table of the newly-found, Harvey went slowly up stairs and knocked at Irene's door. Louisa was chattering delightedly about her cousin, and, sending her down to her tea, he took her seat beside the sofa. Irene lay with her fingers over her eyes, and he said gently:

"You see that I am wiser than you, Irene. I knew that it would do you no good to have company. Next time be advised."

"It was not Electra that harmed me."

"Then you admit that you have been harmed?"

"No; I am low-spirited to-night; I believe that is all."

"You have not studied dialectics yet. People are not low-spirited without a cause; tell me what troubles you."

She turned her face to the wall, and answered:

"Oh! there is nothing which I can tell you, sir."

"Irene, why do you distrust me?"

"I do not; indeed I do not. You must not believe that for one moment."

"You are distressed, and yet will not confide in me."

"It is something which I ought not to tell even my friend—my brother."

"You are sure that it is something I could not remedy?"

"Yes, sir; perfectly sure."

"Then try to forget it, and let me read to you."

He opened the "Rambler," of which she was particularly fond, and began to read. For a while she listened, and in her interest forgot her forebodings, but after a time the long silky lashes swept her cheeks, and she slept. The minister laid down the volume and watched the pure girlish face; noted all its witching loveliness, and thought of the homage which it would win her in coming years. A few more fleeting months, and she would reign the undisputed queen of society. Wealth, intellect, manly beauty, all would bow before her; and she was a woman; would doubtless love and marry, like the majority of women. He set this fact before him and looked it in the face, but it would not answer; he could not realize that she would ever be other than the trusting, noble-hearted, beautiful child which she was to him. He knew as he sat watching her slumber that he loved her above everything on earth; that she wielded a power none had ever possessed before—that his heart was indissolubly linked with her. He had wrestled with this infatuation, had stationed himself on the platform of sound common sense, and railed at and ridiculed this piece of folly. His clear, cool reason gave solemn verdict against the fiercely-throbbing heart, but not one pulsation had been restrained. At his age, with his profession and long-laid plans, this was arrant madness, and he admitted it; but the long down-trodden feelings of his heart, having gained momentary freedom, exultingly ran riot and refused to be reined in. He might just as well have laid his palm on the whitened crest of surging billows in stormy, tropical seas, and bid them sink softly down to their coral pavements. Human passions, hatred, ambition, revenge, love, are despots; and the minister, who for thirty years had struggled for mastery over these, now found himself a slave. He had studied Irene's countenance too well not to know that a shadow rested on it now; and it grieved and perplexed him that she should conceal this trouble from him. As he sat looking down at her a mighty barrier rose between them. His future had long been determined—duty called him to the rude huts of the far West; thither pointed the finger of Destiny, and thither, at all hazards, he would go. He thought that he had habituated himself to sacrifices, but the spirit of self-abnegation was scarcely equal to this trial. Reason taught him that the tenderly-nurtured child of southern climes would never suit him for a companion in the pioneer life which he had marked out. Of course, he must leave her; hundreds of miles would intervene; his memory would fade from her mind, and for him it only remained to bury her image in the prairies of his new home. He folded his arms tightly over his chest, and resolved to go promptly.

The gas-light flashed on Irene's hair as it hung over the side of the sofa; he stooped and pressed his lips to the floating curls, and went down to the library smiling grimly at his own folly. Without delay he wrote two letters, and was dating a third, when his mother came in. Placing a chair for her, he laid down his pen.

"I am glad to see you, Mother; I want to have a talk with you."

"About what, Harvey?" an anxious look settled on her face.

"About my leaving you, and going West. I have decided to start next week."

"Oh, my son! how can you bring such grief upon me? Surely there is work enough for you to do here, without your tearing yourself from us."

"Yes, Mother, work enough, but hands enough also, without mine. These are the sunny slopes of the Vineyard, and laborers crowd to till them; but there are cold, shadowy, barren nooks and corners that equally demand cultivation. There the lines have fallen to me, and there I go to my work. Nay, Mother! don't weep; don't heighten, by your entreaties and remonstrances, the barriers to my departure. It is peculiarly the province of such as I to set forth for this field of operations; men who have wives and children have no right to subject them to the privations and hardships of pioneer life. But I am alone—shall always be so—and this call I feel to be imperative. You know that I have dedicated myself to the ministry, and whatever I firmly believe to be my duty to the holy cause I have espoused, that I must do even though it separate me from my mother. It is a severe ordeal to me—you will probably never know how severe; but we who profess to yield up all things for Christ must not shrink from sacrifice. I shall come back now and then, and letters are a blessed medium of communication and consolation. I have delayed my departure too long already."

"Oh, Harvey! have you fully determined on this step?"

"Yes, my dear Mother, fully determined to go."

"It is very hard for me to give up my only son. I can't say that I will reconcile myself to this separation; but you are old enough to decide your own future; and I suppose I ought not to urge you. For months I have opposed your resolution; now I will not longer remonstrate. Oh, Harvey! it makes my heart ache to part with you. If you were married, I should be better satisfied; but to think of you in your loneliness!" She laid her head on his shoulder and wept.

The minister compressed his lips firmly an instant, then replied:

"I always told you that I should never marry. I shall be too constantly occupied to sit down and feel lonely. Now, Mother, I must finish my letters, if you please, for they should go by the earliest mail."

CHAPTER IX.

The artist stood at the window watching for his pupil's return; it was the late afternoon hour, which they were wont to spend in reading, and her absence annoyed him. As he rested carelessly against the window, his graceful form was displayed to great advantage, and the long brown hair drooped about a classical face of almost feminine beauty. The delicacy of his features was enhanced by the extreme pallor of his complexion, and it was apparent that close application to his profession had made serious inroads on a constitution never very robust. A certain listlessness of manner, a sort of lazy-grace seemed characteristic; but when his pupil came in and laid aside her bonnet, the expression of *ennui* vanished, and he threw himself on a sofa, looking infinitely relieved. She drew near, and without hesitation acquainted him with the discovery of her relatives in New York. He listened in painful surprise, and, ere she had concluded, sprang up. "I understand! they will want to take you; will urge you to share their home of wealth. But, Electra, you won't leave me; surely you won't leave me?"

He put his hands on her shoulders, and she knew from his quick, irregular breathing that the thought of separation greatly distressed him.

"My aunt has not explicitly invited me to reside with her, though I inferred from her manner that she confidently expected me to do so. Irene also spoke of it as a settled matter."

"You will not allow them to persuade you? Oh, child! tell me at once that you will never leave me."

"Mr. Clifton, we must part some day; I can not always live here, you know. Before very long I must go out and earn my bread."

"Never! while I live. When I offered you a home, I expected it to be a permanent one. I intended to adopt you. Here, if you choose, you may work and earn a reputation; but away from me, among strangers, never. Electra, you forget; you gave yourself to me once."

She shuddered, and tried to release herself, but the hands were relentless in their grasp.

"Electra, you belong to me, my child. Whom have I to love but you, my dear pupil? What should I do without you?"

"I have no intention of living with my aunt; I desire to be under obligations to no one but yourself. But I am very proud, and even temporary dependence on you galls me. You are, I believe, the best friend I have on earth, and until I can support myself I will remain under your care; longer than that, it would be impossible. I am bound to you, my generous, kind master, as to no one else."

"This does not satisfy me; the thought that you will leave me, at even a distant day, will haunt me continually—marring all my joy. It can not be, Electra! You gave yourself to me once, and I claim you."

She looked into his eyes, and, with a woman's quick perception, read all the truth. In an instant her countenance changed painfully; she stooped, touched his hand with her lips, and exclaimed:

"Thank you, a thousand times, my friend, my father! for your interest in, and your unvarying, unparalleled kindness to me. All the gratitude and affection which a child could give to a parent I shall always cherish toward you. Since it annoys you, we will say no more about the future; let the years take care of themselves as they come."

"Will you promise me, positively, that you will not go to your aunt?"

"Yes; I have never seriously entertained the thought."

She escaped from his hands, and, lighting the gas, applied herself to her books for the next hour.

If Irene had found the restraint of boarding-school irksome, the separation from Russell was well nigh intolerable to Electra. At first she had seemed plunged in lethargy; but after a time this mood gave place to restless, unceasing activity. Like one trying to flee from something painful, she rushed daily to her work, and regretted when the hours of darkness consigned her to reflection. Mrs. Clifton was quite aged, and though uniformly gentle and affectionate toward the orphan, there was no common ground of congeniality on which they could meet. To a proud, exacting nature like Electra's, Mr. Clifton's constant manifestations of love and sympathy were very soothing. Writhing under the consciousness of her cousin's indifference, she turned eagerly to receive the tokens of affection showered upon her. She knew that his happiness centred in her, and vainly fancied that she could feed her hungry heart with his adoration. But by degrees she realized that these husks would not satisfy her; and a singular sensation of mingled gratitude and impatience arose whenever he caressed her. In his house her fine intellect found ample range; an extensive library wooed her, when not engaged with her pencil, and with eager curiosity she plunged into various departments of study. As might easily have been predicted, from the idealistic tendency of her entire mental conformation, she early selected the imaginative realm as peculiarly her own. Over moth-eaten volumes of mythologic lore she pored continually; effete theogonies and cosmogonies seized upon her fancy, and peopled all space with the gods and heroes of most ancient days. She lived among weird phantasmagoric creations of Sagas and Purānas, and roamed from Asgard to Kinkadulle, having little sympathy or care for the realities that surrounded her. Mr. Clifton's associates were principally artists, and the conversations to which she listened tended to increase her enthusiasm for the profession she had chosen. She had no female companion except Mrs. Clifton, and little leisure to discuss the topics which ordinarily engage girls of her age. The warm gushings of her heart were driven back to their springs, and locked from human gaze; yet she sometimes felt her isolation almost intolerable. To escape from herself she was goaded into feverish activity, and, toiling To-day, shut her eyes to the To-morrow.

She counted the days between Russell's letters; when they arrived, snatched them with trembling fingers, and hastened to her own room to devour them. Once read and folded away, this thought fell with leaden weight upon her heart: "There is so little in this letter, and now I must wait another long week for the next." He never surmised half her wretchedness, for she proudly concealed her discontent, and wrote as if happy and hopeful. The shell of her reserve was beautifully polished and painted, and it never occurred to him that it enclosed dark cells where only wailings echoed. In figure, she was decidedly *petit*, but faultlessly symmetrical and graceful; and the piquant beauty of her face won her the admiration of those who frequented the studio.

Among the artists especially she was a well-established pet, privileged to inspect their work whenever she felt disposed, and always warmly welcomed. They encouraged her in her work, stimulated her by no means dormant ambition, and predicted a brilliant and successful career. Mrs. Clifton was a rigid Roman Catholic; her son a free-thinker, in the broadest significance of the term, if one might judge from the selections that adorned his library shelves. But deep in his soul was the germination of a mystical creed, which gradually unfolded itself to Electra. The simple yet sublime faith of her aunt rapidly faded from the girl's heart; she turned from its severe simplicity to the gorgeous accessories of other systems. The pomp of ceremonial, the bewildering adjuncts of another creed, wooed her overweening, excited fancy. Of doctrine she knew little and cared less; the bare walls and quiet service of the old church at home had for her no attraction; she revelled in dim cathedral light, among mellow, ancient pictures, where pale wreaths of incense curled, and solemn organ-tones whispered through marble aisles. She would sit with folded arms, watching the forms of devotees glide in and out, and prostrate themselves before the images on the gilt altar; and Fancy wafted her, at such times, to the dead ages of imperial Greece, when devout hearts bore offerings to Delphi, Delos, Dodona, and Eleusis. An arch-idolatress she would have been in the ancient days of her Mycenæan namesake—a priestess of Demeter or Artemis. At all hazards this dainty fancy must be pampered, and she gleaned aliment from every source that could possibly yield it, fostering a despotic tendency which soon towered above every other element of her being. The first glimpse of her teacher's Swedenborgian faith was sufficient to rivet her attention. She watched the expansion of his theories, and essayed to follow the profound trains of argumentation, based on physical analogies and correspondences, which led him so irresistibly to his conclusions. But dialectics formed no portion of her intellectual heritage, and her imagination seizing, by a kind of secret affinity, the spiritualistic elements of the system, turned with loathing from the granite-like, scientific fundamentals. Irene would have gone down among the mortar and bricks, measuring the foundations, but Electra gazed upon the exquisite acanthus-wreathings of the ornate capitals, the glowing frescos of the mighty nave, and here was content to rest. Mr. Clifton never attempted to restrain her movements or oppose her inclinations; like a bee she roved ceaselessly from book to book, seeking honey, and, without the safeguard of its unerring instinct, she frequently gathered poison from lovely chalices. Ah, Amy Aubrey! it was an evil day for your orphan charge when Atropos cut the tangled thread of your life, and you left her to follow the dictates of her stormy temperament. Yet otherwise, nature could never have fully woven the pattern; it would have been but a blurred, imperfect design. It was late at night when Electra retired to her room and sat down to collect her thoughts after the unexpected occurrences of the day.

More than one discovery had been made since the sunrise, which she awoke so early to study. She had found relatives, and an opportunity of living luxuriously; but, in the midst of this beautiful *bouquet* of surprises, a serpent's head peered out at her. Once before she thought she had caught sight of its writhing folds, but it vanished too instantaneously to furnish disquiet. Now its glittering eyes held her spell-bound; like the Pentagram in Faust, it kept her in "durance vile." She would fain have shut her eyes had it been possible. Mr. Clifton loved her: not as a teacher his pupil, not as guardian loves ward, not as parent loves child. Perhaps he had not intended that she should know it so soon, but his eyes had betrayed the secret. She saw perfectly how matters stood. This, then, had prompted him, from the first, to render her assistance; he had resolved to make her his wife; nothing less would content him. She twisted her white fingers in her hair, and gazed vacantly down on the carpet, and gradually the rich crimson blood sank out of her face. She held his life in the hollow of her hand, and this she well knew; death hung over him like the sword of Damocles; she had been told that any violent agitation or grief would bring on the hemorrhage which he so much dreaded, and although he seemed stronger and better than usual, the insidious nature of his disease gave her little hope that he would ever be robust. To feign ignorance of his real feelings for her would prove but a temporary stratagem; the time must inevitably come, before long, when he would put aside this veil and set the truth before her. How should she meet it—how should she evade him? Accept the home which Mrs. Young would offer her, and leave him to suffer briefly, to sink swiftly into the tomb? No; her father's family had cast him most unjustly off, withholding his patrimony; and now she scorned to receive one cent of the money which his father was unwilling that he should enjoy. Beside, who loved her as well as Henry Clifton? She owed more to him than to any living being; it would be the part of an ingrate to leave him; it was cowardly to shrink from repaying the debt. But the thought of being his wife froze her blood, and heavy drops gathered on her brow as she endeavored to reflect upon this possibility.

A feeling of unconquerable repulsion sprang up in her heart, nerving, steeling her against his affection. With a strange instantaneous reaction, she thought with loathing of his words of endearment. How could she endure them in future, yet how reject without wounding him? One, and only one, path of escape presented itself—a path of measureless joy. She lifted her hands, and murmured:

"Russell! Russell! save me from this."

When Mr. and Mrs. Young visited the studio the following day, and urged the orphan's removal to their house, she gently but resolutely declined their generous offer, expressing an affectionate gratitude toward her teacher, and a determination not to leave him, at least for the present. Mrs. Young was much distressed, and adduced every argument of which she was mistress, but her niece remained firm; and, finding their entreaties fruitless, Mr. Young said that he would immediately take the necessary steps to secure Robert Grey's portion of the estate to his daughter. Electra sat with her hand nestled in her aunt's, but when this matter was alluded to she rose, and said proudly:

"No, sir; let the estate remain just as it is. I will never accept one cent. My grandfather on his death-bed excluded my father from any portion of it, and since he willed it so, even so it shall be. I have no legal claim to a dollar, and I will never receive one from your generosity. It was the will of the dead that you and my Uncle William should inherit the whole, and, as far as I am concerned, have it you shall. I am poor, I know; so were my parents; poverty they bequeathed as my birthright, and even as they lived without aid from my grandfather so will I. It is very noble and generous in you, after the expiration of nearly twenty years, to be willing to divide with the orphan of the outcast; but I will not, can not, allow you to do so. I fully appreciate and most cordially thank you both for your goodness; but I am young and strong, and I expect to earn my living. Mr. Clifton and his mother want me to remain in his house until I finish my studies, and I gratefully accept his kind offer. Nay, Aunt! don't let it trouble you so; I shall visit you very frequently."

"She has all of Robert's fierce obstinacy.

I see it in her eyes, hear it ringing in the tones of her voice. Take care, child! it ruined your father," said Mrs. Young sorrowfully.

"You should remember, Electra, that an orphan girl needs a protector; such I would fain prove myself."

As Mr. Young spoke he took one of her hands and drew her to him. She turned quickly and laid the other on the artist's arm.

"I have one here, sir; a protector as true and kind as my own father could be."

She understood the flash of his eyes and his proud smile, as he assured her relatives that he would guard her from harm and want so long as he lived, or as she remained under his care. She knew he regarded this as a tacit sealing of the old compact, and she had no inclination to undeceive him at this juncture.

Urging her to visit them as often as possible, and extending the invitation to Mr. Clifton, the Youngs withdrew, evidently much disappointed; and, as the door closed behind them, Electra felt that the circle of doom was narrowing around her. Mr. Clifton approached her, but, averting her head, she lifted the damask curtain that divided the parlor from the studio and effected her retreat, dreading to meet his glance—putting off the evil day as long as possible—trying to trample the serpent that trailed after her from that hour.

CHAPTER X.

"You are better, to-day. Mother tells me."

"Yes, thank you, my foot is much better. You have not been up to see me for two days."

Irene sat in an easy-chair by the open window, and the minister took a seat near her.

"I have not forgotten you in the interim, however." As he spoke he laid a bouquet of choice flowers in her lap. She bent over them with eager delight, and held out one hand, saying:

"Oh, thank you; how very kind you are. These remind me of the greenhouse at home; they are the most beautiful I have seen in New York."

"Irene, the man or woman who is impervious to the subtle, spiritualizing influence of flowers may feel assured that there is something lamentably amiss in either his or her organization or habits of life. They weave rosy links of association more binding than steel, and sometimes of incalculable value. Amid the awful solitude of Alpine glaciers, I recollect the thrill of pleasure which the blue gentians caused me, as I noted the fragile petals shuddering upon the very verge of fields of eternal snow; and among cherished memories of the far East are its acacias and rhododendrons; the scarlet poppies waving like a 'mantle of blood' over Syrian valleys, and the oleanders fringing the gray, gloomy crags and breathing their exquisite fragrance over the silent desolation of that grand city of rock—immemorial Petra. I have remarked your fondness for flowers; cultivate it always; they are evangels of purity and faith, if we but unlock our hearts to their ministry. Callous and sordid indeed must be that soul who fails in grateful appreciation of gifts designed especially to promote the happiness and adorn the dwellings of our race; for, in attestation of this truth, stand the huge, hoary tomes of geology, proving that the pre-Adamic ages were comparatively barren of the gorgeous flowers which tapestried the earth so munificently just ere man made his appearance on the stage. A reverent student of the rocks, who spent his life in listening to the solemn, oracular whispers of their grand granite lips, that moved, Memnon-like, as he flashed the light of Revelation upon them, tells us: 'The poet accepted the bee as a sign of high significance; the geologist, also, accepts her as a sign. Her entombed remains testify to the gradual fitting up of our earth as a place of habitation for a creature destined to seek delight for the mind and eye as certainly as for the grosser senses, and in especial mark the introduction of stately forest-trees and the arrival of the delicious flowers.' A profound thinker and eloquent writer, who is now doing a noble work for his generation by pointing it to unstained sources of happiness, has said of flowers: 'They are chalices of Divine workmanship—of purple and scarlet and liquid gold—from which man is to drink the pure joy of beauty.' There is, you know, a graduated scale of missionary work for all created things; man labors for God and his race through deep, often tortuous, channels, and nature—all animate and inanimate nature—ministers in feebler yet still heaven-appointed processes. The trouble is that, in the rush and din and whirl of life, we will not pause to note these sermons; and from year to year the whispered precepts of faith, hope, and charity fall on deaf ears. Nature is so prodigal of refining, elevating influences, and man is so inaccessible in his isolating, inflated egotism."

He paused, and busied himself in cutting the leaves of a new book, while Irene looked into his calm, noble face, pondering his words; then her eyes went back to the bouquet, and his dwelt once more upon her.

"Irene, you look sober to-day; come, cheer up. I don't want to carry that grave expression away with me. I want to remember your face as I first saw it, unshadowed."

"What do you mean? Are you going to leave home?"

"Yes; day after to-morrow I bid farewell to New York for a long time. I am going to the West to take charge of a church."

"Oh, Mr. Young! surely you are not in earnest? You can not intend to separate yourself from your family?"

She dropped her flowers and leaned forward.

"Yes, I have had it in contemplation for more than a year, and, recently, I have decided to remove at once."

He saw the great sorrow written in her countenance, the quick flutter of her lip, the large drops that dimmed the violet eyes and gathered on the long golden lashes, and far sweeter than Eolian harps was the broken voice:

"What shall I do without you? who will encourage and advise me when you go?"

She leaned her forehead on her hands, and a tear slid down and rested on her chin. The sun was setting, and the crimson light flooding the room bathed her with glory, spreading a halo around her. He held his breath and gazed upon the drooping figure and bewitching face; and in after years, when his dark hair had grown silvery gray, he remembered the lovely sunlit vision that so entranced him, leaving an indelible image on heart and brain. He gently removed the hands, and holding them in his said, in the measured, low tone so indicative of suppressed emotion:

"Irene, my friend, you attach too much importance to the aid which I might render you. You know your duty, and I feel assured will not require to be reminded of it. Henceforth our paths diverge widely. I go to a distant section of our land, there to do my Father's work; and, ere long, having concluded the prescribed course, you will return to your Southern home and take the position assigned you in society. Thus, in all human probability, we shall meet no more, for——"

"Oh, sir! don't say that; you will come back to visit your family, and then I shall see you."

"That is scarcely probable, but we will not discuss it now. There is, however, a channel of communication for separated friends, and of this we must avail ourselves. I shall write to you from western wilds, and letters from you will most pleasantly ripple the monotonous life I expect to lead. This is the last opportunity I shall have to speak with you; let me do so freely, just as I would to Louisa. You are young and rather peculiarly situated; and sometimes I fear that, in the great social vortex awaiting you, constant temptation and frivolous associations will stifle the noble impulses nature gave to guide you. As you grow older you will more fully comprehend my meaning, and find that there are social problems which every true-hearted man and woman should earnestly strive to solve. These will gradually unfold themselves as the web of time unravels before you. You will occupy an elevated stand-point of view, and you must take care that, unlike the great mass of mankind, you do not grow callous.

turning a deaf ear to the cry 'the laborers are few.' It is not woman's place to obtrude herself in the pulpit or harangue from the rostrum; such an abnormal course levels the distinctions which an all-wise God established between the sexes, but the aggregate of her usefulness is often greater than man's. Irene, I want you to wield the vast influence your Maker has given you nobly and for His glory. Let your unobstrusive yet consistent, resolute, unerring conduct leave its impress for good wherever you are known. I would not have you debar yourself from a single avenue of pure enjoyment; far from it. Monkish asceticism and puritanic bigotry I abhor; but there is a happy medium between the wild excesses of so-called fashionable life and the straitlaced rigidity of narrow-minded phariseeism; and this I would earnestly entreat you to select. To discover and adhere to this medium path is almost as difficult as to skip across the Arabic Al-Sirat, of which we read last week. Ultraism is the curse of our race, as exemplified in all departments of society; avoid it, dear child; cultivate enlarged views of life, suppress selfishness, and remember that charity is the key-stone of Christianity."

"I have not the strength which you impute to me."

"Then seek it from the Everlasting source."

"I do, but God does not hear me."

"You are too easily disheartened; strive to be faithful and He will aid you, brace you, uphold you. Will it be any comfort for you to know that I remember you in my prayers, that I constantly bear your name on my lips to the throne of grace?"

"Oh, yes! very great comfort. Thank you, thank you; will you always pray for me? If I thought so it would make me happier."

"Then rest assured that I always shall; and, Irene, when sorrows come upon you—for come they must to all—do not forget that you have at least one firm, faithful friend, waiting and anxious to aid you by every means in his power."

Disengaging her fingers, which still clasped his tightly, he moved his chair backward and took a small blank-book from his pocket, saying:

"You once asked me to give you a catalogue of those works which I thought it advisable for you to study before you plunged into miscellaneous reading. Such a list you will find here, and my experience has enabled me to classify them so as to save you some of the trouble which I had at your age. In examining it, you will see that I have given prominence to the so-called 'Natural Sciences.' As these furnish data for almost all branches of investigation nowadays (there being a growing tendency to argue from the analogy of physics), you can not too thoroughly acquaint yourself with all that appertains to the subject. The writings of Humboldt, Hugh Miller, Cuvier, and Agassiz constitute a thesaurus of scientific information essential to a correct appreciation of the questions now agitating the thinking world; and, as you proceed, you will find the wonderful harmony of creation unfolding itself, proclaiming, in unmistakable accents, that the works of God 'are good.' As time rolls on, the great truth looms up colossal, 'Science and Christianity are handmaids, not antagonists.' Irene, remember:

"A pagan kissing for a step of Pan,
The wild goat's hoof-print on the loamy down,
Exceeds our modern thinker who turns back
The strata—granite, limestone, coal, and clay,
Concluding coldly with 'Here 's law! where 's God?'"

"Can't you stay longer and talk to me?" said Irene, as he gave the blank-book to her and rose.

"No; I promised to address the —— street Sabbath-school children to-night, and must look over my notes before I go." He glanced at his watch, smiled pleasantly, and left her.

The following day was dreary to all in that dwelling; Mrs. Young went from room to room collecting various articles belonging to her son, making no effort to conceal the tears that rolled constantly over her cheeks; and now and then Louisa's sobs broke the sad silence. Harvey was engaged in the library packing his books, and Irene saw him no more till after tea. Then he came up with his mother, and kindly inquired concerning her arm. He saw that she shared the distress of the family, and, glancing over his shoulder at his mother, he said, laughingly:

"She looks too doleful to be left here alone all the evening. Can't we contrive to take her down stairs to the sitting-room? What think you, Mother?"

"Let her decide it herself. Shall Harvey take you down, my dear? It is his last evening at home, you know." Her voice faltered as she spoke.

"I should like to join you all at prayer once more, and I think I could walk down slowly, with a little help. Suppose you let me try? I walked a few steps yesterday, by pushing a chair before me."

"Be very careful not to strain your foot." She wrapped a light shawl around the girl's shoulders, and, leaning on the minister's arm, she limped to the head of the stairs; but he saw, from the wrinkle on her forehead, that the effort gave her pain, and, taking her in his arms as if she were an infant, he replaced her in the chair.

"I see it will not do to carry you down yet. You are not strong enough, and, beside, you ought to be asleep. Irene, would you like for me to read and pray with you before I say good-by?"

"Yes, sir; it would give me great pleasure."

Mrs. Young drew the candle-stand and Bible from its corner, and taking a seat near the arm-chair, Harvey turned over the leaves and slowly read the sixty-third and sixty-fourth chapters of Isaiah. His voice was low and sweet as a woman's, and the calm lofty brow on which the light gleamed was smooth and fair as a child's, bearing no footprints of the thirty years that had crept over it. When the reading was concluded he knelt and prayed fervently for the girl, who sat with her face hidden in her arms; prayed that she might be guided by the Almighty hand into paths of peace and usefulness; that she might be strengthened to do the work required of her. There was no unsteadiness in his tone, no trace of emotion, when he ended his prayer and stood up before her. Irene was deeply moved, and, when she essayed to thank him, found it impossible to pronounce her words. Tears were gliding down her cheeks; he put back the hair, and, taking the face softly in his palms, looked long and earnestly at its fascinating beauty. The great glistening blue eyes gazed into his, and the silky lashes and rich scarlet lips trembled. He felt the hot blood surging like a lava-tide in his veins, and his heart rising in fierce rebellion at the stern interdict which he saw fit to lay upon it; but no token of all this came to the cool, calm surface.

"Good-by, Irene. May God bless you, my dear little friend!"

He drew the face close to his own as though he would have kissed her, but forbore, and merely raising her hands to his lips, turned and left the room. Verily, greater is "he that ruleth his own spirit than he that taketh a city." He left before breakfast the ensuing morning, bearing his secret with him, having given no intimation, by word or look, of the struggle which his resolution cost him. Once his mother had fancied that he felt more than a friendly interest in their guest, but the absolute repose of his countenance and grave serenity of his manner during the last week of his stay dispersed all her suspicions. From a luxurious home, fond friends, and the girlish face he loved better than his life, the minister went forth to his distant post, offering in sacrifice to God, upon the altar of Duty, his throbbing heart and hopes of earthly happiness.

A cloud of sadness settled on the household after his departure, and scarcely less than Louisa's was Irene's silent grief. The confinement grew doubly irksome when his voice and step had passed from the threshold, and she looked forward impatiently to her release. The sprain proved more serious than she had at first imagined, and the summer vacation set in before she was able to walk with ease. Mr. Huntingdon had been apprised of her long absence from school, and one day, when she was cautiously trying her strength, he arrived, without having given premonition of his visit. As he took her in his arms and marked the alteration in her thin face, the listlessness of her manner, the sorrowful gravity of her countenance, his fears were fully aroused, and, holding her to his heart, he exclaimed:

"My Daughter! my Beauty! I must take you out of New York."

"Yes, Father, take me home; do take me home." She clasped her arms around his neck and nestled her face close to his.

"Not yet, Queen. We will go to the Catskill, to Lake George, to Niagara. A few weeks' travel will invigorate you. I have written to Hugh to meet us at Montreal; he is with a gay party, and you shall have a royal time. A pretty piece of business, truly, that you can't amuse yourself in any other way than by breaking half the bones in your body."

"Father, I would rather go home. Oh! I am so tired of this city, so sick of that boarding-school. Do, please, let me go back with you."

"Oh, nonsense, Irene. Lift up your sleeve and let me see your arm; stretch it out; all right, I believe; straight enough. You were walking just now; how is your foot?"

"Almost well, I think; occasionally I have a twinge of pain when I bear my whole weight on it."

"Be sure you do not overtax it for a while. By Monday you will be able to start to Saratoga. Your aunt sent a trunk of clothing and, by the way, here is a letter from her and one from Arnold. The doctor worries considerably about you; is afraid you will not be properly attended to."

Thus the summer programme was determined without any reference to the wishes of the one most concerned, and, knowing her father's disposition, she silently acquiesced. After much persuasion, Mr. Huntingdon prevailed on Louisa's parents to allow her to accompany them. The mother consented very reluctantly, and on the appointed day the party set off for Saratoga. The change was eminently beneficial, and before they reached Canada Irene seemed perfectly restored. But her father was not satisfied. Her unwonted taciturnity annoyed and puzzled him; he knew that beneath the calm surface some strong undercurrent rolled swiftly, and he racked his brain to discover what had rendered her so reserved. Louisa's joyous, elastic spirits probably heightened the effect of her companion's gravity, and the contrast daily presented could not fail to arrest Mr. Huntingdon's attention. On arriving at Montreal the girls were left for a few moments in the parlor of the hotel, while Mr. Huntingdon went to register their names. Irene and Louisa stood by the window looking out into the street, when a happy, ringing voice exclaimed:

"Here you are, at last, Irie! I caught a glimpse of your curls as you passed the dining-room door."

She turned to meet her cousin, and held out her hand.

"Does your majesty suppose I shall be satisfied with the tips of your fingers? Pshaw, Irie! I will have my kiss."

He threw his arm round her shoulder, drew down the shielding hands, and kissed her twice.

"Oh, Hugh! behave yourself! Miss Louisa Young, my cousin, Hugh Seymour."

He bowed, and shook hands with the stranger, then seized his cousin's fingers and fixed his fine eyes affectionately upon her.

"It seems an age since I saw you, Irie. Come, sit down and let me look at you; how stately you have grown, to be sure! More like a queen than ever; absolutely two inches taller since you entered boarding-school. Irie, I am so glad to see you again!" He snatched up a handful of curls and drew them across his lips, careless of what Louisa might think.

"Thank you, Hugh. I am quite as glad to see you."

"Oh, humbug! I know better. You would rather see Paragon any day, ten to one. I will kill that dog yet, and shoot Erebus, too; see if I don't! then maybe you can think of somebody else. When you are glad you show it in your eyes, and now they are as still as violets under icicles. I think you might love me a little, at least as much as a dog."

"Hush! I do love you, but I don't choose to tell it to everybody in Montreal."

Mr. Huntingdon's entrance diverted the conversation, and Irene was glad to escape to her own room.

"Your cousin seems to be very fond of you," observed Louisa, as she unbraided her hair.

"He is very impulsive and demonstrative, that is all."

"How handsome he is!"

"Do you think so, really? Take care, Louisa! I will tell him, and, by way of crushing his vanity, add 'de gustibus, etc., etc., etc.'"

"How old is he?"

"In his twentieth year."

From that time the cousins were thrown constantly together; wherever they went Hugh took charge of Irene, while Mr. Huntingdon gave his attention to Louisa. But the eagle eye was upon his daughter's movements; he watched her countenance, weighed her words, tried to probe her heart. Week after week he found nothing tangible. Hugh was gay, careless; Irene equable, but reserved. Finally they turned their faces homeward, and in October found themselves once more in New York. Mr. Huntingdon prepared to return South and Hugh to sail for Europe, while Irene remained at the hotel until the morning of her cousin's departure.

A private parlor adjoined the room she occupied, and here he came to say farewell. She knew that he had already had a long conversation with her father, and as he threw himself on the sofa and seized one of her hands, she instinctively shrank from him.

"Irene, here is my miniature. I wanted you to ask for it, but I see that you won't do it. I know very well that you will not value it one-thousandth part as much as I do your likeness here on my watch-chain; but perhaps it will remind you of me sometimes. How I shall want to see you before I come home! You know you belong to me. Uncle gave you to me, and when I come back from Europe we will be married. We are both very young, I know; but it has been settled so long. Irie, my beauty, I wish you would love me more; you are so cold. Won't you try?"

He leaned down to kiss her, but she turned her face hastily away and answered, resolutely:

"No, I can't love you other than as my cousin; I would not, if I could. I do not think it would be right, and I won't promise to try. Father has no right to give me to you, or to anybody else. I tell you now I belong to myself, and only I can give myself away. Hugh, I don't consider this settled at all. You might as well know the truth at once; I have some voice in the matter."

Mr. Huntingdon had evidently prepared him for something of this kind on her part, and though his face flushed angrily, he took no notice of the remonstrance.

"I shall write to you frequently, and I hope that you will be punctual in replying. Irie, give me your left hand just a minute; wear this ring till I come back, to remind you that you have a cousin across the ocean."

He tried to force the flashing jewel on her slender finger, but she resisted, and rose, struggling to withdraw her hand.

"No, no, Hugh! I can't; I won't. I know very well what that ring means, and I can not accept it. Release my hand; I tell you I won't wear it."

"Come, Hugh; you have not a moment to spare; the carriage is waiting." Mr. Huntingdon threw open the door, having heard every word that passed. Hugh dropped the ring in his vest-pocket and rose.

"Well, Irie, I suppose I must bid you farewell. Two or three years will change you, my dearest little cousin. Good-by; think of me now and then, and learn to love me by the time I come home."

She suffered him to take both her hands and kiss her tenderly, for her father stood there and she could not refuse; but the touch of his lips burned long after he had gone. She put on her bonnet, and, when her father returned from the steamer, they entered the carriage which was to convey her to the dreary, dreaded school. As they rolled along Broadway Mr. Huntingdon coolly took her hand and placed Hugh's ring upon it, saying, authoritatively:

"Hugh told me you refused to accept his parting gift, and seemed much hurt about it. There is no reason why you should not wear it, and in future I do not wish to see you without it. Remember this, my daughter."

"Father, it is wrong for me to wear it, unless I expected to—"

"I understand the whole matter perfectly. Now, Irene, let me hear no more about it. I wish you would learn that it is a child's duty to obey her parent. No more words, if you please, on the subject."

She felt that this was not the hour for resistance, and wisely forbore; but he saw rebellion written in the calm, fixed eye, and read it in the curved lines of the full upper lip. She had entreated him to take her home, and, only the night before, renewed her pleadings. But his refusal was positive, and now she went back to the hated school without a visible token of regret. She saw her trunks consigned to the porter, listened to a brief conversation between Dr. ——— and her father, and, after a hasty embrace and half-dozen words, watched the tall, soldierly form re-enter the carriage. Then she went slowly up the broad stairway to her cell-like room, and with dry eyes unpacked her clothes, locked up the ring in her jewelry-box, and prepared to resume her studies.

The starry veil concealing the Holy of Holies of her Futurity had swayed just once, and as quickly swept back to its wonted folds; but in that one swift glance she saw, instead of hovering Cherubim, gaunt spectres, woful, appalling as Brimo. At some period of life all have this dim, transient, tantalizing glimpse of the inexorable Three, the mystic Moiræ, weaving with steely fingers the unyielding web of human destiny. Some grow cowardly, striving to wend their way behind or beyond the out-spread net-work, tripping at last, in the midst of the snare; and some, with set teeth and rigid limbs, scorning to dodge the issue, grapple with the Sisters, resolved to wrench the cunning links asunder, trusting solely to the palladium of Will. Irene's little feet had become entangled in the fatal threads, and, with no thought of flight, she measured the length and breadth of the web, nerving herself to battle till the death.

CHAPTER XI.

A halo seems to linger around the haunts of Genius, as though the outer physical world shaped itself in likeness to the Ideal, and at the door of Mr. Clifton's studio crude, matter-of-fact utilitarians should have "put off their shoes from their feet" before treading precincts sacred to Art. It was a long, lofty, narrow room, with a grate at one end and two windows at the other, opening on the street. The walls were stained of a pale olive hue, and the floor was covered with a carpet of green, embroidered with orange sheaves of wheat. In color, the morocco-cushioned chairs and sofas matched it well, and from the broad, massive cornice over the windows—cornice representing writhing serpents in clusters of oak leaves—folds of golden-flowered brocatel hung stiff and stately to the floor. The ceiling rose dome-like in the centre, and here a skylight poured down a flood of radiance on sunny days, and furnished a faint tattoo when rain-drops rattled over its panes. Crowded as the most ancient catacombs of Thebes was this *atelier*, but with a trifle less ghostly tenants. Plaster statues loomed up in the corners, bronze busts and marble *statuettes* crowned mantle and sundry tables and wooden pedestals; quaint antique vases of china, crystal, alabaster, terra-cotta, and wood dark as ebony with age and polished like glass, stood here and there in a sort of well-established regular irregularity, as if snatched from the ashy shroud of Herculaneum, and put down hastily in the first convenient place. An Etruscan vase, time and lichen-stained, was made the base for an unframed piece of canvas, which leaned back against the wall; and another, whose handles were Medusa-heads, and before which, doubtless, some Italian maiden, in the palmy days of Rome, had stood twining the feathery sprays of blossoms whose intoxicating perfume might still linger in its marble depths, was now the desecrated receptacle of a meerschaum and riding-whip. The walls were tapestried with paintings of all sizes, many richly framed, one or two covered with glass, and so dark as to pass, without close examination, for a faithful representation of Pharaoh's ninth plague; some lying helplessly on the olive background, others leaning from the wall at an acute angle, looking threatening, as if fiery souls had entered and stirred up the figures—among which Deianira, bending forward with jealous rage to scan the lovely Iole, destined to prove the Atè of her house. Where a few feet of pale green would have peered forth between large pictures, crayon sketches were suspended; and on the top of more than one carved frame perched stuffed birds of gorgeous tropical hues, a mimic aviary, motionless and silent as if Perseus had stepped in to a choral throng and held up the Gorgon's head. In the centre of the room, under the skylight, stood the artist's easel, holding an unfinished picture, and over its face was drawn a piece of black silk. Farther off was another easel, smaller, and here was the dim outline of a female head traced by the fair, slender fingers of a tyro. It was late October; a feeble flame flickered in the grate; on the rug crouched an English spaniel, creeping closer as the heat died out and the waning light of day gradually receded, leaving the room dusky, save where a slanting line of yellow quivered down from the roof and gilt the folds of black silk. At one of the windows stood Electra, half-concealed by the heavy green and gold drapery, one dimpled hand clinging to the curtains, the other pressed against the panes, as she watched the forms hurrying along the street below. The gas was already lighted on the crowded highways of the great city, and the lamp just beneath the window glared up like an electric eye. She was dressed in half-mourning, in sober gray, with a black crape collar at the throat. "There is no exquisite beauty without some strangeness in the proportions," says Baron Verulam; and the strangeness of Electra's countenance certainly lay in the unusual width between the eyebrows. Whatever significance learned phrenologists or physiognomists attach to this peculiarity, at all events it imparted piquancy to the features that I am striving to show you by that flaming gaslight. Her watching attitude denoted anxiety, and the bloom on her cheek had faded, leaving the whole face colorless. The lower lip was drawn under and held hard and tight by the pearly teeth, while the wide-strained eyes—

Shining eyes like antique jewels set in Parian statue-stone"—

searched every face that passed the window. "That hope deferred maketh the heart sick," she stood there in attestation; yet it was not passive sorrow printed on her countenance—rather the momentary, breathless exhaustion of a wild bird beating out its life in useless conflict with the unyielding wires of its cage. The dying hope, the despairing dread, in that fair young face beggars language, and as the minutes crept by the words burst from her lips: "Will he never, never come!"

For three weeks she had received no letter from Russell; he was remarkably punctual, and this long, unprecedented interval filled her, at first, with vague uneasiness, which grew finally into horrible foreboding. For ten days she had stood at this hour, at the same window, waiting for Mr. Clifton's return from the post-office. Ten times the words "No letter" had fallen, like the voice of doom, on her throbbing heart. "No letter!"—she heard it in feverish dreams, and fled continually from its hissing. Only those who have known what it is to stake their hopes on a sheet of letter-paper; to wake at dawn, counting the hours, till the mail is due, working diligently to murder time till that hour rolls round; to send a messenger, in hot haste, to watch the clock, giving him just so many minutes to go and come; to listen for the sound of returning steps, to meet him at the door with outstretched hands, and receive—"no letter;" only those who have writhed on this rack know the crushing thought with which they pressed cold hands to aching hearts; "another twenty-four hours to be endured before the next mail comes in; what shall I do till then?" These are the trials that plough wrinkles in smooth, girlish brows;

that harden the outline of soft rosy lips; that sicken the weary soul, and teach women deception. Electra knew that Mr. Clifton watched her narrowly, suspiciously; and behind the mask of gay, rapid words, and ringing, mirthless laughter, she tried to hide her suffering. Ah! God pity all who live from day to day hanging upon the brittle thread of hope. On this eleventh day suspense reached its acme, and time seemed to have locked its wheels to lengthen her torture. Mr. Clifton had been absent longer than usual. Most unwittingly we are sometimes grand inquisitors, loitering by the way when waiting hearts are secretly, silently dropping blood. At last an omnibus stopped, and Mr. Clifton stepped out, with a bundle of papers under his arm. Closer pressed the pallid face against the glass; firmer grew the grasp of the icy fingers on the brocatel; she had no strength to meet him. He closed the door, hung up his hat, and looked into the studio; no fire in the grate, no light in the gas-globes—everything cold and dark save the reflection on that front window.

"Electra!"

"I am here."

"No letter."

She stood motionless a moment; but the brick walls opposite, the trees, the lamp-posts spun round, like maple leaves in an autumn gale.

"My owlet! why don't you have a light and some fire?"

He stumbled toward her, and put his hand on her shoulder, but she shrank away, and, lighting the gas, rang for coal.

"There is something terrible the matter; Russell is either ill or dead. I must go to him."

"Nonsense! sheer nonsense; he is busy, that is all. Your cousin has forgotten you for the time; after a while he will write. You are too exacting; young men sometimes find constant, regular correspondence a bore; a letter every week is too much to expect of him. Don't be childish, Electra."

As she noticed the frown on his face, a dark suspicion seized her: "perhaps he had intercepted her letters." Could he stoop to such an artifice?

"Electra, I would try to divert my mind. After all, his letters are short, and, I should judge, rather unsatisfactory."

"What do you know of the length or contents of his letters?"

"I know they are brief, because I occasionally see them open in your hand; I judge that they are unsatisfactory from the cloud on your face whenever they come. But I have no disposition to contest the value of his correspondence with you. That article on *chiaroscuro* has arrived at last; if you feel inclined, you can begin it at once."

"Chiaro-scuro, forsooth! Mockery! She had

quite *chiaro-scuro* enough, and to spare; but the smile on the artist's lips stung her, and, without a word, she took a seat at his side and began to read. Page after page was turned, technicalities slipped through her lips, but she understood as little of the essay as if the language had been Sancrit instead of Saxon; for, like the deep, undying murmur of the restless sea, there rang in her ears, "No letter! no letter!" As she finished the pamphlet and threw it on the table, her hands dropped listlessly in her lap. Mr. Clifton was trying to read her countenance, and, impatient of his scrutiny, she rose to seek her own room. Just then the door-bell rang sharply; she supposed it was some brother-artist coming to spend an hour, and turned to go.

"Wait a minute; I want to——;" he paused, for at that instant she heard a voice which, even amid the din of Shinar, would have been unmistakable to her, and, breaking from him, she sprang to the threshold and met her cousin.

"Oh, Russell! I thought you had forgotten me."

"What put such a ridiculous thought into your head? My last letter must have prepared you to expect me."

"What letter? I have had none for three weeks."

"One in which I mentioned Mr. Campbell's foreign appointment, and the position of secretary which he tendered me. Electra, let me speak to Mr. Clifton."

As he advanced and greeted the artist she heard a quick, snapping sound, and saw the beautiful Bohemian glass paper-cutter her guardian had been using lying, shivered to atoms, on the rug. The fluted handle was crushed in his fingers, and drops of blood oozed over the left hand. Ere she could allude to it he thrust his hand into his pocket and desired Russell to be seated.

"This is a pleasure totally unexpected. What is the appointment of which you spoke?"

"Mr. Campbell has been appointed Minister to ——, and sails next week. I am surprised that you have not heard of it from the public journals; many of them have spoken of it, and warmly commended the selection. I accompany him in the capacity of secretary, and shall, meanwhile, prosecute my studies under his direction."

The gray, glittering eyes of the artist sought those of his pupil, and for an instant hers quailed; but, rallying, she looked fully, steadfastly at him, resolved to play out the game, scorning to bare her heart to his scrutiny. She had fancied that Russell's affection had prompted this visit; now it was apparent that he came to New York to take a steamer, not to see her; to put the stormy Atlantic between them. The foaming draught which she had snatched to her lips so eagerly, so joyfully, was turning to hemlock as she tasted; and though she silently put the cup from her, it was done smilingly; there were no wry faces, no gestures of disgust.

"New York certainly agrees with you, Electra; you have grown and improved very much since you came North. I never saw such color in your cheeks before; I can scarcely believe that you are the same fragile child I put into the stage one year ago. This reconciles me to having given you up to Mr. Clifton; he is a better guardian than I could have been. But tell me something more about these new relatives you spoke of having found here."

Mr. Clifton left the room, and the two sat side by side for an hour, talking of the gloomy past, the flitting present, the uncertain future. Leaning back in his chair, with his eyes fixed on the grate, Russell said, gravely:

"There is now nothing to impede my successful career; obstacles are rapidly melting away; every day brings me nearer the goal I long since set before me. In two years at farthest, perhaps earlier, I shall return and begin the practice of law. Once admitted, I ask no more. Then, and not till then, I hope to save you from the necessity of labor; in the interim, Mr. Clifton will prove a noble and generous friend; and believe me, my cousin, the thought of leaving you so long is the only thing which will mar the pleasure of my European sojourn."

The words were kind enough, but the tone was indifferent, and the countenance showed her that their approaching separation disquieted him little. She thought of the sleepless nights and wretched days she had passed waiting for a letter from that tall, reserved, cold cousin, and her features relaxed in a derisive smile at the folly of her all-absorbing love. Raising his eyes accidentally he caught the smile, wondered what there was to call it forth in the plans which he had just laid before her, and, meeting his glance of surprise, she said, carelessly:

"Are you not going to see Irene before you sail?"

His cheek flushed as he rose, straightened himself, and answered:

"A strange question, truly, from one who knows me as well as you do. Call to see a girl whose father sent her from home solely to prevent her from associating with my family? Through what sort of metamorphosis do you suppose that I have passed, that every spark of self-respect has been crushed out of me?"

"Her father's tyranny and selfishness can never nullify her noble and affectionate remembrance of Aunt Amy in the hour of her need."

"And when I am able to repay her every cent we owe her, then, and not till then, I wish to see her. Things shall change; *mens cujusque is est quisque;* and the day will come when Mr. Huntingdon may not think it degrading for his daughter to acknowledge my acquaintance on the street."

A brief silence ensued, Russell drew on his gloves, and finally said, hesitatingly:

"Dr. Arnold told me she had suffered very much from a fall."

"Yes; for a long time she was confined to her room."

"Has she recovered entirely?"

"Entirely. She grows more beautiful day by day."

Perhaps he wished to hear more concerning her, but she would not gratify him, and, soon after, he took up his hat.

"Mr. Clifton has a spare room, Russell; why can't you stay with us while you are in New York?"

"Thank you; but Mr. Campbell will expect me at the hotel; I shall be needed, too, as he has many letters to write. I will see you to-morrow, and indeed every day while I remain in the city."

"Then pay your visits in the morning, for I want to take your portrait with my own hands. Give me a sitting as early as possible."

"Very well; look for me to-morrow. Good-night."

The week that followed was one of strangely-mingled sorrows and joys; in after years it served as a prominent landmark to which she looked back and dated sad changes in her heart. Irene remained ignorant of Russell's presence in the city, and at last the day dawned on which the vessel was to sail. At the breakfast-table Mr. Clifton noticed the colorlessness of his pupil's face, but kindly abstained from any allusion to it. He saw that, contrary to habit, she drank a cup of coffee, and, arresting her arm as she requested his mother to give her a second, he said gently:

"My dear child, where did you suddenly find such Turkish tastes? I thought you disliked coffee?"

"I take it now as medicine. My head aches horribly."

"Then let me prescribe for you. We will go down to the steamer with Russell, and afterward take a long ride to Greenwood, if you like."

"He said he would call here at ten o'clock to bid us farewell."

"N'importe. The carriage will be ready, and we will accompany him."

At the appointed hour they repaired to the vessel, and, looking at its huge sides, Electra coveted even a deck passage; envied the meanest who hurried about, making all things ready for departure. The last bell rang; people crowded down on the planks; Russell hastened back to the carriage and took the nerveless gloved hand.

"I will write as early as possible; don't be uneasy about me; no accident has ever happened on this line. I am glad I leave you with such a friend as Mr. Clifton. Good-by, Cousin; it will not be very long before we meet again."

He kissed the passive lips, shook hands with the artist, and sprang on board just as the planks were withdrawn. The vessel moved majestically on its way; friends on shore waved handkerchiefs to friends departing, and hands were kissed and hats lifted, and then the crowd slowly dispersed—for steamers sail every week, and people become accustomed to the spectacle. But to-day it was freighted with the last fond hope of a deep and passionate nature; and as Electra gazed on the line of foam whitening the dull surface of the water. the short-lived billows and deep hollows between seemed newly-made graves, whose hungry jaws had closed for ever over the one bright lingering hope which she had hugged to her heart.

"Are you ready to go now?" asked Mr. Clifton.

"Yes, ready, quite ready—for Greenwood."

She spoke in a tone which had lost its liquid music, and with a wintry smile that fled over the ashy face, lending the features no light, no warmth.

He tried to divert her mind by calling attention to various things of interest, but the utter exhaustion of her position and the monosyllabic character of her replies soon discouraged him. Both felt relieved when the carriage stopped before the studio, and as he led her up the steps he said, affectionately:

"I am afraid my prescription has not cured your head."

"No, sir; but I thank you most sincerely for the kind effort you have made to relieve me. I shall be better to-morrow. Good-by till then."

"Stay, my child. Come into the studio, and let me read something light and pleasant to you."

"Not for the universe! The sight of a book would give me brain-fever, I verily believe."

She tried unavailingly to shake off his hand.

"Why do you shrink from me, my pupil?"

"Because I am sick, weary; and you watch me so, that I get restless and nervous. Do let me go! I want to sleep."

An impatient stamp emphasized the words, and, as he relaxed his clasp of her fingers, she hastened to her room, and locked the door to prevent all intrusion. Taking off her bonnet, she drew the heavy shawl closely around her shoulders and threw herself across the foot of the bed, burying her face in her hands lest the bare walls should prove witnesses of her agony. Six hours later she lay there still, with pale fingers pressed to burning, dry eyelids.

Oh, bigotry of human nature! By what high commission, by what royal patent, do men and women essay to judge of fellow-men and sister-women by one stern inexorable standard, unyielding as the measure of Damastes? The variety of emotional and intellectual types is even grater than the physical, and, as the ages roll, we need other criteria. Who shall dare lay finger on fellow-creature and audaciously proclaim: "I have gone down among the volcanic chambers of this soul and groped in its adytum, amid the dust and ruins of its overturned altars and crumbling idols; have fathomed its mysteries, and will tell you, by infallible plummet, the depths thereof." There are sealed cells, where, veiled from scrutiny and sacred as Eleusinia, burns the God-given shechinah of the human soul. As the myriad shells that tessellate old ocean's pavements, as the vast army of innumerable clouds which cea-elessly shift their coloring and their forms at the presto of wizard-winds; as the leaves of the forest that bud and wane in the flush of summer or the howl of wintry storms, so we differ one from another. Linnæus and Jussien, with microscopic aid, have classified and christened; but now and then new varieties startle modern *savans*, and so likewise new types stalk among men and women, whose elements will neither be lopped off nor elongated to meet the established measure.

CHAPTER XII.

Once more the labors of a twelvemonth had been exhibited at the Academy of Design—some to be classed among things "that were not born to die;" others to fall into nameless graves. Many, who had worked faithfully, recognizing the sacredness of their commission, had climbed higher in public estimation; and a few, making mere pastime, or resting upon reputation already earned, had slipped back. Mr. Clifton was represented by an exquisite Œnone, and on the same wall, in a massive oval frame, hung the first finished production of his pupil. For months after Russell's departure she sat before her easel, slowly filling up the outline sketched while his eyes watched her. She lingered over her work, loath to put the final stroke, calling continually upon Memory to furnish the necessary details; and frequently, in recalling transient smiles, the curl of his lip or bending of his brow, palette and brush would slip from her fingers, while she sat weaving the broken yet priceless threads of a hallowed Past. Application sometimes trenches so closely upon genius as to be mistaken for it in its results, and where both are happily blended the bud of Art expands in immortal perfection. Electra spared no toil, and so it came to pass that the faultless head of her idol excited intense and universal admiration. In the catalogue it was briefly mentioned as No. 17—a portrait; first effort of a young female artist." *Connoisseurs*, who had committed themselves by extravagant praise, sneered at the announcement of the catalogue, and, after a few inquiries, blandly asserted that no tyro could have produced it; that the master had wrought out its perfection, and generously allowed the pupil to monopolize the encomiums. In vain Mr. Clifton disclaimed the merit, and asserted that he had never touched the canvas; that she had jealously refused to let him aid her. Incredulous smiles and unmistakable motions of the head were the sole results of his expostulation. Little mercy has a critical world for novices, particularly those clad in woman's garments; few helping hands are kindly stretched toward her trembling fingers, few strengthening words find her in her seclusion; and when these last do come in friendly whispers, are they not hung up "as apples of gold in pictures of silver" along the chequered walls of memory? Cold glances generally greet her earliest works; they are handled suspiciously, the beauties are all extracted, set in a row, and labelled "plagiarisms;" the residue, like dross in crucibles, is handed back as "original, and her undoubted property." Or, perchance, the phraseology varies, and she hears "This book, this statue, this picture, is no unpractised woman's work; we speak advisedly, and pronounce the fact that pen, or rasp, or chisel, or brush, belongs unmistakably to a master—an experienced writer or veteran artist." It is this bent of human nature to load with chaplets well-established favorites of fame, to "whitewash" continually with praise, to jealously withhold the meed of beginners, rendering grudgingly "Cæsar's things to Cæsar," which tips many a pen with gall, and shadows noble pictures with unseemly clouds. Electra was indignant at the injustice meted out to her, and, as might have been expected, rebelled against the verdict. Very little consolation was derived from the argument by which her master strove to mollify her—that the incredulity of the critics was the highest eulogy that could have been pronounced upon her work. Some weeks after the close of the exhibition the Œnone was purchased and the portrait sent home. Electra placed it on the easel once more, and stood before it in rapt contemplation. Down from the arched roof flowed billows of light, bathing her rounded form as in a sea of molten topaz, and kindling a startling, almost unearthly, beauty in the canvas. What mattered the brevity and paucity of Russell's letters now?—what though three thousand miles of tempestuous sea roared and tossed between them?—she had his untarnished image in her heart, his life-like features ever before her. To this shrine she came continually, and laid thereon the offering of a love passionate and worshipping as ever took entire possession of a woman's heart. Coldness, silence, neglect, all were forgotten when she looked into the deep, beautiful eyes, and upon the broad, bold, matchless brow.

> Love is not love
> Which alters, when it alteration finds,
> Or bends with the remover to remove ;
> Oh, no! it is an ever-fixed mark,
> That looks on tempests and is never shaken."

She had not the faintest hope that he would ever cherish a tenderer feeling for her; but love is a plant of strange growth: now lifting its head feebly in rich, sunny spots, where every fostering influence is employed; and now springing vigorous from barren, rocky cliffs, clinging in icy crevices, defying every adverse element, sending its fibrous roots deeper and deeper in ungenial soil; bending before the fierce breath of storms, only to erect itself more firmly; spreading its delicate petals over the edges of eternal snow, self-sustaining, invincible, immortal. A curious plant truly, and one which will not bear transplanting, as many a luckless experiment has proved. To-day, as Electra looked upon her labors, the coils of Time seemed to fall away; the vista of Eternity opened before her, peopled with two forms, which on earth walked widely separate paths, and over her features stole a serene, lifted expression, as if, after painful scaling, she had risen above the cloud-region and caught the first rays of perpetual sunshine.

Time, like a weaver, made strange, dim, confused masses of woof and warf; but in Eternity the earthwork would be turned, and delicate tracery and marvellous coloring, divine gobelins, would come to light. Patience! Away from the loom—let the shuttle fly! "What I do thou knowest not now, but thou shalt know hereafter." Hence to thy barren fields, and till them until the harvest.

Mr. Clifton had watched her for some moments, with lowering brow and jealous hatred of the picture. Approaching, he looked over her shoulder and asked:

"How much longer do you intend to stand here? Pygmalion was not more captivated by his ivory image than you are by your head. Were it Antinous or Apollo, I doubt whether your admiration would be enhanced."

"It is more than Antinous and Apollo," she answered, drawing the folds of silk over the portrait and turning toward him.

"Child, you are an idolatress."

"Perhaps so; but, at least, I am in a goodly company. Many bow down before shrines of their own handiwork; some bring libations to Mammon, some to Fame, some to Ambition, some to Love. Nature intended us to kneel, which is preferable to standing, statue-like, exacting obeisance from others. Which is nobler? But how am I an idolatress? Shall I not prize the features of my cousin, my earliest friend and playmate? Would you have me tear off and cast away the kindly emotions, the warm affections wherewith God clothed me, as badges of humanity?"

"By no means. But would you have a second Ixion's wheel?"

"Aye, sir, when I am weak enough to worship a cloud. Mr. Clifton, I believe I have shaken hands with my rosy-cheeked, sunny-eyed, siren-charmed childhood; and, to-day, standing here a woman, with few ties to bind me to my fellow-creatures, I hold this one jewelled link of the past in the hollow of my hand, and pet it. Why not? Oh, why not? I am but seventeen; this is all that I have left to caress, and soon the waves of coming years will wash this, too, through my fingers. Would you, less merciful than time, snatch it from me prematurely?"

"I would, that in exchange I might heap your hands with untold treasure and joy."

"I think I am less grasping, then, than you. Leave me the little I value; I ask no more, wish no more, will have no more."

She would have left him, but his hand fell heavily on hers.

"Electra, I must speak to you; hear me. You hug a phantom to your heart; Russell does not and will not love you, other than as his cousin."

The blood deserted her face, leaving a grayish pallor, but the eyes sought his steadily, and the rippling voice lost none of its rich cadence.

"Except as his cousin, I do not expect Russell to love me."

"Oh, child! you deceive yourself; this is a hope that you cling to with mad tenacity."

She wrung her hand from his, and drew her figure to its utmost height.

"You transcend your privilege, sir, when you attempt to catechise me thus. I deny the right of any on earth to put such questions to me—to make such assertions."

"Electra, I did not mean to offend you, but the time has come when we must understand each other ——."

"You did not mean to offend me—well, let that pass; another day we will discuss it, if you please," she interrupted, waving him off and turning toward the door.

"No; you must hear me now. I have a right to question you—the right of my long, silent, faithful love. You may deny it, but that matters little; be still, and listen. Did you suppose that I was simply a generous man, when I offered to guard and aid you—when I took you to my house, placed you in my mother's care, and lavished affection upon you? Did you dream that I was disinterested in what I have done to encourage and assist you? Did you imagine I was merely an amiable philanthropist, anxious to help all in difficulty and sorrow? If so, put away the hallucination. Consider me no longer your friend; look at me as I am, a jealous and selfishly exacting man, who stands before you to-day and tells you he loves you. Oh, Electra! From the morning when you first showed me your sketches, you have been more than my life to me. An unconquerable love sprang up then, and it has grown with the months and years, taking sole possession of a heart which never bowed before any other woman. Every hope I have centres in you. I have not deceived myself; I knew that you loved Russell. Nay, don't deny it; I have watched you too long not to probe your mask. I knew that he had your girlish love, but I waited, and hoped my devotion would win you. You were but a child, and I thought the depth and fervor of my affection would out-weigh a childish fancy. When he came here, I saw that the old fascination still kept its hold upon you; but I saw, too, what you saw quite as plainly—that in Russell Aubrey's heart there is room for nothing but ambition. I knew how you suffered, and I believed it was the death-struggle of your love. But instead, I find you, day by day, before that easel—oblivious of me, of everything but the features you cling to so insanely. Do you wonder that I hate that portrait? Do you wonder that I am growing desperate? Where is your womanly pride, that you lavish your love on one totally indifferent to you? Strange paradox that you are!—proud, passionate, exacting, and yet clinging madly to a memory. Have you no mercy, that you doom me to live for ever on the rack? Shall yonder piece of canvas always stand between your heart and mine? If he loved you in return, I could bear it better; but as it is, I am tortured beyond all endurance. I have spent nearly three years in trying to gain your heart; all other aims have faded before this one absorbing love. To-day I lay it at your feet, and ask if I have not earned some reward. Oh, Electra! have you no gratitude?"

A scarlet spot burned on his pale cheeks, and the mild liquid gray eyes sparkled like stars.

It was no startling revelation to her; long before she had seen that this hour of trial must come to both, and now, despite her resolution, his words unnerved her. She dared not look at him; the hollow voice told her too well what effect this excitement was working on his feeble frame.

"Oh, Mr. Clifton! I am grateful; God, who sees my heart, knows that I am. No child ever loved a parent better than I love you."

"It is not filial affection that I ask of you now. I beg you to lay your dear hands in mine, and promise to be my wife. I ask this of you in the name of my devotion. You gave yourself to me years ago, and to-day I beseech you to seal the compact by a final promise. Electra, beware how you answer! Bridge the gulf between us. Give me your hand."

He stretched out his hand, but she drew back a step.

"God forgive me! but I have no such love for you."

A ghastly smile broke over his face, and, after a moment, the snowy handkerchief he passed across his lips was stained with ruby streaks.

"I know that, and I know the reason. But, once more I ask you to give me your hand. Electra, dearest, do not, I pray you, refuse me this. Oh, child! give me your hand, and in time you will learn to love me."

He seized her fingers, and stooped his head till the silky brown beard mingled with her raven locks.

"Mr. Clifton, to marry without love would be a grievous sin; I dare not. We would hate each other. Life would be a curse to both, and death a welcome release. Could you endure a wife who accepted your hand from gratitude and pity? Oh! such a relationship would be horrible beyond all degree. I shudder at the thought."

"But you would learn to love me."

The summer wind shook the window-curtains and rustled the folds of black silk till the drapery slid from the portrait and left it fully exposed to view. She gave one quick glance at the beloved countenance, and, falling on her knees before the easel, raised her clasped hands passionately, and exclaimed:

"Impossible! impossible! You have said that he is my idol, and you make no mistake. He fills my heart so entirely, that I have nothing but reverence and gratitude to offer you. I am young, I know, and you think that this is a girlish fancy which will fade with coming years. I tell you, sir, this love has become part of me. When he went to Europe I said, 'I will tear it out of my heart, and forget him; I will give every thought to my noble Art.' Faithfully I strove to do so; but a little mountain-stream once merged in the pathless ocean, might as well struggle to gather back its tiny wavelets and return to its pebbly channel. I am proud, it humiliates me to acknowledge all this; and nothing on earth could wring it from me but my desire to convince you that it is utterly impossible I can ever love you as you ask.

"I lift my heavy heart up solemnly,
As once Electra her sepulchral urn,
And, looking in thine eyes, I overturn
The ashes at thy feet. Behold, and see
What a great heap of grief lay hid in me,
And how the red wild sparkles dimly burn
Through the ashen grayness. If thy foot in scorn
Could tread them out to darkness utterly,
It might be well, perhaps."

But you can not take Russell's place. None can come between him and my heart."

The yellow light dripped down on her purplish hair, crystalizing into a nimbus, as she knelt before the portrait, lifting her hands, like saints in medieval pictures, fleeing from martyrdom. Shame dyed her cheeks, but a desperate, reckless triumph flashed in the upraised eyes, revealing fully the aversion which his suit had inspired. Unfortunate, deplorable as was her love for a cousin, it seemed for the moment to glorify her, and Mr. Clifton put his hand over his eyes to shut out the vision.

"Electra Grey, you are unwomanly in your unsought love."

She turned her head, and, looking over her shoulder at him, smiled derisively.

"Unwomanly! If so, made such by your unmanliness. Unwomanly! I deny it. Which is most womanly—to yield to the merciless importunity of one to whom I am indebted; to give my hand to him whose touch chills the blood in my veins; to promise to become his wife when the bare thought sickens my soul; to dare to stand before God's altar and take false vows on my lips, or to tell the simple truth? to shield myself from his entreaties, under the holy mantle of a deep, undying love for another? I volunteered no confession; you taxed and taunted me with my affection. Sir, it should have made me sacred in your eyes. Unwomanly! Were you more manly, I had never shocked your maudlin sentiments of propriety."

"And this is my reward for all the tenderness I have lavished on you! When I stooped to beg your hand, to be repulsed with scorn and loathing. To spend three years in faithful effort to win your heart, and reap —— contempt, hatred."

Staggering back, he sank into his arm-chair and closed his eyes a moment, then continued:

"If it were possible that you could be happy, I would not complain; but there is no hope of that. You might as well kneel to my marble Hermes yonder as to Russell. Stranger infatuation never possessed a woman."

"I am not blind; I neither ask nor expect anything from him. Unless you betray my confidence he will never suspect the truth, and I would sooner endure the tortures of Torquemada than that he should know it. But by what process will you demonstrate that, since a rare and royal banquet is for ever shut beyond my reach, it is my duty to sit down in the dust and try to content myself with husks? Sir, my God never intended me to live on crumbs, and I will not. I will be true to my heart; if the vast host of my fellow-creatures should pass away from earth, I will stand alone and conquer solitude as best I may. Not 'one jot, not one tittle' of my nature will I yield for companionship. No mess of pottage will I have, in lieu of my birthright. All or none! Marriage is holy; God, in his wisdom, instituted it with the seal of love; but its desecration with counterfeits makes Tophets, Golgothas, instead of Edens. I know what I have to expect; on my own head be my future. If quarrel there be, it is between Fate and me; you have no concern in it."

"I would not have troubled you long, Electra. It was because I knew that my life must be short at best that I urged you to gild the brief period with the light of your love. I would not have bound you always to me; and, when I asked your hand a few minutes since, I knew that death would soon sever the tie and set you free. Let this suffice to palliate my 'unmanly' pleading. I have but one request to make of you now, and, weak as it may seem, I beg of you not to deny me. You are preparing to leave my house; this I know; I see it in your face, and the thought is harrowing to me. Electra, remain under my roof while I live; let me see you every day, here, in my house. If not as my wife, stay as my friend, my pupil, my child. I little thought I could ever condescend to ask this of any one; but the dread of separation bows me down. Oh, child! I will not claim you long."

She stood up before him with the portrait in her arms, resolved, then and there, to leave him for ever. But the ghastly pallor of his face, the scarlet thread oozing over his lips and saturating the handkerchief with which he strove to staunch it, told her that the request was preferred on no idle pretext. In swift review, his kindness, generosity and unwavering affection passed before her, and the mingled accents of remorse and compassion whispered: "Pay your debt of gratitude by sacrificing your heart. If you can make him happy, you owe it to him."

Without a word she passed him and went up to her own room. It was an hour of sore temptation for one so young and inexperienced; but, placing the portrait on the low mantle, she crossed her arms before it and tried to lay matters in the scale. On one side, years of devotion, the circumstances of the artist's life, his mother's infirmity, confining her sometimes to her bed, often to her room, preventing her from nursing him; the weary season of his tedious illness, the last hours gloomy and miserable, unsoothed by gentle words or tender offices. On the other, stern adherence, unerring obedience to the dictates of her heart, the necessary self-abnegation, the patient attendance at the couch of prolonged suffering, and entire devotion to him. For a time the scales balanced; she could not conquer her repugnance to remaining in his home; then a grave and its monumental stone were added, and, with a groan, she dropped her face in her hands. At the expiration of two hours she locked the portrait from view, and went slowly back to the studio. The house was very quiet; the ticking of the clock was distinctly heard as she pushed the door open and glided in. Involuntarily she drew a long, deep breath, for it was like leaving freedom at the threshold and taking upon herself grievous bonds. The arm-chair was vacant, but the artist lay on one of the sofas, with his face toward the wall, and on a small table beside him stood a crystal bowl of cracked ice, a stained wine-glass, and vial containing some dark purple liquid. Approaching softly, she scanned the countenance, and tears gathered in her eyes as she saw how thin and hollow were the now flushed cheeks; how the lips writhed now and then, as if striving to suppress bitter words. The beautiful brown hair was all tossed back, and she noticed that along the forehead clustered many silver threads. One hand was thrust within his vest, the other thrown up over the head, grasping a fresh handkerchief. Softly she took this hand, and, bending over him, said, in a low, thrilling tone:

"Mr. Clifton, I was passionate and hasty, and said some unkind things which I would fain recall, and for which I beg your pardon. I thank you for the honor you would have conferred on me, and for the unmerited love you offered me. Unless it were in my power to return that love, it would be sinful to give you my hand; but, since you desire it so earnestly, I will promise to stay by your side, to do what I can to make you happy; to prove, by my devotion, that I am not insensible to all your kindness, that I am very grateful for the affection you have given me. I come and offer you this, as a poor return for all that I owe you; it is the most my conscience will permit me to tender. My friend, my master, will you accept it, and forgive the pain and sorrow I have caused you?"

He felt her tears falling on his fingers, and, for a moment, neither spoke; then he drew the hands to his lips and kissed them tenderly.

"Thank you, Electra. I know it is a sacrifice on your part, but I am selfish enough to accept it. Heaven bless you, my pupil."

"In future we will not allude to this day of trial—let it be forgotten; 'let the dead past bury its dead.' I will have no resurrected phantoms. And now, sir, you must not allow this slight hemorrhage to depress you. In a few days you will be stronger, quite able to examine and find fault with my work. Shall I send a note to Dr. LeRoy, asking him to call and see you this evening?"

"He has just left me. Say nothing of the hemorrhage to mother; it would only distress her."

He released her hands, and, stooping over his pillow, she smoothed the disordered hair, and for the first time pressed her lips to his forehead.

Thus she bowed her neck to the yoke, and, with a fixed, unalterable will, entered on the long, dreary ministry to which she felt that duty called.

We shade our eyes, and peer into the dim Unknown, striving to see whither we are tending, and a sudden turn in the way, a sharp angle, brings us face to face with huge, frowning obstacles, that grimly bar all progress in the direction to which our inclinations point. Strange devious paths stretch out at our feet, baffling all our wise conjectures, setting at defiance all our plans and prudential machinations. From breath to breath, from step to step, from hour to hour, is man's sole empire. "Boast not thyself of to-morrow."

CHAPTER XIII.

"Cities give not the human senses room enough," says a latter-day seer, and Electra Grey sometimes felt that her heart and soul were in the stocks, or ironed down to a stake, leaving only a periphery of a few feet. Brick walls and paving-stones uttered no kindly message; hurrying foot-passengers and crowded omnibuses told of the din and strife of life, but whispered no word of cheer, no lesson of uncomplaining fortitude, no exhortation to be strong and patient. She saw colossal Selfishness crushing along its Juggernautic way; Wealth jostled Poverty into the gutter, and Beauty picked a dainty crossing to give a wide berth to Deformity; hard, stern, granite-like faces passed her window day by day; princely equipages, with haughty, supercilious occupants, rolled along the street, and bridal trains and funeral processions mingled in their windings. If man be, indeed, a "microcosm," to what shall I liken that great city wherein dwelt the painter and his pupil? Isis, the great nursing-mother—genial Nature, teeming with soothing influences, and missals of joy and strength, seemed sepulchred—and in her place, a flint-featured, miserly, and most intolerable step-mother frowned upon the luckless young artist. City life? City starvation, rather, she found it, until a long and painful apprenticeship taught her the priceless dietary whereby smiling Plenty beamed upon her. Reared on the outskirts of a country-town, she longed for the freedom and solitude of the old pine-woods at home, and sickened at the thought of spending her life within walls of brick and mortar. She had selected an attic room, with dormer windows looking eastward, and here she daily watched the pale gray dawn struggle with the vapors and shadows of night. "Quiet fields of crimson cirri," fleecy masses of restless, glittering cumuli, or the sweep and rush of "inky-fringed," lowering rain-clouds, alike charmed her. Long before the servants stirred below she was seated at the window, noting the waning shimmer of the Morning-Star as the waves of light rolled up and crested the horizon, whitening the deep dark blue with their sparkling spray. The peculiarities of each sunrise and sunset, were jotted down assiduously:

"Cloud-walls of the morning's gray
Faced with amber column,
Crowned with crimson cupola
From a sunset solemn,"

were sketched with great care, and put aside for future use; and it rarely happened that, on a dull, rainy morning, she came down to breakfast looking other than moody and disappointed, as though her rights had been infringed, her privileges curtailed. Constituted with keen susceptibility to impressions of beauty or sublimity, whether physical, moral, or intellectual, Nature intended her as a thing for gen-shine and holidays, as a darling to be petted; but Fate shook her head, and, with a grimace, set the tender young soul on a bleak exposure, to be hardened and invigorated.

With the characteristic fitfulness of consumption, Mr. Clifton rallied, and, for a time, seemed almost restored; but at the approach of winter the cough increased, and dangerous symptoms returned. Several months after the rejection of his suit, to which no allusion had ever been made, Electra sat before her easel, absorbed in work, while the master slowly walked up and down the studio, wrapped in a warm plaid shawl. Occasionally he paused and looked over her shoulder, then resumed his pace, offering no comment. It was not an unusual occurrence for them to pass entire mornings together without exchanging a word, and to-day the silence had lasted more than an hour. A prolonged fit of coughing finally arrested her attention, and, glancing up, she met his sad gaze.

"This is unpropitious weather for you, Mr. Clifton."

"Yes, this winter offers a dreary prospect."

"There is the doctor now, passing the window. I will come back as soon as his visit is over." She rose hastily to quit the room, but he detained her.

"Do not go—I wish you to remain and finish your work."

Dr. LeRoy entered, and, after questioning his patient, stood on the rug, warming his fingers.

"The fact is, my dear fellow, this is not the place for you. I sent you South four years ago nearly, and saved your life; and, as I told you last week, you will have to take that same prescription again. It is folly to talk of spending the winter here. I can do nothing for you. You must go to Cuba or to Italy. It is of no use to try to deceive you, Harry; you know, just as well as I do, that your case is getting desperate, and change of climate is your last hope. I have told you all this before."

Electra laid down her pallette, and listened for the answer.

"I am sorry you think so, but I can't leave New York."

"Why not?"

"For various good reasons."

"My dear fellow, is your life of any value?"

"A strange question, truly."

"If it is, quit New York in thirty-six hours; if not, remain, 'for various good reasons.' Send to my office for an anodyne. Better take my advice. Good-day."

Passing by the easel, he whispered:

"Use your influence; send him South." And then the two were again alone.

Resting her chin in her hands, she raised her eyes and said:

"Why do you not follow the doctor's advice? A winter South might restore you."

He drew near, and, leaning his folded arms on the top of the easel, looked down into her face.

"There is only one condition upon which I could consent to go; that is in your hands. Will you accompany me?"

She understood it all in an instant, saw the new form in which the trial presented itself, and her soul sickened.

"Mr. Clifton, if I were your sister, or your child, I would gladly go; but, as your pupil, I can not."

"As Electra Grey, certainly not; but, as Electra Clifton, you could go."

"Electra Grey will be carved on my tombstone."

"Then you decide my fate. I remain, and wait the slow approach of death."

"No, before just Heaven! I take no such responsibility, nor shall you thrust it on me. You are a man, and must decide your destiny for yourself; I am a poor girl, having no claim upon, no power over you. It is your duty to preserve the life which God gave you, in the way prescribed by your physician, and I have no voice in the matter. It is your duty to go South, and it will be both weak and wicked to remain here under existing circumstances."

"My life is centred in you; it is worthless, nay, a burden, separated from you."

"Your life should be centred in something nobler, better; in your duty, in your profession. It is suicidal to fold your hands listlessly and look to me, as you do."

"All these things have I tried, and I am weary of their hollowness, weary of life and the world. So long as I have your face here, I care not to cross my own threshold till friendly hands bear me out to my quiet resting-place under the willows of Greenwood. Electra, my darling, think me weak if you will, but bear with me a little while longer, and then this, my shadow, shall flit from your young heart, leaving not even a memory to haunt you. Be patient! I will soon pass away, to another, a more peaceful, blessed sphere."

A melancholy smile lighted his fair waxen features, as waning, sickly sunshine in an autumn evening flickers over sculptured marble in a silent church-yard.

How she compassionated his great weakness as he wiped away the moisture which, even on that cold day, glistened on his forehead.

"Oh! I beseech you to go to Cuba. Go, and get strong once more."

"Nothing will ever help me now. Sunny skies and soft breezes bring no healing for me. I want to die here, in my home, where your hands will be about me; not among strangers, in Cuba or Italy."

He turned to the fire, and, springing up, she left the room. The solemn silence of the house oppressed her; she put on her thickest wrappings, and took the street leading to the nearest park. A steel-gray sky, with slowly-trailing clouds, looked down on her, and the keen, chilly wind wafted a fine snow-powder in her face as she pressed against it. The trees were bare, and the sere grass grew hoary as the first snow-flakes of the season came down softly and shroud-like. The walks were deserted, save where a hurrying form crossed from street to street, homeward-bound; and Electra passed slowly along, absorbed in thoughts colder than the frosting that gathered on shawl and bonnet. The face and figure of the painter glided spectrally before her at every step, and a mighty temptation followed at its heels. Why not strangle her heart? Why not marry him and bear his name, if, thereby, she could make his few remaining months of existence happy, and, by accompanying him South, prolong his life even for a few weeks? She shuddered at the suggestion, it would be such a miserable lot. But then the question arose: "Who told you that your life was given for happiness? Do you imagine your Maker set you on earth solely to hunt your own enjoyment? Suppose duty costs you pain and struggles; is it any the less duty? Nay, is it not all the more urgent duty?" She knew that she could return to the artist, and, with one brief sentence, pour the chrism of joy over his suffering soul; and her great compassion, mild-eyed, soft-lipped, tender-hearted, whispered: Why not? why not?

"Nature owns no man who is not a martyr withal." If this dictum possessed any value, did it not point to her mission? She could no longer shut her eyes and stumble on, for right in her path stood an awful form, with austere lip and fiery eye, demanding a parley, defying all escape; and, calmly, she stood face to face with her Sphinx, considering her riddle. A young, motherless girl, without the girding of a holy religion, a free, untamed soul, yielding allegiance to no creed, hearkening only to the dictates of her tempestuous nature, now confronting the most ancient immemorial Destroyer who haunts the highways of society. Self-immolation, or a poisoning of the spring of joy in the heart of a fellow-creature? Was duty a Moloch, clasping its scorching arms around its devotees?—a Juggernaut, indeed, whose iron wheels drank the life-blood of its victims? "Will you see your benefactor sink swiftly into an early grave, and, standing by with folded arms, persuade yourself that it is not your duty to attempt to save him at all hazards? Can nothing less than love ever sanction marriage?" Such was the riddle hurled before her, and, as she pondered, the floodgates of her sorrow and jealousy were once more lifted—the rush and roar of bitter waters drowned, for a time, the accents of conscience and of reason.

But out of these fierce asphaltic waves arose, Aphrodite-like, a pure, radiant, heavenly form —a child of all climes, conditions, and ages— an immortal evangel; and, as the piercing, sunny eyes of womanly intuition looked upon the riddle, the stony lineaments of the Sphinx melted into air. If womanly eyes rest on this page the answer need not be traced here, for in every true woman's heart the answer is to be found engraved in God's own characters; and, however the rubbish of ignoble motives may accumulate, it can never obliterate the divine handwriting. In the holiest oratory of her nature is enshrined an infallible talisman, an ægis, and she requires no other panoply in the long struggle incident to trials such as shook the stormy soul of the young artist. Faster fell the snow-flakes, cresting the waves of hair like foam, and, setting her teeth firmly, as if thereby locking the door against all compassionating compunctions, Electra left the park and turned into a cross-street, on which was situated an establishment where bouquets were kept for sale. The assortment was meagre at that late hour, but she selected a tiny bunch of delicate, fragrant, hothouse blossoms, and, shielding them with her shawl, hastened home. The studio was brilliant with gas-glare and warm with the breath of anthracite, but an aspect of dreariness, silence, and sorrow predominated. The figures in the pictures shrank back in their frames, the statues gleamed mournfully white and cold, and the emaciated form and face of the painter, thrown into bold relief by the dark green lining of the easy-chair, seemed to belong to realms of death rather than life. On the edge of the low scroll-sculptured mantle, supported at each corner by caryatides, perched a large tame gray owl, with clipped wings folded, and wide, solemn, oracular eyes fastened on the countenance of its beloved master. A bronze clock, of exquisite workmanship, occupied the centre, and represented the Angel of Revelations "*swearing by Him that liveth for ever and ever, that Time should be no longer.*" One hand held the open book, the other a hammer, which gave out the hours with clear metallic ring; and along the base, just underneath the silver-dial-plate, were carved, in German characters, the words of Richter: "And an immeasurably extended hammer was to strike the last hour of Time, and shiver the universe asunder."

With swift, noiseless steps Electra came to the red grate, and, after a moment, drew an ottoman close to the easy-chair. Perhaps its occupant slept; perchance he wandered, with closed eyes, far down among the sombre, dank crypts of memory. She laid her cool fingers on his hand, and held the bouquet before him.

"My dear sir, here are your flowers; they are not as pretty as usual, but sweet enough to atone for lack of beauty."

He fingered them caressingly, laid them against his hollow cheeks, and hid his lips among their fragrant petals, but the starry eyes were fixed on the features of the pupil.

"It is bitter weather out; did you brave it for these? Thank you, but don't expose yourself so in future. Two invalids in a house are quite enough. You are snow-crowned, little one; do you know it? The frosting gleams right royally on that black hair of yours. Nay, child, don't brush it off; like all lovely things it fades rapidly, melts away like the dreams that flutter around a boy in the witchery of a long, still, sunny summer day."

His thin hand nestled in her shining hair, and she submitted to the touch in silence.

"My dove soared away from this dreary ark, and bathed her silver wings in the free air of heaven; returning but to bring me some grateful memorial, an olive-branch, wherewith to deck this gloomy ark of mine. Next time she will soar farther, and find a more tempting perch, and gladden Noah's eyes no more."

"If so, it will be because the high and dry land of God beckons her; and when the deluge is ended, she will be needed no longer."

"For, then, Electra, Noah's haven of rest will be the fair still fields of Eternity."

In this semi-metaphoric strain he often indulged of late, but she felt little inclination to humor the whim, and, interlacing her slight fingers, she answered, half-impatiently:

"Your simile is all awry, sir. Most unfortunately, I have nothing dove-like in my nature."

"Originally you had, but your character has been warped."

"By what, or whom?"

"Primarily, by unhappy extraneous circumstances, influences if you will, which contributed to a diseased development of two passions, that now preponderate over all other elements of your character."

"A diagnosis which I will not accept."

"A true one, nevertheless, my child."

"Possibly; but we will waive a discussion just now. I am, and always intend to be, true to the nature which God gave me."

"A dangerous dogma that. Electra, how do you know that the 'nature' you fondle and plume yourself upon emanated from your Maker?"

"How do you know, sir, that God intended that willows should droop and trail their slender boughs earthward, while poplars, like granite shafts, shoot up, lifting their silver-shimmering leaflets ever to the clouds? Who fingered their germs and directed their course?"

"The analogy will not hold between the vegetable kingdom and the moral and intellectual spheres. Men and women are not cast in particular moulds, bound by iron laws, and labelled, like plants or brutes, Genus ——, Species ——. Moreover, to man alone was given free agency, even to the extent of uprooting, crushing entirely the original impulses implanted by God in the human heart to act as motive power. I have known people insane enough to pluck out the wheat, and culture, into rank luxuriance, the tares in their nature. Child, do you ever look ahead to the coming harvest-time?"

"If I do, it contents me to know that each soul binds up its own sheaves."

"No; angels are reapers, and make up the account for the Lord of the harvest."

"I don't believe that. No third party has any voice in that last, long reckoning. God and the creature only see the balance-sheet."

She rose, and, leaning against the mantle, put out her hand to caress the solemn-eyed solitary pet of the studio. How he came to be the solace and companion of the artist she had never been told, but knew that a strange fellowship linked the gray old favorite with the master, and wondered at the almost human expression with which it sometimes looked from its lofty pedestal upon the languid movements of the painter. "Munin" was the name he ever recognized and answered to, and, when she one day repeated it to herself, puzzling over its significance, Mr. Clifton told her that it meant "memory," in Scandinavian lore, and belonged to one of the favorite birds of Odin. It was one of his many strange whims, fostered by life-long researches among the mythologies of the Old World; and Electra struggled to overcome the undefinable sensation of awe and repulsion which crept over her whenever she met that fascinating stare fixed upon her. As little love had the bird for her, and, though occasionally it settled upon the cross-beam of her easel and watched the slow motion of her brush, they seemed to shrink from each other. Now, as her soft hand touched his feathers, they rumpled, bristled, and he flitted to the artist's knee, uttering a hoarse, prolonged, most melancholy note, as the master caressed him.

"Why are not you and Munin better friends?"

"Because I am not wise enough, or evil-boding in appearance, or sufficiently owlish to suit him, I suppose. He chills my blood sometimes, when I come here, in twilight, before the gas is lighted. I would almost as soon confront Medusa."

She took from the curious oval mosaic table a new book containing her mark, and reseated herself. As she did so, Munin flapped his dusky wings and disappeared through the door opening into the hall, and, shading her face with one hand, she read aloud a passage heavily underlined by a pencil.

"'But this poor, miserable Me! Is *this*, then, all the book I have got to read about God in?' Yes, truly so. No other book, nor fragment of book, than that will you ever find—no velvet-bound missal, nor frankincensed manuscript; nothing hieroglyphic nor cuneiform; papyrus and pyramid are alike silent on this matter; nothing in the clouds above, nor in the earth beneath. That flesh-bound volume is the only revelation that is, that was, or that can be. In that is the image of God painted; in that is the law of God written; in that is the promise of God revealed. Know thyself; for through thyself only thou canst know God. Through the glass darkly; but, except through the glass, in no wise. A tremulous crystal, waved as water, poured out upon the ground; you may defile it, despise it, pollute it at your pleasure, and at your peril; for on the peace of those weak waves must all the heaven you shall ever gain be first seen, and through such purity as you can win for those dark waves must all the light of the risen Sun of Brightness be bent down by faint refraction. Cleanse them, and calm them, as you love your life."

"Mr. Clifton, this epitomizes my creed. There is nothing new in it; I grant you it is old as the Delphian inscription. Two thousand years ago Socrates preached it in the Agora at Athens. Now it shakes off its Greek apparel, and comes to this generation encumbered in loosely-fitting English garments—immemorial Truth peering through modern masks."

He regarded her with an expression of sorrowful tenderness, and his hand trembled as he placed it upon her head.

"This darling creed, this infallible egotism of yours, will fail you in the day of fierce trial. Pagan that you are, I know not what is to become of you. Oh, Electra! if you would only be warned in time."

The warmth of the room had vermilioned her cheeks, and the long black lashes failed to veil in any degree the flash of the eyes she raised to his face. Removing the hand from her head, she took it in both hers, and a cold, dauntless smile wreathed her lips.

"Be easy on my account. I am not afraid of my future. Why should I be? God built an arsenal in every soul before he launched it on the stormy sea of Time, and the key to mine is Will! I am young and healthy; the rich purple blood bubbles through my veins like Chian wine; and, with my heritage of poverty and obscurity, I look fortune's favorites in the eye, and dare them to retard or crush me. A vast caravan of mighty souls, 'whose distant footsteps echo down the corridors of Time,' have gone before me; and step by step I tramp after. What woman has done, woman may do; a glorious sisterhood of artists beckon me on; what Elizabeth Cheron, Sibylla Merian, Angelica Kauffman, Elizabeth Le Brun, Felicie Fauveau, and Rosa Bonheur have achieved, I also will accomplish, or die in the effort. These travelled no royal road to immortality, but rugged, thorny paths; and who shall stay my feet? Afar off gleams my resting-place, but ambition scourges me unflaggingly on. Do not worry about my future; I will take care of it, and of myself."

"And when, after years of toil, you win fame, even fame enough to satisfy your large expectations, what then? Whither will you look for happiness?"

"I will grapple fame to my empty heart, as women do other idols."

"It will freeze you, my dear child. Remember the mournful verdict which Dante gave the world through the lips of Oderigi:

"   Cimabue thought
To lord it over Painting's field; and now
The cry is Giotto's, and his name eclipsed.
Thus hath one Guido from the other snatched
The lettered prize; and he, perhaps, is born,
Who shall drive either from their nest. The noise
Of worldly fame is but a blast of wind
That blows from divers points and shifts its name,
Shifting the point it blows from."

"And, Electra, that chill blast will wail through your lonely heart, chanting a requiem over the trampled, dead hopes that might have garlanded your life. Be warned, oh! daughter of Agamemnon!

"'The earth hath bubbles as the water hath,
And this is of them.'"

"At all events, I will risk it. Thank God! whatever other faults I confess to, there is no taint of cowardice in my soul."

She rose, and stood a moment on the rug, looking into the red net-work of coals, then turned to leave him, saying:

"I must go to your mother now, and presently I will bring your tea."

"You need not trouble. I can go to the dining-room to-night."

"It is no trouble; it gives me great pleasure to do something for your comfort; and I know you always enjoy your supper more when you have it here."

As she closed the door he pressed his face against the morocco lining and groaned unconsciously, and large glittering tears, creeping from beneath the trembling lashes, hid themselves in the curling brown beard.

To see that Mrs. Clifton's supper suited her, and then to read aloud to her for half an hour from the worn family bible, was part of the daily routine which Electra permitted nothing to interrupt. On this occasion she found the old lady seated, as usual, before the fire, her crutches leaning against the chair and her favorite cat curled on the carpet at her feet. Most tenderly did the aged cripple love her son's *protégé*, and the wrinkled sallow face lighted up with a smile of pleasure at her entrance.

"I thought it was about time for you to come to me. Sit down, dear, and touch the bell for Kate. How is Harry?"

"No stronger, I am afraid. You know this is very bad weather for him."

"Yes; when he came up to-day I thought he looked more feeble than I had ever seen him; and, as I sit here and listen to his hollow cough, every sound seems a stab at my heart." She rocked herself to and fro for a moment, and added, mournfully:

"Ah, child! it is so hard to see my youngest boy going down to the grave before me. The last of five, I hoped he would survive me, but consumption is a terrible thing; it took my husband first, then, in quick succession, my other children, and now Harry, my darling, my youngest, is the last prey."

Anxious to divert her mind, Electra adroitly changed the conversation, and when she rose to say good-night, some time after, had the satisfaction of knowing that the old lady had fallen asleep. It was in vain that she arranged several tempting dishes on the table beside the painter, and coaxed him to partake of them; he received but a cup of tea from her hand, and motioned the remainder away. As the servant removed the tray he looked up at his pupil, and said:

"Please wheel the lounge nearer to the grate; I am too tired to sit up to-night."

She complied at once, shook up the pillow, and, as he laid his head upon it, she spread his heavy plaid shawl over him.

"Now, sir, what shall I read this evening?"

"*Arcana Cœlestia*," if you please."

She took up the volume, and began at the place he designated; and, as she read on and on, her rich flexible voice rose and fell upon the air like waves of melody. One of her hands chanced to hang over the arm of the chair, and, as she sat near the lounge, thin hot fingers twined about it, drew it caressingly to the pillow, and held it tightly. Her first impulse was to withdraw it, and an expression of annoyance crossed her features; but, on second thought, she suffered her fingers to rest passively in his. Now and then, as she turned a leaf, she met his luminous eyes fastened upon her; but after a time the quick breathing attracted her attention, and, looking down, she saw that he, too, was sleeping. She closed the book and remained quiet, fearful of disturbing him; and as she studied the weary, fevered face, noting the march of disease, the sorrowful drooping of the mouth, so indicative of grievous disappointment, a new and holy tenderness awoke in her heart. It was a feeling analogous to that of a mother for a suffering child, who can be soothed only by her presence and caresses—an affection not unfrequently kindled in haughty natures by the entire dependence of a weaker one. Blended with this, was a remorseful consciousness of the coldness with which she had persistently rejected, repulsed every manifestation of his devoted love; and, winding her fingers through his long hair, she vowed an atonement for the past in increased gentleness for the remainder of his waning life. As she bent over him, wearing her compassion in her face, he opened his eyes and looked at her.

"How long have I slept?"

"Nearly an hour. How do you feel since your nap?"

He made no reply, and she put her hand on his forehead. The countenance lighted, and he said slowly:

"Ah! yes, press your cool soft little palm on my brow. It seems to still the throbbing in my temples."

"It is late, Mr. Clifton, and I must leave you. William looked in, a few minutes since, to say that the fire burned in your room, but I would not wake you. I will send him to you. Good-night."

She leaned down voluntarily and kissed him, and, with a quick movement, he folded her to his heart an instant, then released her, murmuring huskily:

"God bless you, Electra, and reward you for your patient endurance. Good-night, my precious child."

She went to her own room, all unconscious of the burst of emotion which shook the feeble frame of the painter, long after she had laid her head on her pillow in the sound slumber of healthful youth.

CHAPTER XIV.

The year that ensued proved a valuable school of patience, and taught the young artist a gentleness of tone and quietude of manner at variance with the natural impetuosity of her character. Irksome beyond degree was the discipline to which she subjected herself, but, with a fixedness of purpose that knew no wavering, she walked through the daily dreary routine, keeping her eyes upon the end that slowly but unmistakably approached. In midsummer Mr. Clifton removed, for a few weeks, to the Catskill, and occasionally he rallied for a few hours, with a tenacity of strength almost miraculous. During the still sunny afternoons hosts of gay visitors, summer tourists, often paused in their excursions to watch the emaciated form of the painter leaning on the arm of his beautiful pupil, or reclining on a lichen-carpeted knoll while she sketched the surrounding scenery. Increased feebleness prevented Mrs. Clifton from joining in these outdoor jaunts, and early in September, when it became apparent that her mind was rapidly sinking into imbecility, they returned to the city. Memory seemed to have deserted its throne; she knew neither her son nor Electra, and the last spark of intelligence manifested itself in a semi-recognition of her favorite cat, which sprang to welcome her back as friendly hands bore her to the chamber she was to quit no more till death released the crushed spirit. A letter was found on the *atelier* mantle, directed to Electra in familiar characters, which she had not seen for months. Very quietly she put it in her pocket, and in the solitude of her room broke the seal; found that Russell had returned during her absence, had spent a morning in the studio looking over her work, and had gone South to establish himself in his native town. Ah! the grievous, grievous disappointment. A bitter cry rolled from her lips, and the hands wrung each other despairingly; but, an hour later, she stood beside the artist with unruffled brow and a serene mouth that bore no surface-token of the sorrow gnawing at her heart. Winter came on earlier than usual, with unwonted severity; and, week after week, Electra went continually from one sufferer to another, striving to alleviate pain and to kindle a stray beam of sunshine in the darkened mansion. As one living thing in a charnel-house she flitted from room to room, sometimes shrinking from her own shadow, that glided before her on the polished wall as she went up and down stairs in the dead of night. Unremitted vigil set its pale, infallible signet on her face, but Mr. Clifton either could not or would not see the painful alteration in her appearance; and when Mrs. Young remonstrated with her niece upon the ruinous effects of this tedious confinement to the house, she only answered, steadily: "I will nurse him so long as I have strength left to creep from one room to another."

During Christmas week he grew alarmingly worse, and Dr. LeRoy counted the waning life by hours; but on New Year's eve he declared himself almost well, and insisted on being carried to the studio. The whim was humored, and, wrapped in his silken *robe de chambre*, he was seated in his large cushioned chair, smiling to find himself once more in the midst of his treasures. Turning back the velvet cuff from his attenuated wrist, he lifted his flushed face toward the nurse, and said eagerly:

"Uncover my easel; make William draw it close to me; I have been idle long enough. Give me my palette; I want to retouch the forehead of my hero. It needs a high light."

"You are not strong enough to work. Wait till to-morrow."

"To-morrow! to-morrow! You have told me that fifty times. Wheel up the easel, I say. The spell is upon me, and work I will."

It was the "ruling passion strong in death," and Electra acquiesced, arranging the colors on the palette as he directed, and selecting the brushes he required. Resting his feet upon the cross-beam, he leaned forward and gazed earnestly upon his masterpiece, the darling design which had haunted his brain for years. "Theta" he called this piece of canvas, which was a large square painting representing, in the foreground, the death of Socrates. Around the reclining form of the philosopher clustered Apollodorus, Cebes, Simmias, and Crito, and through the window of the prison came the last slanting, quivering ray of the setting sun, showing the street beyond, where, against the stone wall, near a gleaming guardian Hermes, huddled a mournful group—Xantippe and her weeping children. The details of the picture were finished with pre-Raphaelite precision and minuteness, —the sweep and folds of drapery about the couch, the emptied hemlock cup—but the central figure of the Martyr lacked something, and to these last touches Mr. Clifton essayed to address himself. Slowly, feebly, the transparent hand wandered over the canvas, and Electra heard with alarm the labored breath that came panting from his parted lips. She saw the unnatural sparkle in his sunken eyes almost die out, then leap up again, like smouldering embers swept by a sudden gust, and, in the clear strong voice of other years, he repeated to himself the very words of Plato's Phædo: "For I have heard that it is right to die with good omens. Be quiet, therefore, and bear up."

Leaning back to note the effect of his touches, a shiver ran through his frame, the brush fell from his tremulous fingers, and he lay motionless and exhausted.

Electra threw up the sash, that the wintry air might revive him; and as the red glare of declining day streamed down from the skylight upon the group, she looked from the easy-chair to the canvas, and mutely questioned: "Which is most thanatoid—painter or painted?"

Folding his hands like a helpless, tired child, he raised his eyes to hers and said, brokenly:

"I bequeath it to you; finish my work. You understand me—you know what is lacking; finish my 'Theta,' and tell the world I died at work upon it. Oh! for a fraction of my old strength! One hour more to complete my Socrates! Just one hour! I would ask no more."

She tried to persuade him to return to his own room, but he obstinately refused, and when she insisted, he answered, pleadingly, "No, no; let me stay here. Do let me be quiet here. I hate that gloomy, tomb-like room."

She gave him a powerful cordial which the physician had left, and, having arranged the pillows on the lounge, drew it close to the easel, and prevailed on him to lie down.

A servant was despatched for Dr. LeRoy, but returned to say that a dangerous case detained him elsewhere.

"Mr. Clifton, would you like to have your mother brought down stairs and placed beside you for a while?"

"No; I want nobody but you. Sit down here close to me and keep quiet."

She lowered the heavy curtains, shaded the gas-globe, and, placing a bunch of sweet violets on his pillow, sat down at his side. His favorite spaniel nestled at her feet, and occasionally threw up his head and gazed wistfully at his master. Thus two hours passed, and as she rose to administer the medicine he waved it off, saying:

"Give me no more of it. I won't be drugged in my last hours. I won't have my intellect clouded by opiates. Throw it into the fire and let me rest."

"Oh, sir! can I do nothing for you?"

"Yes; read to me. Your voice lulls me. Read me that letter of Iamblichus to Agathocles, which I marked last summer."

She read it, and, without questioning, laid the book aside and took up a volume of Jacob Behmen, of which he was very fond, selecting, here and there, passages designated by pencil-marks. He had long revelled among the echoless abysses of dim, mediæval, mystical lore, and, strange as it may appear, the quaint old books preserved their spell and riveted the wandering mind, even on the verge of dissolution. She knew that Cornelius-Agrippa, Theophrastus Paracelsus, and Swedenborg held singular mastery over him; but she shrank from all these now, as though they had been bound in flames, and a yearning to comfort him from the sacred lips of Jewish prophets and apostles took possession of her. Passages which she had read to her blind aunt came back to her now, ringing trumpet-toned in her ears, and she rose to bring a bible from Mrs. Clifton's room.

"Where are you going?"

"To your mother's room, for a moment only. I want a book which I left there."

"Sit still. Do not leave me, I beg of you." He drew her back to the seat, and after a short silence said, slowly:

"Electra, are you afraid of death?"

"No, sir."

"Do you know that I am dying?"

"I have seen you as ill several times before."

"You are a brave, strong-hearted child; glazed eyes and stiffened limbs will not frighten you. I have but few hours to live; put your hand in mine, and promise me that you will sit here till my soul quits its clay-prison. Will you watch with me the death of the year? Are you afraid to stay with me and see me die?"

She would not trust herself to speak, but laid her hand in his and clasped it firmly. He smiled, and added:

"Will you promise to call no one? I want no eyes but yours to watch me as I die. Let there be only you and me."

"I promise."

For some moments he lay motionless, but the intensity of his gaze made her restless, and she shaded her face.

"Electra, my darling, your martyrdom draws to a close. I have been merciless in my exactions, I know; you are worn to a shadow, and your face is sharp and haggard; but you will forgive me all, when the willows of Greenwood trail their boughs across my headstone. You have been faithful and uncomplaining; you have been to me a light, a joy, and a glory! God bless you, my pupil. There was a time when, looking at the future that stretched before you, I shuddered on your account. Since then I have learned to know you better; I feel assured your nature will be equal to its trials. You can conquer difficulties, and, better still, you can work and live alone; you can conquer your own heart. I am passing to a higher, purer, happier sphere; but my spirit will hover constantly around you here, in the midst of your work, overlooking you continually, as in the days that have gone by. I have one request to make of you, and unhesitatingly I make it: remain in this house and watch over my poor mother's last hours as you watched over and cheered mine. It is a heavy burden to lay upon you; but you have patiently borne as heavy, and I have no fear that you will desert her when the last of her sons sleep under marble. She will never know that I have gone before her till we meet in another world. In my vest-pocket is the key of my writing-desk. There you will find my will; take charge of it, and put it in LeRoy's hands as soon as possible. Give me some water."

She held the glass to his lips, and, as he sank back, a bright smile played over his face.

"Ah, child! it is such a comfort to have you here—you are so inexpressibly dear to me."

She took his thin hands in hers, and hot tears fell upon them. An intolerable weight crushed her heart, a half-defined, horrible dread, and she asked, falteringly:

"Are you willing to die? Is your soul at peace with God? Have you any fear of Eternity?"

"None, my child, none."

"Would you like to have Mr. Bailey come and pray for you?"

"I want no one now but you."

A long silence ensued, broken only by the heavily-drawn breath of the sufferer. The memory of her aunt's tranquil death haunted the girl, and, finally, the desire to direct his thoughts to God triumphed over every other feeling. She sank on her knees beside the lounge, and a passionate prayer leaped from her pale lips. She had not prayed for nearly four years, and the petition went up to God framed in strange, incoherent language—a plaintive cry to the Father to release, painlessly, a struggling human soul. His fingers clung spasmodically to hers, and, soon after, the head sank on his chest, and she saw that he slept.

The glittering *cortege* of constellations moved solemnly on in their eternal march through the fields of heaven, and in midsky hung a moon of almost supernatural brightness, glaring down through the skylight like an inquisitorial eye. Two hours elapsed; the measured melancholy tick of the clock marked the expiring moments of the old year; the red coals of the grate put on their robe of ashes; the gaslight burned dimly, and flickered now and then as the wind surged through the partially opened window; and there by the couch sat the motionless watcher, noting the indescribable but unmistakable change creeping on, like the shadow which slowly-sailing summer clouds cast down upon green meadows or flowery hill-sides, darkening the landscape. The feeble, thread-like pulse fluttered irregularly, but the breathing became easy and low as a babe's, and occasionally a gentle sigh heaved the chest. Once his lips had moved, and she caught the indistinct words—" Discreet degrees"——, "influx——," "type-creature." She knew that the end was at hand, and a strained, frightened expression came into her large eyes as she glanced nervously round the room, weird and awful in its gloomy surroundings. The damp masses of hair clung to her temples, and she felt heavy drops gathering on her forehead, as in that glance she met the solemn, fascinating eyes of Munin staring at her from the low mantle. She caught her breath, and the deep silence was broken by the metallic tongue that dirged out "twelve." The last stroke of the bronze hammer echoed drearily; the old year lay stark and cold on its bier; Munin flapped his dusky wings with a long, sepulchral, blood-curdling hoot, and the dying man opened his dim, failing eyes, and fixed them for the last time on his pupil.

"Electra, my darling."

"My dear master, I am here."

She lifted his head to her bosom, nestled her fingers into his cold palm, and leaned her cheek against his brow. Pressing his face close to hers, the gray eyes closed, and a smile throned itself on the parted lips. A slight tremor shook the limbs, a soft shuddering breath swept across the watcher's face, and the "golden bowl" was shivered, the "silver cord" was loosed.

She sat there till the iciness of the rigid form chilled her, then laid the head tenderly down on its pillow, and walked to the mantle-piece. The Angel of Time lifted the hammer and struck "one;" and as she glanced accidentally at the inscription on the base, she remembered a favorite quotation which it had often called from the cold lips of the dead painter:

"Time is my fair seed-field, of Time I'm heir."

The seed-time had ended; the calm fields of Eternity stretched before him now; the fruits of the harvest were required at his hands. Were they full of ripe golden sheaves, or——? She shrank from her own questioning, and looked over her shoulder at the dreamless, smiling sleeper.

"His palms are folded on his breast;
There is no other thing expressed,
But long disquiet merged in rest."

The vigil was over, the burden was lifted from her shoulders, the weary ministry here ended; and, shrouding her face in her arms, the lonely woman wept bitterly.

CHAPTER XV

Four years had wrought material changes in the Town of W——; new streets had been opened, new buildings erected, new forms trod the sidewalks new faces looked out of shop-windows and flashing equipages, and new shafts of granite and marble stood in the cemetery to tell of many who had been gathered to their forefathers. The old red school-house, where two generations had been tutored, was swept away to make place for a railroad depot; and, instead of the venerable trees that once overshadowed its precincts, bristling walls of brick and mortar rang with the shrill whistle of the engine, or the sharp continual click of repairing-shops. The wild shout, the rippling laugh of careless, childish glee were banished, and the frolicsome flock of by-gone years had grown to manhood and womanhood, were sedate business-men and sober matrons. If important revolutions had been effected in her early home, not less decided and apparent was the change which had taken place in the heiress of Huntingdon Hill; and having been eyed, questioned, scrutinized by the best families, and laid in the social scales, it was found a difficult matter to determine her weight as accurately as seemed desirable. In common parlance, "her education was finished"—she was regularly and unmistakably "out." Everybody hastened to inspect her, sound her, label her; mothers to compare her with their own daughters; daughters to discover how much they had to apprehend in the charms of the new rival; sons to satisfy themselves with regard to the truth of the rumors concerning her beauty; all with curiosity stamped on their countenances; all with dubiety written there at the conclusion of their visit. Perfectly self-possessed, studiedly polite, attentive to all the punctilios of etiquette, polished and irreproachable in deportment, but cold, reticent, grave, indulging in no familiarities, and allowing none; fascinating by her extraordinary beauty and grace, but tacitly impressing upon all, "Thus far, and no farther." Having lost her aunt two years before her return, the duties of hostess devolved upon her, and she dispensed the hospitalities of her home with an easy though stately elegance, surprising in one so inexperienced. No positive charge could be preferred against her by the inquisitorial circle; even Mrs. Judge Harriss, the self-constituted, but universally acknowledged, autocrat of *beau monde* in W——, accorded her a species of negative excellence, and confessed herself baffled and unable to pronounce a verdict. An enigma to her own father, it was not wonderful that strangers knit their brows in striving to analyze her character, and ere long the cooing of carrier-pigeons became audible: "Her mother had been very eccentric; even before her death it was whispered that insanity hung threateningly over her; strange things were told of her, and, doubtless, Irene inherited her peculiarities." Nature furnishes some seeds with downy wings to insure distribution, and envy and malice, and probably very innocent and mild-intentioned gossip, soon provided this report with remarkable facilities for progress. It chanced that Dr. Arnold was absent for some weeks after her arrival, and no sooner had he returned than he sought his quondam *protégé*. Entering unannounced, he paused suddenly as he caught sight of her standing before the fire, with Paragon at her feet. She lifted her head and came to meet him, holding out both hands, with a warm, bright smile.

"Oh, Dr. Arnold! I am so glad to see you once more. It was neither friendly nor hospitable to go off just as I came home, after long years of absence. I am so very glad to see you."

He held her hands and gazed at her like one in a dream of mingled pain and pleasure, and when he spoke his voice was unsteady.

"You can not possibly be as glad to see me as I am to have you back. But I can't realize that this is, indeed, you, my pet—the Irene I parted with rather more than four years ago. Child, what is it? What have you done to yourself? I called you Queen in your infancy, when you clung to my finger and tottered across the floor to creep into my arms, but tenfold more appropriate does the title seem now. You are not the same Irene who used to toil up my office-steps, and climb upon the tallest chair to examine the skeletons in my cases— the snakes and lizards in my jars. Oh, child! what a marvellous, what a glorious beauty you have grown to be."

"Take care; you will spoil her, Arnold. Don't you know, you old cynic, that women can't stand such flattery as yours?" laughed Mr. Huntingdon.

"I am glad you like me, Doctor; I am glad that you think I have improved; and, since you think so, I am obliged to you for expressing your opinion of me so kindly. I wish I could return your compliments, but my conscience vetoes any such proceeding. You look jaded—overworked. What is the reason that you have grown so gray and haggard? We will enter into a compact to renew the old life; you shall treat me exactly as you used to do, and I shall come to you as formerly, and interrupt labors that seem too heavy. Sit down, and talk to me. I want to hear your voice; it is pleasant to my ears, makes music in my heart, calls up the by-gone. You have adopted a stick in my absence; I don't like the innovation; it hurts me to think that you need it. I must take care of you, I see, and persuade you to relinquish it entirely."

"Arnold, I verily believe she was more anxious to see you than everybody else in W—— except old Nellie, her nurse."

She did not contradict him, and the three sat conversing for more than an hour; then other visitors came, and she withdrew to the parlor. The doctor had examined her closely all the while; had noted every word, action, expression; and a troubled, abstracted look came into his face when she left them.

"Huntingdon, what is it? What is it?"

"What is what? I don't understand you."

"What has so changed that child? I want to know what ails her?"

"Nothing, that I know of. You know she was always rather singular."

"Yes, but it was a different sort of singularity. She is too still and white and cold and stately. I told you it was a wretched piece of business to send a nature like hers, so different from everybody's else, off among utter strangers; to shut up that queer, free, untamed young thing in a boarding-school for four years, with hundreds of miles between her and the few things she loved. She required very peculiar and skilful treatment, and, instead, you put her off where she petrified! I knew it would never answer, and I told you so. You wanted to break her obstinacy, did you? She comes back marble. I tell you now I know her better than you do, though you are her father, and you may as well give up at once that chronic hallucination of 'ruling, conquering her.' She is like steel—cold, firm, brittle; she will break, snap asunder; but bend!— never! never! Huntingdon, I love that child; I have a right to love her; she has been very dear to me from her babyhood, and it would go hard with me to know that any sorrow darkened her life. Don't allow your old plans and views to influence you now. Let Irene be happy in her own way. Did you ever see a contented-looking eagle in a gilt cage? Did you ever know a leopardess kept in a paddock and taught to forget her native jungles?"

Mr. Huntingdon moved uneasily, pondering the unpalatable advice.

"You certainly don't mean to say that she has inherited ——." He crushed back the words; could he crush the apprehension, too?

"I mean to say that, if she were my child, I would be guided by her, instead of striving to cut her character to fit the totally different pattern of my own."

He put on his hat, thrust his hands into his pockets, stood for some seconds frowning so heavily that the shaggy eyebrows met and partially concealed the cavernous eyes, then nodded to the master of the house and son at his buggy. From that day Irene was conscious of a keener and more constant scrutiny on her father's part—a ceaseless *surveillance*, silent, but rigid—that soon grew intolerable. No matter how she employed her time or whither she went, he seemed thoroughly cognizant of the details of her life; and where she least expected interruption or dictation, his hand, firm though gentle, pointed the way, and his voice calmly but inflexibly directed.

Her affection had been in no degree alienated by their long separation, and, through its sway, she submitted for a time; but Huntingdon blood ill brooked restraint, and, ere long, hers became feverish, necessitating release. As in all tyrannical natures, his exactions grew upon her compliance. She was allowed no margin for the exercise of judgment or inclination; her associates were selected, thrust upon her; her occupations decided without reference to her wishes. From the heartless, frivolous routine marked out she shrank in disgust; and, painful as was the alternative, she prepared for the clash which soon became inevitable. He wished her to be happy, but in his own way, in accordance with his views and aims, and, knowing the utter antagonism of taste and feeling which unfortunately existed, she determined to resist. Governed less by impulse than sober second thought and sound reasoning, it was not until after long and patient deliberation that she finally resolved upon her future course, and steadily maintained it. She felt most keenly that it was a painful, a lamentable resolution, but none the less a necessity; and, having once determined, she went forward with a fixedness of purpose characteristic of her family. It was the beginning of a life-long contest, and, to one who understood Leonard Huntingdon's disposition, offered a dreary prospect.

From verbal differences she habitually abstained; opinions which she knew to be disagreeable to him she carefully avoided giving expression to in his presence; and, while always studiously thoughtful of his comfort, she preserved a respectful deportment, allowing herself no hasty or defiant words. Fond of pomp and ceremony, and imbued with certain aristocratic notions, which an ample fortune had always permitted him to indulge, Mr. Huntingdon entertained company in princely style and whenever an opportunity offered. His dinners, suppers, and card-parties were known far and wide, and Huntingdon Hill became proverbial for hospitality throughout the state. Strangers were feted, and it was a rare occurrence for father and daughter to dine quietly together. Fortunately for Irene, the servants were admirably trained; and though this round of company imposed a weight of responsibilities oppressive to one so inexperienced, she applied herself diligently to domestic economy, and soon became familiarized with its details. Her father had been very anxious to provide her with a skilful housekeeper, to relieve her of the care and tedious minutia of such matters; but she refused to accept one, avowing her belief that it was the imperative duty of every woman to superintend and inspect the management of her domestic affairs. Consequently, from the first week of her return, she made it a rule to spend an hour after breakfast in her dining-room pantry, determining and arranging the details of the day.

The situation of the house commanded an extensive and beautiful prospect, and the ancient trees that overshadowed it imparted a venerable and imposing aspect. The building was of brick, overcast to represent granite, and along three sides ran a wide gallery, supported by lofty circular pillars, crowned with unusually heavy capitals. The main body consisted of two stories, with a hall in the centre and three rooms on either side; while two long single-storied wings stretched out right and left—one a billiard-room, the other a greenhouse.

The parlors and library occupied one side—the first opening into the greenhouse; the dining-room and smoking-room were correspondingly situated to the billiard-saloon. The frescoed ceilings were too low to suit modern ideas; the windows were large, and nearly square; the facings, sills, and doors all of cedar, dark as mahogany with age, and polished as rosewood. The tall mantle-pieces were of fluted Egyptian black marble, and along the freshly-tinted walls the elaborate arabesque moulding or cornice hung heavy and threatening. A broad easy flight of white marble steps led up to the richly-carved front-door, with its massive silver knocker bearing the name of Huntingdon in old-fashioned Italian characters; and in the arched niches, on either side of this door, stood two statues, brought from Europe by Mr. Huntingdon's father, and supposed to represent certain Roman penates.

From the hall on the second floor, a narrow, spiral, iron stairway ascended to a circular observatory on the roof, with a row of small columns corresponding with those below, and a tessellated floor of alternating white and variegated squares of marble. Originally the observatory had been crowned by a heavy pagoda-shaped roof, but recently this had been removed and a covering of glass substituted, which, like that of hothouses, could be raised and lowered at pleasure by means of ropes and pulleys. Two generations had embellished this house, and the modern wings forming the cross had been erected within Irene's recollection. In expectation of her return, an entirely new set of furniture had been selected in New York, and arranged some weeks before her arrival—costly carpets, splendid mirrors, plush and brocatel sofas, rich china, and every luxury which wealth and fastidious taste could supply. The grounds in front, embracing several acres, were enclosed by a brick wall, and at the foot of the hill, at the entrance of the long avenue of elms, stood a tall arched iron gate. A smoothly-shaven terrace of Bermuda grass ran round the house, and the broad carriage-way swept up to a mound opposite the door, surmounted by the bronze figure of a crouching dog. On one side of the avenue a beautiful lawn, studded with clumps of trees, extended to the wall; on the other serpentine walks, bordered with low hedges, carved flower-beds of diverse shapes; and here delicate trellis-work supported rare creepers, and airy, elegant arbors and summer-houses were overgrown with vines of rank luxuriance. Everything about the *parterre*, from the well-swept gravel walks to the carefully-clipped hedges, betokened constant attention and lavish expenditure. But the crowning glory of the place was its wealth of trees—the ancient avenue of mighty elms, arching grandly to the sky like the groined nave of some vast cathedral; the circlet of sentinel poplars towering around the house, and old as its foundations; the long, undulating line of venerable willows waving at the foot of the lawn over the sinuous little brook that rippled on its way to the creek; and, beyond the mansion, clothing the sides of a steeper hill, a sombre background of murmuring, solemn, immemorial pines. Such was Irene's home—stately and elegant—kept so thoroughly repaired that, in its cheerfulness, its age was forgotten.

The society of W—— was considered remarkably fine. There was quite an aggregation of wealth and refinement; gentlemen, whose plantations were situated in adjacent counties, resided here, with their families; some, who spent their winters on the seaboard, resorted here for the summer; its bar was said to possess more talent than any other in the state; its schools claimed to be unsurpassed; it boasted of a concert-hall, a lyceum, a handsome court-house, a commodious, well-built jail, and half-a-dozen as fine churches as any country-town could desire. I would fain avoid the term, if possible, but no synonym exists— W—— was, indisputably, an "aristocratic" place.

Thus, after more than four years absence, the summers of which had been spent in travel among the beautiful mountain scenery of the North, the young heiress returned to the home of her childhood. Standing on the verge of nineteen, she put the early garlanded years behind her and looked into the solemn temple of womanhood, with its chequered pavement of light and shadow; its storied friezes, gilded architraves, and fretted shrines, where white-robed bands of devotees enter with uncertain step, all eager, trembling *Mystæ*, soon to become clear-eyed, sad-eyed *Epoptæ*, through the unerring, mystical, sacred initiation of the only true hierophant—Time.

From her few early school associates she had become completely estranged; and the renewal of their acquaintance now soon convinced her that the utter want of congeniality in character and habits of life precluded the possibility of any warm friendships between them. For several months after her return she patiently, hopefully, faithfully studied the dispositions of the members of various families with whom she foresaw that she would be thrown, by her father's wishes, into intimate relationship, and satisfied herself that, among all these, there was not one, save Dr. Arnold, whose counsel, assistance, or sympathy she felt any inclination to claim. Human nature at least is, beyond all cavil, cosmopolitan in its characteristics (barring a few ethnologic limitations); and a given number of men and women similarly circumstanced in Chili, England, Madagascar, Utah, or Burmah would, doubtless, yield a like quota of moral and intellectual idiosyncrasies. In fine, W—— was not in any respect peculiar, or, as a community, specially afflicted with heartlessness, frivolity, brainlessness, or mammonism; the average was fair, reputable in all respects. But, incontrovertibly, the girl who came to spend her life among these people was totally dissimilar in criteria of action, thought, and feeling. To the stereotyped conventional standard of fashionable life she had never yielded allegiance; and now stood (not in the St. Simon, Fourier, Owen, or Leroux sense) a social free-thinker. For a season she allowed herself to be whirled on by the current of dinners, parties, and picnics; but soon her sedate, contemplative temperament revolted from the irksome round, and gradually she outlined and pursued a different course, giving to her gay companions just what courtesy required, no more.

Hugh had prolonged his stay in Europe beyond the period originally designated; and instead of arriving in time to accompany his uncle and cousin home, he did not sail for some months after their return. At length, however, letters were received, announcing his presence in New York and fixing the day when his relatives might expect him.

CHAPTER XVI.

The carriage had been despatched to the depot, a servant stood at the end of the avenue waiting to throw open the gate, Mr. Huntingdon walked up and down the wide colonnade, and Irene sat before the fire in her own room, holding in one palm the flashing betrothal-ring, which she had been forced to wear since her return from New York. She had looked into the rooms to see that all was bright and cheerful, had looped back the curtains in the apartment prepared for Hugh, had filled the vases with flowers that he preferred in his boyhood, and now listened for his approach with complex emotions. The sole companion of her infancy, she would have hailed his arrival with unmixed joy but for the peculiar relationship in which she now stood to him. The few years of partial peace had passed; she knew that the hour drew near when the long-dreaded struggle must begin, and, hopeless of averting it, quietly waited for the storm to break. Dropping the ring in her jewelry-box, she turned the key, and just then her father's voice rang through the house.

"Irene! the carriage is coming up the avenue."

She went slowly down stairs, followed by Paragon, and joined her father at the door. His searching look discovered nothing in the serene face; the carriage stopped, and he hastened to meet his nephew.

"Come at last, eh! Welcome home, my dear boy."

The young man turned from his uncle, sprang up the steps, then paused, and the cousins looked at each other.

"Well, Hugh! I am very glad to see you once more."

She held out her hands, and he saw at a glance that her fingers were unfettered. Seizing them warmly, he bent forward, but she drew back coldly, and he exclaimed:

"Irene! I claim a warmer welcome."

She made a haughty, repellent gesture, and moved forward a few steps to greet the stranger who accompanied him.

"My daughter, this is your uncle, Eric Mitchell, who has not seen you since you were a baby."

The party entered the house, and, seated beside him, Irene gazed with mingled emotions of pain and pleasure upon her mother's only brother. He was about thirty, but looked older, from life-long suffering; had used crutches from the time he was five years of age, having been hopelessly crippled by a fall during his infancy. His features were sharp, his cheeks wore the sallow hue of habitual ill-health, and his fine gray eyes were somewhat sunken. Resting his crutches against the sofa, he leaned back and looked long and earnestly at his niece. Very dimly he remembered a fair flaxen-haired baby whom the nurse had held out to be kissed when he was sent to Philadelphia to be treated for his lameness; soon after he heard of his sister's death, and then his tutor took him to Europe, to command the best medical advice of the Old World.

"From the faint recollection which I have of your mother, I think you strongly resemble her," he said, at last, in a fond, gentle tone.

"I don't know about that, Eric. She is far more of a Huntingdon than a Mitchell. She has many of the traits of your family, but in appearance she certainly belongs to my side of the house. She very often reminds me of Hugh's mother."

Conversation turned upon the misfortune of the cripple; he spoke freely of the unsuccessful experiments made by eminent physicians; of the hopelessness of his case; and Irene was particularly impressed by the calmness and patience with which he seemed to have resigned himself to this great affliction. She could detect no trace of complaining bitterness, or, what was still more to be deplored, the irritable, nervous querulousness so often observed in persons of his situation. She found him a ripe scholar, a profound archæologist, and philosophic observer of his age and generation; and, deeply interested in his quiet, low-toned talk, she felt irresistibly drawn toward him, careless of passing hours and of Hugh's ill-concealed impatience of manner. As they rose from the tea-table her cousin said, laughingly:

"I protest against monopoly. I have not been able to say three words to my lady-cousin."

"I yield the floor, from necessity. My long journey has unfitted me for this evening, and I must bid you all an early good-night."

"Can I do anything for you, Uncle?"

"No, thank you, Irene; I have a servant who thoroughly understands taking care of me. Go talk to Hugh, who has been wishing me among the antipodes."

He shook hands with her, smiled kindly, and Mr. Huntingdon assisted him to his room.

"Irene, come into the library, and let me have a cigar."

"How tenacious your bad habits are, Hugh."

"Smoking belongs to no such category. My habits are certainly quite as tenacious as my cousin's antipathies."

He selected a cigar, lighted it, and drawing a chair near hers, threw himself into it with an expression of great satisfaction. "It is delightful to get back home and see you again, Irene. I felt some regret at quitting Paris, but the sight of your face more than compensates me."

She was looking very earnestly at him, noting the alteration in his appearance, and for a moment his eyes drooped before hers. She saw that the years had been spent, not in study, but in a giddy round of pleasure and dissipation, yet the bright, frank, genial expression of boyhood still lingered, and she could not deny that he had grown up a very handsome man. She knew that he was capable of sudden, spasmodic impulses of generosity, but saw that selfishness remained the great substratum of his character, and her keen feeling of disappointment showed her now how much she had hoped to find him changed in this respect.

"Irene, I had a right to expect a warmer welcome than you deigned to give me."

"Hugh, remember that we have ceased to be children. When you learn to regard me simply as your cousin, and are satisfied with a cousin's welcome, then, and not until then, shall you receive it. Let childish whims pass with the years that have separated us; rake up no germs of contention to mar this first evening of your return. Be reasonable, and now tell me how you have employed yourself since we parted; what have you seen? what have you gleaned?"

He flushed angrily, but the imperturbable face controlled him, even against his will, and, muttering something which she thought sounded very much like an oath, he smoked for some seconds in silence. Without noticing his sullenness, she made some inquiries concerning his sojourn in Paris, and insensibly he found himself drawn into a narration of his course of life. She listened with apparent interest, making occasional good-humored comments, and bringing him back to the subject whenever he attempted a *détour* toward the topic so extremely distasteful to her.

The clock struck eleven; she rose, and said:
"I beg your pardon, Hugh, for keeping you up so late. I ought to have known that you were fatigued by railroad-travel, and required sleep. You know the way to your room; it is the same you occupied before you went to college. Good-night; I hope you will rest well."

She held out her hand carelessly; he took it eagerly, and holding it up to the light said, in a disappointed tone:
"Irene, where is my ring? Why are you not wearing it?"
"It is in my jewelry-box. As I gave you my reasons for not wearing it, when you offered it to me, it is not necessary to repeat them now. Good-night, Hugh; go dream of something more agreeable than our old childish quarrels." She withdrew her fingers and left him.

As she entered her own room and closed the door, she was surprised to find her nurse sitting before the fire, with her chin in her hands, and her keen black eyes fixed on the coals.
"Aunt Nellie, what are you sitting up so late for? You will have another spell of rheumatism, tramping about this time of night."
"I have been in to see Mass' Eric, blessed lamb that he always was and always will be. He is so changed I never would have known him; he was a weak little white-faced cripple when I first saw him twenty years ago. It seems like there is a curse on your family anyhow, both sides. They died off, and have been killed off, on your mother's side, till Mass' Eric is the only one left of all the Mitchells, and, as for Master's family, you and Hugh are the two last. You know some families run out, and I don't think Master ought to try to overturn the Lord's plans. Queen, let things take their course."
"Who has put all this into your head?"
"Nobody put it into my head! I should like to know where my eyes have been these many years? I have n't been so near blind all my life. Don't you suppose I know what Master's been after since you were eighteen months old? Was n't I standing by the bed when Hugh's mother died, and did n't I hear Master promise her that, when you were grown, you and Hugh should marry? Don't I know how your poor dying mother cried, and wrung her hands, and said 'Harm would come of it all, and she hoped you would die while you were a baby?' She had found out what Huntingdon temper was. Poor blessed saint! what a life she did lead between Miss Margaret and Miss Isabella! It is no use to shut your eyes to it, Queen. You might just as well look at it at once. It is a sin for near kin like you and Hugh to marry, and you ought to set your face against it. He is just his mother over again, and you will see trouble, as sure as your name is Irene, if you don't take a stand. Oh! they are managing people! and the Lord have mercy on folks they don't like, for it is n't in Huntingdon blood to forgive or to forget anything. I am so thankful your Uncle Eric has come—he will help to stand between you and trouble. Ah! it is coming, Queen! it's coming! You did n't see how your father frowned when you would n't let Hugh kiss you? I was looking through the window, and saw it all. I have n't had one hour's peace since I dreamed of seeing you and your mother together. Oh, my baby! my baby! there is trouble and sorrow thickening for you; I know it. I have had a warning of it."

She inclined her head on one side, and rocked herself to and fro, much as did early Pelasgic Dodonides in announcing oracular decrees.

"You need not grieve about it; I want nobody to stand between me and trouble. Beside, Nellie, you must remember that, in all my father does, he intends and desires to promote my welfare and to make me happy."
"Did he send you off to that boarding-school for your happiness? You were very happy there, weren't you? It is no use to try to blindfold me; I have lived a little too long. Oh, my baby! your white, white face, and big sorrowful blue eyes follow me day and night; I knew how it would be when you were born. You came into this world among awful signs! the sun was eclipsed! chickens went to roost, as if night had come; and I saw stars in the sky at two o'clock in the day! Oh! I thought, sure enough, judgment-day had come at last; and when they put you in my arms I trembled so I could hardly stand. May God have mercy on you, Queen!"

She shuddered for a moment, as if in the presence of some dread evil, and, rising, wrapped her shawl about her shoulders and left the room.

Irene looked after her retreating form, smiling at the superstitious turn her thoughts had taken, then, dismissing the subject, she fell asleep, thinking of her uncle.

A week passed, varied by few incidents of interest; the new-comers became thoroughly domesticated—the old routine was re-established. Hugh seemed gay and careless—hunting, visiting, renewing boyish acquaintances, and whiling away the time as inclination prompted. He had had a long conversation with his uncle, and the result was that, for the present, no allusion was made to the future. In Irene's presence the subject was temporarily tabooed. She knew that the project was not relinquished—was only veiled till a convenient season, and, giving to the momentary lull its full value, she acquiesced, finding in Eric's society enjoyment and resources altogether unexpected. Instinctively they seemed to comprehend each other's character, and while both were taciturn and undemonstrative, a warm affection sprang up between them.

On Sunday morning, as the family group sat around the breakfast-table waiting for Hugh, who lingered, as usual, over his second cup of chocolate, Mr. Mitchell suddenly laid down the fork with which he had been describing a series of geometrical figures on the fine damask, and said: "I met a young man in Brussels who interested me extremely, and in connection with whom I venture the prediction that, if he lives, he will occupy a conspicuous position in the affairs of his country. He is, or was, Secretary of Mr. Campbell, our Minister to ———, and they were both on a visit to Brussels when I met them. His name is Aubrey, and he told me that he lived here. His talents are of the first order; his ambition unbounded, I should judge; and his patient, laborious application certainly surpasses anything I have ever seen. It happened that a friend of mine, from London, was prosecuting certain researches among the MS. archives at Brussels, and here, immersed in study, he says he found the secretary, who completely distanced him in his investigations, and then, with unexpected generosity, placed his notes at my friend's disposal. His industry is almost incredible. Conversing with Campbell concerning him, I learned that he was a *protégé* of the minister, who spoke of his future in singularly sanguine terms. He left him some time since to embark in the practice of law. Do you know him, Huntingdon?"

"No, sir; but I know that his father was sentenced to the gallows, and only saved himself from it by cutting his miserable throat and cheating the law."

The master of the house thrust back his chair violently, crushing one of Paragon's innocent paws as he crouched on the carpet, and overturning a glass which shivered into a dozen fragments at his feet.

Irene understood the scowl on his brow, but only she possessed the clew, and, lazily sipping his chocolate, Hugh added: "I recollect him very well as a boy; he always had a bookish look, and I met him one day on the boulevard at Paris. He was talking to an *attaché* of the American Legation as I came up, and took no more notice of me than if I had been one of the paving-stones. I could not avoid admiring the cool sublimity of his manner, and as I had snubbed him at school long ago, I put out my hand and said: 'Howdy-do, Aubrey; pray, when did you cross the water?' He bowed as frigidly as Czar Nicholas, and, without noticing my hand, answered: 'Good-morning, Mr. Seymour; I have been in Europe two years,' and walked on. The day after I got home I met him going up the court-house steps, and looked him full in the face; he just inclined his head, and passed me. Confound it! he 's as proud as if he had found a patent of nobility in digging among Belgic archives."

"Nature furnished him with one many years since," replied Eric.

"Yes; and his coat-of-arms should be jack-ketch and a gallows!" sneered Mr. Huntingdon.

Looking at his watch he said, as if wishing to cut the conversation short:

"Irene, if you intend to go to church to-day, it is time that you had your bonnet on. Hugh, what will you do with yourself? Go with Eric and your cousin?"

"No, I rather think I shall stay at home with you. After European cathedrals, our American churches seem excessively plain."

Irene went to her room pondering the conversation. She thought it remarkable that, as long as she had been at home, she had never seen Russell, even on the street.

Unlocking her writing-desk, she took out a tiny note which had accompanied a check for two hundred dollars, and had reached her a few months before she left boarding-school. The firm, round, manly hand ran as follows:

"With gratitude beyond all expression for the favor conferred on my mother and myself, some years since, I now return to Miss Huntingdon the money which I have ever regarded as a friendly loan. Hoping that the future will afford me some opportunity of proving my appreciation of her great kindness,

"I remain, most respectfully,
"Her obliged friend,
"RUSSELL AUBREY.
"NEW YORK, *September 5th*."

She was conscious of a feeling of regret that the money had been returned; it was pleasant to reflect on the fact that she had laid him under obligation; now it all seemed cancelled. She relocked the desk, and, drawing on her gloves, joined her uncle at the carriage. Her father accompanied her so rarely that she scarcely missed him, and during the ride, as Eric seemed abstracted, she leaned back, and her thoughts once more reverted to the unfortunate topic of the breakfast-table. Arriving at church later than was her wont, she found the family pew occupied by strangers, and crossed the aisle to share a friend's, but at that instant a tall form rose in Mr. Campbell's long-vacant pew, stepped into the aisle, and held open the door. She drew back to suffer her uncle to limp in and lay aside his crutches, saw him give his hand to the stranger, and, sweeping her veil aside as she entered, she saw Russell quietly resume his seat at the end of the pew.

Startled beyond measure, she looked at him intently, and almost wondered that she recognized him, he had changed so materially since the day on which she stood with him before his mother's gate. Meantime the service commenced, she gave her hymn-book to her uncle, and at the same moment Russell found the place, and handed her one of two which lay near him. As she received it their eyes met, looked fixedly into each other, and she held out her hand. He took it, she felt his fingers tremble as they dropped hers, and then both faces bent over the books. When they knelt side by side, and the heavy folds of her elegant dress swept against him, it seemed a feverish dream to her; she could not realize that, at last, they had met again, and her heart beat so fiercely that she pressed her hand upon it, dreading lest he should hear its loud pulsations. Lowering her veil, she drew her costly velvet drapery about her and leaned back; and the anthem was chanted, the solemn organ tones hushed themselves, the minister stood up in the pulpit, and his dull tones fell on her ear and brain meaninglesss as the dry patter of dying leaves in an autumn wind. The outline of that tall, broad-shouldered, magnificently turned figure, replete with vigorous muscular strength; the massive, finely-formed head, easily, gracefully poised, like that of a statue; above all, the olive-pale, proud face, unshaded by beard, with regular features sharply yet beautifully cut, like those in the rare gems which Benvenuto Cellini left the world, greeted her now, turn which way she would. The coat was buttoned to the throat, the strong arms were crossed over the deep chest, the piercing black eyes raised and fastened on the pulpit. It has been well said: "The eyes indicate the antiquity of the soul, or through how many forms it has already ascended." If so, his seemed brimful of destiny, and œons old, in that one long unveiling look which they had exchanged; deep, sparkling, and yet indescribably melancholy, something in the expression vividly recalling the Beatrice Cenci; then all analogy was baffled. Electra knew wherein consisted their wonderful charm, and because she put these eyes on canvas *connoisseurs* studied and applauded her work. Now face and figure, cold and unrelenting, stamped themselves on Irene's memory as indelibly as those which laborious, patient lapidaries carve on coral or cornelian. The discourse was ended, the diapason of the organ swelled through the lofty church, priestly hands hovered like white doves over the congregation, dismissing all with blessing. Once more Irene swept back the rich lace veil, fully exposing her face; once more her eyes looked into those of the man who politely held the pew-door open; both bowed with stately grace, and she walked down the aisle. She heard Russell talking to her uncle just behind her, heard the inquiries concerning his health, the expression of pleasure at meeting again, the hope which Eric uttered that he should see him frequently during his stay in W———. Without even a glance over her shoulder, she proceeded to the carriage, where her uncle soon joined her—taking the front seat instead of sharing the back one, as is customary. He scrutinized his niece's countenance, but it baffled him, as on the first night of his arrival; the serene, colorless face showed not the slightest symptom of emotion of any kind. Neither spoke till they approached the cottage on the road-side, then she extended her hand and said, indifferently:

"Your European acquaintance, the quondam secretary, formerly lived in that little three-roomed house hid among the vines yonder."

"When I spoke of him this morning you did not mention having known him. I inferred from your manner that he was a stranger to you."

"He is a stranger now. I knew him long ago, when we were children, and met him to-day for the first time in some years."

"There is something peculiarly commanding in his appearance. He impresses me with respect and involuntary admiration, such as no man of his age ever excited before, and I have travelled far and wide, and have seen the lordliest of many lands."

"Years have greatly changed him. He is less like his mother than when I knew him in his boyhood."

"He is an orphan, I learned from Campbell."

"Yes."

She pulled the check-cord, and, as the driver stopped, she leaned out of the window, pointing to a mossy tuft on the margin of the little brook just at the foot of the hill.

"Andrew, if you are not afraid to leave your horses, get me that cluster of violets just this side of the sweet-gum tree. They are the very earliest I have seen."

He gathered them carefully and placed them in the daintily-gloved, out-stretched hand. She bent over them an instant, then divided the tiny bunch with her uncle, saying: "Spring has opened its blue eyes at last."

She met his searching gaze as calmly as the flowerets, and as they now neared the house, he forbore any further allusion to the subject, which he shrewdly suspected engaged her thoughts quite as fully as his own.

CHAPTER XVII.

"Irene, it is past midnight."

She gave no intimation of having heard him.

"Irene, my child, it is one o'clock."

Without looking up she raised her hand toward the clock on the mantle, and answered, coldly:

"You need not sit up to tell me the time of night; I have a clock here. Go to sleep, Uncle Eric."

He rested his shoulder against the door-facing, and, leaning on his crutches, watched her.

She sat there just as he had seen her several times before, with her arms crossed on the table, the large celestial globe drawn near, astronomical catalogues scattered about, and a thick folio open before her. She wore a loose wrapper, or robe de chambre, of black velvet, lined with crimson silk and girded with a heavy cord and tassel. The sleeves were very full, and fell away from the arms, exposing them from the dimpled elbows, and rendering their pearly whiteness more apparent by contrast with the sable hue of the velvet, while the broad round collar was pressed smoothly down, revealing the polished turn of the throat. The ivory comb lay on the table, and the unbound hair, falling around her shoulders, swept over the back of her chair and trailed on the carpet. A miracle of statuesque beauty was his queenly niece, yet he could not look at her without a vague feeling of awe, of painful apprehension; and, as he stood watching her motionless figure in its grand yet graceful *pose*, he sighed involuntarily. She rose, shook back her magnificent hair, and approached him. Her eyes, so like deep, calm azure lakes, crossed by no ripple, met his, and the clear, pure voice echoed through the still room.

"Uncle Eric, I wish you would not sit up on my account; I do not like to be watched."

"Irene, your father forbade your studying until this hour. You will accomplish nothing but the ruin of your health."

"How do you know that? Do statistics prove astronomers short-lived? Rather the contrary. I commend you to the contemplation of their longevity. Good-night, Uncle; starry dreams to you."

"Stay, child; what object have you in view in all this laborious investigation?"

"Are you sceptical of the possibility of a devotion to science merely for science's sake? Do my womanly garments shut me out of the Holy of Holies, debar me eternally from sacred arcana, think you? Uncle Eric, once for all, it is not my aim to—

"————brush with extreme flounce
The circle of the sciences.'

I take my heart, my intellect, my life, and offer all upon the altar of its penetralia. You men doubt women's credentials for work like mine; but this intellectual bigotry and monopoly already trembles beneath the weight of stern and positive results which women lay before you—data for your speculations—alms for your calculation. In glorious attestation of the truth of female capacity to grapple with some of the most recondite problems of science stand the names of Caroline Herschel, Mary Sommerville, Maria Mitchel, Emma Willard, Mrs. Phelps, and the proud compliment paid to Madame Lepaute by Clairant and Lalande, who, at the successful conclusion of their gigantic computations, declared: 'The assistance rendered by her was such that, without her, we never should have dared to undertake the enormous labor in which it was necessary to calculate the distance of each of the two planets, Jupiter and Saturn, from the comet, separately for every degree, for one hundred and fifty years.' Uncle Eric, remember—

"'————Whoso cures the plague,
Though twice a woman, shall be called a leech;
Who rights a land's finances is excused
For touching coppers, though her hands be white.'"

She took the volume she had been reading, selected several catalogues from the mass, and, lighting a small lamp, passed her uncle and mounted the spiral staircase leading to the observatory. He watched her tall form slowly ascending, and, in the flashing light of the lamp she carried, her black dress and floating hair seemed to belong to some veritable Urania—some ancient Egyptian Berenice. He heard her open the glass door of the observatory, then the flame vanished, and the click of the lock fell down the dark stairway as she turned the key. With a heavy sigh the cripple returned to his room, there to ponder the singular character of the woman whom he had just left, and to dream that he saw her transplanted to the constellations, her blue eyes brightening into stars, her waving hair braiding itself out into brilliant, rushing comets. The night was keen, still, and cloudless, and, as Irene locked herself in, the chill from the marble tiles crept through the carpet to her slippered feet. In the centre of the apartment rose a wooden shaft bearing a brass plate, and to this a telescope was securely fastened. Two chairs and an old-fashioned oaken table, with curious carved legs, comprised the furniture. She looked at the small siderial clock, and finding that a quarter of an hour must elapse before she could make the desired observation, drew a chair to the table and seated herself. She took from the drawer a number of loose papers, and prepared the blank-book for registering the observation; then laid before her a slate covered with figures, and began to run over the calculation. At the close of fifteen minutes she placed herself at the telescope, and waited patiently for the appearance of a small star which gradually entered the field; she noted the exact moment and position, transferred the result to the register, and after a time went back to slate and figures. Cautiously she went over the work, now and then having recourse to pen and paper; she reached the bottom of the slate and turned it over, moving one finger along the lines. The solution was wrong; a mistake had been made somewhere; she pressed her palm on her forehead, and thought over the whole question; then began again. The work was tedious, the calculation subtle, and she attached great importance to the result; the second examination was fruitless as the first; time was wearing away; where could the error be? Without hesitation she turned back for the third time, and commenced at the first, slowly, patiently threading the maze. Suddenly she paused and smiled; there was the mistake, glaring enough, now. She corrected it, and working the sum through, found the result perfectly accurate, according fully with the tables of Leverrier by which she was computing. She carefully transferred the operation from slate to paper, and, after numbering the problem with great particularity, placed all in the drawer and turned the key. It was three o'clock; she opened the door, drew her chair out on the little gallery, and sat down, looking toward the East. The air was crisp but still, unswayed by current waifs; no sound swept its crystal waves save the low, monotonous distant thunder of the Falls, and the deep, cloudless blue ocean of space glowed with its numberless argosies of stellar worlds. Constellations which, in the purple twilight, stood sentinel at the horizon, had marched in majesty to mid-heaven, taken reconnoissance thence, and as solemnly passed the opposite horizon to report to watching gazers in another hemisphere. "Scouts stood upon every headland, on every plain;" mercilessly the inquisitorial eye of science followed the heavenly wanderers; there was no escape from the eager, sleepless police who kept vigil in every clime and country; as well call on Boötes to give o'er his care of Ursa-Major, as hopelessly attempt to thrust him from the ken of Cynosura. From her earliest recollection, and especially from the hour of entering school, astronomy and mathematics had exerted an overmastering influence upon Irene's mind. The ordinary text-books only increased her interest in the former science, and while in New York, with the aid of the professor of astronomy, she had possessed herself of all the most eminent works bearing upon the subject, sending across the Atlantic for tables and selenographic charts which were not to be procured in America.

Under singularly favorable auspices she had pursued her studies perseveringly, methodically, and, despite her father's prohibition, indefatigably. He had indulged, in earlier years, a *penchant* for the same science, and cheerfully facilitated her progress by rearranging the observatory so as to allow full play for her fine telescope; but, though proud of her proficiency, he objected most strenuously to her devoting so large a share of her time and attention to this study, and had positively interdicted all observations after twelve o'clock. Most girls patronize certain branches of investigation with fitful, spasmodic vehemence, or periodic impulses of enthusiasm; but Irene knew no intermission of interest, she hurried over no details, and, when the weather permitted, never failed to make her nightly visit to the observatory. She loved her work as a painter his canvas, or the sculptor the marble one day to enshrine his cherished ideal; and she prosecuted it, not as a mere pastime, not as a toy, but as a life-long labor, for the labor's sake. To-night, as her drooping palms nestled to each other, and her eyes searched the vast jewelled dome above, Thought, unwearied as the theme it pondered, flew back to the dim gray dawn of Time, "When the morning-stars sang together, and all the sons of God shouted for joy." In panoramic vision she crossed the dusty desert of centuries, and watched with Chaldean shepherds the pale, sickly light of waning moons on Shinar's plains; welcomed the gnomon (first-born of the great family of astronomic apparatus); toiled over and gloried in the Zaros; stood at the armillary sphere of Ju, in the days of Confucius; studied with Thales, Anaximander, and Pythagoras; entered the sacred precincts of the school of Crotona, hand in hand with Damo, the earliest woman who bowed a devotee at the starry shrine, and, with her, was initiated into its esoteric doctrines; puzzled with Meton over his lunar cycle; exulted in Hipparchus' gigantic labor, the first collection of tables, the earliest reliable catalogues; walked through the Alexandrine school of *savans*, misled by Ptolemy; and bent with Uliegh Beigh over the charts at Samarcand. In imagination she accompanied Copernicus and Tycho-Brahe, and wrestled with Kepler in the titanic struggle that ended in the discovery of the magnificent trinity of astronomical laws framed by the Divine Architect when the first star threw its faint shimmer through the silent wastes of space. Kepler's three laws were an unceasing wonder and joy to her, and with fond, womanly pride she was wont to recur to a lonely observatory in Silesia, where, before Newton rose upon the world, one of her own sex, Maria Cunitz, launched upon the stormy sea of scientific literature the "*Urania Propitia*." The Congress of Lilienthal possessed far more of interest for her than any which ever sat in august council over the fate of nations, and the names of Herschel, Bessel, Argelander, Struve, Arago, Leverrier, and Maedler were sacred as Persian *telefin*. From the "Almagest" of Ptolemy, and the "Cométographie" of Pingré, to the "Mécanique Céleste," she had searched and toiled; and now the sublime and almost bewildering speculations of Maedler held her spell-bound. The delicate, subtle, beautiful problem of parallax had heretofore exerted the strongest fascination over her; but this magnificent hypothesis of a "central sun," from the monarch of computations at Dorpat, seized upon her imagination with painful tenacity. From the hour when Kepler stretched out his curious fingers, feeling for the shape of planetary orbits, or Leverrier groped through abysses of darkness for the unknown Neptune, which a sceptical world declared existed only in his mathematical calculations, no such daring or stupendous speculation had been breathed as this which Maedler threw down from his Russian observatory. Night after night she gazed upon the pleiades, singling out Alcyone, the brilliant central sun of the mighty astral system, whose light met her eager eyes after the long travel of five hundred and thirty-seven years; and, following in the footsteps of the great speculator, she tried to grasp the result, that the period of one revolution of our sun and system around that glittering centre was eighteen million two hundred thousand years.

The stony lips of geology asserted that our globe was growing old, thousands of generations had fallen asleep in the bosom of mother-earth, the ashes of centuries had gathered upon the past, were creeping over the present; and yet, in the face of catacombs, and mummies, and mouldering monuments, chiselled in the infancy of the human race, mathematics unrolled her figured scroll, and proclaimed that Time had but begun; that chiliasms must elapse, that æons on æons must roll away, before the first revolution of the starry universe could be completed about its far-off Alcyone centre. What mattered human labors, what need of trophies of human genius, of national grandeur, or individual glory? Eighteen millions of years would level all in one huge, common, shapeless ruin. In comparison with the mighty mechanism of the astral system, the solar seemed a mere tiny cluster of jewels set in some infinite abyss; the sun shrank into insignificance, the moon waned, the planets became little gleaming points of light, such as her diamond-ring threw off when held under gas-chandeliers. Perish the microcosm in the limitless macrocosm, and sink the feeble earthly segregate in the boundless, rushing, choral aggregation! She was oppressed by the stupendous nature of the problem; human reason and imagination reeled under the vastness of the subject which they essayed to contemplate and measure; and to-night, as she pondered in silent awe the gigantic, overwhelming laws of God's great *Cosmos*, by some subtle association there flashed upon her memory the sybillic inscription on the Temple of Neith at Saïs: "I am all that has been, all that is, all that will be. No mortal has ever raised the veil which conceals me; and the fruit I have produced is the sun." Had Maedler, with telescopic insight, climbed by mathematical ladders to the starry adyta of nature, and triumphantly raised the mystic veil? With a feeling of adoration which no language could adequately convey she gazed upon nebulæ, and suns, and systems; and with the solemn reflection that some, like Cassiopeia's lost jewel, might be perishing, wrapped in the last conflagration, while their light still journeyed to her, she recalled the feverish yet sublime vision of the great German dreamer: "Once we issued suddenly from the middle of thickest night into an aurora borealis—the herald of an expiring world—and we found, throughout this cycle of solar systems, that a day of judgment had indeed arrived. The suns had sickened, and the planets were heaving, rocking, yawning in convulsions; the subterraneous waters of the great deeps were breaking up, and lightnings that were ten diameters of a world in length ran along from zenith to nadir; and, here and there, where a sun should have been, we saw, instead, through the misty vapor, a gloomy, ashy-leaden corpse of a solar body, that sucked in flames from the perishing world, but gave out neither light nor heat. Then came eternities of twilight that revealed but were not revealed; on the right hand and on the left towered mighty constellations, that by self-repetitions and answers from afar, that by counter-positions built up triumphal gates, whose architraves, whose archways—horizontal, upright—rested, rose at altitude by spans—that seemed ghostly from infinitude. Without measure were the architraves, past number were the archways, beyond memory the gates. Suddenly, as thus we rode from infinite to infinite, and tilted over abyssmal worlds, a mighty ary arose, that systems more mysterious, that worlds more billowy, other heights and other depths, were coming, were nearing, were at hand. Then the angel threw up his glorious hands to the heaven of heavens, saying: 'End is there none to the universe of God. Lo! also, there is no beginning.'"

Among the mysteries of the Crotona school the Samian sage had taught the "music of the spheres," and to-night Irene dwelt upon the thought of that grand choir of innumerable worlds, that mighty orchestra of starry systems,

"Look how the floor of heaven
Is thick inlaid with patines of bright gold:
There 's not the smallest orb which thou behold'st
But in his motion like an angel sings,
Still quiring to the young-eyed cherubims.
Such harmony is in immortal souls;
But whilst this muddy vesture of decay
Doth grossly close it in, we can not hear it."

unceasingly to the Lord of glory, till her firm lips relaxed, and the immortal words of Shakspeare fell slowly from them:

That the myriad members of the shining archipelago were peopled with orders of intelligent beings, differing from our race even as the planets differ in magnitude and physical structure, she entertained not a doubt; and as feeble Fancy struggled to grasp and comprehend the ultimate destiny of the countless hosts of immortal creatures (to which our earthly races, with their distinct, unalterable types, stood but as one small family circle amid clustering worlds) her wearied brain and human heart bowed humbly, reverently, worshippingly before the God of Revelation, who can "bind the sweet influences of Pleiades, or loose the bands of Orion; bring forth Mazzaroth in his season, and guide Arcturus with his sons." Kneeling there, with the twinkling light of stars upon her upturned face, she prayed earnestly for strength and grace and guidance from on High, that she might so live and govern herself that, when the season of earthly probation ended, she could fearlessly pass to her eternal home and joyfully meet the awful face of Jehovah.

The night was almost spent; she knew from the "celestial clock-work" that Day blushed just beyond the horizon; that, ere long, silver-gray fingers would steal up the quiet sky, parting the sable curtains; and, taking the lamp, she hung the observatory-key upon her girdle, and glided noiselessly down the stairway to her own apartment.

Paragon slept on the threshold, and raised his head to greet her; she stooped, stroked his silky ears, and closed the door, shutting him out. Fifteen minutes later she, too, was sleeping soundly; and an hour and a half afterward, followed by that faithful guardian "dweller of the threshold," she swept down the steps, and, amid the matin-chant of forest-birds, mounted Erebus and dashed off at full gallop for the customary ride. No matter what occurred to prevent her sleeping, she invariably rode before breakfast when the weather permitted; and as her midnight labors left few hours for repose, she generally retired to her room immediately after dinner and indulged in the luxury of a two hours' nap. Such was a portion of the regimen she had prescribed for herself on her return from school, and which she suffered only the inclemency of the weather to infringe.

CHAPTER XVIII.

"Surely, Uncle Eric, there is room enough in this large, airy house of ours to accommodate my mother's brother? I thought it was fully settled that you were to reside with us. There is no good reason why you should not. Obviously, we have a better claim upon you than anybody else; why doom yourself to the loneliness of a separate household? Reconsider the matter."

"No, Irene; it is better that I should have a quiet little home of my own, free from the inevitable restraint incident to residing under the roof of another. My recluse nature and habits unfit me for the gay young associates who throng this house, making carnival-time of all seasons."

"I will change the library, and give you two rooms on this floor, to avoid stair-steps; I will build you a wall of partition, and have your doors and windows hermetically sealed against intrusion. No sound of billiard-ball, or dancing feet, or noisy laughter shall invade your sanctuary. Not St. Simeon, of isolated memory, could desire more complete seclusion and solitude than that with which I shall indulge you."

"It is advisable that I should go."

"I appreciate neither the expediency nor necessity."

"Like all other crusty, self-indulgent bachelors, I have many whims, which I certainly do not expect people to bear patiently."

"You are neither crusty nor self-indulgent, that I have discovered; as for your whims, I have large charity, and will humor them."

"Irene, I want a house of my own, to which I can feel privileged to invite such guests, such companions, as I deem congenial, irrespective of the fiats of would-be social autocrats and the social ostracism of certain *cliques*."

She was silent a moment, but met his keen look without the slightest embarrassment, and yet when she spoke he knew, from her eyes and voice, that she fully comprehended his meaning.

"Of course, it is a matter which you must determine for yourself. You are the best judge of what conduces to your happiness; but I am sorry, very sorry, Uncle Eric, that, in order to promote it, you feel it necessary to remove from our domestic circle. I shall miss you painfully."

"Pardon me, but I doubt the last clause. You lean on no one sufficiently to note the absence of their support."

"Do you recognize no difference between a parasitic clinging and an affectionate friendship—a valued companionship based on congenial tastes and sympathies?"

"Unquestionably, I admit and appreciate the distinction; but you do not meet me full-eyed, open-handed, on this common platform of congeniality, strengthened as it is, or should be, by near relationship. You confront me always with your emotional nature mail-clad, and make our intercourse a mere intellectual fencing-match. Now, mark you, I have no wish to force your confidence; that is a curious and complex lock, which only the golden key of perfect love and trust should ever open; and I simply desire to say that your constitutional reticence or habitual reserve precludes the hope of my rendering you either assistance or sympathy by my continued presence."

"Uncle Eric, it arises from no want of trust in you, but in the consciousness that only I can help myself. I have more than once heard you quote Wallenstein; have so soon forgotten his words:

"'Permit her own will.
For there are sorrows,
Where, of necessity, the soul must be
Its own support. A strong heart will rely
On its own strength alone.'"

"But, my dear girl, you certainly are no Thekla?"

Was there prescience in his question, and a quick recognition of it in the quiver which ran across her lips and eyelids?

"The Fates forbid that I should ever be!"

"Irene, in the name and memory of your mother, promise me one thing: that if sorrows assail you, and a third party can bear aught on his shoulders, you will call upon me."

"A most improbable conjunction of circumstances; but, in such emergency, I promise to afflict you with a summons to the rescue. Uncle Eric, I think I shall never gall any shoulders but my own with the burdens which God may see fit to lay on them in the coming years."

He looked pained, puzzled, and irresolute; but she smiled, and swept her fingers over the bars of her bird-cage, toying with its golden-throated inmate.

"Have you any engagement for this morning?"

"None, sir. What can I do for you?"

"If you feel disposed, I should be glad to have you accompany me to town; I want your assistance in selecting a set of china for my new home. Will you go?"

A shadow drifted over the colorless tranquil face as she said, sadly:

"Uncle Eric, is it utterly useless for me to attempt to persuade you to relinquish this project and remain with us?"

"Utterly useless, my dear child."

"I will get my bonnet, and join you at the carriage."

Very near the cottage formerly occupied by Mrs. Aubrey stood a small brick house, partially concealed by poplar and sycamore trees, and surrounded by a neat, well-arranged flower-garden. This was the place selected and purchased by the cripple for his future home. Mr. Huntingdon had opposed the whole proceeding, and invited his brother-in-law to reside with him; but beneath the cordial surface the guest felt that other sentiments rolled deep and strong. He had little in common with his sister's husband, and only a warm and increasing affection for his niece now induced him to settle in W——. Some necessary repairs had been made, some requisite arrangements completed regarding servants, and to-day the finishing touches were given to the snug little bachelor establishment. When it was apparent that no arguments would avail to alter the decision, Irene ceased to speak of it, and busied herself in various undertakings to promote her uncle's comfort. She made pretty white curtains for his library-windows, knitted bright-colored worsted lamp-mats, and hemmed and marked the contents of the linen-closet. The dining-room pantry she took under her special charge, and at the expiration of ten days, when the master took formal possession, she accompanied him, and enjoyed the pleased surprise with which he received her donation of cakes, preserves, catchups, pickles, etc., etc., neatly stowed away on the spotless shelves.

"I shall make a weekly pilgrimage to this same pantry, and take an inventory of its contents. I intend to take good care of you, though you have moved off, Diogenes-like."

She stepped forward, and arranged some glass jars which stood rather irregularly.

"How prim and old maidish you are!" laughed her uncle.

"I never could bear to see things scattered in that helter-skelter style; I like bottles, jars, plates, and dishes drilled into straight lines, not leaning in and out, in that broken-rank fashion. I am not given to boasting, but I will say that no housekeeper can show a nicer, neater pantry than my own."

"What have you in that basket?"

"Flowers from the greenhouse. Come into the library, and let me dress your new vases."

He followed her into the next room, and watched her as she leisurely and tastefully disposed her flowers; now searching the basket for a sprig of evergreen, and now bending obstinate stems to make stiff clusters lean lovingly to each other. Placing the vases on the mantle, she stepped back to inspect the effect, and said, gravely:

"How beautiful they are! Let me always dress your vases, Uncle. Women have a knack of intertwining stems and grouping colors; our fingers were ordained for all such embroidery on the coarse gray serge of stern, practical every-day life. You men are more at home with state papers, machine-shops, navies, armies, political economy, and agricultural chemistry than with fragile azaleas and golden-dusted lilies."

Before he could reply she turned and asked:

"What do these large square boxes in the hall contain?"

"Books which I gathered in Europe and selected in New York; among them many rare old volumes, which you have never seen. Come down next Monday, and help me to number and shelve them; afterward, we will read them together. Lay aside your bonnet, and spend the evening with me."

"No, I must go back; Hugh sent me word that he would bring company to tea."

He took her hand and drew her close to his chair, saying gently:

"Ah, Irene! I wish I could keep you always. You would be happier here, in this little unpretending home of mine, than presiding as mistress over that great palatial house on the hill yonder."

"There you mistake me most entirely. I love, better than any other place on earth, my stately, elegant, beautiful home. Not Fontainebleau. Windsor, Potsdam; not the vineyards of Shiraz, or the gardens of Damascus, could win me from it. I love every tree, every creeper, every foot of ground from the frontgate to the brink of the creek. If you suppose that I am not happy there, you err egregiously."

"My intuitions rarely deceive me."

"At least, Uncle Eric, they play you false in this instance. Why, sir, I would not give my grand old avenue of primeval elms for St. Peter's nave. Your intuitions are full of cobwebs; have them well swept and dusted before I see you Monday. Good-night, Uncle; I must really go. If you find we have forgotten anything, send Willis up for it."

He kissed her fingers tenderly, and, taking her basket, she left him alone in his new home.

A few weeks passed without incident; Hugh went to New Orleans to visit friends, and Mr. Huntingdon was frequently absent at the plantation.

One day he expressed the desire that Judge Harris' family should dine with him, and added several gentlemen, "to make the party merry." Irene promptly issued the invitations, suppressing the reluctance which filled her heart; for the young people were not favorites, and she dreaded Charlie's set speeches and admiring glances, not less than his mother's endless disquisitions on fashion and the pedigree of all the best families of W—— and its vicinage. Grace had grown up very pretty, highly accomplished, even-tempered, gentle-hearted, but full of her mother's fashionable notions, and, withal, rather weak and frivolous. She and Irene were constantly thrown into each other's society, but no warmth of feeling existed on either side. Grace could not comprehend her companion's character, and Irene wearied of her gay, heedless chitchat. As the latter anticipated, the day proved very tiresome; the usual complement of music was contributed by Grace, the expected quantity of flattering nothings gracefully uttered by her brother, the customary amount of execrable puns handed around the circle for patronage, and Irene gave the signal for dinner. Mr. Huntingdon prided himself on his fine wines, and, after the decanters had circulated freely, the gentlemen grew garrulous as market-women.

Irene was gravely discussing the tariff question with Mr. Herbert Blackwell (whom Mrs. Harris pronounced the most promising young lawyer of her acquaintance), and politely listening to his stereotyped reasoning, when a scrap of conversation at the opposite end of the table attracted her attention.

"Huntingdon, my dear fellow, I tell you I never made a mistake in my life, when reading people's minds; and if Aubrey has not the finest legal intellect in W——, I will throw up my judgeship. You have seen Campbell,

I suppose? He returned last week, and, by the way, I half-expected to meet him to-day; well, I was talking to him about Aubrey, and he laughed his droll, chuckling laugh, snapped his bony fingers in my face, and said:

"Aye! aye, Harris! let him alone; hands off! and I will wager my new office against your old one that he steps into your honor's shoes. Now you know perfectly well that Campbell has no more enthusiasm than a brick wall or a roll of red tape; but he is as proud of the young man as if he were his son. Do you know that he has taken him into partnership?"

"Pshaw! he will never commit such a faux pas."

"But he has; I read the notice in this morning's paper. Pass the madeira. The fact is, we must not allow our old prejudices to make us unjust. I know Aubrey has struggled hard; he had much to contend—"

"Hang Campbell and the partnership! He will find that he has played the fool before he gets rid of his precious pet. Miss Grace, do let me fill your glass? My young prude there at the head of the table just sips hers as if she feared it was poisoned. Mrs. Harris, you have no sherry; permit me."

"The young man's antecedents are most disgraceful, Mr. Huntingdon, and I told the judge last night that I was surprised at Mr. Campbell's infatuation," chimed in Mrs. Harris over her golden sherry.

"Whose antecedents, Mother?"

"My dear, we were speaking of Russell Aubrey, and the stigma on his name and character."

"Oh, yes! His father was sentenced to be hung, I believe, and committed suicide in prison. But what a splendid, dark-looking man he is! Decidedly the most superb figure and eyes in W——. Shy, though! shy as a school girl; will cross the street to avoid meeting a body. When he finds that he can not dodge you, he gives you the full benefit of his magnificent eyes, and bows as haughtily as Great Mogul. Maria Henderson goes into raptures over his figure."

With head slightly inclined, and eyes fixed on Mr. Blackwell's face, Irene had heard all that passed, and as the gentleman paused in his harangue to drain his glass, she rose and led the way to the parlors. The gentlemen adjourned to the smoking-room, and in a short time Mrs. Harris ordered her carriage, pleading an engagement with Grace's mantua-maker as an excuse for leaving so early. With a feeling of infinite relief the hostess accompanied them to the door, saw the carriage descend the avenue, and, desiring one of the servants to have Erebus saddled at once, she went to her room and changed the rich dinner-dress for her riding-habit. As she sprang into the saddle, and gathered up the reins, her father called from the open window, whence issued curling wreaths of blue smoke:

"Where now, Irene?"

"I am going to ride; it threatened rain this morning, and I was afraid to venture."

He said something, but without hearing she rode off, and was soon out of sight, leaving the town to the left, and taking the road that wound along the river-bank—the same where, years before, she had cantered with Grace, Hugh, and Charlie. It was a windless, sunny April afternoon; trees were freshly robed in new-born fringy foliage, green and glistening; long grassy slopes looked like crinkled velvet, starred with delicate pale blue houstonias; wandering woodbine trailed its coral trumpets in and out of grass and tangled shrubs, and late wood-azaleas loaded the air with their delicious, intoxicating perfume. Irene felt unwontedly depressed; the day had wearied her; she shook the reins, and the beautiful horse sprang on in a quick gallop. For a mile farther they dashed along the river bank, and then, reining him up, she leaned forward and drew a long, deep breath. The scene was surpassingly quiet and beautiful; on either side wooded hills came down, herd-like, to the edge of the stream, to lave their thirsty sides and listen to the continual solemn monotone of the foaming falls; here a small flock of sheep browsed on the young waving grass, and there contented-looking cows, with glossy satin skins, sauntered homeward—taking the road with as much precision as their Swiss sisters to the tune of *Ranz des Vaches;* the broad river sweeping down its rocky pavement, and, over all, a mellow April sky of intense blue, with whiffs of creamy vapor, sinuous as floss silk. Close to the margin of the river grew a luxuriant mass of ivy, and now the dark shining foliage was flecked with tiny rosy buds and well-blown waxen petals, crimped into fairy-like cups, and tinted as no Sèvres china ever will be. Urging Erebus into the thicket, Irene broke as many clusters as she could conveniently carry; dragged a long tangled wreath of late jasmine from its seclusion, fastened it across the pommel of the saddle, and turned her horse's head homeward. The sight of these ivy cups recalled the memory of her Aunt Margaret; they had been her favorite flowers, and as thought now took another channel, she directed her way to the graveyard. She always rode rapidly, and, ere long, Erebus' feet drew sparks from the rocky road leading up the hill-side to the cemetery-gate. Dismounting, she fastened the reins to one of the iron spikes, and, gathering the folds of her habit over her arm, carried her flowers to the family burying-ground. It was a large square lot, enclosed by a handsome railing and tall gate, bearing the name of "Huntingdon" in silver letters. As she approached, she was surprised to find a low brick wall and beautiful new marble monument close to her father's lot, and occupying a space which had been filled with grass and weeds a few weeks previous. While she paused, wondering whose was the new monument, and resolved to examine it, a tall form stepped from behind the column and stood, with folded arms, looking down at the grave. There was no mistaking face or figure; evidently he was unaware of her presence, though she was near enough to mark the stern sorrow written on his countenance. She glided forward and opened the heavy gate of her own enclosure; with difficulty she pushed it ajar, and with a sudden, sharp, clanging report it swung back, and the bolt slid to its rusty place. He lifted his eyes then, and saw her standing a few yards from him; the rich soft folds of the Marie Louise blue riding-dress trailed along the ground; the blue velvet hat, with its long drooping plume, had become loosened by the exercise, and, slipping back, left fully exposed the dazzling white face and golden glory of waving hair. She bowed, he returned the silent token of recognition, and she moved forward to her aunt's tomb, wreathing it with the flowers which Miss Margaret had loved so well. The sun was low, leaning upon the purple crest of a distant hill; the yellow light flashed over the forest of marble pillars, and their cold polished surfaces gave back the waning glare, throwing it off contemptuously, as if sunshine were a mockery in that silent city of the dead. Sombre sacred guardian cedars extended their arms lovingly over the marble couches of fair young sleepers in God's Acre, and venerable willows wept over many a stela, whose inscription lichen-footed Time had effaced. Here slept two generations of the Huntingdons, and the last scion of the proud old house stood up among the hoarded bones of her ancestry, glancing round at the moss-stained costly mausoleums, and noting the fact that the crowded lot had room for but two more narrow beds—two more silent citizens—her father and herself. It was a reflection which she had little inclination to linger over, and, retaining a beautiful cluster of ivy and jasmine, she left the enclosure, keeping her eyes fixed on the ground.

As she passed the new lot the gate swung open, and Russell stood before her.

"Good-evening, Miss Huntingdon."

"Good-evening, Mr. Aubrey."

The name sounded strange and harsh as she uttered it, and involuntarily she paused and held out her hand. He accepted it; for an instant the cold fingers lay in his warm palm, and as she withdrew them he said, in the rich mellow voice which she had heard in the church:

"Allow me to show you my mother's monument."

He held the gate open, and she entered and stood at his side. The monument was beautiful in its severe simplicity—a pure, faultless shaft, crowned with a delicately-chiselled wreath of poppy leaves, and bearing these words in gilt letters: "Sacred to the memory of my mother, Amy Aubrey." Just below, in black characters, "*Resurgam;*" and, underneath the whole, on a finely-fluted scroll, the inscription of St. Gilgen. After a silence of some moments Russell pointed to the singular and solemn words, and said, as if speaking rather to himself than to her:

"I want to say always, with Paul Flemming, 'I will be strong,' and therefore I placed here the inscription which proved an evangel to him, that when I come to my mother's grave I may be strengthened, not melted, by the thronging of bitter memories."

She looked up as he spoke, and the melancholy splendor of the deep eyes stirred her heart as nothing had ever done before.

"I have a few flowers left; let me lay them as an affectionate tribute, an '*in memoriam*' on your mother's tomb—for the olden time, the cottage-days, are as fresh in my recollection as in yours."

She held out the woodland bouquet; he took it, and strewed the blossoms along the broad base of the shaft, reserving only a small cluster of the rosy china-cups. Both were silent; but, as she turned to go, a sudden gust blew her hat from her head, the loosened comb fell upon the grass, and down came the heavy masses of hair. She twisted them hastily into a coil, fastened them securely, and received her hat from him, with a cool:

"Thank you, sir; when did you hear from Electra?"

They walked on to the cemetery-gate, and he answered:

"I have heard nothing for some weeks. Have you any message? I am going to New York in a few days, to try to persuade her to return to W—— with me."

"I doubt the success of your mission; W—— has little to tempt an artist like your cousin. Be kind enough to tender her my love and best wishes for the realization of her artistic dreams."

They had reached the gate where Erebus waited, when Russell took off his hat reverently, and pointed to the western sky all "aflame." Masses of purple, scarlet, gold, amber, and pure, pale, opaline green blended in one magnificent conflagration; and toward the zenith tortuous feathery braids and dashes of blood-red cirri, gleaming through the mild, balmy air like coral reefs in some breezeless oriental sea.

"No soft, neutral, sober 'Graiæ' there," said Irene, lifting her hand to the glowing cloud-panorama.

He took up the quotation promptly, and added:

"'The Angel of the Sea' is abroad on his immemorial mission, the soft wings droop still with dew, and the shadows of their plumes falter on the hill; strange laughings and glitterings of silver streamlets, born suddenly, and twined about the mossy heights in trickling tinsel, answering to them as they wave. The coiled locks of 'hundred-headed Typhon' leave no menace yonder."

He paused, and turning suddenly, with a piercing look at his companion, continued:

"Miss Huntingdon, 'on what anvils and wheels is the vapor pointed, twisted, hammered, whirled as the potter's clay? By what hands is the incense of the sea built up into domes of marble?'"

"I see that you follow assiduously the beck of Nature's last anointed hierophant, and go in and out with the seer, even among the cherubim and seraphim of his metropolitan cathedral, with its 'gates of rock, pavements of cloud, choirs of stream, altars of snow, and vaults of purple, traversed by the continual stars.'"

"Yes; I am a reverent student and warm admirer of John Ruskin. I learned to love him first through the recommendations of my cousin; then for his gorgeous, unapproachable word-painting."

While they talked, the brilliant pageant faded, the coral banks paled to snowy lines, as if the blue waves of air were foam-crested, and in the valley below rose the dusky outline of dark-haired, wan-browed, gray-clad Twilight, stealing her "sober livery" over the flushed and fretted bosom of the murmuring river.

"You have a long walk to town," said Irene, as Russell arranged her horse's reins.

"I shall not find it long. It is a fine piece of road, and the stars will be up to light it."

He held out his hand to assist her; she sprang easily to the saddle, then leaned toward him, every statue-like curve and moulding of her proud ivory face stamping themselves on his recollection as she spoke.

"Be so good as to hand me my glove; I dropped it at your feet as I mounted. Thank you. Good-evening, Mr. Aubrey; take my best wishes on your journey and its mission."

"Good-by, Miss Huntingdon." He raised his hat, and, as she wheeled off, the magnetic handsome face followed, haunted her. Erebus was impatient, out of humor, and flew up the next steep hill as if he, too, were haunted. Glancing back as she reached the summit, Irene saw the erect, stern, solitary figure at the extremity of the wooded vista, and in that mystical dim light he looked a colossal avenging Viking.

Once more, as in childhood, she heard the whirr of the loom of Destiny; and to-night, catching sight of the Parcæ fingers, she knew that along the silver warp of her life ran dark alien threads, interweaving all in one shapeless, tangled web.

On through gathering gloom dashed horse and rider, over the little gurgling stream, through the gate, up the dark, rayless avenue to the door-step. The billiard-room was a blaze of light, and the cheerful sound of mingled voices came out at the open window, to tell that the gentlemen had not yet finished their game. Pausing in the hall, Irene listened an instant to distinguish the voices, then ascended the long, easy staircase. The lamp threw a mellow radiance on the steps, and as she reached the landing Hugh caught her in his arms and kissed her warmly. Startled by his unexpected appearance, she recoiled a step or two and asked, rather haughtily:

"When did you get home?"

"Only a few moments after you left the house. Do change your dress quickly, and come down. I have a thousand things to say."

She waited to hear no more, but disengaged herself and went to her room.

"Now, child! why will you do so? What makes you stay out so late, and then come thundering back like a hurricane? I never did like that horse's great big saucy, shining, devilish eyes. I tell Andrew constantly I wish he would manage to break his legs while he is jumping over all the fences on the place. You scare me nearly to death about your riding; I tell you, Beauty, that black satan will break your neck yet. Your grandfather was flung from just such a looking brute, and dragged till he was dead; and some day that everlasting long hair of yours will drag you to your grave. Here it is now, all streaming down your back; yes—just as I expected—not a blessed hair-pin left in it; done galloped 'em all clean out. You will ride yourself into eternity. Sit down, and let me comb it out; it is all in a tangle, like ravelled yellow silk."

Nellie looked cloudy, moody, and her mistress offered no resistance to her directions.

"Mass' Hugh's come."

"Yes; I know it."

"But you don't know supper is almost ready, do you? Presently you will hear your father's voice sounding like a brass trumpet down stairs, if you ar'n't ready. There! John rings that bell as if he had the dead to raise!"

"That will do, Aunt Nellie, only give me a handkerchief."

She went down, and met her father at the dining-room door.

"Come, Queen; we are waiting for you."

He looked at her fondly, took her hand, and drew her to the table; and, in after years, she recalled this occasion with mournful pleasure as the last on which he had ever given her his pet name.

"... There are fatal days, indeed.
In which the fibrous years have taken root
So deeply, that they quiver to their tops
Whene'er you stir the dust of such a day."

CHAPTER XIX.

"Come out on the colonnade; the air is delicious." As he spoke, Hugh drew his cousin's arm through his, and led the way from the tea-table.

"You had company to dine to-day?"

"Yes; if I had known that you were coming home to-day, I would have postponed the invitation till to-morrow. Grace expressed much disappointment at your absence."

"Indeed! Of course I am duly grateful. What a pretty, sweet little creature she is! So sprightly, so vivacious, so winning; so charmingly ignorant of 'Almacantar' and 'Azimuth,' and all such learned stupidity. Unlike some royal personages of my acquaintance, who are for ever soaring among the stars, she never stretches my brains the hundredth part of an inch to comprehend her delightful prattle. Like Dickens' 'Dora,' she regards any attempt to reason with her as a greater insult than downright scolding. Your solemn worshipper was also present, I believe?"

"To whom do you allude?"

"Your tedious, tiresome, pertinacious shadow, Herbert Blackwell, of course! Do you know that I detest that man most cordially?"

"For what reason?"

"I really do not feel in the mood to enumerate all his peccadilloes and disagreeable traits; but it is supremely ridiculous to see the way in which he hovers round you, like one of those large black moths about the hall-lamp."

"Come, come, Hugh! Mr. Blackwell is a man whom I respect and esteem, and you shall not make him a target for your merriment."

"Oh, doubtless! my Czarina! and, as a reward for your consideration, he would fain confer on you his distinguished hand and fortune. It is quite a respectable farce to watch him watching you."

"I wish you had a tithe of his industry and perseverance. Did it ever occur to you that life is given for nobler purposes and loftier aspirations than hunting, fishing, horse-racing, gambling, and similar modes of murdering time which you habitually patronize?"

"You are too young to play the *role* of Mentor, and those rare red lips of yours were never meant for homilizing. Irene, how long do you intend to keep me in painful suspense?"

"I am not aware that I have in any degree kept you in suspense."

"At all events, you know that you torture me with cool, deliberate cruelty."

"I deny your charge most solemnly."

"My dear Irie, let us understand each other fully, for——."

"Nay, Hugh—be honest; there is no misapprehension whatever. We thoroughly understand each other already."

"You shall not evade me; I have been patient, and the time has come when we must talk of our future. Irene, dearest, be generous, and tell me when will you give me, irrevocably, this hand, which has been promised to me from your infancy?"

He took the hand and carried it to his lips, but she forcibly withdrew it, and, disengaging her arm, said, emphatically:

"Never, Hugh. Never."

"How can you trifle with me, Irene? If you could realize how impatient I am for the happy day when I shall call you my wife, you would be serious, and fix an early period for our marriage."

"Hugh, why will you affect to misconceive my meaning? I am serious; I have pondered, long and well, a matter involving your life-long happiness and mine, and I tell you, most solemnly, that I will never be your wife."

"Oh, Irene! your promise! your sacred promise!"

"I never gave it! On the contrary, I have never failed to show you that my whole nature rebelled against the most unnatural relation forced upon me. I can not, shall not, hold myself bound by the promise of another made when I was an unconscious infant. I know the family compact, sealed by my father's word, at your mother's death-bed, making two little irresponsible children parties to a thoroughly selfish, ignoble contract, which is revolting to me. Your future and mine were adumbrated from my cradle, and that which only we could legitimately decide was usurped and predetermined. You have known, for years, that I loathed the heartless betrothal and ignored its restrictions; my unalterable determination was very apparent when you returned from Europe. You were kept in no suspense; you understood me then as fully as now; and it is ungenerous, unmanly, to press a suit which you can not fail to know is extremely disagreeable to me."

"My dear Irene, have you, then, no love for me? I have hoped and believed that you hid your love behind your cold mask of proud silence. You must, you do love me, my beautiful cousin!"

"You do not believe your own words; you are obliged to know better. I love you as my cousin, love you somewhat as I love Uncle Eric, love you as the sole young relative left to me, as the only companion of my lonely childhood; but other love than this I never had, never can have, for you. Hugh, my cousin, look fearlessly at the unvarnished truth; neither you nor I have one spark of that affection which alone can sanction marriage. We are utterly unlike in thought, taste, feeling, habits of life, and aspirations; I have no sympathy with your pursuits, you are invariably afflicted with *ennui* at the bare suggestion of mine. Nature stamped us with relentless antagonisms of character; I bow to her decree rather than to man's word. Dante painted no purgatory dark enough to suit the wretchedness that would result from such an unholy union as ours would be. Think of it, Hugh; a loveless marriage; a mere moneyed partnership; a sort of legal contract; the only true union being of bank-stock, railroad-shares, and broad plantations."

She leaned against one of the pillars with her arms folded, and a cold, merciless smile curling the beautiful mouth.

"Indeed, you wrong me! my worshipped cousin. You are dearer to me than everything else on earth. I have loved you, and you only, from my boyhood; you have been a lovely idol from earliest recollection!"

"You are mistaken, most entirely mistaken; I am not to be deceived, neither can you hoodwink yourself. You like me, you love me, in the same quiet way that I love you; you admire me, perhaps, more than any one you chance to know just now; you are partial to my beauty, and, from long habit, have come to regard me as your property, much in the same light as that in which you look upon your costly diamond buttons, or your high-spirited horses, or rare imported pointers. After a fashion you like me, Hugh; I know you do; and, my cousin, it would be most lamentable and unnatural if you had not some affection for me; but love such as a man should have for the woman whom he makes his life-companion, and calls by the sacred name of wife, you have not one atom of. I do not wish to wound you, but I must talk to you as any reasonable woman would on a question of such great importance; for I hold it no light thing for two souls to burden themselves with vows which neither can possibly perform. Hugh, I abhor shams! and I tell you now that I never will be a party to that which others have arranged without my consent."

"Ah! I see how matters stand. Having disposed of your heart, and lavished your love elsewhere, you shrink from fulfilling the sacred obligations that make you mine. I little dreamed that you were so susceptible, else I had not left you feeling so secure. My uncle has not proved the faithful guardian I believed him when I entrusted my treasure, my affianced bride, to his care."

Bitter disappointment flashed in his face and quivered in his voice, rendering him reckless of consequences. But though he gazed fiercely at her as he uttered the taunt, it produced not the faintest visible effect; the cloudless chiselled face still wore its quiet smile of mild irony, and the low clear voice preserved its sweetness.

"You do my father rank injustice, Hugh. Not Ladon was more faithful or tireless than he has been."

"He can not deny that the treasure has been stolen, nevertheless."

"He probably can and will deny that the golden treasure has been snatched from his guardianship. Another Atlas or a second Hercules would be needed for such a theft."

The application stung him; he crimsoned, and retorted with a degree of bitterness of which he was probably unconscious at the moment:

"You, at least, dare not deny my charge, my truthful, constant *fiancée!*"

"Either you overestimate my supposed offence or underrate my courage; there are few honorable things which I dare not do."

"Confess, then, who stands between your heart and mine. I have a right to ask; I will know."

"You forget yourself, my cousin. Your right is obviously a debatable question; we will waive it, if you please. I have told you already, and now I repeat it for the last time, I will not go with you to the altar, because neither of us has proper affection for the other to warrant such a union; because it would be an infamous pecuniary contract, revolting to every true soul. I do not want your estate, and you should be content with your ample fortune without coveting my inheritance, or consenting to sell your manhood to mammon. I would not suit you for a wife; go find some more congenial spirit, some gentle, clinging girl, who will live only in your love, and make you forget all else in her presence. I have no fancy for the Gehenna our married life would inevitably prove. Henceforth there is no margin for misapprehension; understand that we meet in future as cousins, only as cousins, acknowledging no other relationship, no other tie save that of consanguinity; for I do not hesitate to snap the links that were forged in my babyhood, to annul the unrighteous betrothal of other hands. Hugh, cherish no animosity against me; I merit none. Because we can not be more, shall we be less than friends?"

She held out her hand, but he was too angry to accept it, and asked, haughtily:

"Shall I break this pleasant piece of information to my uncle? Or do you feel quite equal to the task of blighting all his long-cherished hopes, as well as mine?"

"I leave it in your hands; consult your discretion, or your pleasure; to me it matters little. Remember my earnest request, that you bear me no malice in the coming years. Good-night, my cousin."

She turned to leave him, but he caught her dress, and exclaimed, with more tenderness than he had ever manifested before:

"Oh, Irene! do not reject me utterly! I can not relinquish you. Give me one more year to prove my love; to win yours. If your proud heart is still your own, may I not hope to obtain it, by ———."

"No, Hugh! no. As well hope to inspire affection in yonder mute marble guardians. Forgive me if I pain you, but I must be candid at every hazard." She pointed to the statues near the door, and went through the greenhouse to the library, thence to the observatory, expecting, ere long, to be joined by her father. Gradually the house became quiet, and, oppressed with the painful sense of coming trouble, she sought her own room just as the clock struck twelve. Pausing to count the strokes, she saw a light gleaming through the key-hole of her father's door, opposite her own, and heard the sound of low but earnest conversation mingled with the restless tramp of pacing feet. She was powerfully tempted to cross the passage, knock, and have the ordeal ended then and there; but second thought whispered, "To-morrow will soon be here; be patient." She entered her room, and, wearied by the events of the day, fell asleep, dreaming of the new lot in the cemetery, and the lonely, joyless man who haunted it.

As she adjusted her riding-habit the following morning, and suffered Andrew to arrange her stirrup, the latter said, good-humoredly:

"So, Mass' Hugh got the start of you? It is n't often he beats you."

"What do you mean?"

"He started a while ago, and, if he drives as he generally does, he will get to his plantation in time for dinner."

"Did Father go, too?"

"No ma'm; only Mass' Hugh, in his own buggy."

In the quiet, leafy laboratory of Nature there is an elixir of strength for those wise enough to seek it; and its subtle, volatile properties continually come to the relief of wearied, overtaxed brains, and aching, oppressed hearts. The human frame, because of its keen susceptibility to impressions from the external world, and its curious adaptation thereunto, becomes, like the strings of an Æolian harp, attuned perfectly to the breath that sweeps it, and is by turns the exponent of stormy passion or holy resignation. Thus, from the cool serenity, the dewy sparkle, and delicate perfume of the early morning, Irene derived a renewal of strength such as no purely human aid could have furnished. She remembered now the sibyllic words of the young minister: "*You, too, must tread the wine-press alone,*" and felt that the garments of her soul were taking the dye, the purple stain of the wine of trial. Doubtless he had alluded to a different ordeal, but she knew that all the future of her earthly existence was to receive its changeless hue from this day, and she could entertain but a modicum of doubt as to what that hue would prove. Returning from her ride, she stood a moment on the front-step, looking down the avenue. The Bermuda terrace blazed in the sunlight like a jewelled coronal, the billowy sea of foliage, crested by dewy drops, flashed and dripped as the soft air stirred the ancient trees, the hedges were all alive with birds and butterflies, the rich aroma of brilliant and countless flowers, the graceful curl of smoke wreathing up from the valley beyond, the measured musical tinkle of bells as the cows slowly descended the distant hills, and, over all, like God's mantling mercy, a summer sky—

"'As blue as Aaron's priestly robe appeared
To Aaron, when he took it off to die.'"

Involuntarily she stretched out her arms to the bending heavens and her lips moved, but no sound escaped to tell what petition went forth to the All-Father. She went to her room, changed her dress, and joined her father at the breakfast-table. Half-concealed behind his paper, he took no notice of her quiet "good-morning," seeming absorbed in an editorial. The silent meal ended, he said, as they left the table:

"I want to see you in the library."

She followed him without comment; he locked the door, threw open the blinds, and drew two chairs to the window, seating himself immediately in front of her. For a moment he eyed her earnestly, as if measuring her strength; and she saw the peculiar sparkle in his falcon-eye, which, like the first lurid flash in a darkened sky, betokened tempests. "Irene, I was very much astonished to learn the result of an interview between Hugh and yourself; I can scarcely believe that you were in earnest, and feel disposed to attribute your foolish words to some trifling motive of girlish coquetry or momentary pique. You have long been perfectly well aware that you and your cousin were destined for each other; that I solemnly promised the marriage should take place as soon as you were of age; that all my plans and hopes for you centred in this one engagement. I have not pressed the matter on your attention of late, because I knew you had sense enough to appreciate your position, and because I believed you would be guided by my wishes in this important affair. You are no longer a child; I treat you as a reasonable woman, and now I tell you candidly it is the one wish of my heart to see you Hugh's wife."

He paused, but she made no answer, and, taking one of her hands, he continued:

"My daughter, I can not believe that you, on whom I have lavished so much love and tenderness, can deliberately refuse to accede to my wishes, can disappoint my dearest hopes. Of course, in all that I do or counsel, I am actuated only by a desire to promote your happiness. My dear child, I have a right to direct you, and surely your affection for your only parent will induce you to yield to his wishes."

He tightened his clasp of her cold hand, and leaned toward her.

"Father, my happiness will not be promoted by this marriage, and if you are actuated solely by this motive, allow me to remain just as I am. I should be most miserable as Hugh's wife; most utterly miserable."

"Why so?"

"For reasons which I gave him last night, and which it is hardly necessary for me to recapitulate, as he doubtless repeated them to you."

"Let me hear them, if you please."

"Our characters are totally dissimilar; our tastes and opinions wide as the poles asunder; our natures could not possibly harmonize; and, more than all, we do not love each other as people should who stand at the altar and ask God's blessing on their marriage. I suppose, sir, that Hugh tells you he loves me; perhaps he likes me better than any one else beside himself, but the deep, holy affection which he ought to feel for the woman whom he calls his wife has no existence in his heart. It will prove a mere temporary disappointment, nothing seriously touching his happiness; for, I assure you, that is not in my keeping."

"And if I answer that I know the contrary to be true?"

"Father, I should still adhere to my own opinion; and, even were I disposed to accept your view of it, my own feelings would stand an everlasting barrier to our union. I do not love Hugh, and—I must tell you, sir, that I think it wrong for cousins to marry."

"You talk like a silly child; I thought you had more sense. Your objections I have listened to; they are imaginary and trifling; and I ask you, as a father has a right to ask his child, to waive these ridiculous notions, and grant the only request I have ever made of you. Tell me, my daughter, that you will consent to accept your cousin, and thereby make me happy."

He stooped and kissed her forehead, watching her countenance eagerly.

"Oh, Father! do not ask this of me! Anything else! anything else."

"Answer me, my darling child; give me your promise."

His hold was painful, and an angry pant mingled with the pleading tones. She raised her head and said, slowly:

"My father, I can not."

He threw her hand from him, and sprang up.

"Ingrate! do you mean to say that you will not fulfil a sacred engagement?—that you will break an oath given to the dead?"

"I do not hold myself bound by the oaths of another, though he were twice my father. I am responsible for no acts but my own. No one has the right to lay his hand on an unconscious infant, slumbering in her cradle, and coolly determine, for all time, her destiny. You have the right to guide me, to say what I shall not do without your consent, but I am a free-born American, thank God! I did not draw my breath in Circassia, to be bartered for gold by my father. I, only, can give myself away. Why should you wish to force this marriage on me? Father, do you think that a woman has no voice in a matter involving her happiness for life? Is one of God's holy sacraments to become a mere pecuniary transaction?—only a legal transfer of real estate and cotton bales? Oh, my father! would you make yourself and your child parties to so ignoble, so loathsome a proceeding?"

"Oh! I suspected that your cursed obstinacy would meet me here, as well as elsewhere in your life. You have been a source of trouble and sorrow from your birth; but the time has come to end all this. I will not be trifled with; I tried to reason with you, to influence you through your affections, but it seems you have none. If I resort to other measures now, you have only yourself to thank. Irene, there can be peace between us but upon one condition; I have set my heart on seeing you Hugh's wife; nothing less will satisfy me. I warn you, as you value your own happiness, not to thwart me; it is no trivial risk that you run. I tell you now, I will make you suffer severely if you dare to disobey me in this matter. You know that I never menace idly, and if you refuse to hear reason I will utterly disinherit you, though you are my only child. Ponder it well. You have been raised in luxury, and taught to believe yourself one of the wealthiest heiresses in the state; contrast your present position, your elegant home, your fastidious tastes gratified to the utmost; contrast all this, I say, with poverty—imagine yourself left in the world without one cent! Think of it! think of it! My wealth is my own, mark you, and I will give it to whom I please, irrespective of all claims of custom. Now the alternative is fully before you, and on your own head be the consequences. Will you accede to my wishes, as any dutiful child should, or will you deliberately incur my everlasting displeasure? Will you marry Hugh?"

Both rose, and stood confronting each other; his face burning with wrath, every feature quivering with passion; hers white and rigid as a statue's, with only a blue cord-like crescent between the arching brows to index her emotion. Steadily the large violet eyes looked into those that regarded her so angrily; there was no drooping of the long silken fringes; no moisture dimming their depths; then they were raised slowly, as if to the throne of God, registering some vow, and, pressing her hands over her heart, she said, solemnly:

"Father, I will not marry Hugh, so help me God!"

Silence fell between them for several moments; something in that fixed, calm face of his child awed him, but it was temporary, and, with a bitter laugh, he exclaimed:

"Oh, very well! Your poverty be upon your own head in coming years, when the grave closes over me. At my death every cent of my property passes to Hugh, and with it my name, and between you and me, as an impassable gulf, lies my everlasting displeasure. Understand that, though we live here in one house, as father and child, I do not, and will not, forgive you. You have defied me; now eat the bitter fruit of your disobedience."

"I have no desire to question the disposition of your wealth; if you prefer to give it to my cousin, I am willing—perfectly willing. I would rather beg my bread from door to door, proud though I am; I would sooner soil my Huntingdon hands by washing or cooking, than soil my soul with perjury, or sell myself for gold. It is true, I love elegance and luxury; I enjoy wealth as well as most people do, I suppose; but poverty does not frighten me half so much as a loveless marriage. Give Hugh your fortune if you wish, but, Father! Father! let there be no estrangement between you and me. I can bear everything but your displeasure; I dread nothing so much as the loss of your love. Oh, Father! forgive a disappointment which my conscience would not permit me to avert. Forgive the pain which, God knows, I would not have caused you, if I could have avoided it without compromising principle. Oh, my Father! my Father! let not dollars and cents stand between you and your only child. I ask nothing now but your love."

She drew nearer, but he waved her off and said, with a sneering laugh:

"Away with all such cant! I gave you the choice, and you made your selection with your eyes fully open. Accept poverty as your doom, and with it my eternal displeasure. I intend to make you suffer for your obstinacy. You shall find, to your sorrow, that I am not to be trifled with, or my name is not Leonard Huntingdon. Now go your way, and find what a thorny path you have made for yourself."

He pointed to the door as he had done, years before, when the boarding-school decree went forth, and without remonstrance she left him and sat down on the steps of the greenhouse. Soon after, the sound of his buggy-wheels told her that he had gone to town, and, leaning her cheek on her hand, she recalled the painful conversation from first to last. That he meant all he had threatened, and more, she did not question for an instant, and, thinking of her future, she felt sick at heart. But with the shame and sorrow came, also, a thrill of joy; she had burst the fetters; she was free. Wounded affection bled freely, but brain and conscience exulted in the result. She could not reproach herself; she resolved not to reproach her father, even in thought. Hers was not a disposition to vent its griefs and troubles in tears; these had come to her relief but three or four times in the course of a life, and on this occasion she felt as little inclination to cry as to repine idly over what could not be rectified. Her painful reverie was interrupted by the click of approaching crutches, and she rose to meet her uncle.

"Do not get up, Irene; I will sit here beside you. My child, look at me—are you sick?"

"No, Uncle Eric; what put that absurd notion into your head? I rode past your door two hours ago, and was powerfully tempted to stop and breakfast with your bachelorship."

He regarded her anxiously, noting the singular crescent on her pale forehead, and connecting it with the scowling face of his brother-in-law, which had passed him on the avenue. He knew that something very unusual had excited the calm, inflexible woman till the hot blood swelled that vein, but he forebore all question.

"What are you thinking of, Uncle Eric?"

"Only of a line in a poem which I was reading last night. Shall I quote it for you?

"'A still Medusa, with mild milky brows
All curdled ———.'"

She looked in his face, smiled, and passed her hand over her forehead, hiding the blue cord.

"Ah! a gentle way of reading me a lecture on ill-temper. I lay no claim to saintship, you know, and when I am out of humor my face won't play the hypocrite. I am no Griselda; obviously none of my name can ever expect canonization on that score. Come to the conservatory; the lemons are in full bloom, and marvellously sweet. Put your hand on my shoulder, and come down slowly."

"Where is Hugh? I thought he came home yesterday?"

"He started to his plantation at daylight. Take care, sir; these flags are slippery with dew; your crutches are unsafe."

CHAPTER XX.

"To-whit—to-whoo!" Munin stretched his broad gray wings, and, quitting the mantle-piece, perched upon the top of the easel, gazing down at the solitary artist, and uttering all the while a subdued melancholy note of complaint, as if to attract her attention. She looked up and held out her hand coaxingly.

"Munin! Munin! what do you want? You haunt me like my shadow. Poor pet, true to your name, you pine for your master."

The ruffled plumes smoothed themselves, the plaint was hushed. He fluttered to her shoulder, received her soft, caressing touches with evident satisfaction, nestled his beak in her shining hair, and then, as if soothed and contented, flitted to the open window. Resuming her brush, Electra leaned forward and continued her work. "*Laborare est orare;*" if so, no more ardent devotee ever bowed at the shrine of toil, bearing sacrificial offerings. Thoughts, hopes, aspirations, memories, all centred in the chosen profession; to its prosecution she brought the strength and energy of an indomitable will, the rich and varied resources of a well-stored, brilliant intellect. It was evident that she labored *con amore,* and now the expectation of approaching triumph lent additional eagerness to her manner. The fingers trembled, the eyes sparkled unwontedly, a deeper, richer crimson glowed on the smooth cheeks, and the lips parted and closed unconsciously. The tantalizing dreams of childhood, beautiful but evanescent, had gradually embodied themselves in a palpable, tangible, glorious reality; and the radiant woman exulted in the knowledge that she had but to put forth her hand and grasp it. The patient work of twelve months drew to a close; the study of years bore its first fruit; the last delicate yet quivering touch was given; she threw down palette and brush, and, stepping back, surveyed the canvas. The Exhibition would open within two days, and this was to be her contribution. A sad-eyed Cassandra, with pallid, prescient, woe-struck features—an overmastering face, wherein the flickering light of divination struggled feebly with the human horror of the To-Come, whose hideous mysteries were known only to the royal prophetess. In mute and stern despair it looked out from the canvas, a curious, anomalous thing—cut adrift from human help, bereft of aid from heaven—yet, in its doomed isolation, scorning to ask the sympathy which its extraordinary loveliness extorted from all who saw it. The artist's pride in this, her first finished creation, might well be pardoned, for she was fully conscious that the cloud-region of a painful novitiate lay far beneath her; that henceforth she should never miss the pressure of long-coveted chaplets from her brow; that she should bask in the warm, fructifying rays of public favor; and measureless exultation flashed in her beautiful eyes. The torch of Genius burned brightly, as, buoyant and eager, she took her place in the great lampadrome of life; but would it endure till the end? Would it light up the goal standing upon the terminus of Time?

The door opened, and Russell came into the studio. She was not expecting him; his sudden appearance gave her no time to adjust the chilling mask of pride, and all her uncontrolled affection found eloquent language in the joyful face.

"Russell! my own dear Russell!"

He drew his arm around her and kissed her flushed cheek, and each looked at the other, wondering at the changes which years had wrought.

"Electra, you have certainly improved more than any one I ever knew. You look the impersonation of perfect health; it is needless to ask how you are." And again his lips touched the beaming face pressed against his shoulder. Her arms stole tremblingly around his neck, past indifference was forgotten in the joy of his presence, and she murmured:

"I thought I should not see you before I left America. I can not tell you what a pleasure this surprise is to me. Oh, Russell!

I longed inexpressibly to be with you once more. Thank you, a thousand times, for coming to me at last."

"Did you suppose that I intended to let you put the Atlantic between us without making an effort to see you again? Were you unjust enough to believe that I had forgotten the only relative whom I love? My dear little sceptic, I have come to prove my affection, and put yours to the test."

He pressed her closer to his heart, but suddenly she shrank from him, unclasped his arm, and, wheeling two chairs to the window, said, hurriedly:

"Sit down, and let me look at you. You have grown so tall and commanding that I am half-afraid of my own cousin. You are less like Aunt Amy than formerly."

"Allow me to look at your painting first, for it will soon be too dark to examine it. This is the Cassandra of which you wrote me."

He stood before it for some moments in silence, and she watched him with breathless eagerness—for his opinion was of more value to her than that of all the *dilettanti* and *connoisseurs* who would soon inspect it. Gradually his dark, cold face kindled, and she had her reward.

"It is a masterly creation; a thing of wonderful and imperishable beauty; it is a great success—as such the world will receive it—and hundreds will proclaim your triumph. I am proud of it, and doubly proud of you."

He held out his hand, and, as she put her fingers in his, her head drooped and hot tears blinded her. Praise from the lips she loved best stirred her womanly heart as the applause of the public could never do; and, in after years, when grief and loneliness oppressed her, these precious words rang sweet and silvery through the darkened chambers of her soul, working miracles of comfort infinitely beyond the potent spell of Indian O-U-M or mystic Agla. Without perceiving her emotion he continued, with his eyes fixed on the picture:

"Some day you must make me a copy, and I will hang it over the desk in my office, where I can feast my eyes on its rare loveliness and my ears with your praises from all who see it. How long have you been at work upon it?"

"I can't recall the time when it first took hold of my imagination; it paced by my side when I was a child, brooded over me in my troubled dreams, looked out from the pomp of summer clouds and the dripping drab skies of winter, floated on snow-flakes, and flashed in thunder-storms; but I outlined it about a year ago. For my Exhibition picture, I wavered long between this and an unfinished Antigone; but finally decided in favor of Cassandra."

"And selected wisely. While in Europe I saw, in a private house, an exquisite head of the '*Erythræan Sybil*,' which somewhat resembles your painting. The position is almost identical—the nose, mouth, and chin very similar; but the glory of this Cassandra is the supernatural eyes, brimful of prescience. It might afford matter for curious speculation, however, and some time we will trace the subtle law of association of ideas by which two artists, separated by the Atlantic and by centuries, chanced, under totally different circumstances, to portray similarly the two distinct prophetesses who both foretold the doom of Troy."

"If such is the case, the world will be very sceptical of the coincidence. I did not even know that there was an '*Erythræan Sybil*,' much less a picture of her; so much for ignorance! The critics who knew that I did not paint your portrait, simply because it was well done, will swear that I stole the whole of my Cassandra," answered Electra, perplexed and troubled.

"You need not look so rueful, and plough your forehead with that heavy frown. In all probability I am the only person in New York who has seen the other picture; and, granting the contrary, the resemblance might not be detected. If you suffer it to annoy you, I shall be sorry that I mentioned it. Yet, I doubt not, the withering charge of plagiarism has often been hurled in the face of an honest worker quite as unjustly as it would be in your case. Very startling coincidences sometimes occur most innocently; but carping envy is a thrifty plant, and flourishes on an astonishingly small amount of soil."

"Who painted that Sibyl?"

"It is not known positively. Travelling through the northern part of France, I was detained some hours at a village, and employed the delay in rambling about the suburbs. Following a winding road it brought me to the enclosure of a chateau, and I leaned on the fence and admired the *parterre*, which was uncommonly pretty. The owner happened to be among his flower-beds, saw me, and, with genuine French politeness and urbanity, insisted that I should enter and rest myself while he gathered me a bouquet of mignonette and pinks. The afternoon was warm, and I asked for a glass of water. He took me into the house, and on the parlor wall hung this picture. It riveted my attention, and flattered, doubtless, by my evident admiration, he gave me its history. His father had found it at a picture-shop in Germany, I forget now exactly where, and bought it for a Dolce, but doubted its genuineness; and my host, who seemed thoroughly *au fait* in Art matters, asserted that it belonged to a much earlier school. That is all that I or the owner know of it; so dismiss the subject from your mind."

"I shall not, I promise you. Give me minute directions, and I will hunt up chateau, mignonette, gentlemanly proprietor, Sibyl, and all. Who knows but metempsychosis may be true after all, and that the painter's soul possesses me bodily, striving to portray the archetype which haunted him in the last stage of existence? According to Vaughan, the Portuguese have a superstition that the soul of a man who has died leaving some duty unfulfilled, or promised work unfinished, is frequently known to enter into another person, and, dislodging for a time the rightful soul-occupant, impel him unconsciously to complete what was lacking."

"You are growing positively paganish, Electra, from constant association with the dead deities of classic ages, and I must reclaim you. Come, sit down, and tell me something of your life since the death of your friend, Mr. Clifton."

"Did you receive my last letter, giving an account of Mrs. Clifton's death?"

"Yes; just as I stepped upon the platform of the cars it was handed to me. I had heard nothing from you for so long, that I thought it was time to look after you."

"You had started, then, before you knew that I was going to Europe?"

"Yes."

He could not understand the instantaneous change which came over her countenance—the illumination, followed as suddenly by a smile, half-compassionate, half-bitter. She pressed one hand to her heart, and said:

"Mrs. Clifton never seemed to realize her son's death, though, after paralysis took place, and she became speechless, I thought she recovered her memory in some degree. She survived him just four months, and, doubtless, was saved much grief by her unconsciousness of what had occurred. Poor old lady! she suffered little for a year past, and died, I hope, without pain. I have the consolation of knowing that I did all that could be done to promote her comfort. Russell, I would not live here for any consideration; nothing but a sense of duty has detained me this long. I promised him that I would not forsake his mother. But you can have no adequate conception of the feeling of desolation which comes over me when I sit here during the long evenings. He seems watching me from picture-frames and pedestals; his face—his pleading, patient, wan face—haunts me perpetually. And yet I tried to make him happy; God knows I did my duty."

She sprang up and paced the room for some moments, with her hands behind her, and tears glittering on her cheeks. Pausing at last on the rug, she pointed to a large square object closely shrouded, and added:

"Yonder stands his last picture, unfinished. The day he died he put a few feeble strokes upon it, and bequeathed the completion of the task to me. For several years he worked occasionally on it, but much remains to be done. It is the 'Death of Socrates.' I have not even looked at it since that night; I do not intend to touch it until after I visit Italy; I doubt whether my hand will ever be steady enough to give the last strokes. Oh, Russell! the olden time, the cottage-days seem far, far off to me now!"

Leaning against the mantle-piece she dropped her head on her hand, but when he approached and stood at the opposite corner he saw that the tears had dried.

"Neither of us has had a sunny life, Electra; both have had numerous obstacles to contend with; both have very bitter memories. Originally there was a certain parallelism in our characters, but with our growth grew the divergence. You have preserved the nobler part of your nature better than I; for my years I am far older than you; none of the brightness of my boyhood seems to linger about me. Contact with the world is an indurating process; I really did not know how hard I had grown, until I felt my heart soften at sight of you. I need you to keep the kindly charities and gentle amenities of life before me, and, therefore, I have come for you. But for my poverty, I never would have given you up so long; I felt that it would be for your advantage, in more than one respect, to remain with Mr. Clifton until I had acquired my profession. I knew that you would enjoy privileges here which I could not give you in my straitened circumstances. Things have changed; Mr. Campbell has admitted me to partnership; my success I consider an established fact. Give up, for a season, this projected tour of Europe; wait till I can go with you, till I can take you; go back to W—— with me. You can continue your pursuits, if you wish it; you can prosecute them here as well as here. You are ambitious, Electra; so am I; let us work together."

She raised her head and looked up at the powerful, nobly-proportioned form, the grand, kingly face, calm and colorless; the large, searching black eyes, within whose baffling depths lay all the mysteries of mesmerism, and a spasm of pain seized her own features. She shaded her brow, and answered:

"No, Russell, I could not entertain that thought an instant."

"Are you too proud to accept a home from me?"

"Not too proud, exactly; but, as long as I have health, I mean to make a support. I will not burden you."

"What bunglers you women are at logic! The thought of living on my charity affrights you, and yet you fly from me to the cold charity of the world—for what is so fleeting, fickle public favor—fitful public patronage or praise?"

"Full value received for benefit rendered is not charity; beside, Russell, you too, seek and subsist upon this same fickle public favor."

"Partially, I grant you; but I ground my claims far deeper than you; I strike down, taking root in the substratum of selfishness. Interest, individual interest, is the outpost of which I am paid to be the sentinel; stern necessity is my guardian angel, compelling all men to see that my wages are inviolate. I stand in the great brain market-place, and deal with mankind in the normal, every-day manifestations of avarice, selfishness, or hate; profit and loss the theme—dollars or blood the currency. M. Quetelet, one of the most eminent statisticians of Europe, has proved that, in a given population, a given number of crimes will annually be committed; so you see that, in this market, also, production keeps pace with consumption, and legal counsel is necessitated. On the contrary, you address yourself to a class of emotions fluctuating and short-lived—common to comparatively few—involving no questions of utility—luxuries, not necessities. Yours is a profession of contingencies; not so mine; for injustice, duplicity, theft, are every-day, settled certainties. A man will give me one-half of his estate to save the other, which the chicane of his neighbor threatens."

"And if that villanous, avaricious neighbor had employed you half an hour before the injured man sought to engage your services?"

"Why, then, the lawyer next in his estimation gets the case, and it is resolved into a simple question of his superior adroitness, acumen, and industry, or mine. The world is hard upon lawyers, its faithful servants, and holds them up as moral monsters to the very children whose mouths their labor fills with bread. An erroneous and most unjust impression prevails that a lawyer of ability, plus extensive practice, equals Bacon, Jeffries, Impey, or some other abnormal disgrace to jurisprudence; whereas, the sole object of the institution of law is to secure right, justice, and truth. You are opening your lips to ask if the last is not often wilfully suppressed? Remember that even the Twelve found a Judas among their number, and the provision of counsel is to elicit truth, and all the truth, on both sides. I bring testimony in defence of all that is susceptible of proof in my client's favor, and it is the business of the opposite counsel to do likewise; if he neglects his duty, or, through lack of intellect, suffers me to gain the case, even against real justice, am I culpable? I did my duty; he failed to defend his cause, however righteous, and on his shoulders rest the turpitude."

"Ah, Russell! you have taken a diploma in the school of sophistry."

"I am content that you should think so, since a recent great historian has decided that the Sophists were a sadly maligned sect, and, instead of becoming a synonyme of reproach, merited the everlasting gratitude of mankind, as the tireless public teachers of Greece—the walking-school system of Athens in her imperial, palmy days."

"I never will believe that! I wish to heaven archæologists would let the dust of Athens rest, instead of ploughing it up periodically with the sacrilegious shares of newfangled theories."

"And thereby exhuming the mouldering bones of some of your favorite divinities, I suppose? The literary philhellenism of the present age, and especially its philologic tendency, is fast hunting the classic spectres of the heroic times into primeval shade. Old-fogyism in literature is considered, I believe, quite as unpardonable as in politics. Take care how you handle the Sophists, for I hold that they differed in but one respect from your hero, Socrates."

"You shall not insult his memory by any such disgraceful association," interrupted his cousin.

"And that difference," he continued, without heeding her, "consists in the fact that they taught for money, while he scorned to accept remuneration. Sydney Smith maintains that 'Socrates invented common-sense two thousand years ago, as Ceres invented the plough, and Bacchus intoxication.' I should receive the *dictum* more readily if he had pocketed the honest wages of his talents, instead of deluding himself with the belief that he was the heaven-appointed regenerator of Athens, and making his labors purely eleemosynary, to the possible detriment of his family. Who knows but that, after all, Xantippe deserved a place in martyrology, having been driven to paroxysms of rage and desperation by an empty purse or wretched household derangements, victimized by her husband's cosmopolitan mission; for it is a notorious fact that men who essay to manage the opinions of the world invariably neglect their domestic affairs, and allow them to run to ruin."

"Five years ago you would not have said that, Russell, and I think it questionable whether you believe it all now. I hold my profession a nobler one than yours, and dispute your predicate that it involves no utility. Whatever tends to exalt, to purify, to ennoble, is surely useful; and æsthetics, properly directed, is one of the most powerful engines of civilization. See what it wrought for Athens."

"You mistake effect for cause. The freedom of Athens was the lever which raised it to such a pitch of glory; as a sequence, the arts flourished and beauty was apotheosized. When freedom perished the arts received their death-blow, and, impotent to preserve the prosperity of the city, shed a lingering halo around its melancholy but majestic ruins. That æsthetics and utility are synonymes is an axiom which might find acceptation in 'Bensalem;' but in this intensely practical, mechanical epoch of human history, and this money-making quarter of the globe, you must educate the masses up to an entirely different level before you can expect them to receive it."

"And, so far as my feeble influence extends, or my limited ability will permit, I purpose to become such a teacher. Do not laugh at me, Russell, I beg of you."

"I smile at the beautiful dream, rather than the enthusiastic dreamer. So, doubtless, dreamed Phidias, Praxiteles, and the Rhodian Trio, and only a few time-corroded blocks of marble remain in attestation. *Cui bono?*"

"Yours and mine!—for dead nations, and for generations yet unborn, who shall gaze upon their noble and imperishable monuments. You are worse than Goth or Vandal, if you can ignore their softening, spiritualizing influence—for even they, rude and untutored, bowed before their immortal beauty. What has come over you, Russell, hardening your nature, and sealing the sources of genial, genuine appreciation?"

"The icy breath of experience, the crystalizing touch of years. You must not be so severe upon me, Electra; many a time, since we parted, I have left my desk to watch a gorgeous sunset, and for a few minutes fancy myself once more leaning on the garden-gate of my early home. I love beauty, but I subordinate it to the practical utilities of life. I have little time for æsthetic musings; I live among disenchanting commonplace realities. It is woman's province and prerogative to gather up the links of beauty, and bind them as a garland round her home; to fill it with the fragrance of dewy flowers, the golden light of western skies, the low soothing strains of music, which can chant all care to rest; which will drown the clink of dollars and cents, and lead a man's thoughts to purer, loftier themes. Ah! there is no apocalypse of joy and peace like a happy home, where a woman of elegance and refinement goes to and fro. This recalls the object of my visit. You say, truly, that full value received for benefit rendered is not charity; apply your principle, come to W——, share my future, and what fortune I may find assigned me. I have bought the cottage, and intend to build a handsome house there some day, where you and Mr. Campbell and I can live peacefully. You shall twine your æsthetic fancies all about it, to make it picturesque enough to suit your fastidious artistic taste. Come, and save me from what you consider my worse than vandalian proclivities. I came here simply and solely in the hope of prevailing on you to return with me. I make this request, not because I think it will be expected of me, but for more selfish reasons—because it is a matter resting very near my heart."

"Oh, Russell! you tempt me."

"I wish to do so. My blood beats in your veins; you are the only relative I value, and were you indeed my sister I should scarcely love you more. With all a brother's interest, why should I not claim a brother's right to keep you with me—at least until you find your Pylades, and give him a higher claim before God and man? Electra, were I your brother you would require no persuasion; why hesitate now?"

She clasped her hands behind her, as if for support in some fiery ordeal, and, gathering up her strength, spoke rapidly, like one who fears that resolution will fail before some necessary sentence is pronounced.

"You are very kind and generous, Russell, and for all that you have offered me I thank you from the depths of a full heart. The consciousness of your continued interest and affection is inexpressibly precious; but my disposition is too much like your own to suffer me to sit down in idleness, while there is so much to be done in the world. I, too, want to earn a noble reputation, which will survive long after I have been gathered to my fathers; I want to accomplish some work, looking upon which, my fellow-creatures will proclaim: 'That woman has not lived in vain; the world is better and happier because she came and labored in it.' I want my name carved, not on monumental marble only, but upon the living, throbbing heart of my age! stamped indelibly on the generation in which my lot is cast. Perhaps I am too sanguine of success; a grievous disappointment may await all my ambitious hopes, but failure will come from want of genius, not lack of persevering, patient toil. Upon the threshold of my career, facing the loneliness of coming years, I resign that hope with which, like a golden thread, most women embroider their future. I dedicate myself, my life, unreservedly to Art."

"You believe that you will be happier among the marble and canvas of Italy than in W—— with me?"

"Yes; I shall be better satisfied there. All my life it has gleamed afar off, a glorious land of promise to my eager, longing spirit. From childhood I have cherished the hope of reaching it, and the fruition is near at hand. Italy! bright *alma mater* of the art to which I consecrate my years. Do you wonder that, like a lonely child, I stretch out my arms toward it? Yet my stay there will be but for a season. I go to complete my studies; to make myself a more perfect instrument for my noble work, and then I shall come home—come, not to New York, but to my own dear native South, to W——, that I may labor under the shadow of its lofty pines and within hearing of its murmuring river—dearer to me than classic Arno or immortal Tiber. I wrote you that Mr. Clifton had left me a legacy, which, judiciously invested, will defray my expenses in Europe, where living is cheaper than in this country. Mr. Young has taken charge of the money for me, and has kindly offered to attend to my remittances. Aunt Ruth's friends, the Richardsons, consented to wait for me until after the opening of the Exhibition of the Academy of Design, and one week from to-morrow we expect to sail."

"What do you know of the family?"

"Nothing, except that the lady, who is an old friend of my aunt, is threatened with consumption, and has been advised to spend a year or two in Florence. Aunt Ruth took me to see her the other day; she seems intelligent and agreeable, and, I dare say, I shall find her kind and pleasant enough."

"Since such is the programme you have marked out, I trust that no disappointments await you, and that all your bright dreams may be realized. But, if it should prove otherwise, and you grow weary of your art, sick of isolation, and satiated with Italy, remember that I shall welcome you home, and gladly share with you all that I possess. You are embarking in an experiment which thousands have tried before you, and wrecked happiness upon; but I have no right to control your future, and certainly no desire to discourage you. At all events, I hope our separation will be brief."

A short silence followed, broken at last by Electra, who watched him keenly as she spoke.

"Tell me something about Irene. Of course, in a small town like W———, you must see her frequently."

"By no means. I think I have seen her but three times since her childhood — once riding with her father, then accidentally at church, and again, a few evenings before I left, at the graveyard, where she was dressing a tombstone with flowers. There we exchanged a few words for the first time, and this reminds me that I am bearer of a message yet undelivered. She inquired after you, and desired me to tender you her love and best wishes."

He neither started nor changed color at the mention of Irene's name, but straightened himself, and buttoned to the throat the black coat, which, from the warmth of the room, he had partially loosened.

"Is she not a great belle?"

"I presume few women have been more admired than she is. I hear much of her beauty and the sensation which it creates wherever she goes; but the number of her suitors is probably limited, from the fact that it is generally known she is engaged to her cousin, young Seymour."

"I can not believe that she loves him."

"Oh! that is not necessary to latter-day matrimonial contracts; it is an obsolete clause, not essential to legality, and utterly ignored. She is bound, hand and foot, and her father will immolate her on the altar of Money."

He smiled bitterly, and crossed his arms over his chest.

"You mistake her character, Russell. I know her better, and I tell you there is none of the Iphigenia in her nature."

"At least I do not mistake her father's, and I pity the woman whose fate rests in his iron grasp."

"She holds hers in her own hands, small and white though they are; and, so surely as the stars shine above us, she will marry only where she loves. She has all the will which has rendered the name of her family proverbial. I have her here in crayons; tell me what you think of the likeness."

She took down a portfolio and selected the head of her quondam playmate, holding it under the gaslight, and still scrutinizing her cousin's countenance. He took it, and looked gravely, earnestly, at the lovely features.

"It scarcely does her justice; I doubt whether any portrait ever will. Beside, the expression of her face has changed materially since this was sketched. There is a harder outline now about her mouth, less of dreaminess in the eyes, more of cold *hauteur* in the whole face. If you desire it, I can, in one line of Tennyson, photograph her proud beauty, as I saw her mounted on her favorite horse the week that I left home:

"'Faultily faultless, icily regular, splendidly null!'"

He laid the drawing back in the open portfolio, crossed the room, and took up his hat.

"Where are you going, Russell? Can't you spend the evening with me at Aunt Ruth's?"

"No, thank you; I must go. There is to be a great political meeting at Tammany Hall tonight, and I am particularly anxious to attend."

"What! are you, too, engaged in watching the fermentation of the political vat?"

"Yes; I am most deeply interested; no true lover of his country can fail to be so at this juncture."

"How long will you be in New York?"

"Since I can not persuade you to return with me, my stay here will be shortened. One of our courts meets soon, and, though Mr. Campbell will be there to attend to the cases, I want, if possible, to be present. I shall return day after to-morrow. And now goodnight; I will see you early in the morning."

The door closed behind him, and she remained standing for some time just as he left her. Slowly the folded hands shrank from each other, and dropped nerveless to her side; the bright glow in her cheeks, the dash of crimson on her lips, faded from both; the whole face relaxed into an expression of hopeless agony. Lonely as Moses when he calmly climbed Nebo to die, she bowed herself a despairing victim upon the grim, flint-fronted altar of Necessity.

Curiously subtle and indomitable is woman's heart—so often the jest of the flippant and unthinking, the sneer of the unscrupulously calculating, or mercilessly cynical. It had long been no secret to this woman that she occupied the third place in her cousin's affections—was but a dweller of the vestibule. Her pride had been tortured, her vanity sorely wounded; yet, to-night, purified from all dross, love rose invincible, triumphant, from the crucible of long and severe trial—sublime in its isolation, asking, expecting no return—

"Self-girded with torn strips of hope."

Such is the love of a true woman. God help all such, in this degenerate world of ours, so cursed with shams and counterfeits.

Raising her tearless, shadowy eyes to the woeful face of her Cassandra, Electra extended her arms and murmured:

"Alone henceforth! a pilgrim in foreign lands! a solitary worker among strangers. So be it! I am strong enough to work alone. So be it!"

The flaming sword of the Angel of Destiny waved her from the Eden of her girlish day-dreams, and by its fiery gleam she read the dim, dun future; saw all—

"The long mechanic pacings to and fro,
The set gray life, and apathetic end."

CHAPTER XXI.

"Don't you know that even granite millstones finally grind themselves into impalpable powder? You give yourself no rest, Aubrey, and human machinery wears rapidly."

"But if the powder ground be golden?"

"The dust is but dust still, despite its glitter, and fills men's eyes and dims their vision like any other dust; ending often in a moral ophthalmia past cure."

"'The plague of gold strikes far and near,
And deep and strong it enters.
This purple clamor which we wear,
Makes madder than the centaur's;
Our thoughts grow blank, our words grow strange,
We cheer the pale gold-diggers;
Each soul is worth so much on 'Change,
And marked, like sheep, with figures.
Be pitiful, O God!'"

"I should really dislike to think that you had become a confirmed, inveterate chrysologist. Take time, Aubrey! take time; you are overworked, and make months press upon your brow more heavily than years on most men's. After all, my dear fellow, as Emerson says, 'Politics is a deleterious profession, like some poisonous handicrafts.' I sometimes feel like drawing a long breath for you; it wearies me to look at you—you are such a concentrated extract of work! work! Simply for this reason, I sent for you to come and take a cup of tea with me."

"I have been too much engaged of late to spare an evening to merely social claims. A man whose life rests at his feet, to be lifted to some fitting pedestal, has little leisure for the luxury of friendly visiting."

The two were in Eric Mitchell's pleasant library. Russell sat in an arm-chair, and the master of the house reclined on a lounge drawn near the hearth. The mellow glow of the lamp, the flash and crackle of the fire, the careless, lazy posture of the invalid, all betokened quiet comfort, save the dark fixed face and erect, restless figure of the guest.

"But, Aubrey, a man who has already achieved so much should be content to rest a while, and move more slowly."

"That depends altogether on the nature and distance of his goal."

"And that goal is—what?"

"Men call it by a variety of names, hoping to escape Lucifer's fate by adroitly cloaking Lucifer's infirmity."

"Yes; and whenever I look at you toiling so ceaselessly, climbing so surely to eminence, I am forcibly reminded of Macaulay's fine passage on the hollowness of political life: 'A pursuit from which, at most, they can only expect, by relinquishing liberal studies and social pleasures, by passing nights without sleep and summers without one glimpse of the beauty of nature, they may attain that laborious, that invidious, that closely-watched slavery which is mocked with the name of power.' You have not asked my opinion of your speech."

"I was not aware that you heard it."

"Of course not, but I read it; and, let me tell you, it was a great speech, a masterly argument, that will make a lasting impression upon the people. It has greatly changed the vote of this county already."

"You mistake appearances; the seed fell in good soil, but party spirit came, as fowls of the air, and devoured them."

"At any rate, it produced a profound impression on public opinion and startled some of our political patriarchs."

"No, a mere transitory effect; they have folded their arms and gone to sleep again. I am, of course, gratified by your favorable appreciation of my effort, but I differ with you as to its result. The ploughshare of naked truth must thoroughly subsoil the mind of the Southern states before the future of the country is realized in any degree; as yet, the surface has been but slightly grazed. The hydra-headed foe of democracy is slowly but certainly coiling around our American eagle, and will crush it, if not scared promptly. But, Mr. Mitchell, the 'flaming brands' are not ready."

"To what hydra do you allude?"

"Demagogism, of course. Cleon was the prototype of a numerous class; the school is flourishing vigorously at the North, and no longer a stranger here. The people must root it out speedily, or the days of our national existence are numbered."

"History proves it an invariable concomitant of democracy; rather a rank offshoot from than antagonistic to it."

"You confound the use and abuse of a system. Civilization is, indisputably, a blessing to our race, yet an abuse of the very improvements and discoveries that constitute its glory entails incalculable sorrow and swells criminal statistics. The march of medical science has induced the administering of deadly poisons with the happiest results, when skilfully directed; yet it sometimes happens that fatal effects follow an overdose. Powerful political levers should be handled judiciously—not thrown into the clutches of ignorant empirics."

"Universal suffrage is not your hobby, then?"

"On the contrary, I hold, with one of the most brilliant statesmen this country ever produced, that 'it is the Greek horse introduced into the citadel of American liberties and sovereignty.'"

"On my honor, I am astounded at hearing you quote and endorse a *dictum* of Hamilton. The millennium can't be far off, when democrats seek illustration from federalism!"

"Bigotry in politics is as indefensible as in religion or science. Truth is a sworn foe to monopolists; is the exclusive right of no one organization or party that ever waxed and waned. I am a democrat; I believe in liberal, enlarged, but not universal suffrage; it is a precious boon, and should be hedged about with cautious restrictions. The creation of the ephori was a sort of compromise measure, a concession to appease the people of Sparta, and, as an extension of the elective franchise, was most deplorable in its results. Universal suffrage always recalls to my mind the pithy criticism of Anacharsis, the Scythian philosopher, on the Solonian code, which lodged too much power in the hands of the people: 'Wise men debate, but fools decide.' Mr. Mitchell, it matters little whether we have one or one hundred million tyrants if our rights are trampled; it is a mere question of taste whether you call the despot Czar, Dictator, or Ballot-box. The masses are electrical, and valuable principles of government should be kept beyond the reach of explosion."

"And, except in a powerful centralization, where could you place them for safety?"

"They are already deposited in the constitution. I would, in order to secure them, extend our naturalization laws so as to restrict the foreign vote, limit the right of suffrage by affixing a property qualification, make the tenure of our judiciary offices for life or good behavior, and lengthen the term of administration of our chief magistrate, thereby diminishing the frequency of popular elections, which, in offering premiums for demagogism, has been a prolific cause of mischief. In examining the statistics of the Northern and Western states recently, and noting the dangerous results of the crude foreign vote, I was forcibly reminded of a passage in Burke's 'Reflections on the French Revolution:' 'Those who attempt to level never equalize. In all societies, consisting of various descriptions of citizens, some description must be uppermost. The levellers, therefore, only change and pervert the natural order of things; they load the edifice of society by setting up in the air what the solidity of the structure requires to be on the ground.' The day is not far distant, I fear, when European paupers, utterly ignorant of our institutions, will determine who shall sit in the presidential chair, and how far the constitution shall be observed. These are grave truths, which the enlightened body of the American people should ponder well; but, instead, they are made mere catch-words for party purposes, and serve only to induce a new scramble for office. It requires no extraordinary prescience to predict that the great fundamental principles of this government will soon become a simple question of arithmetic—will lie at the mercy of an unscrupulous majority. The surging waves of Northern faction and fanaticism already break ominously against our time-honored constitutional dykes, and if the South would strengthen her bulwarks there is no time to be slept or wrangled away."

As he spoke, Russell's eyes fell upon a large oval vase on the mantle-piece filled with rare exotics, whose graceful tendrils were tastefully disposed into a perfumed fringe. Rising, he looked carefully at the brilliant hues, and said, as he bent to inhale their fragrance:

"Where do you grow such flowers at this season?"

"Irene brings them almost every day from the greenhouse on the hill. She takes a peculiar pleasure in arranging them in my vases. I think she stood a half-hour yesterday twining and bending those stems the way she wanted them to hang. They are so brittle that I snap the blossoms off, but in her hands they seem pliable enough."

Russell withdrew the fingers which had wandered caressingly amid the delicate leaves, and, reseating himself, took a book from his pocket.

"Mr. Mitchell, I dare say you recollect a discussion which we had, some months ago, regarding the Homeric unity question? Since that time I have been looking into Payne Knight's views on the subject, and am more than ever convinced that the German theory is incorrect. I will read a portion of his argument, and leave the book for you to examine at your leisure."

"By all means! But I thought your red-tape gyves kept you from archæologic researches?"

"It is true they do bind me tighter than I sometimes relish; but we are all in bondage, more or less, and, since one must submit to tyranny, I prefer a stern master." He drew his chair nearer the lamp and began to read aloud. Nearly a half-hour passed thus, when the library-door was opened hastily and Irene came in, dressed magnificently in party costume. She stood a moment, irresolute and surprised, with her eyes fixed on Russell's, then both bowed silently, and she came to the fire.

"How are you, Uncle Eric? You look flushed—feverish." She laid her cold pearly hand on his forehead and stood at his side.

"Tolerably comfortable, thanks to Mr. Aubrey, who has made me almost forget my headache. You will be fashionably late at the party to-night."

"Yes! as usual; but for a better reason than because I wish to be fashionable. I wanted to know how you were, and, as Father was not quite ready, I came in advance and sent the carriage back for him and Hugh. I was not aware that you were in Mr. Aubrey's hands for the evening. You were reading, I believe; pardon my intrusion, and do not let me interrupt you."

"Sit down, Irene; here, child, where I can look at you. We can both bear such an interruption."

Russell closed the volume, but kept his finger in the leaves, and his fascinated eyes went back to the face and form of the heiress. The dress was of heavy blue silk, with an overskirt and bertha of rich white lace, looped with bunches of violets and geranium leaves. The rippling hair was drawn smoothly over the pure brow and coiled at the back of the head under a blue and silver netting, from which fuchsias of turquoise and pearl hung low on the polished neck. The arms and shoulders gleamed like ivory as the lamplight glowed over her; and, save the firm, delicate crimson lips, there was no stain of color in the cold but superbly beautiful face. It was the first time they had met since that evening at the cemetery, many months before. Lifting her splendid violet eyes, she met his gaze an instant, and, tapping the book, Russell asked, with quiet nonchalance:

"Where do you stand, Miss Huntingdon, in this vexed Wolfian controversy concerning the authorship of the Iliad and Odyssey?"

"I would render unto Cæsar the things that are Cæsar's."

"Equivocal, of course!—a woman's answer," laughed her uncle.

"Explicitly, then, I believe that, as Scott absorbed the crude minstrelsy of Scotland, and reproduced national songs and legends under a fairer, sweeter form, so Homer, grand old blind eclectic, gathered the fragmentary myths of heroic ages, and, clothing them with the melody of wandering Greek rhapsodists, gave to the world his wonderful epic—the first and last specimen of composite poetic architecture."

"You ascribe the Odyssey, then, to a different author and a later period?" asked Mr. Mitchell.

"I am too little versed in philology to determine so grave a question. My acquaintance with Greek is limited, and I am not competent to the task of considering all the evidence in favor of the identity of authorship."

She put on her white cashmere cloak and stood still a moment, listening.

"Good-night, Uncle Eric; the carriage is coming. I believe I should know the tramp of those horses amid a regiment of cavalry."

"Why need you hurry off? Let your father come in."

"I will spare him that trouble. Goodnight, Mr. Aubrey."

She turned to leave the room, but, in gathering her cloak around her, dropped her fan. Russell stooped to pick it up, and, as he restored it, there hands met. His brow flushed, but not even the pale pearly glow of a seashell crept to her cheek. Again she raised her eyes to his, and a haughty, dazzling smile flashed over her face as she inclined her head.

"Thank you, sir."

There was a brief silence, broken by Eric, when the sound of the carriage had died away.

"Irene is the only perfectly beautiful woman I ever saw; and yet, Aubrey, it makes me sad to watch her countenance."

"Whenever I see her I can not avoid recalling an old Scandinavian myth, she realizes so fully my ideal Iduna standing at the portals of Valhalla, offering apples of immortality."

He returned at once to his book and read several pages, occasionally pausing to call attention to some special passage; finally he rose and took his hat.

"It is early yet, Aubrey; don't go."

"Thank you; I must fulfil another engagement."

"A word before you leave; will you be a candidate for the legislature?"

"Yes; I was waited upon by a committee to-day, and my name will be announced to-morrow. Good-night."

Slowly he walked back to town, and, once upon the main street, took a new pair of gloves from his pocket, fitted them carefully, and directed his steps to the elegant residence, whose approach was well-nigh blocked up with carriages. This was the second time that he had been invited by the Hendersons, and he had almost determined to decline as formerly, but something in Irene's chill manner changed his resolution. He knew, from various circumstances, that the social edict against him was being revoked in fashionable circles; that because he had risen without its permission, aid, or countenance, and in defiance of its sneers, the world was beginning to court him. A gloomy scowl sat on his stern lips as he mounted the steps of the mansion from which his meek and suffering mother had borne bundles of plain work, or delicate masses of embroidery, for the mother and daughter who passed her in the street with a supercilious stare. *Beau monde* suddenly awoke to the recollection that, "after all, Mrs. Aubrey belonged to one of the wealthiest and first families in the state." At first Russell had proudly repelled all overtures, but gradually he was possessed by a desire to rule in the very circle which had so long excluded his family. Most fully he appreciated his position and the motives which actuated the social autocrats of W———; he was no longer the poor disgraced clerk, but the talented young lawyer, and prospective heir of Mr. Campbell's wealth. Bitterly, bitterly came memories of early trial, and now the haughtiness of Irene's manner stung him as nothing else could possibly have done. He was at a loss to comprehend this change in one who had dared so much in order to assist his family, and proud defiance arose in his heart. It was ten o'clock; the *fete* was at its height; the sound of music, the shimmer of jewels, and rustle of costly silks mingled with the hum of conversation and the tread of dancing feet as Russell deposited hat and overcoat in the dressing-room and entered the blazing parlors. The quadrille had just ended, and gay groups chattered in the centre of the room; among these, Maria Henderson, leaning on Hugh's arm, and Grace Harris, who had been dancing with Louis Henderson. As Russell crossed the floor to speak to the host and hostess all eyes turned upon him, and a sudden hush fell on the merry dancers.

"Coaxed at last within the pale of civilization! how did you contrive it, Louis?" asked Maria.

"Oh! he declined when I invited him; but I believe father saw him afterward and renewed the request. Do observe him talking to mother; he is as polished as if he had spent his life at court."

"He is a man whom I never fancied; but that two hours speech of his was certainly the finest effort I ever listened to. Cæsar's ambition was moderate in comparison with Aubrey's; and, somehow, even against my will, I can't help admiring him, he is so coolly independent," said Hugh, eyeing him curiously.

"I heard father say that the democrats intend to send him to the legislature next term, and the opposition are bothered to match him fully. By the way, they speak of Mr. Huntingdon for their candidate. But here comes your hero, Miss Maria." As he spoke, Charlie Harris drew back a few steps, and suffered Russell to speak to the young lady of the house. Irene stood not far off, talking to the governor of the state, who chanced to be on a brief visit to W———, and quite near her Judge Harris and her father were in earnest conversation. Astonished at the sudden apparition, her eyes followed him as he bowed to the members of the central group; and, as she heard the deep rich voice above the buzz of small-talk, she waited to see if he would notice her. Soon Governor G——— gave her his arm for a promenade, and she found herself, ere long, very near Maria, who was approaching with Russell. He was saying something at which she laughed delightedly; just then his eye fell on Irene; there was no token of recognition on the part of either; but the governor, in passing, put out his hand to shake Russell's, and asked for Mr. Campbell. Again and again they met during the ensuing hour, but no greeting was exchanged; then he disappeared. As Irene leaned against the window-frame in the crowded supper-room she heard Charlie Harris gaily bantering Maria on the events of the evening.

"What have you done with Aubrey? I will challenge him before to-morrow morning, for cutting me out of my *schottische* with his prosy chat."

"Oh! he left a half-hour ago; excused himself to mother on the plea of starting off to court at daybreak. He is perfectly fascinating; don't you think so, Grace? Such eyes and lips! and such a forehead!"

"Don't appeal to me for corroboration, I beg of you, Maria, for you really gave nobody else an opportunity of judging. Take a friendly hint, and do not betray your admiration so publicly," answered the friend, pouting her pretty childish lip.

"I see clearly that the remainder of us may as well go hang ourselves at once for any future favor we can expect, since My Lord Aubrey condescends to enter the lists. Miss Irene, I have not heard you rhapsodizing yet about the new sensation."

"I rarely rhapsodize about anything, sir."

"To whom does he allude?" asked Governor G———, good-humoredly."

"To Mr. Aubrey, who is no stranger to you, I believe."

"Ah! Campbell's partner. I have had some correspondence with him recently, and when I met him at his office yesterday I was no longer surprised at the tone of his letters. His intellect is one of the keenest in the state; his logical and analytical powers are of the rarest order. I shall watch his career with great interest. Campbell may justly be proud of him."

If she had felt any inclination to reply, the expression of her father's face discouraged her. He had joined them in time to hear the governor's eulogium, and she saw a sneer distort his features as he listened. During the drive homeward Mr. Huntingdon suddenly interrupted a strain of Hugh's nonsense by exclaiming:

"People have certainly lost common-sense! Their memory is not as long as my little finger."

"What is the matter, sir? With what recent proof of imbecility have they favored you?"

"The idea of that upstart wheedling this community is utterly preposterous. His impudence is absolutely astounding. I am astonished that Henderson should give him countenance!"

"The world has strange criteria to determine its verdicts. His father was sentenced to be hung for committing murder; and my uncle, Clement Huntingdon, who deliberately shot a man dead in a duel, was received in social circles as cordially as if his hands were not blood-stained. There was more of palliation in the first case (one of manslaughter), for it was the hasty, accidental work of a moment of passion; in the last a cool, premeditated taking of human life. But the sensitive, fastidious world called one brutal and disgraceful, and the other 'honorable satisfaction,' in which gentlemen could indulge with impunity by crossing state lines. *O tempora! O mores!*"

As Irene uttered these words she involuntarily crushed her bouquet and threw it from her, while Hugh expected an explosion of wrath on the part of his uncle. He merely muttered an oath, however, and smoked his cigar in sullen silence, leaving the cousins to discuss the events of the party during the remainder of the ride.

Once more in his own room, at the quiet boarding-house, Russell lighted the gas-burner over a small desk and sat down to a mass of papers. The apartment was cold; the fire had long since died out; the hearth looked ashy and desolate. There was nothing home-like or cozy in the aspect of the room; the man lived at his office, and this was but a place to pass the brief unconscious hours of sleep. He had no home-life, no social existence; was fast becoming callous, impervious, to the gentler emotions and kindly sympathies which domestic ties foster and develop. No womanly touch left pleasant traces here, as in Eric's home; no graceful, luxurious trifles met the eye; all things were cold and prim and formal. He had no kindred and few friends, but unbounded aspiration stood in lieu of both. Fortunately for him, his great physical strength enabled him to pursue a course of study which men of feebler constitution could never have endured. On the desk lay several volumes, carefully annotated for future reference—Ricardo, Malthus, Say, and Smith. To these he turned, and busied himself in transferring such excerpts as suited his purpose to an unfinished MS. designed for future legislative service. The brilliant smile which lighted his face an hour before, imparting an irresistible charm, had wholly faded, leaving the features to their wonted grave immobility—the accustomed non-committalism of the business-man of the world. The measured tones of the watchman on the town-tower recalled him, finally, from the cold realm of political economy; he closed the books, took off his watch, and wound it up. It wanted but three hours to dawn; but he heeded it not; the sight of the massive old watch brought vividly back the boyish days of sorrow, and he sat thinking of that morning of shame, when Irene came close to him, nestling her soft little hand in his, and from some long-silent, dark, chill chamber of memory leaped sweet, silvery, childish echoes:

"Oh, Russell! if I could only help you!"

With an involuntary sigh he arose, and, walking to the chimney, leaned his elbow on the mantle. But it would not answer; the faint, delicious perfume of violets seemed to steal up from the gray ashes on the hearth, and the passionless, peerless face of a queenly woman followed him from the haunts of fashion. The golden-haired dream of his early youth had lost none of her former witchery: she only shared the mastery of his heart with stern, unrelaxing Ambition, and the gulf which divided them only enhanced the depth, the holiness of his love for her. Since his return from Europe he had accustomed himself to think of her as Hugh's wife; but he found it daily more difficult to realize that she could willingly give her hand to her heedless, self-indulgent cousin; and now the alteration in her manner toward him perplexed and grieved him. Did she suspect the truth, and fear that he might presume on her charity in by-gone years? To his proud spirit this was a suggestion singularly insulting, and he had resolved to show her in future that he claimed not even a nod of recognition. Instead of avoiding her as formerly, he would seek occasions to exhibit an indifference which he little thought that her womanly heart would rightly interpret. He had found it more difficult than he supposed to keep his attention chained to Maria's and Grace's gay nonsense; to prevent his eyes from wandering to the face whose image was enshrined in his lonely heart; and now, with complex feelings of tenderness and angry defiance, he sought his pillow for a short respite before the journey that waited but for daylight.

For a few weeks all W———— was astir with interest in the impending election; newspaper columns teemed with caustic articles, and Huntingdon and Aubrey clubs vilified each other with the usual acrimony of such occasions. Mr. Campbell's influence was extensive, but the Huntingdon supporters were powerful, and the result seemed doubtful until the week previous to the election, when Russell, who had as yet taken no active part, accepted the challenge of his opponent to a public discussion. The meeting was held in front of the court-house, the massive stone steps serving as a temporary rostrum. The night was dark and cloudy, but huge bonfires, blazing barrels of pitch, threw a lurid glare over the broad street, now converted into a surging sea of human heads.

Surrounded by a committee of select friends Mr. Huntingdon sat, confident of success; and when the hiss of rockets ceased, he came forward and addressed the assembly in an hour's speech. As a warm and rather prominent politician, he was habituated to the task, and bursts of applause from his own party frequently attested the effect of his easy, graceful style and pungent irony. Blinded by personal hate, and hurried on by the excitement of the hour, he neglected the cautious policy which had hitherto been observed, and finally launched into a fierce philippic against his antagonist—holding up for derision the melancholy fate of his father, and sneeringly denouncing the " audacious pretensions of a political neophyte."

Groans and hisses greeted this unexpected peroration, and many of his own friends bit their lips and bent their brows in angry surprise, as he took his seat amid an uproar which would have been respectable even in the days of the builders of Babel. Russell was sitting on the upper step, with his head leaning on his hand and his eyes fixed on the mass of upturned, eager faces, listening patiently to the lengthy address, expecting just what he was destined to hear. At the mention of his family misfortunes he lifted his head, rose, and, advancing a few steps, took off his hat and stood confronting the speaker in full view of the excited crowd. And there the red light, flaring over his features, showed a calm, stern, self-reliant man, who felt that he had nothing to blush for in the past or to dread in the future. When the tirade ended, when the tumult ceased and silence fell upon the audience, he turned and fixed his deep, glowing eyes full on the face of his opponent for one moment, smiling haughtily; then, as Mr. Huntingdon quailed before his withering gaze, he crossed his arms over his chest and addressed the meeting.

He came, he said, to discuss questions of grave import to the state, not the pedigree or antecedents of his antagonist, with which, he supposed, the public had no concern. He could not condescend to the level of the gentleman; was not a proficient, not his equal in slang phrases, or gross, vulgar vituperation, and scorned to farther insult the good taste of his hearers by acquainting them with the contemptible motives of individual hatred which had induced his opponent to forget what the rules of good-breeding and etiquette imperatively demanded. He would not continue to disgrace the occasion by any refutation of the exceedingly irrelevant portion of the preceding harangue, which related to purely personal matters and was unworthy of notice, but asked the attention of his hearers, for a few moments, while he analyzed the platform of his party. Briefly he stated the issues dividing the people of the state; warned the opposition of the probable results of their policy, if triumphant; and, with resistless eloquence, pleaded for a firm maintenance of the principles of his own party. He was, he averred, no alarmist, but he proclaimed that the people slept upon the thin heaving crust of a volcano which would inevitably soon burst forth; and the period was rapidly approaching when the Southern states, unless united and on the alert, would lie bound at the feet of an insolent and rapacious Northern faction. He demanded that, through the legislatures, the states should appeal to Congress for certain restrictions and guarantees, which, if denied, would justify extreme measures on the part of the people. The man's marvellous magnetism was never more triumphantly attested; the mass, who had listened in profound silence to every syllable which passed his lips, now vented their enthusiasm in prolonged and vociferous applause and vehement cries of "Go on! go on!" The entire absence of stereotyped rhodomontade rendered his words peculiarly impressive, as he gave them utterance with no visible token of enthusiasm. He did not lash the passions of the populace into a passing phrensy, but effectually stirred the great deep of sober feeling and sound sense. With his elegant, graceful delivery, and polished, sparkling diction, he stood, as it were, on some lofty cool pedestal, and pointed unerringly to coming events, whose shadows had not yet reached them, of which they had not dreamed before, and it was not wonderful that the handsome young speaker became an idol to be worshipped afar off.

As he descended the steps and disappeared amid the shouts of the crowd, Judge Harris turned to Mr. Huntingdon and said, with ill-concealed annoyance:

"You have lost your election by your confounded imprudence."

"That remains to be seen, sir," was the petulant rejoinder.

"It is a foregone conclusion," muttered Dr. Arnold, buttoning his overcoat and looking around for his cane.

"I have sworn a solemn oath that I will trample the upstart out of existence, at least politically!"

"As well try to trample on the stars yonder! Your speech ruined you, I am afraid!"

The judge walked off, pondering a heavy bet which he had relative to the result.

By sunrise on the day of the election the roads leading to town were crowded with voters making their way to the polls. The drinking-saloons were full to overflowing; the sidewalks thronged with reeling groups as the day advanced. Because the Huntingdon side bribed freely, the Aubrey partisans felt that they must, from necessity, follow the disgraceful precedent. Not a lady showed her face upon the street; drinking, wrangling, fighting, was the order of the day. Windows were smashed, buggies overturned, and the police exercised to the utmost. Accompanied by a few friends, Mr. Huntingdon rode from poll to poll, encouraging his supporters and drawing heavily upon his purse, while Russell remained quietly in his office, well assured of the result. At five o'clock, when the town polls closed, Russell's votes showed a majority of two hundred and forty-four. Couriers came in constantly from country precincts, with equally favorable accounts, and at ten o'clock it was ascertained, beyond doubt, that he was elected. Irene and her uncle rode down to learn the truth, and, not knowing where to find Mr. Huntingdon, stopped the carriage at the corner of the main street and waited a few moments. Very soon a rocket whizzed through the air, a band of music struck up before Russell's office, and a number of his adherents insisted that he should show himself on the balcony. A crowd immediately collected opposite, cheering the successful candidate and calling for a speech. He came out, and, in a few happy, dignified words thanked them for the honor conferred, and pledged himself to guard most faithfully the interests committed to his keeping. After the noisy constituents had retired he stood talking to some friends, when he chanced to recognize the fiery horses across the street. The carriage-top was thrown back, and by the neighboring gaslight he saw Irene's white face turned toward him, then the horses sprang off. Mr. Campbell noticed, without understanding, the sudden start and bitter though triumphant smile that crossed his face in the midst of pleasant gratulations.

"Go home, Andrew. I know now what I came to learn."

Irene sank back and folded her mantle closer around her.

"Is Master elected?"

"No."

"Your father's speech, last week, was most unfortunate in every respect," said her uncle, who felt indignant and mortified at the course pursued by his brother-in-law.

"We will not discuss it, if you please, Uncle Eric, as it is entirely useless now."

"Don't you think that Aubrey deserves to succeed?"

"Yes."

Her dreary tone disconcerted him, and he offered no further comment, little suspecting that her hands were pressed hard against her heart and that her voiceless sorrow was: "Henceforth we must be still more estranged; a wider gulf, from this night, divides us."

The din, the tumult of the day, had hushed itself, and deep silence brooded over the sleeping town, when, by the light of the newly-risen moon, Russell leaned upon the little gate and gazed on the neglected cottage, overgrown with vines and crumbling to ruin. A sweet, resigned face smiled at him once more from the clustering tendrils that festooned the broken window, where, in other years, his mother had been wont to sit at work, watching for his return; and, in this hour of his first triumph, as he sought the hallowed spot and thoughts of her long martyrdom, recollection rolled its troubled waves over his throbbing, exultant heart, until the proud head dropped on the folded arms and tears fell upon the mouldering gate.

"Oh, Mother! Mother! if you could have lived to see this day—to share my victory!"*

"Ghost-like I paced round the haunts of my childhood,
Earth seemed a desert I was bound to traverse,
Seeking to find the old familiar faces.
   *   *   *   *   *   *
All, all are gone, the old familiar faces!"

CHAPTER XXII.

'The icy breath of winter, the mild wandering airs of spring, the luxurious *laissez-nous-faire* murmurs of summer, and the solemn moan of autumn had followed each other in rapid succession. Two years rolled on, stained with the tears of many, ringing with the songs and laughter of a fortunate few. The paths of some had widened into sunny pastures, flower-starred, Cridavana meadows; others had grown narrower still, choked with the *débris* of dead hopes, which the tide of time drifted from the far-off glittering peaks of early aspirations. The witchery of Southern spring again enveloped W———, and Irene stood on the lawn surveying the "greenery of the out-door world" that surrounded her. Peach and plum orchards on the slope of a neighboring hill wore their festal robes of promise, and as the loitering breeze stole down to the valley they showered rosy perfumed shells, tiny *avant couriers* of abundant fruitage. The air was redolent with delicate distillations from a thousand flowery laboratories, stately magnolias rustled their polished shimmering leaves, long-haired acacias trailed their fringy shadows over the young wavering grass-blades; and, far above the soft green wilderness of tangled willows, regal pines spread out their wind-harps, glittering in the sunshine like spiculæ of silver. A delicious languor brooded in the atmosphere; the distant narrow valleys were full of purple haze; beyond and above the town, that nestled so peacefully along the river banks, the marble fingers of the cemetery gleamed white and cold; and afar off, and over all, was heard the measured music of factory bells, chanting a hymn to sacred and eternal Labor. With her brown straw hat in one hand and a willow-basket filled with flowers in the other, Irene leaned against the glossy trunk of an ancient wild-cherry tree, and looked in dreamy abstraction down the long shadowy vista of venerable elms. Paragon lay panting on the grass at her feet, now and then snapping playfully at the tame pigeons who had followed their mistress out upon the lawn, fluttering and cooing continually around her; and a few yards off a golden pheasant and two peacocks sunned their gorgeous plumage on the smoothly-cut hedges.

> ".   .   .   Some faces show
> The last act of a tragedy in their regard,
> Though the first scenes be wanting;"

and in this woman's sad but intensely calm countenance a joyless life found silent history. The pale forehead bore not a single line, the quiet mouth no ripple-marks traced by rolling years; but the imperial eyes, coldly blue as the lonely ice-girt Märjelen-See, revealed, in their melancholy crystal depths, the dreary isolation of soul with which she had been cursed from infancy. Her face was an ivory tablet inscribed with hieroglyphics which no social, friendly Champollion had yet deciphered. Satiated with universal homage, weary of the frivolity of the gay circle surrounding her, and debarred from all hope of affectionate, sympathetic intercourse with her father, her real life was apart from the world in which report said that she ruled supreme. She wandered in the primeval temples of nature, and ministered, a solitary priestess, at the silent, blazing shrine of Astronomy. The soft folds of her white muslin dress stirred now and then, and the blue ribbons that looped back her braided hair fluttered like mimic pennons in the breeze; but the clematis bells which clustered around her cameo-pin were unshaken by the slow pulsations of her sad heart. She felt that her life was passing rapidly, unimproved, and aimless; she knew that her years, instead of being fragrant with the mellow fruitage of good deeds, were tedious and joyless, and that the gaunt, numbing hand of *ennui* was closing upon her. The elasticity of spirits, the buoyancy of youth, had given place to a species of stoical mute apathy; a mental and moral paralysis was stealing over her.

The slamming of the ponderous iron gate attracted her attention, and she saw a carriage ascending the avenue. As it reached a point opposite to the spot where she stood it halted, the door was thrown open, and a gentleman stepped out and approached her. The form was not familiar, and the straw hat partially veiled the features, but he paused before her and said, with a genial smile:

"Don't you know me?"

"Oh, Harvey! My brother! My great guardian angel!"

A glad light kindled in her face, and she stretched out her hands with the eagerness of a delighted child. Time had pressed heavily upon him; wrinkles were conspicuous about the corners of his eyes and mouth, and the black hair had become a steely gray. He was not

"A little sunburnt by the glare of life,"

but weather-beaten by its storms; and, in lieu of the idiosyncratic placidity of former days, a certain restlessness of expression betokened internal disquiet. Holding her hands, he drew her nearer to him, scrutinized her features, and a look of keen sorrow crossed his own as he said, almost inaudibly:

"I feared as much! I feared as much! The shadow has spread."

"You kept Punic faith with me, sir; you promised to write and failed. I sent you one letter, but it was never answered."

"Through no fault of mine, Irene; I never received it, believe me. True, I expected to write to you frequently when I parted with you, but subsequently determined that it would be best not to do so. Attribute my silence, however, to every other cause than want of remembrance."

"Your letters would have been a great stay and comfort to me."

"Precisely for that reason I sent none. I knew that you must rely upon yourself; that I could not properly judge of the circumstances which surrounded and influenced you. One, at least, of my promises has been faithfully fulfilled: I have prayed for you as often as for myself in all these years of separation."

"God only knows how I have wanted, how I have needed you, to guide and strengthen me."

She raised the two hands that still held hers and bowed her forehead upon them.

"You had a better Friend, dear child, always near you, who would have given surer guidance and borne all your burdens. What I most dreaded has come to pass. You have forgotten your God."

"No! indeed, no! but He has forsaken me."

"Come and sit down here, and tell me what the trouble is."

He led her to a circular seat surrounding a venerable oak, and placed himself where he could command a full view of her face.

"Mr. Young, you must have had a hard life out West: you have grown old so fast since I saw you. But you have been doing good, and that is sufficient recompense."

"I have, of course, endured some hardships inseparable from such a long sojourn on the frontier, but my labors have been so successful that I forget everything in my great reward. Many a fair June day I have wished that you could see my congregation, as we stood up to sing in a cool shady grove of beech or hackberry, offering our orisons in 'God's first temples.' No brick and mortar walls, but pavements of God's own living green, and dome of blue, and choir of sinless consecrated birds. My little log-cabin in the far West is very dear to me, for around it cluster some of the most precious reminiscences of my life. The greatest of my unsatisfied wants was that of congenial companionship. I betook myself to gardening in self-defence, and finer annuals you never saw than those which I raised on my hill-side. My borders I made of mignonette, and the rusty front of my cabin I draped with beautiful festoons of convolvulus. My hermitage was pleasant enough, though humble indeed."

"Tell me the secret of your quiet contentment. By what spell do you invoke the atmosphere of happy serenity that constantly surrounds you?"

"It is neither occult nor cabalistic; you will find it contained in the few words of Paul: 'Be ye steadfast, unmovable, always abounding in the work of the Lord; forasmuch as ye know that your labor is not in vain in the Lord.' There is nothing recondite in this injunction; all may comprehend and practice it."

"It may seem so to you, who dispense peace and blessings wherever you move; but to me, alone and useless, cut off from such a sphere of labor, it might as well be locked up in Parsee. I thought once that God created every human being for some particular work—some special mission. That, in order that the vast social machinery of the world might move harmoniously, each had his or her allotted duties, in accordance with the great fundamental law of economy—'division of labor.' But, like many other youthful theories, I have been compelled to part with this also."

"Rather hold fast to it, for the precious truth it is. Do you not find, on reflection, that the disarrangement, the confusion in this same social mill proves that some of the human cogs are broken, or out of place, or not rendering their part? I am older than you, and have travelled farther, and I have yet to see the New Atlantis, where every member of society discharges fully the duties assigned.

"'I might say, in a world full of lips that lack bread,
And of souls that lack light, there are mouths to be fed,
There are wounds to be healed, there is work to be done,
And life can withhold love and duty from none!'"

"Irene, 'why stand ye here all the day idle?' Why wait afar off to glean, where you should be a busy reaper in God's whitening harvest-fields?—closing your ears to the eager cry, 'The harvest is plentiful, but the laborers are few!'"

A wintry smile flitted over her lips and she shook her head.

"Ah, sir! long ago I marked out a different programme; but my hands are tied. I am led along another path; I can do nothing now."

"You owe allegiance first to your Maker. What stands between you and your work? Irene, tell me what is this dark cloud that shuts out sunshine from your heart and throws such a chill shadow over your face?"

He drew down the hand with which she shaded her eyes, and bent his head till the gray locks touched her cheek. She did not shrink away, but looked at him steadily, and answered:

"It is a cloud that enveloped me from the hour of my birth, and grows denser each year; I can neither escape from nor dissipate it. It will not break in storms and clear away; but, perchance, as I go down to my tomb the silver lining may show itself. The sun was eclipsed when I first opened my eyes in this world, and my future was faithfully adumbrated. I am not superstitious, but I can not be blind to the striking analogy—the sombre symbolism."

His grave face was painfully convulsed as he listened to her, and it was with difficulty that he restrained himself from drawing the head to his shoulder and revealing all the depth and strength of love which had so long ruled his heart and saddened his life. But he merely enclosed her hand in both his with a gentle pressure, and said:

"Carry out your metaphor, and at least you must admit that, though the sun was eclipsed, stars come out to light you."

"But, at best, one shivers and gropes through the cold light of stars, and mine have all set in a clouded sky. You only are left to me; you shine on me still, undimmed, all the brighter for my gloom. Oh! if I could have you always. But as well stretch out my hands to clutch the moon."

He started, and looked at her wistfully, but the utter passionlessness of her face and manner showed him all too plainly the nature of her feelings and her ignorance of his own.

"Irene, you deal in similies and vague generalities. Has absence shaken your confidence in me? Be frank; tell me what this haunting trouble is, and let me help you to exorcise it."

"You can not. All the Teraphim of the East would not avail. Let it suffice that, many years since, I displeased my father in a trifling matter; and, as I grew older, my views and wishes conflicted with his. I disappointed a darling plan which he had long cherished, and we are estranged. We live here, father and daughter, in luxury; we give and go to parties and dinners; before the world we keep up the semblance of affection and good feeling; but he can not, will not, forgive me. I have ceased to ask or to expect it; the only possible condition of reconciliation is one to which I can never consent; and, for more than two years, he has scarcely spoken to me except when compelled to do so. I pass my days in a monotonous round, wishing for tomorrow, and my nights yonder, among the stars. I have little money to dispense in charity; I dress richly, but the materials are selected by my father, who will have my clothing of the costliest fabrics, to suit his elegant and fastidious taste. Though an only child, and presumptive heiress of one of the finest estates at the South, I have not a dime in the world which I can call my own, except a small sum which he voluntarily allows me per annum. Mark you, I do not complain of my father—

for, in the twinkling of an eye, I could change this unnatural position of affairs in my home ; I only mention some stern facts to prove to you that my hands are tied. It was once the fondest desire of my life to expend the fortune that I supposed belonged to me in alleviating suffering and want, and making people happy around me ; but, like other dewy sparkles of childhood, this hope vanished as the heat and strife of life overtook me."

She spoke in a low, measured tone, unshaken by emotion, and the expression of dreary abstraction showed that she had long accustomed herself to this contemplation of her lot. The minister was deeply moved as he watched her beautiful calm features, so hushed in their joylessness, and he passed his hand across his eyes to wipe away the moisture that so unwontedly dimmed them. He pressed her fingers to his lips and said, encouragingly:

"'Lift thyself up! oh, thou of saddened face!
Cease from thy sighing, draw from out thy heart
The joyful light of faith.'"

"You asked me once to be your brother; my dear child, let me prove myself such now; let me say that, perhaps, it is your duty to yield obedience to your father's wishes, since this deplorable alienation results from your refusal. You never can be happy, standing in this unnatural relation to an only parent. Because it is painful, and involves a sacrifice on your part, should you consider it any the less your duty? Has he not a right to expect that his wishes should guide you?"

She rose instantly, and, withdrawing her hands, folded them together and replied, with an indescribable mingling of *hauteur* and sorrow:

"Has he a right to give my hand to a man whom I do not love? Has he a right to drag me to the altar, and force me to swear to ' love and honor' one whom I can not even respect? Could you stand by and see your father doom your sister to such a miserable fate? I would consent to die for my father to-morrow, if thereby I might make him happy; but I can not endure to live, and bring upon myself the curse of a loveless marriage; and, God is my witness, I never will!"

Her eyes gleamed like blue steel, and the stern, gem-like features vividly reminded him of a medal of the noble Medusa which he had frequently examined and admired while in Rome. In that brief flash he saw, with astonishment, that beneath the studiedly calm exterior lay an iron will, and a rigidity of purpose which he had never conjectured belonged to her character.

"Forgive me, Irene; I retract my words. Ignorant of the nature of the demand, I should not have presumed to counsel you. Keep true to the instincts of your own heart, and you will never go far astray in the path of duty. May God bless and comfort you! Other friends can lend you no assistance in these peculiar circumstances."

He could not trust himself to say more, for feelings too painful for utterance stirred the depths of his soul.

For some moments silence reigned; then, standing before him, Irene said, with touching pathos:

"My friend, I am so desolate! so lonely! I am drifting down the current of life aimless, hopeless, useless! What shall I do with my future? I believe I am slowly petrifying; I neither suffer nor enjoy as formerly; my feelings are deadened; I am growing callous, indifferent to everything. I am fast losing sympathy for the sorrows of others, swallowed up in self, oblivious of the noble aspirations which spanned the early years like a bow of promise. I am cut off from companionship; have no friend, save an uncle, to whom I could put out my hand for support. People talk of the desolation of Western wilds and Eastern deserts; but, oh! God knows there is no isolation comparable to that of a woman who walks daily through halls of wealth and gay salons, knowing that no human being understands or truly sympathizes with her. My prophet! as you long ago foretold, I am 'treading the wine-press alone.' Once more I ask you, what shall I do with my life?"

"Give it to God."

"Ah! there is neither grace nor virtue in necessity. He will not accept the worthless thing thrown at His feet as a *dernier ressort*. Once it was my choice, but the pure, clear-eyed faith of my childhood shook hands with me when you left me in New York."

For a short while he struggled with himself, striving to overcome the unconquerable impulse which suddenly prompted him, and his face grew pallid as hers as he walked hastily across the smooth grass and came back to her. Her countenance was lifted toward the neighboring hill, her thoughts evidently far away, when he paused before her and said, unsteadily:

"Irene, my beloved! give yourself to me. Go with me into God's vineyard; let us work together, and consecrate our lives to His service."

The mesmeric eyes gazed into his, full of wonder, and the rich ruby tint fled from her lips as she pondered his words in unfeigned astonishment, and, shaking her regal head, answered slowly:

"Harvey, I am not worthy. I want your counsel, not your pity."

"Pity! you mistake me. If you have been ignorant so long, know now that I have loved you from the evening you first sat in my study looking over my foreign sketches. You were then a child, but I was a man, and I knew all that you had so suddenly become to me. Because of this great disparity in years, and because I dared not hope that one so tenderly nurtured could ever brave the hardships of my projected life, I determined to quit New York earlier than I had anticipated, and to bury a foolish memory in the trackless forests of the far West. I ought to have known the fallacy of my expectation; I have proved it since. Your face followed me; your eyes met mine at every turn; your glittering hair swept on every breeze that touched my cheek. I battled with the image, but it would not avail; I resolved not to write to you, but found that the dearest part of my letters from home consisted of the casual allusions which they contained to you. Then came tidings from Louisa that you were probably married—had long been engaged to your cousin; and, though it wrung my heart to think of you as the wife of another, I schooled myself to hope that, for your sake, it might be true. But years passed; no confirmation reached me; and the yearning to look on your dear face once more took possession of me. My mother wrote, urging me to visit her this summer, and I came out of my way to hear of and to see you. The world sneers at the possibility of such love as mine, and I doubt not that it is very rare among men; but, through all the dreary separation, I have thought of you as constantly, and fondly, and tenderly as when I first met you in my father's house. Irene, you are young, and singularly beautiful, and I am a gray-haired man, much, much older than yourself; but, if you live a thousand years, you will never find such affection as I offer you now. There is nothing on earth which would make me so happy as the possession of your love. You are the only woman I have ever seen whom I even wished to call my wife—the only woman who, I felt, could lend new charm to life and make my quiet hearth happier by her presence. Irene, will you share my future? Can you give me what I ask?"

The temptation was powerful—the future he held out enticing indeed. The strong, holy, manly love, the noble heart and head to guide her, the firm, tender hand to support her, the constant, congenial, and delightful companionship—all this passed swiftly through her mind; but, crushing all in its grasp, came the memory of one whom she rarely met, but who held undisputed sway over her proud heart.

Drawing close to the minister, she laid her hands on his shoulder, and, looking reverently up into his fine face, said, in her peculiarly sweet clear voice:

"The knowledge of your priceless, unmerited love makes me proud beyond degree; but I would not mock you by the miserable and only return I could make you—the affection of a devoted sister. I would gladly, thankfully go with you to your Western home, and redeem my past by my future—but, as your wife, I could not; and, without the protection of your honored name, it would not be permitted me to accompany you. I look up to you as to no other human being; I revere and love you, Harvey; and, oh! I wish that I could pass my life at your side, cheered by your smile, doing some good in the world. That I do not love you as you wish is my great misfortune; for I appreciate most fully the noble privilege you have tendered me. I do not say what I earnestly wish could happen, that you will find some one else who can make you happy, because I feel that no woman whom I have ever met is worthy of being your wife. But I trust that the pain I may give you now will soon pass away, and that, in time, you will forget one who is utterly undeserving of the honor you have conferred on her to-day. Oh, Harvey! do not. I beg of you. let one thought of me ever disquiet your noble, generous heart."

A shiver crept over her still face, and she drooped her pale forehead. She felt two tears fall upon her hair, and in silence he bent down and kissed her softly, tenderly, as one kisses a sleeping babe.

"Oh, Harvey! do not let it grieve you, dear friend!"

He smiled sadly, as if not daring to trust himself in words; then, after a moment, laying his hands upon her head, in the baptism of a deathless love, he gently and solemnly blessed her. When his fingers were removed she raised her eyes, but he had gone; she saw only the retreating form through the green arches of the grand old avenue.

"Unlike are we, unlike. O princely heart!
Unlike our uses and our destinies.
Our ministering two angels look surprise
On one another as they strike athwart
Their wings in passing.
The chrism is on thine head—on mine the dew,
And death must dig the level where these agree."

CHAPTER XXIII.

Says D'Alembert: "The industry of men is now so far exhausted in canvassing for places that none is left for fulfilling the duties of them;" and the history of our government furnishes a melancholy parallel. The regular quadrennial storm had swept over the nation; caucuses had been held and platforms fiercely fought for, to be kicked away, plank by plank, when they no longer served as scaffolding by which to climb to office. Buchanan was elected, but destined to exemplify, during his administration, the truth of Tacitus' words: "He was regarded as greater than a private man whilst he remained in privacy, and would have been deemed worthy of governing if he had never governed." The heat of the canvass cooled, people settled down once more to a condition of lethargic indifference—bought and sold, sowed and reaped, as usual—little realizing that the temporary lull, the perfect calm, was treacherous as the glassy green expanse of waters which, it is said, sometimes covers the location of the all-destroying mælstrom of Moskoe. Having taken an active and prominent part in the presidential campaign, and made frequent speeches, Russell found himself again opposed by Mr. Huntingdon, who was equally indefatigable during the exciting contest. The old feud received, if possible, additional acrimony, and there were no bounds to the maledictions heaped upon the young and imperturbable legislator by his virulent antagonist. Many predicted a duel or a street rencounter; but weeks passed, and though, in casual meetings, Mr. Huntingdon's glare of hate was always answered by a mocking smile of cold disdain, the cloud floated off without breaking into bloody showers.

Mr. Mitchell's health had failed so rapidly, as winter approached, that Dr. Arnold persuaded him to try the efficacy of a sea-voyage, and he had accordingly sailed from New Orleans in a vessel bound for Genoa. Irene begged the privilege of accompanying him, but her father peremptorily refused; and she saw her uncle depart, and superintended the closing of his house, with silent sorrow, and the feeling of one who knows that the night is deepening around her. In the course of the political cataclysm much chaff came to the surface, and whirled along with portentous alacrity; gossip seemed to have received a new impetus, and among the most important *on-dits* was that of Irene's speedy marriage to her cousin. Hundred-tongued rumor was busy, too, with the mysterious fact that Russell had placed a handsome iron railing around the humble home of his boyhood; had removed the little three-roomed crumbling dwelling and planted shade-trees. Much curiosity was excited, and the only plausible solution at which the kindly inquiring public arrived was that he intended to marry somebody. But whom? He occasionally visited at Judge Harris' and Mr. Henderson's, and, as he had been seen last at the house of the former, by a species of not very abstruse ratiocination it was finally decided, and promulgated as a social edict, that the talented young lawyer would soon claim Grace's hand at the altar. In less than twenty-four hours all of fashionable W———— had discussed the young lady's brilliant future, and were ready to tender their congratulations to the ambitious man, who was utterly unconscious of the commotion which his individual plans and actions had induced. This insatiable mania for obtaining information about other people's affairs and purposes, this ridiculous and contemptible tittle-tattle, this news mongering, scandal-peddling proclivity, characteristic of cities, towns, villages, and even country neighborhoods, should certainly have been included by the Massachusetts seer in his catalogue of "social inflictions which the magistrate can not cure or defend you from, and which must be intrusted to the restraining force of custom, and proverbs, and familiar rules of behavior impressed on young people in their school-days;" and I trust I may be allowed the additional suggestion, "by mothers around the hearthstone." But, unfortunately, the admirable adage, "*il faut attendre le boiteux*," finds no acceptation in *beau monde*.

Late in the afternoon of Christmas-day Irene went into the greenhouse to gather a bouquet for an invalid friend in town, and had almost accomplished her errand when the crash and whir of wheels drew her to the window that looked out upon the lawn. Her father had gone to the plantation early that morning, and she had scarcely time to conjecture whom the visitor would prove, when Hugh's loud voice rang through the house, and, soon after, he came clattering in, with the end of his pantaloons crammed into his boots and his whip trailing along in true boyish fashion. As he threw down his hat, scattering the petals of a snowy camellia, and drew near his cousin, she saw that his face was deeply flushed and his eyes somewhat bloodshot.

"Hugh! what are you doing here? Father expected you to overtake him at Crescent Bend; you said last night that you would start by five o'clock."

"Merry Christmas, my beauty! I have come for my Christmas gift. Give it to me, like the queen you are."

He stooped, as if to kiss her, but she shrank back instantly and said, gravely:

"You ought not to make promises which you have no idea of keeping; Father will be annoyed, and wonder very much what has happened. He was anxious that you should go with him."

"Oh! confound the plantation! I wish it would sink! Of all other days none but Christmas will suit him to tramp down there through mud and mire. The fact is, I did not go to sleep till four o'clock, and nobody ought to be unchristian enough to expect me to wake up in an hour. You may be quiet, though, for I am on my way now to that paradise of black mud. I only stopped to get a glimpse of you, my Sappho! my Corinna! so don't homilize, I pray you."

"Better wait till daylight, Hugh; you know the state of the roads and condition of the bridges. It will be safer, and an economy of time, to defer it till morning, since you have made it so late."

"No; I must go to-night, for I have an engagement to ride with Maria Henderson, and I can't get back in time if I wait till to-morrow morning. I want to start back day after to-morrow. As for time, Wildfire will make it the better for the darkness; he is as much afraid of night and shadows as if he had a conscience, and had maltreated it, master-like. I shall convince him that all Tam O'Shanter's witches are in full pursuit and his matchless heels his only salvation."

A shade of apprehension settled on her face, and, placing the bouquet in a basket, she turned to her cousin, saying:

"Indeed, you can not be insane enough to drive that horse such a night as this weather threatens. If go you will, in the face of a coming rain, leave Wildfire here, and drive one of the carriage-horses instead. I shall be uneasy if you start with that vicious, unmanageable incarnation of lightning. Let me ring the bell and direct Andrew to make the change."

She stepped into the parlor adjoining and laid her fingers on the bell-cord, but he snatched up the hand and kissed it several times.

"No! I'll be hanged if I don't drive my own pearl of Arabia! I can manage him well enough; and, beside, what do you care whether he breaks my neck or not? Without compunction you broke my heart, which is much the greater catastrophe."

"Come into the library; you don't know what you are saying."

She drew him into the room, where a warm fire burned cheerfully, and made him sit down.

"Where did you go last night when you left here? Tell me."

"To Harry Neal's; a party of us were invited there to drink eggnog, and, of course, found something stronger afterward. Then we had a game or so of poker, and ——, the grand *finale* is, that I have had a deuced headache all day. Ah, my sweet saint! how shocked you are, to be sure! Now, don't lecture, or I shall be off like a flash."

Without answering, she rang the bell and quietly looped back the heavy crimson curtains.

"What is that for? Have you sent for John or old Nellie to carry me up stairs, like other bad boys sent to bed in disgrace, without even the cold comfort of supper?"

"Hush, Hugh! hush."

Turning to John, who opened the door and looked in, she said:

"Tell William to make some strong coffee as soon as possible. Mass' Hugh has a headache, and wants some before he leaves."

"Thank you, my angel! my unapproachable Peri! Ugh! how cold it is. Pardon me, but I really must warm my feet."

He threw them carelessly on the fender of the grate.

"Shall I get you a pair of slippers?"

"Could not afford the luxury; positively have not the time to indulge myself."

With a prolonged yawn he laid his head back and closed his eyes. An expression of disgust was discernible in his companion's countenance, but it passed like the shadow of a summer cloud, and she sat down at the opposite side of the fireplace, with her eyes bent upon the hearth and the long silky lashes sweeping her cheeks. A silence of some minutes ensued; finally Hugh rapped startlingly on his boot with the ivory handle of his whip, and exclaimed:

"A Quaker-meeting is no part of my programme! What the mischief are you thinking about?—looking as solemn as an archbishop in canonicals!"

"Do you really want to know what I am thinking of?"

"Of course I do, if it is not something as supernal and far-off as the stars, which you have taken under your special protection and patronage."

"I was thinking of a passage which I read yesterday, and wishing that it could be framed and hung up in every dwelling. Emerson says: 'Goethe said well, "nobody should be rich but those who understand it." They should own who can administer, not they who hoard and conceal; not they who, the greater proprietors they are, are only the greater beggars; but they whose work carves out work for more, opens a path for all. For he is the rich man in whom the people are rich, and he is the poor man in whom the people are poor; and how to give all access to the masterpieces of art and nature is the problem of civilization.' Weighed in this balance, how many of our millionaires, think you, would find Belshazzar's warning traced on their walls?"

"All of which, I suppose, I am to interpret into a polite circumlocutory way of telling me that I am a worthless spendthrift, squandering away a fortune which I don't deserve, and a disgrace to my fair cousinly Lady Bountiful? When do you contemplate mounting a pedestal, marble image that you are, folding those incomparable hands of yours, and encouraging idolatry? I promise you I shall fall down and worship most irreproachably. But, seriously, Irene, if you do not admire my style of living, why don't you take me in hand, as is your privilege, and make me a model of strait-laced propriety?"

"You might, with very great advantage to yourself, take a little common-sense in hand. Of course, Hugh, you are your own master, but it frequently pains me to see you throwing away your life and privileges so recklessly. You might do a vast amount of good with your money, if you felt disposed to employ it benevolently and judiciously."

"Well, whose fault is it? I offered to make you my banker, and let you dispense charities for both of us, and you snatched back your dainty fingers in haughty refusal. If I play Prodigal to the end of the chapter, you are responsible for it."

"Begging your pardon, sir, I am no scapegoat for any of your shortcomings. Shoulder your own peccadilloes, if you please. But here comes your coffee. Put the waiter on the table, John, and tell Andrew to take Mass' Hugh's buggy."

"Do nothing of the kind! but send somebody to open that everlasting gate, which would not have disgraced ancient Thebes. Are you classical, John? Be off, and see about it; I must start in five minutes."

"Hugh, be reasonable for once in your life; you are not in a proper condition to drive that horse. For my sake, at least, be persuaded to wait till morning. Will you not remain, to oblige me?"

"Oh, hang my condition! I tell you I must and I will go, if all the stars fall and judgment-day overtakes me on the road. What splendid coffee you always have! The most fastidious of bashaws could not find it in his Moorish heart to complain."

He put on his hat, buttoned his costly fur coat, and, flourishing his whip, came close to his cousin.

"Good-by, Beauty. I hate to leave you; upon my word I do; but duty before pleasure, my heavenly-eyed monitress. I have not had my Christmas present yet, and have it I will."

"On one condition, Hugh: that you drive cautiously and moderately, instead of thundering down hills and over bridges like some express-train behind time. Will you promise?"

"To be sure I will! everything in the world; and am ready to swear it, if you are sceptical."

"Well then, good-by, Hugh, and take care of yourself."

She allowed him to press his hot lips to hers, and, accompanying him to the door, saw him jump into the frail open-topped buggy. Wildfire plunged and sprang off in his usual style, and, with a crack of the whip and wave of his hat, Hugh was fairly started.

Seven hours later Irene sat alone at the library table, absorbed in writing an article on Laplace's Nebular Theory for the scientific journal to which she occasionally contributed over the signature of "Sabæan." Several books, with close "marginalias," were scattered around, and the "Mécanique Céleste" and a volume of "Cosmos" lay open before her. The servants had gone to rest; the house was very still, the silence unbroken save by the moan of the wind and the melancholy tapping of the poplar branches against the outside. The sky was black, gloomy as Malbolge; and, instead of a hard, pattering rain, a fine, cold mist drizzled noiselessly down the panes. Wrapped in her work, Irene wrote on rapidly till the clock struck twelve. She counted the strokes, saw that there remained but one page uncopied, and concluded to finish the MS. At last she affixed her *nom de plume*, numbered the pages, and folded the whole for transmission. The fire was still bright; and, with no inclination to go to sleep, she replaced the books on their respective shelves, turned up the wick of the lamp, and sat down close to the grate to warm her stiffened fingers. Gradually her thoughts wandered from the completed task to other themes of scarcely less interest. The week previous she had accompanied Hugh to an operatic concert given by the Parodi troupe, and had been astonished to find Russell seated on the bench in front of her. He so rarely showed himself on such occasions, that his appearance elicited some comment. They had met frequently since the evening at Mr. Mitchell's, but he pertinaciously avoided recognizing her; and, on this particular night, though he came during an interlude to speak to Grace Harris, who sat on the same row of seats with Irene, he never once directed his eyes toward the latter. This studied neglect, she felt assured, was not the result of the bitter animosity existing between her father and himself; and though it puzzled her for a while, she began finally to suspect the true nature of his feelings, and, with woman's rarely-erring instincts, laid her finger on the real motive which prompted him. The report of his engagement to Grace had reached her some days before, and now it recurred to her mind like a haunting spectre. She did not believe for an instant that he was attached to the pretty, joyous girl whom rumor gave him; but she was well aware that he was ambitious of high social position, and feared that he might possibly, from selfish, ignoble reasons, seek an alliance with Judge Harris' only daughter, knowing that the family was one of the wealthiest and most aristocratic in the state. She recollected, with unutterable scorn, the frequent sneers at his blind mother, in which Grace, Charlie, and even Mrs. Harris had indulged in the season of trial and adversity; and, pondering all that she had silently endured because of her sympathy with him and his mother, a feeling of bitterness, heretofore unknown, rose in her heart. True, impassable barriers divided them; but she could not endure the thought of his wedding another—it tortured her beyond all expression. With a suffocating sensation she unfastened the cameo-pin that held her *robe de chambre* at the throat, and threw back the collar. Taking out her comb, she shook down her hair, gathered it up in her hands, and tossed it over the back of her chair, whence it fell to the floor, coiling there in glittering rings. Life had seemed dreary enough before; but, with this apprehension added, it appeared insupportable, and she was conscious of a degree of wretchedness never dreamed of or realized heretofore. Not even a sigh escaped her; she was one of a few women who permit no external evidences of suffering, but lock it securely in their own proud hearts, and in silence and loneliness go down into the "ghoul-haunted," darkened chambers to brood over it, as did the Portuguese monarch the mouldering remains of his murdered wife. The painful reverie might, perhaps, have lasted till the pallid dawn looked in with tearful eyes at the window, but Paragon, who was sleeping on the rug at her feet, started up and growled. She raised her head and listened, but only the ticking of the clock was audible, and the wailing of the wind through the leafless poplars.

"Down, Paragon! hush, sir!"

She patted his head soothingly, and he sank back a few seconds in quiet, then sprang up with a loud bark. This time she heard an indistinct sound of steps in the hall, and thought: "Nellie sees my light through the window, and is coming to coax me up stairs." Something stumbled near the threshold, a hand struck the knob as if in hunting for it, the door opened softly, and, muffled in his heavy cloak, holding his hat in one hand, Russell Aubrey stood in the room. Neither spoke, but he looked at her with such mournful earnestness, such eager yet grieved compassion, that she read some terrible disaster in his eyes. The years of estrangement, all that had passed since their childhood, was forgotten; studied conventionalities fell away at sight of him standing there, for the first time, in her home. She crossed the room with a quick, uncertain step, and put out her hands toward him—vague, horrible apprehension blanching the beautiful lips, which asked shiveringly:

"What is it, Russell? what is it?"

He took the cold little hands tremblingly in his, and endeavored to draw her back to the hearth, but she repeated:

"What has happened? Is it Father, or Hugh?"

"Your father is well, I believe; I passed him on the road yesterday. Sit down, Miss Huntingdon; you look pale and faint."

Her fingers closed tightly over his; he saw an ashen hue settle on her face, and, in an unnaturally calm, low tone, she asked:

"Is Hugh dead? Oh, my God! why don't you speak, Russell?"

"He did not suffer much; his death was too sudden."

Her face had such a stony look that he would have passed his arm around her, but could not disengage his hand; she seemed to cling to it as if for strength.

"Won't you let me carry you to your room, or call a servant? You are not able to stand."

She neither heeded nor heard him.

"Was it that horse; or how was it?"

"One of the bridges had been swept away by the freshet, and, in trying to cross, he missed the ford. The horse must have been frightened and unmanageable, the buggy was overturned in the creek, and your cousin, stunned by the fall, drowned instantly; life was just extinct when I reached him."

Something like a moan escaped her as she listened.

"Was anything done?"

"We tried every means of resuscitation, but they were entirely ineffectual."

She relaxed her clasp of his fingers and moved toward the door.

"Where are you going, Miss Huntingdon? Indeed you must sit down."

"Russell, you have brought him home; where is he?"

Without waiting for an answer, she walked down the hall and paused suddenly at sight of the still form resting on a gray travelling-blanket, with a lantern at his head and an elderly man, a stranger, sitting near, keeping watch. Russell came to her side, and, drawing his arm around her, made her lean upon him. He felt the long, long lingering shudder which shook the elegant, queenly figure; then she slipped down beside the rigid sleeper and smoothed back from the fair brow the dripping curling auburn hair.

"Hugh, my cousin! my playmate! Snatched away in an hour from the life you loved so well. Ah! the curse of our house has fallen upon you. It is but the beginning of the end. Only two of us are left, and we, too, shall soon be caught up to join you."

She kissed the icy lips which a few hours before had pressed hers so warmly, and, rising, walked up and down the long hall. Russell leaned against the wall, with his arms crossed over his chest and his head bent low, waiting for her to speak again. But, calm and tearless, she walked on and on, in profound silence, till he grew restless at the strange sound of her hair trailing along the oil-cloth, and once more approached her.

"Are you entirely alone?"

"Yes, except the servants. Oh, Russell! how am I to break this to my father? He loves that boy better than everything else; infinitely better than he ever loved me. How shall I tell him that Hugh is dead—dead?"

"A messenger has already gone to inform him of what has happened, and this distressing task will not be yours. Herbert Blackwell and I were riding together, on our return from T——, when we reached the ford where the disaster occurred. Finding that all our efforts to resuscitate were useless, he turned back, and went to your father's plantation to break the sad intelligence to him."

His soothing, tender tone touched some chord deep in her strange nature, and unshed tears gathered for the first time in her eyes.

"As you have no friend near enough to call upon at present, I will, if you desire it, wake the servants, remain, and do all that is necessary until morning."

"If you please, Russell; I shall thank you very much."

As her glance fell upon her cousin's gleaming face her lip fluttered, and she turned away and sat down on one of the sofas in the parlor, dropping her face in her hands. A little while after the light of a candle streamed in, and Russell came with a cushion from the library lounge and his warm cloak. He wrapped the latter carefully about the drooping form, and would have placed her head on the silken pillow, but she silently resisted without looking up, and he left her. It was a vigil which she never forgot; the slow hours crushed her as they rolled, the very atmosphere seemed filled with the curse which brooded inexorably over the ancient house, and when, at last, the eastern sky blanched, and the wan forehead of the day lifted itself sadly up, it seemed, indeed, as if—

> "The dim red morn had died, her journey done,
> And with dead lips smiled at the twilight plain,
> Half-fallen across the threshold of the sun,
> Never to rise again."

Shaking off her covering, Irene passed into the greenhouse and broke clusters of jasmine and spicy geranium leaves, and, thus engaged, her glance fell upon the dashed camellia petals which Hugh had ruined so recklessly the previous evening. They seemed fitting symbols, as they lay in withering heaps, of the exuberant life so suddenly cut short—the gay, throbbing heart so unexpectedly stilled.

> "* * * Life struck sharp on death,
> Makes awful lightning."

And she felt a keen pang at sight of his cambric handkerchief, which had been dropped unconsciously between two branching fuchsias. As she stooped and picked it up his name stared at her, and the soft folds gave out the powerful breath of bergamot, of which he was particularly fond. She turned away from the wealth of beauty that mocked her sorrow, and walk on to the library.

The fire had died out entirely, the curtains were drawn back to let in the day, on the library-table the startling glare of white linen showed the outlines of the cold young sleeper, and Russell slowly paced the floor, his arms crossed, as was their habit, and his powerful form unweariedly erect. She stood by the table, half-irresolute, then folded down the sheet and exposed the handsome, untroubled face. She studied it long and quietly, and with no burst of emotion laid her flowers against his cheek and mouth, and scattered the geraniums over his pulseless heart.

"I begged him not to start yesterday, and he answered that he would go, if the stars fell and judgment-day overtook him. Sometimes we are prophets unawares. His star has set—his day has risen! Have mercy on his soul! oh, my God!"

The voice was low and even, but wonderfully sweet, and in the solemn morning-light her face showed itself gray and bloodless; no stain of color on the still lips, only the blue cord standing out between the brows, sure signet of a deep distress which found no vent. Russell felt a crushing weight lifted from his heart; he saw that she had "loved her cousin, cousinly—no more;" and his face flushed when she looked across the table at him, with grateful but indescribably melancholy eyes, which had never been closed during that night of horror.

"I have come to relieve you, Russell, from your friendly watch. Few would have acted as you have done, and for all your generous kindness to poor Hugh I thank you most earnestly, as well for my father as myself. The day may come, perhaps, when I shall be able to prove my gratitude and the sincerity of my friendship, which has never wavered since we were children together. Until that day, farewell, Russell; but believe that I rejoice to hear of your successes."

She held out her hand, and, as he took it in his, which trembled violently, he felt, even then, that there was no quiver in the icy white fingers, and that his name rippled over her lips as calmly as that of the dead had done just before. She endured his long, searching gaze, like any other Niobe, and he dropped the little pearly hand and quitted the room. She heard his quick step ring changes down the long hall and stony steps, and, when all was still again, she knelt beside the table, and crossing her arms over it, bowed her face upon them. Now and then the servants looked in, but crept away awed, closing the door stealthily; and as the day advanced, and the news of what had happened flew through the town, friends came to offer assistance and condolence. But none dared disturb or address the kneeling figure, veiled by waving hair and giving no more sign of life than the form before her. At ten o'clock Mr. Huntingdon returned, and, with his hat drawn over his eyes, went straight to the library. He kissed the face of the dead passionately, and his sob and violent burst of sorrow told his child of his arrival. She lifted her rigid face and extended her arms, pleadingly.

"Father! Father! here, at least, you will forgive me!"

He turned from her sternly, and answered, with bitter emphasis:

"I will not! But for *you*, he would have been different, and this would never have happened."

"Father, I have asked for love and pardon for the last time. Perhaps, when you stand over my dead body, you may remember that you had a child who had a right to your affection. God knows, if it were possible, I would gladly lay my weary head down to rest, here on Hugh's bier, and give him back to your arms. Life is not so sweet to me that I would not yield it up to-day without a murmur."

She bent down and kissed her cousin, and, with a hard, bitter expression in her countenance, went up to her own room, locking out Paragon and old Nellie, who followed cautiously at her heels.

"For the drift of the Maker is dark, an Isis hid by the veil.
Who knows the ways of the world, how God will bring them about."

CHAPTER XXIV

"Where are you going, Irene?"

"Only to the Factory-row."

"For what, I should like to know?"

"To see Bessie Davis, who has been very ill."

"Fiddle-stick! I want the carriage myself. I promised to send down to the hotel for Judge Peterson, who is coming to spend the night here."

"Of course, Father, if you want Andrew I do not wish to interfere with your arrangements. I did not know that you intended to use the carriage. John, tell Andrew to drive the horses back to the stable-yard until called for, and have Erebus saddled at once. Unpack that flat basket I left on the pantry-shelf, and put the things into one with a handle, that I can carry in my hand. The egg-basket will do very well; it has a cover."

She went to her room, changed her dress for her riding-habit, and came down to the front door, where her father sat smoking.

"What are you going to do with that basket? Erebus won't suffer you to carry it."

"Yes, sir; he will suffer just what I please to take. I have a bottle of wine, some jelly, and some light bread for poor Mrs. Davis."

"What sort of wine?"

"Not your high-priced sherry or port, but a pint bottle of madeira. Tighten that girth for me, Andrew, if you please; the saddle turned the last time I rode."

"I'll bet that you will let that basket fall before you get to the gate, and lose every drop in it. It is all nonsense! sheer nonsense!"

She made no reply, but mounted the beautiful spirited animal, who arched his neck and curveted at sight of the basket. Patting his mane soothingly, she hung the basket securely on the pommel of the saddle and rode off.

"He is wilder to-day than he was when I first bought him; he will break her neck yet, I have n't a doubt," muttered Mr. Huntingdon, looking after her.

"No he won't, Master; she can tame him down any minute. Last week she wanted to ride, but he had got out into the creek-pasture and I could n't catch him. I raced him for a half-hour up and down, and could n't come near him; I tried him with corn and fodder, but he ran like a deer. I give it up, sir, and told Miss Irene he was in one of his tantrums and I could do nothing with him. She just put on her hat and walked over to the pasture, and the minute he saw her coming he neighed two or three times, and, before I could get to her, she had her hand on his mane, patting him, and he was rubbing his head against her. Miss Irene can tame anything in this world, she has such a steady, conquering look in her eyes."

Such were Andrew's reassuring words, as, with his hat on the back of his head and both hands thrust into his deep pockets, he stood watching his young mistress until a turn in the road obscured both horse and rider, then walked back to the stable.

It was a cold afternoon in November—

"And Autumn, laying here and there
A fiery finger on the leaves,"

had kindled her forest conflagration. Golden maples and amber-hued cherries, crimson dogwoods and scarlet oaks shook out their flame foliage and waved their glowing boughs, all dashed and speckled, flecked and rimmed with orange and blood, ghastly green, and tawny brown. The hectic spot burned everywhere, save on the solemn sombre pines that lifted themselves defiantly far above the fevered region of decay. Royal clusters of golden-rod were blackened and seared by the lips of an early frost, and pallid starry asters shivered and dropped their faded petals as the wind bowed their fragile heads. The smoky atmosphere, which had hung all day in purple folds around the distant hills, took a golden haze as the sun sank rapidly; and to Irene's gaze river and woodland, hill-side and valley, were brimmed with that weird "light which never was on sea or land." Her almost "Brahminical" love of nature had grown with her years, but a holier element mingled with her adoration now; she looked beyond the material veil of beauty, and bowed reverently before the indwelling Spiritual Presence. Only during these silent hours of communion afforded by her solitary rides was the shadow lifted from her heart, and at such times immemorial Cybele's fingers, soft and warm, touched the still face, and the icy lines melted. Since Hugh's death, nearly a year before, she had become a recluse—availing herself of her mourning-dress to decline all social engagements; and during these months a narrow path opened before her feet, she became a member of the church which she had attended from infancy, and her hands closed firmly over her life-work. The baffling Sphinx that had so long vexed her sat no more at the cross-roads of her existence; she found an Œdipus in the far more than cabalistic words:

"Thy path is plain and straight, that light is given.
Onward in faith! and leave the rest to heaven."

Sorrow and want hung out their signs among the poor of W——, and here, silently, but methodically, she had become, not a ministering angel certainly, but a generous benefactress, a noble, sympathetic friend—a counsellor whose strong good sense rendered her advice and guidance valuable indeed. By a system of rigid economy she was enabled to set apart a small portion of money, which she gave judiciously, superintending its investment; kind, hopeful words she scattered like sunshine over every threshold; and here and there, where she detected smouldering aspiration or incipient appreciation of learning, she fanned the spark with some suitable volume from her own library, which, in more than one instance, became the germ, the spring of "a joy for ever." Frequently her father threw obstacles in her way, sneering all the while at her "sanctimonious freaks." Sometimes she affected not to notice the impediments, sometimes frankly acknowledged their magnitude, and climbed right over them, on to her work. Among the factory operatives she found the greatest need of ameliorating touches of every kind. Improvident, illiterate, in some cases almost brutalized, she occasionally found herself puzzled as to the proper plan to pursue; but her womanly heart, like the hidden jewelled levers of a watch, guided the womanly hands unerringly.

This evening, as she approached the row of low whitewashed houses, a crowd of children swarmed out, as usual, to stare at her. She rode up to a door-step, where a boy of some fourteen years sat sunning himself, with an open book on his knee and a pair of crutches beside him. At sight of her a bright smile broke over his sickly face, and he tried to rise.

"Good-evening, Philip; don't get up. How are you to-day?"

"Better, I thank you, ma'm; but very stiff yet."

"The stiffness will pass off gradually, I hope. I see you have not finished your book yet; how do you like it?"

"Oh! I could bear to be a cripple always, if I had plenty like it to read."

"You need not be a cripple; but there are plenty more, just as good and better, which you shall have in time. Do you think you could hold my horse for me a little while? I can't find a suitable place to tie him. He is gentle enough if you will only hold the reins."

"Certainly, ma'm; I shall be glad to hold him as long as you like."

She dismounted, and, taking her basket, placed the bridle in the boy's hand, saying encouragingly, as Erebus put up his ears and looked vicious:

"Don't be afraid of him. Speak to him quietly if he gets restless, and if you can't keep him in order, call me; I am going in next door."

He smiled assent, wrapped the bridle round his wrist, and returned eagerly to his treasure, Simms' "Life of Nathaniel Greene," while Irene passed into the adjoining house. Some sick-rooms are inviting, from the costly display of marble, rosewood, velvet, and silver; from the tasteful arrangement of books and flowers; from the air of delicacy and affectionate consideration which pervades them. But those where poverty stands grim and gaunt on the hearth are rarely enticing, and to this dreary class belonged the room where Bessie Davis had suffered for months, watching the sands of life run low and the shadow of death growing longer across the threshold day by day. The dust and lint of the cotton-room had choked the springs of life, and on her hollow cheeks glowed the autograph of consumption. She stretched out her wasted hand and said:

"Ah, Miss Irene! I heard your voice outside, and it was pleasant to my ears as the sound of the bell when work-hours are over. I am always glad to see your face, but this evening I was longing for you, hoping and praying that you would come. I am in trouble."

"About what, Mrs. Davis? Nothing serious, I hope; tell me."

"I don't know how serious it is going to be. Johnnie is sick in the next room, taken yesterday; and, about noon to-day, Susan had to knock off work and come home. Hester is the only one left, and you know she is but a baby to work. I don't like to complain of my lot, God knows, but it seems hard if we are all to be taken down."

"I hope they will not be sick long. What is the matter with Johnnie?"

"Dear knows! I am sure I don't; he complains of the headache and has fever, and Susan here seems ailing the same way. She is as stupid as can be—sleeps all the time. My children have had measles and whooping-cough and chicken-pox and scarlet-fever, and I can't imagine what they are trying to catch now. I hear that there is a deal of sickness showing itself in the Row."

"Have you sent for the doctor?" asked Irene, walking around to the other side of the bed and examining Susan's pulse.

"Yes, I sent Hester; but she said he told her he was too busy to come."

"Why did you not apply to some other physician?"

"Because Dr. Brandon has always attended me, and, as I sent for him first, I didn't know whether any other doctor would like to come. You know some of them have very curious notions about their dignity."

"And sometimes, while they pause to discuss etiquette, humanity suffers. Susan, let me see your tongue. Who else is sick in the Row, Mrs. Davis?"

"Three of Tom Brown's children, two of Dick Spencer's, and Lucy Hall, and Mary Moorhead. Miss Irene, will you be good enough to give me a drink of water? Hester has gone to try to find some wood, and I can't reach the pitcher."

"I brought you some jelly; would you like a little now, or shall I put it away in the closet?"

"Thank you; I will save it for my Johnnie, he is so fond of sweet things; and, poor child! he sees 'em so seldom now-a-days."

"There is enough for you and Johnnie too. Eat this, while I look after him and see whether he ought to have any this evening."

She placed the saucer filled with the tempting amber-hued delicacy on the little pine table beside the bed and went into the next room. The boy, who looked about seven or eight years old, lay on a pallet in one corner, restless and fretful, his cheeks burning and his large brown eyes sparkling with fever.

"Johnnie, boy! what is the matter? Tell me what hurts you?"

"My head aches so badly," and tears came to the beautiful childish eyes.

"It feels hot. Would you like to have it bathed in cold water?"

"If you please, ma'm. I have been calling Hettie, and she won't hear."

"Because she has gone out. Let me see if I can't do it just as well as Hettie."

She hunted about the room for a cloth, but, finding nothing suitable, took her cambric handkerchief, and, after laving his forehead gently for ten or fifteen minutes, laid the wet folds upon it, and asked, smilingly:

"Does n't that feel pleasant?"

"Ever so nice, ma'm—if I had some to drink."

She put the dripping gourd to his parched lips, and, after shaking up his pillow and straightening the covering of his pallet, she promised to see him again soon, and returned to his mother.

"How does he appear to be, Miss Irene? I had him moved out of this room because he said my coughing hurt his head, and his continual fretting worried me. I am so weak now, God help me!" and she covered her eyes with one hand.

"He has some fever, Mrs. Davis, but not more than Susan. I will ask Dr. Arnold to come and see them this evening. This change in the weather is very well calculated to make sickness. Are you entirely out of wood?"

"Very nearly, ma'm—a few sticks left."

"When Hester comes keep her at home. I will send you some wood. And now, how are you?"

"My cough is not quite so bad; the pectoral holds it a little in check; but I had another hemorrhage last night, and I am growing weaker every day. Oh, Miss Irene! what will become of my poor little children when I am gone? That is such an agonizing thought." She sobbed as she spoke.

"Do not let that grieve you now. I promise you that your children shall be taken care of. I will send a servant down to stay here to-night, and perhaps some of the women in the Row will be willing to come in occasionally and help Hester till Susan gets able to cook. I left two loaves of bread in the closet, and will send more in the morning, which Hester can toast. I shall go by town and send Dr. Arnold out."

"I would rather have Dr. Brandon, if you please."

"Why?"

"I have always heard that Dr. Arnold was so gruff and unfeeling that I am afraid of him. I hate to be snapped up when I ask a question."

"That is a great mistake, Mrs Davis. People do him injustice. He has one of the kindest, warmest hearts I ever knew, though sometimes he is rather abrupt in his manner. If you prefer it, however, I will see your doctor. Good-by; I will come again to-morrow."

As she took her bridle from Philip's hand the boy looked up at her with an expression bordering on adoration.

"Thank you, Philip; how did he behave?"

"Not very well; but he is beautiful enough to make up for his wildness."

"That is bad doctrine; beauty never should excuse bad behavior. Is your mother at home?"

"No, ma'm."

"When she comes, ask her I say please to step in now and then and overlook things for Mrs. Davis; Susan is sick. Philip, if it is not asking too much of you, Johnnie would like for you to sit by him till his little sister comes home, and wet that cloth which I left on his head. Will you?"

"Indeed I will; I am very glad you told me. Certainly I will."

"I thought so. Don't talk to him; let him sleep if he will. Good-by."

She went first to a wood-yard on the river and left an order for a cord of wood to be sent immediately to No. 13. Factory-row; then took the street leading to Dr. Brandon's office. A servant sat on the step whistling merrily, and, in answer to her question, he informed her that his master had just left town, to be absent two days. She rode on for a few squares, doubling her veil in the hope of shrouding her features, and stopped once more in front of the door where stood Dr. Arnold's buggy."

"Cyrus, is the doctor in his office?"

"Yes, Miss Irene."

"Hold my horse for me."

She gathered the folds of her riding-habit over her arm and went up stairs. Leaning far back in his chair, with his feet on the fender of the grate, sat Dr. Arnold, watching the blue smoke of his meerschaum curl lazily in faint wreaths over his head; and, as she entered, a look of pleasant surprise came instantly into his cold, clear eyes.

"Bless me! Irene, I am glad to see you. It is many a day since you have shown your face here; sit down. Now, then, what is to pay? You are in trouble, of course; you never think of me except when you are. Has old Nellie treated herself to another spell of rheumatism, or Paragon broke his leg, or small-pox broke out anywhere; or, worse than all, have the hawks taken to catching your pigeons?"

"None of these catastrophes has overtaken me; but I come, as usual, to ask a favor. If you please, I want you to go up to the Factory-row this evening. Mrs. Davis, No. 13, has two children very sick, I am afraid. I don't like the appearance of their tongues."

"Humph! what do you know about tongues, I should like to be informed?"

"How to use my own, sir, at least, when there is a necessity for it. They are what you medical *savans* call typhoid tongues; and from what I heard to-day, I am afraid there will be a distressing amount of sickness among the operatives. Of course you will go, sir?"

"How do you know that so well? Perhaps I will, and perhaps I won't. Nobody ever looks after me, or cares about the condition of my health; I don't see why I must adopt the whole human race. See here, my child! do not let me hear of you at the Row again soon; it is no place for you, my lily. Ten to one it is some low, miserable typhus fever showing itself, and I will take care of your precious pets only on condition that you keep away, so that I shall not be haunted with the dread of having you, also, on my hands. If I lay eyes on you at the Row, I swear I will write to Leonard to chain you up at home. Do you hear?"

"I shall come every day, I promise you that."

"Oh! you are ambitious of martyrdom! But typhus-fever is not the style, Queen. There is neither *eclat* nor glory in such a death."

A sad smile curved her mouth as she answered slowly:

"Indeed you wrong me, Doctor. I am not ready to die; I am not fit for eternity; my work has but begun."

"Why do you think so, my dear child? What sin have you ever committed?"

"Sins of omission, sir, foot up as heavily as those of commission."

"Don't tread upon my Antinomianistic toes, if you please! they are tender. Wherein have you failed to do your duty?"

"God and my own soul only sit in assize upon my derelictions."

"Irene, I have watched you for years with hungry, eager eyes; and of late I have followed you in your rounds among the poor. You are inaugurating a new system; the fashion is, to organize societies, flame in print as officer, president, treasurer, as the case may be, and placard the members and purposes of the or-organization. Left hand industriously puffs what right hand doeth. Is it not so? One of your own sex, the greatest, strongest, noblest of your learned women-singers, pithily tells you:

'There is too much abstract willing, purposing, In this poor world. We talk by aggregates,
And think by systems. . . . If we pray at all,
We pray no longer for our daily bread,
But next century's harvests. If we give,
Our cup of water is not tendered till
We lay down pipes and found a company:
With branches. A woman can not do the thing she ought.
Which means whatever perfect thing she can,
In life, in art, in science, but she fears
To let the perfect action take her part
And rest there; she must prove what she can do
Before she does it—prate of woman's rights,
Of woman's mission, woman's function, till
The men (who are prating, too, on their side) cry—
"A woman's function plainly is—to talk.
Poor souls, they are very reasonably vexed!
They can not hear each other speak.'"

"I tell you, Queen, I have watched these associations all my life: I am getting old now, and I am as completely nauseated with their cant and phariseeism as Macaulay was with that of the seventeenth century Puritans. Self-glorification has a deal of influence over our modern Dorcases."

"I think, sir, that you are unjust in some instances; your cynical lenses distort the facts. Judiciously-conducted charitable societies greatly facilitate matters, by systematizing the work and inducing punctuality. I grant that the evils you speak of are much to be deprecated; and, to complete your own lengthy quotation:

"'I'd whisper—Soft, my sister! not a word!
By speaking we prove only we can speak;
Which he, the man here, never doubted. What
He doubts is, whether we can *do* the thing
With decent grace we've not yet done at all:
Now do it!'"

"Doctor, I wish you were more of an optimist."

He took one of her hands, spread out the ivory fingers on his broad palm, and said, in a lower tone:

"My Chaldean priestess, who says that I am not as orthodox on optimism as Leibnitz himself? Don't you know that I am a sort of latter-day troglodyte, very rarely airing my pet creeds for the benefit of the public? That was a wise law of Solon's which declared 'every man infamous who, in seditious or civil dissensions of the state, remained neuter, and refused to side with either party;' but I do not regard it as expedient or incumbent upon me to advertise my individual *status* on all ethical schisms. What is it to the public whether I endorse 'Candide' or Leibnitz's 'Theodicea'?"

"One thing I certainly do know, with great regret, that your seeming austerity, your roughness of manner, renders you very unpopular; whereas you should be universally beloved."

"Really! have I become a bugbear in my old age?"

"Not that exactly, sir; but I wish, if it were possible, that you would not mask your really kind, generous, sympathizing heart by such repellent, abrupt conduct in sick-rooms, where people expect gentleness and consideration on the part of a physician. I know you are often annoyed by senseless and ridiculous questions; but I wish, for your own sake, that you could be a little more patient with poor, weak human nature."

"Child, I am not gregarious; never was. I touch my hat to the world, and it is welcome to think just what it chooses of me."

"No, sir; far from touching your hat, you stand aloof, scowling at your race, smiling grimly at the struggling, drowning men and women around you, as if we were not all one great family, designed by God to assist and cheer each other. Every man—"

"Pardon me, Queen; but I am not one of those deluded, self-complacent human beings who actually lay the 'flattering unction' to their souls that they were sent into this world for some particular purpose—some special mission. I want you distinctly to understand, child, that I don't consider myself appointed to any work but that of attending to my own affairs and taking care of myself."

"Then you admit yourself a marred, imperfect block, rejected by the Divine Architect as unworthy of a place in the grand social temple. God clothed you with human affections and sympathies that, in accordance with the fundamental law of social existence, you might extend a helping hand to your fellow-creatures."

He moved restlessly, and his gray shaggy brows met in a heavy frown.

"I believe, Irene, I am entirely innocent of any agrarian or socialistic tendency."

"And so, I trust, am I. But, sir, because I abhor Brook-Farm I will not take refuge in the cave of Trophonius."

He looked up at her with one of his steely, probing glances, then the brows unbent, and he drew her hand caressingly across his cheek.

"Well, child, we won't quarrel over my bearishness. If you will keep that hard, frozen look away from your lips, and smile now and then as you used to do in your childhood when I held you on my knee, I will promise to try and unearth myself, to seal up my gnome habitation, and buy me a tub which I can drag after me into the sunlight. Is it a bargain?"

"That is problematical, Doctor. But it is getting late, and I wish, if you please, you would go at once to the Row."

"Stop! if any good is accomplished among those semi-savages up yonder, who is to have the credit? Tell me that."

"God shall have the thanks; you all the credit as the worthy instrument, and I as much of the gratification as I can steal from you. Are you satisfied with your wages, my honored Shylock? Good-night."

"Humph! it is strange what a hold that queer, motherless child took upon my heart in her babyhood, and tightens as she grows older.

'That souls are dangerous things to carry straight Through all the spilt saltpetre of the world'

who will question? Not I, surely; and yet I know that girl will take hers safely to the terminus of time, pure, with no smut or smell of gunpowder. A pearl before swine! But, I swear, untrampled to the end."

He shook the ashes from his pipe, put it away behind the clock, and went down to his buggy. Before breakfast the following morning, while Irene was in the poultry-yard feeding her chickens and pigeons, pheasants and peafowls, she received a note from Dr. Arnold containing these few scrawling words:

"If you do not feel quite ready for the day of judgment, avoid the Row as you would the plagues of Egypt. I found no less than six developed cases of rank typhus.
"Yours,
"HIRAM ARNOLD."

She put the note in her pocket, and, while the pigeons fluttered and perched on her shoulders and arms, cooing and pecking at her fingers, she stood musing—calculating the chances of contagion and death if she persisted. Raising her eyes to the calm blue sky, the perplexed look passed from her countenance, and, fully decided regarding her course, she went in to breakfast. Mr. Huntingdon was going to a neighboring county with Judge Peterson, to transact some business connected with Hugh's estate, and, as the buggy came to the door, he asked carelessly:

"What did Cyrus want?"

"He came to bring me a note from the doctor, concerning some sick people whom I asked him to see."

"Oh—! John, put my overcoat in the buggy. Come, Judge, I am ready."

As he made no inquiry about the sick she volunteered no explanation, and he bade her good-by with manifest cold indifference. She could not avoid congratulating herself that, since he must take this journey soon, he had selected the present occasion to be absent, for she was well aware that he would violently oppose her wishes in the matter of the Row. When Dr. Arnold met her, late in the afternoon of the same day, at little Johnnie's side, his surprise and chagrin found vent, first in a series of oaths, then, scowling at her like some thunder-cloud with the electricity expended, he said:

"Do you consider me a stark idiot, or a shallow quack?"

"Neither, sir, I assure you."

"Then, if I know anything about my business, I wrote you the truth this morning, and you treat my advice with cool contempt. You vex me beyond all endurance! Do you want to throw yourself into the jaws of Death?"

"No, sir; far from it; but I had incurred the risk before I was aware that there was any. Besides, I really do not think I shall take the fever. I believe a good resolution is a powerful preventive, and that, you know, I have."

"The deuce you have! you obstinate, ungovernable piece of marble! Look here, Irene, I shall go straight to your father and let him know the facts. It is my duty, and I mean to do it."

"I don't think you will, for he started to B—— county this morning. And now, Doctor, you may just as well quit scolding me, for I have made up my mind to nurse Johnnie, come what will."

"Yes! I will warrant you have! and you may as well go make up your shroud, too—for you will want it, I am thinking."

"Well, my life, at least, is my own, even if it should prove the price."

"Oh! is it, indeed? What has become of that pretty doctrine you preached to me yesterday? I thought you belonged to the whole human fraternity? Your life yours, indeed!"

"You forget, Doctor; 'greater love hath no man than this, that he lay down his life for his friends.'"

She slipped her hand into his and looked up, smiling and calm, into his harsh, swarthy face.

"My child, you made a mistake; your life belongs to me, for I saved it in your infancy. I cradled you in my arms, lest Death should snatch you. I have a better right to you than anybody else in this world. I don't want to see you die; I wish to go first."

"I know what I owe you, Doctor; but I am not going to die, and you have scolded me enough for one time. Do make peace."

"Remember, I warned you, and you would not heed."

From that hour she kept faithful vigil in No. 13—passing continually from one bedside to another. Susan's attack proved comparatively light, and she was soon pronounced convalescent; but little Johnnie was desperately ill, and for several nights Irene sat at his pillow, fearing that every hour would be his last. While his delirium was at its height Hester was taken violently, and on the morning when Irene felt that her labor was not in vain and that the boy would get well, his little sister, whom she had nursed quite as assiduously, grew rapidly worse, and died at noon. As is frequently observed in such diseases, this increased in virulence with every new case. It spread with astonishing celerity through the Row, baffling the efforts of the best physicians in W——; and finally, the day after Hester's death, as Irene sat trying to comfort the poor mother, a neighbor came in, exclaiming:

"Oh, Miss Irene! Philip Martin is down, too. He caught the fever from his mother, and his father says won't you please come over."

She went promptly, though so wearied she could scarcely stand, and took a seat by the bed where tossed the poor boy in whom she had taken such an interest since the accident which crushed his leg in the machinery and rendered him a temporary cripple.

"He has been talking about you constantly, Miss Irene, and calling for you. Philip, my son, here is Miss Irene."

He smiled and turned, but there was no recognition in the hot eyes, and after an instant he muttered on incoherently.

"You must go home, Miss Huntingdon; you are worn-out. His father can watch him till his mother gets stronger," said Dr. Brandon, who was fully acquainted with her unremitting attendance at the next house.

"No, I must stay with Philip; perhaps he will know me when he wakes."

A hope doomed to disappointment, for he raved for four days and nights, calling frantically for the serene, sad woman who sat at his pillow, bending over him and laying her cold hand on his scorched brow. On the fifth day, being free from fever and utterly prostrated, he seemed sinking rapidly; but she kept her fingers on his pulse, and, without waiting for the doctor's advice, administered powerful stimulants. So passed two hours of painful anxiety; then Philip opened his eyes languidly, and looked at her.

"Philip, do you know me?"

"Yes—Miss Irene."

She sank back as if some strong supporting hand had suddenly been withdrawn from her; and, observing that she looked ghastly, Mr. Martin hastily brought her a glass of water. Just then Dr. Brandon entered, and examined his patient with evident surprise.

"What have you done to him, Miss Huntingdon?"

"Since daylight I have been giving him ammonia and brandy; his pulse was so feeble and thready I thought he needed it, and I was afraid to wait for you."

"Right! and you saved his life by it. I could not get here any earlier, and if you had delayed it until I came it would probably have been too late. You may call him your patient after this."

She waited no longer, but staggered to the door; and Andrew, seeing how faint she was, came to meet her and led her to the carriage. The ten days of watching has told upon her; and when she reached home and Nellie brought her wrapper and unlaced her shoes, she fell back on her lounge in a heavy, death-like sleep. Mr. Huntingdon had been expected two days before, but failed to arrive at the time designated; and, having her fears fully aroused, Nellie despatched a messenger for Dr. Arnold.

CHAPTER XXV

"Do you see any change, Hiram?"

"None for the better."

Mr. Huntingdon dropped his head on his hand again, and Dr. Arnold resumed his slow walk up and down the carpet. The blue damask curtains had been looped back from the western window, and the broad band of yellow belting in the sky threw a mellow light over the bed where lay the unconscious heiress of the grand old Hill. Fever rouged the polished cheeks usually pure as alabaster, and touched the parted lips with deeper scarlet, lending a brilliant and almost unearthly beauty to the sculptured features. Her hair, partially escaping from confinement, straggled in crumpled rings and folds across the pillow, a mass of golden netting; and the sparkling eyes wandered from one object to another as if in anxious search. The disease had assumed a different type, and, instead of raving paroxysms, her illness was characterized by a silent, wakeful unconsciousness, while opiates produced only the effect of increasing her restlessness. A week had passed thus—during which time she had recognized no one, and though numerous lady friends came to offer assistance, all were refused permission to see her. Mr. Huntingdon was utterly ignorant of the duties of a nurse; and though he haunted the room like an unlifting shadow, Dr. Arnold and Nellie took entire charge of the patient. The former was unremitting in his care, sitting beside the pillow through the long winter nights, and snatching a few hours sleep during the day. Watching her now, as he walked to and fro, he noticed that her eyes followed him earnestly, and he paused at the bedside and leaned over her.

"Irene, what do you want? Does my walking annoy you?"

No answer.

"Won't you shut your eyes, my darling, and try to go to sleep?"

The deep brilliant eyes only looked into his with mocking intentness. He put his fingers on the lids and pressed them gently down, but she struggled, and turned away her face. Her hands crept constantly along the snowy quilt as if seeking for something, and taking them both he folded them in his and pressed them to his lips, while tears, which he did not attempt to restrain, fell over them.

"You don't think she is any worse, do you?" asked the father, huskily.

"I don't know anything, except that she can't lay this way much longer."

His harsh voice faltered and his stern mouth trembled. He laid the hands back, went to the window, and stood there till the room grew dusky and the lamp was brought in. As Nellie closed the door after her the doctor came to the hearth and said, sharply:

"I would not be in your place for John Jacob Astor's fortune."

"What do you mean by that?"

"I mean that, if you have any conscience left, you must suffer the pains of purgatory for the manner in which you have persecuted that child."

"In all that I have ever done I have looked only to her good—to her ultimate happiness. I know that she—"

"Hush, Leonard! hush! You know very well that you have been down on your knees before the Golden Calf ever since that girl opened her eyes in this plagued world of trouble! You are no more fit to be a father than I am to be a saint! You have tyrannized and fretted her poor innocent soul nearly out of her ever since she was big enough to crawl. Why the d—l could not you let the child have a little peace? I told you how it would end; but oh, no! you could see nothing but the gilt face of your bellowing god! You tormented her so about Hugh that anybody else would have hated the poor fellow. Mind you, she never opened her lips to me with reference to that matter in her life; she would have been gibbeted first. But I am not blind entirely; I knew what was going on; I knew that the proud, sensitive bird was hunted and could find no spot to rest upon. There are ninety-nine chances to one that she has come to her rest at last. You will feel pleasantly when you see her in her shroud."

His hard face worked painfully, and tears glided down the wrinkled cheek and hid themselves in his gray beard. Mr. Huntingdon was much agitated, but an angry flush crossed his brow as he answered, hastily:

"I am the best judge of my family matters. You are unjust and severe. Of course, I love my child better than anybody else."

"Heaven preserve her from such love as you have lavished on her! She is very dear to me. I understand her character; you either can not or will not. She is the only thing in this world that I do really love. I have fondled her from the time when she was a week old, and it hurts me to see her suffer as she has done ever since you posted her off among strangers in New York. It will go hard with me to lay her down, in all her loveliness, in the grave. My pet, my violet-eyed darling!"

He shaded his face and swallowed a sob, and for some moments neither spoke. After a while the doctor buttoned up his coat and took his hat.

"I am going down to my office to get a different prescription. I will be back soon."

"Mrs. Harris and Mrs. Clark said that they would sit up to-night. Hiram, you must be worn-out, losing so much sleep."

"Tell Mrs. Harris and Mrs. Clark to go to Egypt! Do you suppose I want two such gossip-hawks perched over my dove? I am going to sit up myself. Give Irene a spoonful of that mixture in the small vial at seven o'clock."

Contrary to his phlegmatic habit, the doctor had taken counsel of his fears until he was completely unnerved, and he went home more than usually surly and snappish. As he entered his office Russell advanced to meet him from the window, whence, for nearly an hour, he had been watching for his arrival.

"Good-evening, Doctor."

"What do you want?"

"How is Miss Huntingdon?"

"What is Miss Huntingdon to you?"

"She was one of my mother's best friends, though only a little girl at the time."

"And you love her for your mother's sake, I suppose? Truly filial."

"For that matter, she is beautiful enough to be very easily loved for her own sake, judging from the number of her devoted admirers. But I certainly am very grateful for her kindness to my mother, years ago."

"And well you may be, Aubrey! She paid dearly for her friendly interest in your family."

"In what respect, sir?"

"In more respects than I choose to recapitulate. Did you ever know where she got the two hundred dollars which she gave your mother?"

"I presume she took it from her own purse."

"She borrowed it from me, and paid me back gradually in the money that her father gave her, from time to time, while she was at boarding-school. Cyrus! you stupid! bring me some coffee."

"How is she to-night? Rumors are so unreliable, that I came to you to find out the truth."

"She is going to die, I am afraid."

A sudden pallor overspread Russell's face, but he sat erect and motionless, and, fastening his keen eyes upon him, the doctor added:

"She is about to be transplanted to a better world, if there is such a place. She is too good and pure for this cursed, pestiferous earth."

"Is the case so utterly hopeless? I cannot, I will not, believe it!" came indistinctly from the young man's bloodless lips.

"I tell you I know better! She stands on a hair stretched across her grave. If I don't succeed to-night in making her sleep (which I have been trying to accomplish for two days), she can't possibly live. And what is that whole confounded crew of factory savages in comparison with her precious life?"

"Is it true that her illness is attributable to nursing those people?"

"Yes. D—l take the Row! I wish the river would swallow it up."

"Is she conscious?"

"Heaven only knows; I don't. She lies with her eyes wide open, looking at everything as if she were searching for something which she had lost, but never speaks, and understands nothing, except to swallow the medicine when I put the spoon to her lips."

"If I could only see her!" exclaimed Russell, and an expression of such intense agony settled on his features, usually so inflexible, that his companion was startled and astonished. The doctor regarded him a moment with perplexity and compassion mingled in his own face; then light broke upon him, and, rising, he laid his hand heavily on Russell's shoulder.

"Of course, Aubrey, you don't visit at that house?"

"Of course not."

"Do you meet her often?"

"I have not seen her for nearly a year. Not since the night in which Hugh Seymour was drowned."

He rose, and turned away to screen his countenance from the scrutiny to which it was subjected, for the painful shock baffled all his efforts at self-control and he felt that his face would betray him.

"Where are you going, Aubrey?"

"Back to my office."

"Is there any message which you would like for me to deliver to her, if she should recover her consciousness? You may trust me, young man."

"Thank you; I have no message to send. I merely called to ask after her. I trust she will yet recover. Good-night."

He walked on rapidly till he reached the door of his office. The gas was burning brightly over his desk, and red-tape and legal-cap beckoned him in; but fathomless blue eyes, calm as mid-ocean, looked up at him, and, without entering, he turned, and went through the cold and darkness to the cemetery, to his mother's tomb. She had been his comfort in boyish sorrows, and habit was strong; he went to her grave for it still.

When Russell left him Dr. Arnold took from his pocket the only solace he had ever known—his meerschaum. While he smoked, and mixed some powders in a marble mortar, memory industriously ran back, raking amid the ashes of the by-gone for here a word and there a look, to eke out the Ariadne thread which his imagination was spinning. The possibility of an attachment between Irene and the blind widow's son had never occurred to him before; but that Russell's unmistakable emotion could be referable simply to gratitude to his mother's benefactress was an explanation of which he was disposed to be very sceptical. If this surmise should prove correct, what were Irene's feelings toward the popular young politician? Here he was absolutely without data; he could recall nothing to assist him; but, comprehending the bitter animosity existing between the lawyer and her father, he sighed involuntarily, knowing the hopelessness of any such attachment on either or both sides. Determined to satisfy himself of the truth at the earliest opportunity he carefully weighed out the powder and rode back to the Hill. He could perceive no change, unless it were a heightening of the carmine on cheeks and lips and an increased twitching of the fingers, which hunted so pertinaciously about the bedclothes.

"That everlasting picking, picking at everything, is such an awful bad sign," said poor Nellie, who was crying bitterly at the foot of the bed—and she covered her face with her apron to shut out the sight.

"You 'pick' yourself off to bed, Nellie! I don't want you snubbing and groaning around, day and night."

"I am afraid to leave her a minute. I am afraid when my poor baby shuts her eyes she never will open 'em again till she opens 'em in heaven."

"Oh, go along to sleep! you eternal old stupid. I will wake you up, I tell you, if she gets worse."

He mixed one of the powders and stooped down.

"Irene—Irene, take this for me, won't you, dear?"

She gave no intimation of having heard him till he placed the wineglass to her mouth and raised her head tenderly; then she swallowed the contents mechanically. At the expiration of an hour he repeated the dose, and at ten o'clock, while he sat watching her intently, he saw the eyelids begin to droop, the long silky lashes quivered and touched her cheeks. When he listened to her breathing, and knew that at last she slept, his gray head sank on his chest and he murmured, inaudibly, "thank God!" Patient as a woman, he kept his place at her side, fearing to move lest he should wake her; the dreary hours of night wore away; morning came, gloriously bright, and still she slept. The flush had faded, leaving her wan as death, and the little hands were now at rest. She looked like the figures which all have seen on cenotaphs, and anxiously and often the doctor felt the slow pulse, that seemed weary of its mission. He kept the room quiet and maintained his faithful watch, refusing to leave her for a moment. Twelve o'clock rolled round, and it appeared, indeed, as if Nellie's prognostication would prove true, the sleeper was so motionless. At three o'clock the doctor counted the pulse, and, reassured, threw his head back against the velvet lining of the chair and shut his aching eyes. Before five minutes had elapsed he heard a faint sweet voice say, "Paragon." Springing to his feet, he saw her put out her hand to pat the head of her favorite, who could not be kept out of the room, and howled so intolerably when they chained him that they were forced to set him free. Now he stood with his paws on the pillow and his face close to hers, whining with delight. Tears of joy almost blinded the doctor as he pushed Paragon aside and said, eagerly:

"Irene, one dog is as good as another! You know Paragon; do you know me, Queen?"

"Certainly—I know you, Doctor."

"God bless you, Beauty! You have n't known me for a week."

"I am so thirsty—please give me some water."

He lifted her head and she drank eagerly, till he checked her.

"There—we have n't all turned hydropathists since you were taken sick. Nellie! I say, Nellie! you Witch of Endor! bring some wine-whey here. Irene, how do you feel, child?"

"Very tired and feeble, sir. My head is confused. Where is father?"

"Here I am, my daughter."

He bent down with trembling lips and kissed her, for the first time since the day of their estrangement, nearly three years before. She put her arms feebly around his neck, and as he held her to his heart she felt a tear drop on her forehead.

"Father, have you forgiven me?"

He either could not or would not answer, but kissed her again warmly; and, as he disengaged her arms and left the room, she felt assured that, at last, she had been forgiven. She took the whey silently, and, after some moments, said:

"Doctor, have you been sitting by me a long time?"

"I rather think I have!—losing my sleep for nearly ten days, you unconscionable young heathen."

"Have I been so ill as to require that? I have a dim recollection of going on a long journey, and of your being by my side all the way."

"Well, I hope you travelled to your entire satisfaction and found what you wanted—for you were feeling about as if hunting for something the whole time. Oh! I am so thankful that you know me once more. Child, you have cost me a deal of sorrow. Now be quiet, and go to sleep again; at least don't talk to Nellie or Paragon. I shall take a nap on the sofa in the library."

She regained her strength very slowly, and many days elapsed before she was able to leave her room. One bright sunny morning she sat before the open window, looking down on the lawn where the pigeons flashed in and out of the hedges, and now and then glancing at the bouquet of choice hothouse flowers in the vase beside her. In her lap lay a letter just received from Harvey Young—a letter full of fond remembrance, grave counsel, and gentle encouragement—and the unbent lines about her mouth showed that her mind was troubled.

The doctor came in and drew up a chair.

"I should like to know who gave you leave to ride yesterday?"

"Father thought that I was well enough, and the carriage was close and warm. I hope, sir, that I shall not be on your hands much longer."

"What did I tell you? Next time don't be so hard-headed when you are advised by older and wiser persons. I trust you are quite satisfied with the result of your eleemosynary performances at the Row."

"Far from it, Doctor. I am fully acclimated now, and have nothing to fear in future. I am very sorry, sir, that I caused you all so much trouble and anxiety; I did not believe that I should take the fever. If Philip had not been so ill I should have come out safely; but, I suppose, my uneasiness about him unnerved me in some way—for, when I saw that he would get well, all my strength left me in an instant. How is he, sir?"

"Oh! the young dog is as well as ever; limps around now without his crutches. Comes to my office every day to ask after his blessed Lady Bountiful."

Leaning forward carelessly, but so as to command a full view of her face, he added:

"You stirred up quite an excitement in town, and introduced me generally to society. People, who never inflicted themselves on me before, thought it was incumbent on them to hang around my door to make inquiries concerning my fair patient. One night I found even that statue of bronze and steel, Russell Aubrey, waiting at my office to find out whether you really intended translation."

A change certainly passed swiftly over her countenance; but it was inexplicable, indescribable; an anomalous lightening of the eye and darkening of the brow. Before he could analyze it her features resumed their wonted serenity, and he found her voice unfluttered.

"I was not aware that I had so many friends; it is a pleasant discovery, and almost compensates for the pain of illness. Take care, Doctor! You are tilting my flowers out of their vase."

"Confound the flowers, Queen! They are always in the way. It is a great pity there is such Theban-brother affection between your father and Aubrey. He has any amount of fine feeling hid away under that dark, Jesuitical, non-committal face of his. He has not forgotten your interest in his mother, and when I told him that I thought you had determined to take your departure from this world he seemed really hurt about it. I always liked the boy, but I think he is a heretic in politics."

Looking steadily at him as he spoke, she smiled coldly, and answered:

"It is very apparent that this fierceness of party spirit, this bitter political animosity, is driving the ship of State on the rock of Ruin. The foamy lips of the breakers are just ahead, but you men will not open your eyes to the danger."

"Better get some of you wise women to pilot us, I dare say!" sneered her companion, provoked at her unsatisfactory manner and inflexible features.

"It is not our calling, Doctor; but I promise you, if the experiment were tried, that you would find no Palinurus among us. We have no desire to thrust ourselves into the forum, like Roman women 'storming at the Oppian Law and crushing Cato;' still less to imitate Hortensia and confronting august Triumvirs in the market-place, harangue against the tax, however unjust. Practically, women should have as little to do with politics as men with darning stockings or making puff-paste; but we should be unworthy of the high social *status* which your chivalry accords us were we indifferent to the conduct of public affairs.

'Man for the field, and woman for the hearth:
Man for the sword, and for the needle she:
Man with the head, and woman with the heart:
Man to command, and woman to obey.'

Such is the judicious arrangement of nature—a wise and happy one, indubitably. We bow before it, and have no wish to trench on your prerogatives; but we do protest against your sleeping on your posts, or lulling yourselves with dreams of selfish ambition when Scylla and Charybdis grin destruction on either side."

"Phew—Queen! who told you all that? Has Aubrey indoctrinated you in his 'fire-eating,' schismatic principles? What platform do you propose to mount?"

"None, sir, but that of the constitution—ignoring both whig and democratic additions, which make it top-heavy. I don't like latter-day political carpentering. I want to see Nestors in the councils of my country, not nerveless imbeciles, or worthless, desperate political gamesters."

"You rabid little Jacobin! Don't you think that, Portia-like, you might completely transmogrify yourself, and get into Congress and Cabinet long enough to write '*Mene, mene*' on their walls?"

"They would have no Daniel there, even if I should, which is no business of mine. Doctor, I claim to be no politician; a thousand years will scarcely produce another De Staël. I am simply a true lover of my country—anxious in view of its stormy, troubled future."

"Aubrey has not proselyted you, then, after all?"

She had unlocked her writing-desk, and, without seeming to hear his last words, handed him a letter.

"Here is a letter from Uncle Eric, which I received yesterday. It contains a message for you about some medical books and journals."

He muttered something indistinctly, put the letter in his pocket, and took her hand.

"Irene—what is the matter, dear child? Your pulse is entirely too quick."

"That is nothing new, Doctor. Father insists that I shall drink port-wine, and it does not suit me—keeps my head aching continually."

"Try porter instead."

She shook her head wearily.

"I need nothing, sir, but to be let alone."

He smoothed back her hair and said, hastily:

"You will never get what you need. Oh, child! why won't you trust me?"

"Why—Doctor! I do."

"Hush! don't tell me that! I know better. You steel that white face of yours, and lock your confidence from the old man who loves you above all other things."

She drew down his hand from her head and leaned her cold cheek upon it.

"You misunderstand me, sir; I repose the most perfect confidence in you. If I were in trouble, and wanted help or a favor of any kind, I would apply to you sooner than to any other human being—for you have always been more patient with my whims than even my own father—and I should be worse than an ingrate if I had not the most complete trust in you. My dear, kind friend, what have I done to fret you?"

He did not reply, but searched her countenance sorrowfully.

"Doctor, tell me one thing. You nursed me constantly while I was unconscious, and I want to know whether I said anything during my delirium that surprised or annoyed you."

"No; the trouble was that you sealed your lips hermetically. Are you afraid now that you divulged some secret which I may betray?"

"I am not afraid of your betraying anything—never had such a thought. When do you think that I may take a horseback ride with impunity? I am so tired of the house."

"Not for a week, at least. You must be prudent, Irene, for you are not strong yet, by a great deal."

"I wanted to talk to you, this morning, about something very near my heart; but you are going."

"I can wait, my child. What is it?"

"To-morrow will do as well. I want you to aid me in getting a bill passed by the legislature appropriating a school-fund for this county. Perhaps you can obtain Mr. Aubrey's influence with the members of the lower house."

"Perhaps I'll go to the North Pole to cool a glass of amontillado for your majesty! I'll be hanged if I have anything to do with it! Why the deuce can't you ask Mr. Aubrey yourself?"

"Because, in the first place, you know very well that I never see him, and I could not ask him, even if I should meet him; and, beside, I do not wish to be known at all in the affair. It is not a woman's business to put forward legislative bills."

"Indeed! Then why are you meddling with other people's business?"

"Our legislators seem to have forgotten one grand and good maxim of Lycurgus: 'Children are the property of the state, to whom alone their education should be intrusted.' They have forgotten that our poor require educating, and I simply desire some of their constituents to call their attention to the oversight. Doctor, I know you will do it."

"I will first see myself floundering like Pharaoh! I'll rake out nobody's chestnuts! Not even yours, child! Put down that window; the air is too chilly. You are as cold as an iceberg and as blue as a gentian."

The doctor had scarcely taken his departure when Nellie's turbaned head showed itself at the door.

"That factory-boy, Philip, is down stairs; be brought back a book, and wants to see you. He seems in trouble; but you don't feel like being bothered to-day, do you?"

"Did he ask to see me?"

"Not exactly; but showed very plainly he wanted to see you."

"Let him come up."

As he entered she rose and held out her hand.

"Good-morning, Philip; I am glad you are well enough to be out again."

He looked at her reverently, and, as he noticed the change her illness had wrought, his lips quivered and his eyes filled.

"Oh, Miss Irene! I am so glad you are better. I prayed for you all the time while you were so very ill."

"Thank you. Sit down and tell me about the sick."

"They are all better, I believe, ma'm, except Mrs. Davis. She was wishing yesterday that she could see you again."

"I shall go there in a day or two. You are walking pretty well without your crutches. Have you resumed your work?"

"I shall begin again to-morrow."

"It need not interfere with your studies. The nights are very long now, and you can accomplish a great deal if you feel disposed to do so."

He did not answer immediately, and, observing the cloud on his countenance, she added:

"Philip, what is the matter? You look troubled; can I do anything for you?"

A deep flush mantled his sallow cheek, and, drooping his head as if in humiliation, he said, passionately:

"Oh, Miss Irene! You are the only friend I have. I am so mortified I can hardly look anybody in the face. Father is drinking again worse than ever, and is so violent that mother won't stay at home; she has gone across the river for a few days. I have done all I could, but I can't influence him."

"Where is he now?"

"The police put him in the guard-house last night for creating a disturbance. I suppose, when the Mayor holds court, he will be fined and turned out. Miss Irene, I feel like jumping into the river and drowning myself. It is so horrible to be ashamed of my own father!"

He dropped his face in his hands, and she saw that he trembled violently.

"You must struggle against such feelings, Philip; though it is certainly very mortifying to know that your father has been arrested. If you conduct yourself properly, people will respect you all the more because of your misfortune."

"No, Miss Irene! they are always holding it up to me. Hard as I try to do right, they are continually sneering at me, and sometimes it makes me almost desperate."

"That is unjust and ungenerous. No one, who has any refinement or goodness of heart, will be guilty of such behavior. I do not know positively that I can assist you, but I think it possible I can obtain a situation for your father as carpenter on a plantation in the country, if he will promise to abstain from drinking. I have heard that he was a very good mechanic, and in the country he would not meet with such constant temptation. Do you suppose that he will be willing to leave town?"

"Oh, yes, ma'm! I think so; he is generally very repentant when he gets sober. If you please, Miss Irene, I should be so glad if you would talk to him, and persuade him to take the pledge before he starts. I believe he would join the Temperance society if you asked him to do it. Oh! then I should have some heart to work."

"You and your mother must try to influence him, and in a few days I will talk to him. In the meantime I will see about the situation, which is a very desirable one. I am very sorry, Philip, that this trouble has occurred again; I know that it is very painful, but you must endeavor to be patient and hopeful, and to bear up bravely. Brighter days will soon come, I trust."

He took his cap from the carpet, rose, and looked at her with swimming eyes.

"Oh, Miss Irene! I wish I could tell you all I feel. I thank you more than I can ever express, and so does mother."

"You have finished your book, I see; don't you want another? Nellie will show you the library, and on the lower book-shelf, on the right-hand side of the door, you will find a large volume in leather binding—'Plutarch.' Take it with you and read it carefully. Good-by. I shall come down to the Row to-morrow or next day."

As she heard his halting step descend the stairs she leaned back wearily in her chair, and, closing her eyes, these words crept almost inaudibly over her pale lips:

> But go to! thy love
> Shall thant itself, its own beatitudes,
> After its own life-working. A child's kiss
> Set on thy sighing lips, shall make thee glad;
> A poor man served by thee, shall make thee rich;
> A sick man helped by thee, shall make thee strong."

CHAPTER XXVI.

"Well, Irene, what is your decision about the party at Mrs. Churchhill's to-night?"

"I will go with you, Father, if it is a matter of so much interest to you; though, as I told you yesterday, I should prefer declining the invitation as far as I am concerned."

"It is full time for you to go into society again. You have moped at home long enough."

"'Moped' is scarcely the right word, Father."

"It matters little what you call it, the fact is the same. You have shut yourself in till you have grown to look like a totally different woman. Indeed, Irene, I won't permit it any longer; you must come out into the world once more. I am sick of your black looks; let me see you in colors to-night."

"Will not pure white content you, Father?"

"No; I am tired of it; wear something bright."

Mr. Huntingdon smoked his after-breakfast cigar, half-reclined on the upper step, and Irene walked up and down the wide colonnade, enjoying the cool, dewy, fragrant June day, whose sun was rapidly mounting in heaven. The air was of that peculiar stillness found only in southern summer mornings, but now and then its holy calm was rippled by the contented ringing whistle of a partridge far down among the grassy orchard-depths, and by the peaceful chime of doves cooing soft and low, one to another, in the thickest shadows of the dripping grove. True summer sounds—sure concomitants of June. Frail, foam-like cloud-navies in line-of-battle, as if piloted by dubious, treacherous winds, sailed lazily across the sea of intense blue, staring down covetously at a ripening field of flashing wheat which bowed and wavered in a long billowy sweep and swell as the mild June breeze stole over it; and on a neighboring hill-side, where sickles had been busy a few days before, the royal yellow shocks stood thick and tall in crowded ranks, like golden gods of Plenty.

Ah! rare June day, impearled and purpled, freshly glowing from the robing hands of Deity, serenely regal on her southern throne as Sheba's brown queen.

"Irene, sit here on the step, where I can see you without twisting my head off of my shoulders. Now, then—what is the matter with you?"

"Nothing unusual, Father."

"Don't evade me. Why can't you look and act like other girls of your age?"

"Probably because I feel differently. But to what do you allude? In what respect have I displeased you?"

"Oh! in a thousand. You never would look at things in their proper light. Why did you treat William Bainbridge so coldly yesterday evening? You know very well that he came here expressly to see you."

"And, for that reason, sir, I felt it my duty to receive the visit coolly."

"You disappointed all my plans for you once; but let me tell you, if you are not a downright simpleton, you will accept the offer William Bainbridge came here to make. You are aware of the warm friendship which has always existed between the governor and myself, and his son is considered the finest match in the state. If you live a thousand years you will never have a better offer, or another as good; and I do hope, my daughter, that you will not be insane enough to reject him.'"

"Father, why are you so anxious to get rid of your only child?"

"I am not; but you must marry some time, and I know very well such an opportunity as this will not recur."

"Don't you think, sir, that you and I could live always happily here without planting a stranger at our fireside? Father, let us understand each other fully. I speak deliberately and solemnly—I shall never marry."

Mr. Huntingdon started up from his indolent posture and surveyed his daughter keenly.

Her spotless muslin morning-dress swept down the marble steps, its wide sleeves falling away from the rounded dazzling arms, and a black cord and tassel girding the waist. The geranium-leaves fastened at her throat were unstirred as the silver-dusted lilies sleeping, lotos-like, on some lonely tarn; and the dewy Lamarque roses twined in her coiled hair glittering and kindled into faint opaline flushes as the sunshine quivered into their creamy hearts. One hand held a steel ring, to which half-a-dozen keys were attached—the other toyed unconsciously with the heavy tassel, and the hushed face, with its deep holy eyes, was lifted to meet her father's.

"Nonsense, Irene! I have heard fifty women say that same thing, and have danced at their weddings six months later."

"I do not doubt it. But, Father, no one will ever dance at mine."

"And pray why have n't you as good a right to marry and be happy as other women?"

"The abstract right, and the will to use it, are different, Father; and, as regards happiness, I love my own beautiful home too well to desire to change it for any other. Let me be quiet here—I ask no more."

"But, Irene, I can't be expected to live always, even were my society sufficient for you, which is not true."

"Death yields allegiance to no decree of man. I may find Hugh in another world before you are called to quit this."

Her father shuddered, and smoked silently for several seconds; then the crash of wheels on the shelled avenue startled both.

"Here comes Bainbridge now. I promised him that you would play a game of billiards with him this morning. For heaven's sake, Irene! be reasonable for once in your life; let me hear no more such stuff as you have been talking, but treat the man civilly, and give him what he will ask."

The handsome suitor came up the steps rather dubiously, as if fearful of his welcome; and the heiress rose composedly and received him with graceful, polished, imperturbable reserve. A few months before, in compliance with her father's earnest request, she had accompanied him to the capital of the state, and during this brief visit met and completely fascinated Mr. Bainbridge, whose attentions were susceptible of but one interpretation. He was a year her senior—a chivalric, agreeable, gay young man, who had grown up without selecting a profession, knowing that his ample fortune would more than suffice for his maintenance. He was the only son of the governor; his character was unimpeachable, his nature magnanimous, and many of his impulses were truly noble—but his intellect was far inferior to hers. He could no more comprehend her than some long-inurned Assyrian scroll, for which the cipher-key is wanting; and in the midst of his devotion she was conscious of no feeling save that of utter indifference, sometimes waxing into impatience at his frequent visits. She had studiously avoided encouraging his attentions, but he either could not or would not interpret her cold reticence.

The morning was spent over the billiard-table, and at last, foiled by her skilful guiding of the fragmentary conversation, Mr. Bainbridge having been refused the honor of escorting her to the party, took his leave, expressing the hope that in a few hours he should see her again.

"Well?" said Mr. Huntingdon, seating himself at the luncheon-table.

"Well, Father; we played till I was heartily tired."

"But the result of the visit, Irene?"

"The result was that I beat him three games out of five. John, where is the claret? You have forgotten it; here are the keys."

"Pshaw! I mean, did Bainbridge come to the point."

"I took most of the points from him."

"Confound your quibbling! Did you accept him?"

"I am happy to be able to tell you, sir, that he did not afford me an opportunity."

"Then I will be sworn it was your fault—not his!"

A short silence ensued; Irene sat, seemingly abstracted, dipping her slender hand in a ruby-colored Bohemian finger-bowl. Presently John returned; she took the bottle from him, and, filling her father's glass, said, earnestly:

"Father, I have a favor to ask at your hands; are you in a mood for concessions?"

"'That depends—,' as Guy Darrell says. What is it? Do you want a new collar for Paragon, or a bran new pigeon-box twice the size of the old one? Something unreasonable, I will warrant. You never want what you ought to have. Speak out, my bleached gentile Esther!"

"I do want another pigeon-box badly, but that is not to be asked for to-day. Father, will you give me that large beautiful vacant lot, with the old willow-tree, on the corner of Pine street and Huntingdon avenue, opposite the court-house?"

"Upon my word! I must say you are very modest in your request. What the deuce do you want with it?"

"I know that I am asking a good deal, sir; but I want it as a site for an orphan-asylum. Will you give it to me?"

"No! I'll be hanged if I do! Are you going entirely deranged? What business have you with asylums, I should like to know? Put all of that ridiculous stuff out of your head. Here is something for which I sent to Europe. Eric selected it in Paris, and it arrived yesterday. Wear it to-night."

He drew a velvet case from his pocket and laid it before her. Touching the spring, the lid flew open, and on the blue satin lining lay the blazing coils of a magnificent diamond necklace and bracelets.

"How beautiful! how splendidly beautiful!"

She bent over the flashing mass in silent admiration for some time, examining the delicate setting, then looked up at her father.

"What did they cost?"

"Why do you want to know that?"

"I am pardonably curious on the subject."

"Well, then, I was silly enough to give seven thousand dollars for them."

"And what is the value of that lot I asked for?"

"Five thousand dollars."

"Father, these diamonds are the finest I ever saw. They are superbly beautiful; a queen might be proud of them, and I thank you most earnestly for such a gorgeous present; but, if you will not be offended, I will be candid with you—I would a thousand times rather have the lot than the jewels."

The expression of blank astonishment with which these words were received would have been ludicrous but for the ominous thickening of his brows.

"Father, do not feel hurt with me, or attribute my conduct to any want of gratitude for your indulgent kindness. If I love the smiles of happy children more than the radiance of those costly gems, and would rather wear in my heart the contented faces of well-cared-for orphans than on my neck these glittering diamonds, may I not at least utter my preference without offending you? When I think of the better use to which this money might be applied, the incalculable good it would effect, I shrink from hoarding it up on my person to dazzle the eyes of my associates, to incite some to imitate the lavish expenditure, and to awaken in others envious discontent at their inability to cover themselves with similar splendor. The result of such an example on our society would be like dropping a pebble into some crystal lakelet sleeping in evening sunshine; the wavering ring would widen till the entire glassy surface was shivered into spinning circles and dashed on the rocky shore beyond. Father, forgive me if I have said anything disagreeable to you. I shall be grieved indeed if, on the occasion of your too generous indulgence, any dissension arise between us. Tell me that you are not angry with me."

She laid her fingers on his arm, but he shook off the touch, and, scowling sullenly, snatched the velvet case from her hand and stamped out of the room—slamming the door so violently that the glasses on the table rang out a tinkling chime and the red wine in the bottle danced a saraband.

He went to town, and she met him no more till she was attired for the party. Standing before the mirror in her own room she arranged the flowers in her hair, and, when the leaves were disposed to suit her fastidious taste, she took up a pearl set which he had given her years before, intending to wear it. But just then, raising her eyes, she saw her father's image reflected in the glass. Without turning she put up her arms, and laying her head back on his shoulder said, eagerly:

"My dear, dear Father, do let us be reconciled."

Clouds and moodiness melted from his handsome features as he bent over her an instant, kissing her fondly; then his hands passed swiftly over her neck, an icy shower fell upon it, and she was clothed with light.

"My beautiful child, wear your diamonds as a seal of peace. I can't let you have the Pine street lot—I want it for a different purpose; but I will give you three acres on the edge of town, near the depot, for your asylum whim. It is a better location every way for your project."

"Thank you, Father. Oh! thank you, more than words can express."

She turned her lips to one of the hands still lingering on her shoulder.

"Irene, look at yourself. Diana of Ephesus! what a blaze of glory!"

"Father, it would not require much stretch of imagination to believe that, by some descendental metempsychosis, I had become an exhumed member of the sacred gnomides, torn ruthlessly from my sisterhood in Cerro do Frio or the cold dreary caverns of the Agathyrsi."

"The metamorphosis is not sufficiently complete without your bracelets. Put them on and come down; the carriage is ready. Where is your bouquet-holder? Give it to me; I will fasten the flowers in while you draw on your gloves."

Two days before, the marriage of Charles

Harris and Maria Henderson had been celebrated with considerable pomp, and the party to-night was given in honor of the event by Mrs. Churchhill, a widowed sister of Judge Harris. She had spent several years in Paris, superintending the education of a daughter, whom she had recently brought home to reside near her uncle and dazzle all W—— with her accomplishments.

At ten o'clock there stood beneath the gas-lights in her elegant parlor a human fleshy antithesis, upon which all eyes were riveted—Salome Churchhill—a dark imperious beauty, of the Cleopatra type, with very full crimson lips, passionate or pouting as occasion demanded; brilliant black eyes that, like August days, burned, dewless and unclouded, a steady blaze; thick shining black hair elaborately curled, and a rich tropical complexion, clear and glowing as the warm blood that pulsed through her rounded graceful form. She wore a fleecy fabric. topaz-colored, with black lace trimmings; yellow roses gemmed her hair, and topaz and ruby ornaments clasped her throat and arms. An Eastern queen she looked, exacting universal homage, and full of fiery jealousy whenever her eyes fell upon one who stood just opposite. A statuesque face, pure and calm as any ever cut from Pentelic quarry, and cold as its dews—the delicately-carved features borrowing no color from the glare around her, the polished shoulders and perfect arms gleaming frigidly in the rainbow-light of her diamonds, and the bronze hair caught up by a pearl comb, with here and there a cluster of clematis bells drooping toward her neck. Irene's dress was an airy blue *tulle*, flounced to the waist, and without trimming save the violet and clematis clusters. Never had her rare beauty been more resplendent—more dazzlingly chilly; it seemed the glitter of an arctic iceberg lit by some low midnight sun, and, turn whither she would, fascinated groups followed her steps. Salome's reputation as a brilliant *belle* had become extended since Irene's long seclusion, yet to-night, on the reappearance of the latter, it was apparent to even the most obtuse that she resumed her sway—the matchless cynosura of that social system. Fully conscious of the intense admiration she excited she moved slowly from room to room, smiling once or twice when she met her father's proud look of fond triumph fixed upon her.

Leaning against the window to rest, while Charles Harris went in search of a glass of water, she heard her name pronounced by some one on the gallery.

"They say Irene Huntingdon is positively going to marry Bainbridge. Splendid match both sides. Won't she shine at the governor's mansion? I wonder if she really grieved much for Seymour? How perfectly lovely she is; and Huntingdon is so proud of her. By the way, Neal, have you heard the last gossip?"

"About whom? I have been away a month, you must remember, and am behind the times. Do tell me."

"Well, the very latest report is that, after all, Aubrey never fancied Grace Harris, as the quidnuncs asserted—never addressed her, or anybody else—but is now sure enough about to bear off *belle* Salome, the new prize, right in the face of twenty rivals. I should really like to hear of something which that man could not do, if he set himself to work in earnest. I wonder whether it ever recurs to him that he once stood behind Jacob Watson's counter?"

"But Aubrey is not here to-night. Does not affect parties, I believe?"

"Rarely shows himself; but you mistake; he came in not twenty minutes ago, and you should have seen what I saw—the rare-ripe red deepen on Salome's cheeks when he spoke to her."

Irene moved away from the window, and soon after was about to accompany Charlie to the hall, when Mr. Bainbridge came up and claimed her hand for the cotillon forming in the next room. As they took their places on the floor she saw that Salome and Russell would be *vis-a-vis*. With an effort she raised her eyes to those of the man whom she had seen last at Hugh's bier; he drooped his head very slightly, she inclined hers; then the band smote their instruments, violin and piano, and the crash of music filled the house.

Irene moved mechanically through the airy mazes of the dance, giving apparent attention to the low-toned, half-whispered observations of her devoted partner, but straining her ear to catch the mellow voice which uttered such graceful fascinating nothings to Salome. Several times in the course of the cotillon Russell's hand clasped hers, but even then he avoided looking at her, and seemed engrossed in conversation with his gay partner. Once Irene looked up steadily, and as she noted the expression with which he regarded his companion she wondered no longer at the rumor she had heard, and acknowledged to herself that they were, indeed, a handsome couple. Dr. Arnold, whom Mrs. Churchhill had coaxed into "showing himself," had curiously watched this meeting, and, observing Russell's marked attentions, puzzled over the question: "Does he really care for that fire-fly, or is he only trying to make Irene jealous?" He looked long and earnestly at both, then sighed heavily. What did that haughty blue-robed woman know of jealousy? How absurd such a suggestion seemed when she turned her smiling passionless face full upon him. The dance ended; Irene found herself seated on a sofa at the window of the deserted library, and Russell and Salome walked slowly up and down the veranda in front of it. Mr. Bainbridge had manœuvred for this opportunity, and, seated beside Irene, he eagerly and eloquently pleaded his cause, assuring her of a devotion which should know no diminution, and emphasizing the fact that he had possessed himself of her father's sanction.

She made no attempt to interrupt him, but sat erect and motionless, with one hand partially shielding her face and the other pressed hard against her heart, where a dull continual pain was gnawing. Every few minutes Russell passed the window, his noble head bent down to the beautiful companion on his arm. Irene could see the outline of his features distinctly, and her soul sickened as she watched him and reasoned concerning the future. He would probably marry somebody, and why not Salome? She could not expect him to remain single always, and he could never be more than a stranger to her. After his marriage, what a blank her life would be; to love him still would be sinful. She moved her fingers slightly and looked fixedly at the handsome man beside her, entreating her to give him the privilege of making her life happy. For an instant she wavered. The world held nothing for her but dreariness at best; she was weary of alienation and contention; why not accede to her father's wishes, and thus repair the grievous disappointment of other days? William Bainbridge loved her, and perhaps if she were his wife the sanctity of her vows might strengthen her in tearing another image from her heart. She took her future in the palm of her hand and pondered. At this moment the couple on the veranda paused in front of the window, to allow the promenading crowd to pass, and Russell looked in, with a brilliant smile on his countenance. It seemed to mock her with a "Marry him if you dare!" The two passed on into the parlors, and closing her eyes a moment, as if shutting out some hideous vision, Irene briefly, but firmly and irrevocably, declined the flattering offer; and rising, left him with his disappointment. She looked about for Dr. Arnold, but he had disappeared; her father was deep in a game of euchre; and as she crossed the hall she was surprised to see Philip leaning against the door-facing and peering curiously into the parlors.

"Philip, what are you doing here?"

"Oh, Miss Irene! I have been hunting for you ever so long. Mrs. Davis is dying, and Susan sent me after you. I went to your house two hours ago, and they said you were here. I ran back and told mother you could not come. But Mrs. Davis worried so, they sent me here. She says she won't die in peace unless she sees you. She wrung her hands, and asked me if you would not have time enough to go to parties when she was in her grave? Will you come, ma'm?"

"Of course. Philip, find Andrew and the carriage, and I will meet you at the side door in five minutes."

She went to the dressing-room, asked for pencil and paper, and wrote a few lines, which she directed the servant to hand immediately to her father—found her shawl, and stole down to the side door. She saw the dim outline of a form sitting on the step, in the shadow of clustering vines, and asked:

"Is that you, Philip? I am ready."

The figure rose, came forward into the light, hat in hand, and both started visibly.

"Pardon me, Mr. Aubrey. I mistook you in the darkness for another."

Here Philip ran up the steps.

"Miss Irene, Andrew says he can't get to the side gate for the carriages. He is at the front entrance."

"Can I assist you, Miss Huntingdon?"

"Thank you; no."

"May I ask if you are ill?"

"Not in the least—but I am suddenly called away."

She passed him, and accompanied Philip to the carriage. A few minutes rapid driving brought them to the Row, and, directing Andrew to return and wait for her father, Irene entered the low small chamber where a human soul was pluming itself for its final flight home. The dying woman knew her even then in the fierce throes of dissolution, and the sunken eyes beamed as she bent over the pillow.

"God bless you! I knew you would come. My children—what will become of them? Will you take care of them? Tell me quick."

"Put your mind at rest, Mrs. Davis. I will see that your children are well cared for in every respect."

"Promise me!" gasped the poor sufferer, clutching the jewelled arm.

"I do promise you most solemnly that I will watch over them constantly. They shall never want so long as I live. Will you not believe me, and calm yourself?"

A ghastly smile trembled over the distorted features, and she bowed her head in assent. Irene poured some cordial into a glass and put it to her lips, but she refused the draught, and, joining her emaciated hands, muttered half-inaudibly:

"Pray for me once more. Oh! pray for me, my best friend."

Kneeling on the bare floor in the midst of a sobbing group, Irene prayed long and earnestly; and gradually, as her sweet voice rolled through the room, a peaceful look settled on the dying mother's face. At last the petition ended and silence reigned, broken only by the smothered sobs of Susan and little Johnnie, who clung to Irene's hand and buried his face in her dress as she still knelt at the bedside.

"Mrs. Davis, don't you feel that you will soon be at rest with God?'

"Yes; I am going home happy—happy."

She closed her eyes and whispered:

"Sing my—hymn—once—more."

Making a great effort to crush her own feelings, Irene sang the simple but touching words of "Home Again," and though her voice faltered now and then, she sang it through—

knowing, from the expression of the sufferer's face, that the spirit was passing to its endless rest.

It was a strange scene. The poverty of the room—the emaciated form, with sharp, set features—the magnificently beautiful woman kneeling there in her costly festal-robes, with the light of the tallow candle flickering over her diamonds, setting her neck and arms on fire—and the weeping girl and wailing curly-haired boy, whose tearful face was hidden in the full flounces of blue *tulle*. "Passing strange," thought the proud man of the world, who had followed her from the scenes of festivity and now stood in the door-way listening with hushed breath, to the prayer she had put up, to the words of the hymn she had sung so sorrowfully, and gazing in silent adoration upon the face and form of the kneeling woman. Now one of the beautiful arms stole around the trembling child who clung to her so tenaciously, and she gently lifted the chestnut curls from his flushed face.

"Don't sob so, Johnnie. Your mother is in heaven, where there is no sorrow, or sickness, or trouble. She will be very happy there; and if you are as good and patient as she was, you will meet her in heaven when God calls you to die."

"Oh! is she dead? Miss Irene, is my mother dead?"

"My dear little boy, she has gone to our Father in heaven, who will make her happier than she could possibly be in this world."

A passionate burst of sorrow followed the discovery of the melancholy truth, and rising from the floor Irene seated herself on a chair, taking the child on her lap and soothing his violent grief. Too young to realize his loss, he was easily comforted, and after a time grew quiet. She directed Susan to take him into the next room and put him on his pallet; and when she had exchanged a few words with Philip's mother about the disposition of the rigid sleeper, she turned to quit the apartment, and saw Russell standing on the threshold. Had the dead mother suddenly stepped before her she would scarcely have been more astonished and startled.

He extended one hand, and hastily taking hers, drew her to the door of the narrow dark hall, where the newly-risen moon shone in.

"Come out of this charnel-house into the pure air once more. Do not shrink back—trust yourself with me this once, at least."

The brick walls of the Factory rose a hundred yards off in full view of the Row, and leading her along the river bank he placed her on one of the massive stone steps of the building.

"What brought you here to-night, Mr. Aubrey?"

"An unpardonable curiosity concerning your sudden departure—an unconquerable desire to speak to you once more."

"You witnessed a melancholy scene."

"Yes—melancholy indeed; but not half so sad as one which memory held before me while I watched yonder pale corpse grow rigid. The veil of the Past was rent, and I stood again over my own dead mother. For me there is no Lethe. *In memoriam* creeps in sombre characters over all that I look upon."

A waning June moon, in its last quarter, struggled feebly up the eastern sky, "hounded by a few dim stars," and the spectral light fell like a dying smile upon the silent scene—the broad swift river flashing below, champing with foamy lips on the rocky bit that barred its current, and breaking into shimmering silver cataracts as it leaped triumphantly over a gray ledge of granite and thundered down into the basin beyond, churning itself into diamond spray, that wreathed and fluttered in gleaming threads like a bridal veil streaming on some mild May breeze. The shining shafts of water gave back the ghastly light as huge mirrors might, and from the dark depths of foliage on the opposite bank and the lofty aisles of pine-clad hills stretching far westward and overtopping all, the deep solemn monotone of the everlasting Fall echoed and re-echoed, chanting to the quiet night a sacred "*in cœlo quies.*"

Standing with uncovered head in the weird light, Russell's piercing eyes were fixed on his companion.

"You do not know why I came here, Miss Huntingdon?"

"You told me why."

"No. But you shall know. I came here overmastered by some 'Imp of the Perverse,' led by an irresistible desire to see you alone, to look at you, to tell you what I have almost sworn should never pass my lips—what you may consider unmanly weakness—nay, insanity, on my part. We are face to face at last, man and woman, with the golden bars of conventionality and worldly distinction snapped asunder. I am no longer the man whom society would fain flatter, in atonement for past injustice; and I choose to forget, for the time, that you are the daughter of my bitterest deadly foe—my persistent persecutor. I remember nothing now but the crowned days of our childhood, the rosy dawn of my manhood, where your golden head shone my Morning Star. I hurl away all barriers, and remember only the one dream of my life—my deathless, unwavering love for you. Oh, Irene! Irene! why have you locked that rigid cold face of yours against me? In the hallowed days of old you nestled your dear hands into mine, and pressed your curls against my cheek, and gave me comfort in your pure, warm, girlish affection; how can you snatch your frozen fingers from mine now, as though my touch were contamination? Be yourself once more—give me one drop from the old over-flowing fountain. I am a lonely man; and my proud, bitter heart hungers for one of your gentle words, one of your sweet, priceless smiles. Irene, look at me! Give it to me!"

He sat down on the step at her feet and raised his dark magnetic face, glowing with the love which had so long burned undimmed, his lofty full forehead wearing a strange flush.

She dared not meet his eye, and drooped her head on her palms, shrinking from the scorching furnace of trial, whose red jaws yawned to receive her. He waited a moment, and his low, mellow voice rose to a stormy key.

"Irene, you are kind and merciful to the poor wretches in the Row. Poverty—nay, crime, does not frighten away your compassion for them; why are you hard and cruelly haughty only to me?"

"You do not need my sympathy, Mr. Aubrey, and congratulations on your great success would not come gracefully from my lips. Most unfortunate obstacles long since rendered all intercourse between us impossible, still my feeling for you has undergone no change. I am, I assure you, still your friend."

It cost her a powerful effort to utter these words, and her voice took a metallic tone utterly foreign to it. Her heart writhed and bled and moaned in the gripe of her steely purpose, but she endured all calmly—relaxing not one jot of her bitter resolution.

"My friend! Mockery! God defend me from such henceforth. Irene, I looked at you to-night in all your wonderful, incomparable loveliness as you hung upon the arm of your acknowledged lover, and the possibility of your becoming that man's wife absolutely maddened me. I felt that I could never endure that horrible reality, and I resolved to know the truth. Other lips deceive, but yours never can. Tell me, have you promised your hand to Bainbridge? Will you ever give it to him?"

"Such questions, Mr. Aubrey, you have no right to propound."

"Right! does my worshipping love give me no right to relieve myself from torture, if possible? Oh! relentless, beautiful idol, that you are! I have cheated myself with a heavenly dream—have hugged to my soul the hope that, after all, I was more to you than you designed to show—that far down in your proud heart you, too, cherished memories of other days. Irene, you loved me once—nay, don't deny it! You need not blush for the early folly which, it seems, you have interred so deeply; and though you scorn to meet me even as an equal, I know, I feel, that I am worthy of your love—that I comprehend your strange nature as no one else ever will—that, had such a privilege been accorded me, I could have kindled your heart, and made you supremely happy. Cursed barriers have divided us always; fate denied me my right. I have suffered many things; but does it not argue,

at least, in favor of my love, that it has survived all the trials to which your father's hate has subjected me? To-night I could forgive him all! all! if I knew that he had not so successfully hardened, closed your heart against me. My soul is full of bitterness which would move you, if one trait of your girlish nature remained. But you are not my Irene! The world's queen, the dazzling idol of the ball-room, is not my blue-eyed, angelic Irene of old! I will intrude upon you no longer. Try at least not to despise me for my folly; I will crush it; and if you deign to remember me at all in future, think of a man who laughs at his own idiotcy and strives to forget that he ever believed there lived one woman who would be true to her own heart, even though the heavens fell and the world passed away!"

He rose partially, but her hand fell quickly upon his shoulder and the bowed face lifted itself, stainless as starry jasmines bathed in equatorial dews.

"Mr. Aubrey, you are too severe upon yourself and very unjust to me. The circumstances which conspired to alienate us were far beyond my control; I regret them as sincerely as you possibly can, but as unavailingly. If I have individually occasioned you sorrow or disappointment, God knows it was no fault of mine! We stand on the opposite shores of a dark, bridgeless gulf; but before we turn away to be henceforth strangers, I stretch out my hand to you in friendly farewell!—deeply regretting the pain which I may have innocently caused you and asking your forgiveness. Mr. Aubrey, remember me as I was, not as I am. Good-by, my friend. May God bless you in coming years and crown your life with the happiness you merit, is the earnest prayer of my heart."

The rare blue cord on her brow told how fiercely the lava-flood surged under its icy bands, and the blanched lip matched her cheek in colorlessness; save these tokens of anguish, no other was visible.

Russell drew down the hand from his shoulder and folded it in both his own.

"Irene, are we to walk different paths henceforth—utter strangers? Is such your will?"

"Such is the necessity which must be as apparent to you as to me. Do not doubt my friendship, Mr. Aubrey; but doubt the propriety of my parading it before the world."

He bent his cheek down on her cold hand, then raised it to his lips once, twice—laid it back on her lap, and, taking his hat, walked away toward town.

Two blithe crickets chirped merrily somewhere in the brick pavement round the door; a solitary mocking-bird, perched on the limb of a neighboring china-tree, warbled his sweet varied notes as if in answer; the mellow diapason of the Falls rose soothingly over all, and the blue-robed woman sat still as the stone steps of the Factory, watching the vanishing dying sparkles of a crystal draught of joy which Fate had rudely dashed at her feet, sternly denying the parched eager lips.

For some time she remained just as Russell had left her, then the white arms and dry eyes were raised to the midnight sky.

"My God! my God! strengthen me in my desolation!"

She put back the folds of hair that, damp with dew, clung to her gleaming temples, and recrossing the wide road or street, entered the chamber of death. Low-spoken words crept to and fro between Mrs. Martin and two middle-aged, sad-faced women of the Row, who sat around the candle on the little pine table, clipping and scalloping a jaconet shroud. As Irene approached the scissors rested and all looked up.

"Where is Philip, Mrs. Martin? I shall ask him to walk home with me, and not wait for the carriage."

"I expect he is asleep, Miss Irene—but I will wake him."

"You need not; I think I hear wheels. Yes; they are coming for me. Mrs. Martin, I will see you about Susan and Johnnie tomorrow or next day; meantime, I leave them in your care. Good-night."

"What a white angel she is!—almost as pale as the poor creature on the bed yonder. I catch my breath sometimes when she looks like she did just now."

All three sighed simultaneously, and the dull click, click, began again.

It was not the carriage which Irene met at the door, but Dr. Arnold's buggy.

"Irene, are you ready to go home?"

"Yes. Mrs. Davis is dead."

"As I was leaving Mrs. Churchhill's your father told me where you were, and I thought I would come after you. Put on your shawl and jump in. You are in a pretty plight, truly, to stand over a death-bed! 'Vanity of vanities! all is vanity!' Here, let me wrap that gauze cloud around your head. Now then!"

The top of the buggy had been lowered, and as they rode homeward she leaned her head back, turning her face to the sickly moonlight.

"Irene, did Aubrey come up here with you?"

"No, sir. He was at the Row for a while, however. You must have met him returning."

"I did; what did he want here?"

"You must ask him if you are curious. It is no business of either yours or mine to watch his movements."

"I wonder he was able to tear himself from that brown Sybil, Salome. What a splendid dark pair they will be some day, when he makes her Mrs. Aubrey!"

Surgeon-like, he was pressing his finger heavily on the wound, but no flinching could be detected—no moan of pain; and he was startled by a singular short, quick laugh, which sounded to his ear like the sudden snapping of a musical string. It was the first time he had heard her laugh since her return from New York.

"Sage of Sinope! how long since your transmigration into a latter-day news-monger?"

"News-monger be hanged! It is a transparent fact that Aubrey intends to marry the daughter of Herodias. Don't you believe it, Irene?"

"Doctor, I believe I have dropped my bouquet-holder. I am sorry to give you so much trouble, but Uncle Eric bought it for me in Geneva, and I should dislike to lose it. Give me the reins. Yonder it is, in the sand—I see its glitter."

Fulminating inaudible plagues on the chased silver toy, the doctor picked it up and placed it in her hand.

"Drop yourself out next, won't you, when you have another question to dodge?"

"What is the matter? Who has fretted you, sir? Were you cheated out of your supper by coming after me?"

"You fret me beyond all patience—slipping everlastingly through my fingers. Child, answer me one thing truly; are you going to marry Bainbridge, as everybody believes, and as Leonard led me to suppose?"

"No, Dr. Arnold; I shall never marry Mr. Bainbridge."

"If he does not suit your fastidious taste, pray who will, Queen?"

"You might, perhaps, if you were thirty-five years younger, and a trifle less surly. Doctor, come in, and let me give you a glass of wine; it is very late and you must be tired."

"No—but I will light my pipe at the hall-lamp."

They went into the house, and as he filled and lighted his pipe his cavernous eyes ran curiously over her.

"How you have blazed to-night! Your diamonds are superb."

"Yes, sir."

"Go to sleep at once, child. You look as if you had seen a ghost. What has knotted up your forehead in that style?"

"I have looked upon a melancholy death to-night, and have seen two helpless children orphaned. Come and see me soon; I want to consult you about an orphan-asylum for which father has given me a lot. Good-night, sir; I am very much obliged to you for your kindness in bringing me home. Nobody else is half so considerate and thoughtful."

In her own room she took off the jewels, withered violets, and moist *tulle*—and, drawing on her dressing-gown, went up to the observatory and sat down on the threshold of one of the glass doors looking eastward.

"Think of a man who laughs at his own idiotcy and strives to forget that he ever believed there lived one woman who would be true to her own heart, though the heavens fell and the world passed away!"

These words of scorn were the burning shares over which her bare feet trod, and his bitter accents wailed up and down her lonely heart, mournful as the ceaseless cry of "*El Alma Perdida*" in moonless, breezeless Amazonian solitudes. Through the remainder of that cloudless night she wrestled silently—not like the Jewish patriarch, with angels—but with Despair, grim as Geryon. At last, when the sky flushed rosily, like an opal smitten with light, and holy Resignation—the blessing born only of great trial like hers—shed its heavenly chrism over the worn and weary, bruised and bleeding spirit, she gathered up the mangled hopes that might have gladdened and gilded and glorified her earthly career, and pressing the ruins to her heart, laid herself meekly down, offering all upon the God-built altar of Filial Obedience.

In the

> ". . . early morning, when the air
> Was delicate with some last starry touch,"

she opened the door of her father's room and approached the bed. The noise wakened him, and, raising himself on his elbow, he looked wonderingly at her.

"What is the matter, Irene? You look as if you had not closed your eyes."

"Father, you took me in your arms last night, and kissed me as you have not done before for years; but I feared that when Mr. Bainbridge told you what passed between us at Mrs. Churchhill's you would again close your heart against me. Do not! oh, do not! Because I prefer to remain at home with you rather than accept his brilliant offer, ought you to love me less? I have spent a sorrowful, a wretched night, and, like a weary child, I have come to you to find rest for my heart. Oh, Father! my father! do not cast me off again! Whom have I in the world but you? By the memory of my sainted mother I ask—I claim your love!"

"You are a strange girl, Irene; I never did understand you. But I don't want to drive you from me if you prefer to live here single. There shall be peace between us, my dear daughter." He leaned forward and laid his hand caressingly on her head as she knelt at his bedside pleading with uplifted arms.

> "And her face is lily-clear.
> Lily-shaped and dropped in duty
> To the law of its own beauty.
> And a forehead, fair and saintly,
> Which two blue eyes undershine
> Like meek prayers before a shrine."

CHAPTER XXVII.

The treacherous four years lull was broken at last by the mutter of the storm which was so soon to sweep over the nation, prostrating all interests and bearing desolation to almost every hearthstone in our once happy, smiling land of constitutional freedom. Sleepless watchmen on the tower of Southern Rights—faithful guardians, like William L. Yancey, who had stood for years, in advance of public opinion, lifting their warning voices far above the howling waves of popular faction and party strife, pointing to the only path of safety—now discerned the cloud upon the horizon, and at the selection of delegates to the Charleston Convention hedged our cause with cautious resolutions. Among the number appointed was Russell Aubrey; and during the tempestuous debates which ushered in the war of 1861 his earnest, eloquent pleadings on the question of a platform rang through his state, touching the master-chord that thrilled responsive in the great heart of the people. When demagogism triumphed in that convention, and the Democratic party was rent into hopeless fragments, Russell returned, to stump the state in favor of the only candidate whom he believed the South could trust with her liberties; and during the arduous campaign that ensued, he gathered fresh laurels and won a brilliant reputation. Aside from individual ambitious projects, the purest patriotism nerved him to his ceaseless labors. He was deeply impressed with the vital consequences of the impending election; and as the conviction forced itself upon his mind that, through the demoralization of the Northern wing of Democracy, Lincoln would be elected, he endeavored to prepare the masses for that final separation which he foresaw was inevitable. During that five months campaign faction, fanaticism, demagogism, held high revel—ran riot through the land. Seward cantered toward Washington on the hobby labelled Emancipation, dragging Lincoln at his heels; and Breckinridge, our noble standard-bearer, with the constitution in his hand, pressed on to save the sacred precincts of the capitol from pollution. The gauntlet had been thrown down by the South at Charleston and Baltimore: "The election of a sectional President will be the signal for separation." The North sneered at the threat, derided the possibility, and in frantic defiance the die was cast. The 6th of November dawned upon a vast populous empire, rich in every resource, capable of the acme of human greatness and prosperity, claiming to be the guardian of peaceful liberty. It set upon a nation rent in twain, between whose sections yawned a bottomless, bridgeless gulf, where the shining pillars of the temple of Concord had stood for eighty years; and a grating sound of horror shuddered through the land as the brazen, blood-clotted doors of Janus flung themselves suddenly wide apart. Lincoln was elected. Abolitionism, so long adroitly cloaked, was triumphantly clad in robes of state—shameless now, and hideous; and while the North looked upon the loathsome face of its political Mokanna, the South prepared for resistance.

No surer indication of the purpose of the Southern people could have been furnished than the temper in which the news was received. No noisy outbursts, expending resolve in empty words—no surface excitement—but a stern calm gloom, set lips, heavy bent brows, appropriate in men who realized that they had a revolution on their hands; not indignation-meetings, with fruitless resolutions—that they stood as body-guard for the liberty of the Republic, and would preserve the trust at all hazards. It would seem that, for a time at least, party animosities would have been crushed; but, like the Eumenides of Orestes, they merely slept for a moment, starting up wolfish and implacable as ever; and even here, in many instances, the old acrimony of feeling showed itself. Bitter differences sprung up at the very threshold on the *modus operandi* of Southern release from Yankee-Egyptian bondage. Separate "state action" or "co-operation" divided the people, many of whom were earnestly impressed by the necessity and expediency of deliberate, concerted, simultaneous action on the part of all the Southern states, while others vehemently advocated this latter course solely because the former plan was advanced and supported by their old opponents. In this new issue, as if fate persistently fanned the flame of hate between Mr. Huntingdon and Russell Aubrey, they were again opposed as candidates for the State Convention. Ah! will the ghost of Faction ever be laid in this our republican land? Shall this insatiate immemorial political Fenris for ever prey upon the people?

W—— was once more convulsed, and strenuous efforts were made by both sides. Russell was indefatigable in his labors for prompt, immediate state action, proclaiming his belief that co-operation was impracticable before secession; and it was now that his researches in the dusty regions of statistics came admirably into play, as he built up his arguments on solid foundations of indisputable calculation.

For the first time in her life Irene openly confronted her father's wrath on political grounds. She realized the imminence of the danger, dreaded the siren song of co-operation, and dauntlessly discussed the matter without hesitation. The contest was close and heated, and resulted somewhat singularly in the election of a mixed ticket—two Secessionists being returned, and one Co-operationist, Mr. Huntingdon, owing to personal popularity.

While the entire South was girding for the contest, South Carolina, ever the *avant courrier* in the march of freedom, seceded: and if doubt had existed before, it vanished now from every mind—for all felt that the gallant state must be sustained. Soon after, Russell and Mr. Huntingdon stood face to face on the floor of their own state convention, and wrestled desperately. The latter headed the opposition, and so contumacious did it prove that, for some days, the fate of the state lay in dangerous equilibrium. Finally the vigilance of the Secessionists prevailed, and, late in the afternoon of a winter day, the ordinance was signed.

Electricity flashed the decree to every portion of the state, and the thunder of artillery and blaze of countless illuminations told that the people gratefully and joyfully accepted the verdict. W—— was vociferous; and as Irene gazed from the colonnade on the distant but brilliant rows of lights flaming along the streets, she regretted that respect for her father's feelings kept the windows of her own home dark and cheerless.

Revolution is no laggard, but swift-winged as Hermes; and in quick succession seven sovereign states, in virtue of the inherent rights of a people acknowledging allegiance only to the fundamental doctrine that all just governments rest on the consent of the governed, organized a provisional government, sprang, Pallas-like, upon the political arena, and claimed an important *role* in the grand drama of the nineteenth century. It was not to be expected that a man of Mr. Huntingdon's known acerbity of temper would yield gracefully to a defeat against which he had struggled so earnestly, and he submitted with characteristic sullenness.

Great contrariety of opinion prevailed concerning the course of the Federal government—many deluding themselves with the belief that the separation would be peaceful. But Russell had stated his conviction at the time of Lincoln's election, that no bloodless revolution of equal magnitude had yet been effected, and that we must prepare to pay the invariable sacrificial dues which liberty inexorably demands.

So firm was this belief, that he applied himself to the study of military tactics, in anticipation of entering the army; and many a midnight found him bending over Hardee, Mahan, Gilham, Jomini, and Army Regulations.

The 12th and 13th of April were days of unexampled excitement throughout the Southern states. The discharge of the first gun from Fort Moultrie crushed the last lingering vestiges of "Unionism" and welded the entire Confederacy in one huge homogeneous mass of stubborn resistance to despotism. With the explosion of the first shell aimed by General Beauregard against Fort Sumter burst the frail painted bubble of "Reconstruction," which had danced alluringly upon the dark surging billows of revolution. W—— was almost wild with anxiety; and in the afternoon of the second day of the bombardment, as Irene watched the avenue, she saw her father driving rapidly homeward. Descending the steps, she met him at the buggy.

"Beauregard has taken Sumter. Anderson surrendered unconditionally. No lives lost."

"Thank God!"

They sat down on the steps, and a moment after the roar of guns shook the atmosphere, and cheer after cheer went up the evening sky.

"Act 1, of a long and bloody civil war," said Mr. Huntingdon, gravely.

"Perhaps so, Father; but it was forced upon us. We left no honorable means untried to prevent it, and now it must be accepted as the least of two evils. Political bondage—worse than Russian serfdom—or armed resistance; no other alternative, turn it which way you will; and the Southern people are not of stuff to deliberate as to choice in such an issue. God is witness that we have earnestly endeavored to avert hostilities—that the blood of this war rests upon the government at Washington; our hands are stainless."

"I believe you are right, and to-day I have come to a determination which will doubtless surprise you."

He paused, and eyed her a moment.

"No, Father; I am not surprised that you have determined to do your duty."

"How, Irene? What do you suppose that it is?"

"To use Nelson's words, the Confederacy 'expects that every man will do his duty;' and you are going into the army."

"Who told you that?"

"My own heart, Father; which tells me what I should do were I in your place."

"Well, I have written to Montgomery, to Clapham, to tender my services. We were at West Point together; I served under him at Contreras and Chepultepec, and he will no doubt press matters through promptly. The fact is, I could not possibly stay at home now. My blood has been at boiling heat since yesterday morning, when I read Beauregard's first dispatch."

"Did you specify any branch of the service?"

"Yes; I told him I preferred artillery. What is the matter? Your lips are as white as cotton. Courage failing you already, at thought of grape, shell, and canister?"

A long shiver crept over her, and she shielded her face with her hands. When she met his eagle eye again her voice was unsteady.

"Oh, Father! if I were only a man, that I might go with you—stand by you under all circumstances. Could n't you take me anyhow? Surely a daughter may follow her father, even on the battle-field?"

He laughed lightly, and swept his fingers over her head.

"Could n't you learn a little common-sense, if you were to try? Do you suppose I want all this gold braid of yours streaming in my face while I am getting my guns into position? A pretty figure you would cut in the midst of my battery! Really, though, Irene, I do not believe that you would flinch before all the cannon of Borodino. My blood beats at your heart, and it has never yet shown a cowardly drop. If you were a boy, I swear you would not disgrace my name in any conflict. By the way, what shall I do with you? It won't do to leave you here all alone."

"Why not, Father? Home is certainly the proper place for me, if you cannot take me with you."

"What! with nobody but the servants?"

"They will take better care of me than anybody else. Nellie and Andrew and John are the only guardians I want in your absence. They have watched over me all my life, and they will do it to the end. Give yourself no trouble, sir, on my account."

"I suppose your Uncle Eric will be home before long; he can stay here till I come back —or—till the troubles are over. In the meantime, you could be with the Harrises, or Hendersons, or Mrs. Churchhill."

"No, sir; I can stay here, which is infinitely preferable on many accounts. I will, with your permission, invite Mrs. Campbell to shut up the parsonage in her husband's absence and remain with me till Uncle Eric returns. I have no doubt that she will be glad to make the change. Do you approve the plan?"

"Yes. That arrangement will answer for the present, and Arnold will be here to take care of you."

At the close of a week a telegraphic despatch was received, informing Mr. Huntingdon of his appointment as major in the provisional army of the Confederacy, and containing an order to report immediately for duty.

Some days of delay were consumed in necessary preparations for an indefinite absence. Sundry papers were drawn up by Judge Harris—an old will was destroyed, a new one made—and explicit directions were reiterated to the overseer at the plantation. More reticent than ever, Irene busied herself in devising and arranging various little comforts for her father, when he should be debarred from the luxuries of home. No traces of tears were ever visible on her grave, composed face; but several times, on coming suddenly into the room, he found that her work had fallen into her lap and that her head was bowed down on her arms. Once he distinguished low pleading words of prayer. She loved him with a devotion very rarely found between father and child, and this separation cost her hours of silent agony, which even her father could not fully appreciate.

Having completed his arrangements, and ordered the carriage to be in readiness at daylight next morning to convey him to the depot, he bade her good-night much as usual and retired to his own room.

But thought was too busy to admit of sleep. He turned restlessly on his pillow, rose, and smoked a second cigar, and returned, to find himself more wakeful than ever. The clock down stairs in the library struck one; his door opened softly, and, by the dim moonlight struggling through the window, he saw Irene glide to his bedside.

"Why don't you go to sleep, Irene?"

"Because I can't. I am too miserable."

Her voice was dry, but broken, faltering.

"I never knew you to be nervous before; I thought you scorned nerves? Here, my daughter—take this pillow, and lie down by me."

She put her arm about his neck, drawing his face close to hers, and he felt her lips quiver as they touched his cheek.

"Father, when you know exactly where you are to be stationed, won't you let me come and stay somewhere in the vicinity, where I can be with you if you should be wounded? Do promise me this; it will be the only comfort I can have."

"The neighborhood of an army would not be a pleasant place for you; beside, you could do me no good even if I were hurt. I shall have a surgeon to attend to all such work much better than your inexperienced hands could possibly do it. I am surprised at you, Irene; upon my word, I am. I thought you wanted me to go into service promptly?"

"So I do, Father. I think that every man in the Confederacy who can leave his family should be in our army; but a stern sense of duty does not prevent people from suffering at separation and thought of danger. I should be unworthy of my country if I were selfish enough to want to keep you from its defence; and yet I were unworthy of my father if I could see you leave home, under such circumstances, without great grief. Oh! if I could only go with you! But to have to stay here, useless and inactive!"

"Yes—it is bad to be obliged to leave you behind, but it can't be helped. I should feel much better satisfied if you were married and had somebody to take care of you in case anything happens to me. It is your own fault that you are not; I never could understand what possessed you to discard Bainbridge. Still, that is past, and I suppose irreparable, and now you must abide by your own choice."

"I am satisfied with my choice; have no regrets on any score, save that of your departure. But, Father, the future is dark and uncertain; and I feel that I want an assurance of your entire reconciliation and affection before you go. I came here to say to you that I deeply regret all the unfortunate circumstances of my life which caused you to treat me so coldly for a season—that if in anything I have ever seemed obstinate or undutiful it was not because I failed in love for you, but from an unhappy difference of opinion as to my duty under very trying circumstances. Father, my heart ached very bitterly under your estrangement—the very memory is unutterably painful. I want your full, free forgiveness now for all the trouble I have ever occasioned you. Oh, Father! give it to me!"

He drew her close to him and kissed her twice.

"You have my forgiveness, my daughter—though I must tell you that your treatment of poor Hugh has been a continual source of sorrow and keen disappointment to me. I never can forget your disobedience in that matter. I do not believe you will ever be happy, you have such a strange disposition; but, since you took matters so completely in your own hands, you have only yourself to reproach. Irene, I very often wonder whether you have any heart—for it seems to me that if you have, it would have been won by the devotion which has been lavished on you more than once. You are the only woman I ever knew who appeared utterly incapable of love; and I sometimes wonder what will become of you when I am dead."

"God will protect me. I look continually to his guardianship. Father, do not be offended if I beg you most earnestly to give some thought to Him who has blessed you so abundantly in the privileges of this world, and to prepare for that future into which you may be ushered, at any moment, from the battle-field. You have never allowed me to speak to you on this subject; but oh, my dear father! it is too solemn a question to be put aside any longer. If you would only pray for yourself, my mind would be eased of such a weight of anxiety and apprehension. Oh! that the spirit of my mother may join in my prayers before the Throne in your behalf!"

He unclasped her arm and turned his face away, saying, coldly:

"Do you consider it your privilege to tell me that I am so wicked there is no hope for me in the next world, if there be one?"

"No! no! Father! but it is enjoined, as the duty of even the purest and holiest, to acknowledge their dependence on God and to supplicate His mercy and direction. It is true, I pray constantly for you, but that is a duty which our Maker requires every individual to perform for himself. Do not be displeased, Father; if it were anything less than your eternal happiness I should not presume to question your conduct. I can only hope and trust that your life will be spared, and that some day you will, without offence, suffer me to talk to you of what deeply concerns my peace of mind. I won't keep you awake any longer, as you have a tedious journey before you. Good-night, my dear father."

She kissed him tenderly and left him, closing the door softly behind her.

A spectral crescent moon flickered in the sky, and stars still burned in the violet East, when the carriage drove to the door and Irene followed her father to the steps.

Even in that dim, uncertain gray light he could see that her face was rigid and haggard, and tears filled his cold brilliant eyes as he folded her to his heart.

"Good-by, Beauty. Cheer up, my brave child! and look on the bright side. After all. I may come back a brigadier-general, and make you one of my staff officers! You shall be my adjutant, and light up my office with your golden head. Take care of yourself till Eric comes, and write to me often. Good-by, my dear, my darling daughter."

She trembled convulsively, pressing her lips repeatedly to his.

"Oh, may God bless you, my father, and bring you safely back to me!"

He unwound her arms, put her gently aside, and stepped into the carriage.

William, the cook, who was to accompany him, stood sobbing near the door, and now advancing, grasped her hand.

"Good-by, Miss Irene. May the Lord protect you all till we come back!"

"William, I look to you to take care of Father, and let me know at once if anything happens."

"I will, Miss Irene. I promise you I will take good care of Master, and telegraph you if he is hurt."

He wrung her hand, the carriage rolled rapidly away, and the sorrow-stricken, tearless woman sat down on the steps and dropped her head in her hands. Old Nellie drew near, wiping her eyes and essaying comfort.

"Don't fret so, child. When trouble comes it will be time enough to grieve over it. Master was in the Mexican war, and never had a scratch; and maybe he will be as lucky this time. Don't harden your face in that flinty way. You never would cry like other children, but just set yourself straight up, for all the world like one of the stone figures standing over your grandfather's grave. Try to come and take a nap; I know you have n't shut your eyes this night."

"No—I can't sleep. Go in, Nellie, and leave me to myself."

The shrill scream of the locomotive rang through the still, dewy air, and between two neighboring hills the long train of cars dashed on, leaving a fiery track of sparks as it disappeared around a curve. Oppressed with a horrible dread, against which she struggled in vain, Irene remained alone, and was only aroused from her painful reverie by the low musical cooing of the pigeons, already astir. As they fluttered and nestled about, she extended her arms, and catching two of the gentlest to her heart, murmured, mournfully:

"Come, messengers of peace! bring me resignation. Teach me patience and faith."

The empty carriage came slowly up the avenue, as if returning from a funeral, and passed to the stable-yard; birds chirped, twittered, sang in the wavering, glistening tree-tops; the sun flashed up in conquering splendor, and the glory of the spring day broke upon the world.

"'To-day thou girdest up thy loins thyself,
And goest where thou would'st: presently
Others shall gird thee.' said the Lord, 'to go
Where thou would'st not.'"

CHAPTER XXVIII.

To those who reside at the convulsed throbbing heart of a great revolution a lifetime seems compressed into the compass of days and weeks, and men and women are conscious of growing prematurely old while watching the rushing, thundering tramp of events, portentous with the fate of nations. W—— presented the appearance of a military camp rather than the peaceful manufacturing town of yore. Every vacant lot was converted into a parade-ground—and the dash of cavalry, the low, sullen rumbling of artillery, and the slow, steady tread of infantry echoed through its wide, handsome streets. Flag-staffs were erected from public buildings, private residences, and at the most frequented corners, and from these floated banners of all sizes, tossing proudly to the balmy breeze the new-born ensign of freedom—around which clustered the hopes of a people who felt that upon them, and them only, now devolved the sacred duty of proving to the world the capacity of a nation for self-government. In view of the iniquitous and impossible task which it had insanely set itself to accomplish, the government at Washington had swept aside all constitutional forms, in order to free its hands for the work of blood—had ultimated in complete despotism. The press was thoroughly muzzled—freedom of speech was erased from the list of American privileges; the crowded cells of Bastile Lafayette, McHenry, and Warren wailed out to the civilized world that *habeas corpus* was no more; and, terror-stricken at the hideous figure of Absolutism carved by the cunning fingers of Lincoln and Seward, and set up for worship at Washington, Liberty fled from her polluted fane and sought shelter and shrine on the banner of the Confederacy, in the dauntless, devoted hearts of its unconquerable patriots. Fondly and proudly was the divinity guarded. Smiling flowery valleys rang with pæans that rose high above the din of deadly strife—and rugged, lonely hills and purple mountains lifted themselves to the God of battle, like huge smoking altars red with the noble blood of slaughtered heroes. Loathing and detestation succeeded the old affection for the Federal government, and "Union" became everywhere the synonyme of political duplicity, despotism, and the utter abrogation of all that had once constituted American freedom and rendered the republic, in earlier years, the civil Pharos of Christendom. The Confederacy realized that the hour had arrived when the historic Sphinx must find an Œdipus, or Democratic republican liberty would be devoured, swept away, with the *debris* of other dead systems. Lifting their eyes to God for blessing, the men of the South girded on their swords and resolved, calmly and solemnly, to prove that Œdipus—to read, and for ever set at rest the haunting, vexing riddle. Another adjective than "Spartan" must fleck with glory the pages of future historians, for all the stern resolution and self-abnegation of Rome and Lacedæmon had entered the souls of Southern women. Mothers closed their lips firmly to repress a wail of sorrow as they buckled on the swords of their first-born, and sent them forth with a "Godspeed!" to battle for the right; fond wives silently packed their husbands' knapsacks, with hands that knew no faltering; and sisters, with tearless eyes, bent by the light of midnight-lamps over canteens which their thoughtful care covered for brothers who were to start to the scene of action on the morrow. A nation of laboring, nimble-fingered, prayerful-hearted, brave-spirited women, and chivalric, high-souled, heroic men, who had never learned that Americans could live and not be free. Grant us our reward, O God! the independence of the land we hold so dear.

W—— gave her young men liberally; company after company was equipped, furnished with ample funds by the munificence of citizens who remained, and sent forward to Virginia, to make their breasts a shield for the proud old "Mother of Presidents." The battle of Bethel was regarded as part of an overture to the opera of Blood, yclept "Subjugation," and people watched in silence for the crimson curtain to rise upon the banks of the Potomac. Russell Aubrey had succeeded in raising a fine full company for the war, as contra-distinguished from twelve months volunteers; and to properly drill and discipline it, he bent all the energy of his character. It was made the nucleus of a new regiment, recruits gathered rapidly, and when the regiment organized, preparatory to starting for Virginia, he was elected colonel, with Herbert Blackwell for lieutenant-colonel, and Charles Harris was appointed adjutant. They were temporarily encamped on the common between the railroad depot and Mr. Huntingdon's residence, and from the observatory or colonnade Irene could look down on the gleaming tents and the flag-staff that stood before the officers' quarters. *Reveille* startled her at dawn, and *tattoo* regularly warned her of the shortness of summer nights. As the fiery carriage-horses would not brook the sight of the encampment, she discarded them for a time, and when compelled to leave home rode Erebus, at no slight risk of her life—for he evinced the greatest repugnance to the sound of drum or fife.

One afternoon she went over to the Row, and thence to the Factory. A new company had been named in honor of her father; uniforms and haversacks were to be furnished, and Mr. Huntingdon had intrusted her with the commission. Selecting the cloth and accomplishing her errand, she returned by way of the orphan-asylum, whose brick walls were rapidly rising under her supervision. One of the workmen took her horse, and she went over the building, talking to the principal mechanic about some additional closets which she desired to have inserted. Dr. Arnold chanced to be passing, but saw Erebus at the gate, stopped, and came in.

"I was just going up to the Hill to see you, Queen—glad I am saved the trouble. Here, sit down a minute; I will clear these shavings away. When did you hear from Leonard?"

"I had a letter yesterday. He was well, and on outpost duty near Manassas."

"Well, I shall join him very soon."

"Sir?"

"I say I shall join him very soon; don't you believe it? Why should n't I serve my country as well as younger men? The fact is, I am going as surgeon of Aubrey's regiment. It would never do to have the handsome colonel maimed for life through the awkwardness of a new-fledged M.D. Miss Salome would spoil her superb eyes with crying—which catastrophe would, doubtless, distress him more than the loss of a limb—eh, Irene?"

She looked at him, betraying neither surprise nor regret.

"When will you leave W——?"

"Day after to-morrow morning; can't get transportation any sooner. Aubrey has received orders to report at once to General Beauregard. Child, have you been sick?"

"No, sir. I am glad you are going with the regiment; very glad. Every good surgeon in the Confederacy should hasten to the front line of our armies. Since you leave home, I am particularly glad that you are going to Manassas, where you can be near Father."

"Humph! Do you suppose that I am a patent life-preserver against minie balls and grape-shot?"

"I know you will do all that skill and affection can suggest, and I shall feel much better satisfied."

He mused a moment, watching her furtively.

"I suppose you have heard of the performance for to-morrow?"

"No, sir. To what do you allude?"

"The daughter of Herodias is preparing to dance."

"I don't understand you, Doctor."

"Oh, don't you, indeed? Well, then, she intends to present a splendid regimental flag with her own brown hands; and, as Aubrey is to receive it, the regiment will march to Mrs. Churchhill's, where the speeches will be delivered. Will you attend?"

"Scarcely, I presume, as I am not invited.

I knew that Salome was having an elegant flag made, but was not aware that to-morrow was appointed for the ceremony of presentation."

"Who will look after you when I am gone? You are the only tie I have here. I can't bear to leave you."

"I dare say I shall get on very well; and, beside, you, of course, must go and do your duty, no matter what happens."

"But you will be so lonely and isolated till Eric comes."

She smiled suddenly, strangely, yet with no tinge of bitterness.

"That is nothing new. I have been solitary all my life."

"And it is your own fault. You might have married like other people, and been happier."

"You are mistaken in assuming that I am not happy in my home."

"Hush, Irene! hush! I know the signs of true happiness, if I don't possess it myself. You never murmur; oh, no!—you are too proud! You don't droop like some poor, weak, sickly souls; oh, no!—you are too stately and regal. You will live and die a model of reticent chill propriety; and when you are in your shroud your placid, treacherous face will bear no witness that you were cheated out of your rights in this world."

Again she smiled, and laid her hand on his.

"What a pity you mistook your forte in early life; with such a fertile imagination, not physic, but fiction, was your calling. When will you come to see me? I want you to take a parcel to father for me; and then I want to have a long talk."

"I know what the long talk amounts to. You need not hold out any such rosy-cheeked apples of Sodom as a bait. I am coming, of course, after the flag-ceremonies, where I am expected. At one o'clock I will be at the Hill—perhaps earlier. Where now?"

"I must go by Mrs. Baker's to see about giving out some sewing for the 'Huntingdon Rifles.' I can't do it all at home, and several families here require work. I shall expect you at one o'clock—shall have lunch ready for you. By the way, Doctor, is there anything I can do for you in the sewing line? It would give me genuine pleasure to make something for you, if you will only tell me what you need. Think over your wants."

She had caught up her reins, but paused, looking at him. He averted his head quickly.

"I will tell you to-morrow. Good-evening."

Turning from the town, she took a narrow sandy road leading among low, irregular hills, and after passing a thicket of sweet-gum, bay, and poplar, that bordered a clear, brawling, rocky-bosomed stream which ran across the road, she rode up to a three-roomed log-house. Two small children, with anomalous bluish-white hair, were playing marbles in the passage, and a boy, apparently ten years of age, was seated on the ground, whistling "Dixie" and making split baskets, such as are generally used on plantations for picking cotton. He threw down his work and ran to open the gate, which was tied with a piece of rope.

"How do you do, Hanson? Is your mother at home?"

"Yes, ma'm."

She gave him her bridle and entered the house, in one of the rooms of which she found a tall, muscular, powerful-looking woman kneeling on the floor and engaged in cutting out work from a roll of striped cloth. Putting her grayish hair behind her ears, she paused, looked up, and, with scissors in hand, said, bluntly:

"Be seated, Miss Irene. I have n't time, or I would get up. Lucinda, bring some water fresh from the spring, and if your grandmother is awake, tell her Miss Irene is here."

"I see you have not finished your contract, Mrs. Baker."

"Very nearly, ma'm. I will finish off and send in the last lot of these haversacks by twelve o'clock to-morrow. The captain was out to-day to hurry me up; said the regiment had orders to leave day after to-morrow. I gave him my word he should have them by noon, and that is something I never break."

"Have you heard from your husband since I saw you?"

Again the busy scissors paused.

"Not a word. But my boy, Robert, has had a terrible spell of fever in Lynchburg. I received a few lines from the doctor of the hospital yesterday. Thank God! he was better when the letter was written. His father knows nothing of it. I can't find out exactly where Mr. Baker's company is. They are doing good service, I hope, somewhere—making their mark on the Union wretches in the Virginia valley. I want to hear that my husband had a hand in burning Wheeling."

"I believe you told me that you were from Virginia."

"Yes, ma'm; but not from that part of it, I want you to understand. I was born in Amelia, thank my stars! and that is as true as steel."

"It must be a great trial to you to have your husband and son so far off, and yet separated."

"Of course I hate to have them away, and times are hard for such a family as mine, with little means of support; but I don't grieve. Every man has to do his duty now, and every woman, too. I told Stephen I thought I could take care of the children and myself—that I would rather live on acorns, than that he should not serve his country when it needed him; and I told Robert, when I fixed him off, that I never would die contented if he and his father did not both do something to distinguish themselves in this war. I am a poor woman, Miss Irene, but no soul loves the Confederacy better than I do, or will work harder for it. I have no money to lend our government, but I give my husband and my child—and two better soldiers no state can show."

"You have done your part nobly, and I trust both your dear ones will be spared and brought safely back to you. How is your mother to-day?"

"Very feeble. I was up nearly all night with her. She had one of her bad spells. Have some water; it is sweet and cold."

"Do you want any more work this week?"

"Yes ma'm; I should like some after to-morrow. Do you know where I can get any?"

"I can give you seventy-five flannel over-shirts, and the same number of haversacks; but you could scarcely finish them all in time, and I thought I would send you the shirts and let Mrs. Pritchard take the haversacks."

"I shall be very glad to get them. You are not raising a company yourself, Miss Irene?"

"Oh, no! but there is a new company named 'Huntingdon Rifles' for my father, and he wishes to give them everything they need. When can you come in to see me about cutting out the shirts?"

"Day after to-morrow morning, quite early, if it will suit you."

"That will suit me very well. Here is that remedy for asthma, which I mentioned to you once before. If you will try it faithfully, I have no doubt it will at least relieve your mother of much suffering. If you can't find the ingredients here, let me know, and I can get them from the plantation."

As the kneeling figure received the slip of paper she rose, and tears gathered in the large clear gray eyes.

"Thank you, Miss Irene; it is very good of you to remember my poor old mother so constantly. I am afraid nothing will ever do her much good; but I am grateful to you, and will try your remedy faithfully. I want to thank you, too, for the good you have done Hanson; I never saw a boy so changed. He is up by daylight Sunday mornings, getting all things in trim, so that he can be off to Sabbath-school. I have always tried to teach my children to be honest and upright, but I am afraid I did not do my duty fully; I am afraid they were neglected in some respects, till you began with them in Sabbath-school."

"Your children all learn very readily, but Hanson is particularly bright. I am very glad to have him in my class; he is one of my best pupils."

As she went homeward a shadow fell upon her face—a shadow darker than that cast by the black plume in her riding-hat—and once or twice her lips writhed from their ordinary curves of beauty. Nearing the encampment she lowered her veil, but saw that dress-parade had been dismissed; and as she shook the reins and Erebus quickened his gallop, she found herself face to face with the colonel, who had just mounted his horse and was riding toward town. She looked at him and bowed; but, in passing, he kept his eyes fixed on the road before him, and in the duskiness his face seemed colder and more inflexible than ever. Such had been the manner of their occasional meetings since the interview at the Factory, and she was not surprised that this, her first greeting, was disregarded. The public believed that an engagement existed between him and Salome, and the attentions heaped upon him by the family of the latter certainly gave color to the report. But Irene was not deceived; she had learned to understand his nature, and knew that his bitterness of feeling and studied avoidance of herself betokened that the old affection had not been crushed. Struggling with the dictates of her heart and a sense of the respect due to her father's feelings, she passed a sleepless night in pacing the gallery of the observatory. It was a vigil of almost intolerable perplexity and anguish. Under all its painful aspects she patiently weighed the matter, and at sunrise next morning, throwing open the blinds of her room, she drew her rose-wood desk to the window, and wrote these words:

"COL. AUBREY:

"Before you leave W—— allow me to see you for a few moments. If your departure is positively fixed for to-morrow, come to me this afternoon, at any hour which may be most convenient.

"Respectfully,
"IRENE HUNTINGDON.

"Huntingdon Hill, June, 1861."

As the regiment prepared to march to Mrs. Churchhill's residence, the note was received from Andrew's hands. Returning his sword to its scabbard, the colonel read the paper twice, three times—a heavy frown gathered on his forehead, his swarthy cheek fired, and, thrusting the note into his pocket, he turned toward his regiment, saying hastily to the servant:

"You need not wait. No answer is expected."

At the breakfast-table Irene opened a hasty missive from Salome, inviting her to be present at the presentation of the flag and begging a few choice flowers for the occasion. Smiling quietly, she filled the accompanying basket with some of the rarest treasures of the green-house, added a bowl of raspberries which the gardener had just brought in, and sent all, with a brief line excusing herself from attending.

The morning was spent in writing to her father, preparing a parcel for him, and in superintending the making of a large quantity of blackberry jelly and cordial for the use of the hospitals.

About noon Dr. Arnold came and found her

engaged in sealing up a number of the jars, all neatly labelled. The day was warm; she had pushed back her hair from her brow as she bent over her work; the full sleeves were pinned up above the elbow, and she wore a white check-muslin apron to protect her dress from the resin and beeswax.

"In the name of Medea and her Colchian caldron! what are you about, Irene?"

"Fixing a box of hospital stores for you to take with you."

"Fixing! you Yankee! crucify that word! I detest it. Say arranging, getting up, putting in order, aggregating, conglomerating, or what you will, but save my ears from 'fixing!' How do I know that all that trash was n't boiled in a brass kettle and is not rank poison?"

"Because I always use a porcelain kettle, sir. Here is a glass; try some of my 'trash.' I am determined to receive you 'cordially.'"

"Take my advice, Queen, and never attempt another pun so long as life and reason are spared to you. It is an execrable, heathenish, uncivil practice, which should be tabooed in all well-regulated respectable families. As a class, your punsters are a desperate, vinegar-souled set. Old Samuel Johnson treated the world to a remarkably correct estimate of the whole sorry tribe. Just a half-glass more. You have spilled a drop on your immaculate apron. Well, your pun and your cordial are about on a par; not exactly either—for one has too much spice, and the other none at all."

"Well, then, Fadladeen, I will reconsider, and send the box to a Richmond hospital."

"No; give it to me. The poor fellows who are to use it may not be so fastidious. How much longer do you intend to sit here? I did not come to make my visit to the pantry."

"I have finished, sir. Let me wash my hands and I will give you some lunch in the dining-room."

"No; I lunched with the Israelites. Salome was brilliant as a Brazilian fire-fly, and presented her banner quite gracefully. Aubrey looked splendidly in his uniform; was superbly happy in his speech—always is. Madam did the honors inimitably, and, in fine—give me that fan on the table—everything was decidedly *comme il faut*. You were expected, and you ought to have gone; it looked spiteful to stay away. I should absolutely like to see you subjected to 212° Fahrenheit, in order to mark the result. Here I am almost suffocating with the heat, which would be respectable in Soudan, and you sit there bolt upright, looking as cool as a west wind in March. Beauty, you should get yourself patented as a social refrigerator, 'Warranted proof against the dog-days.' What rigmarole do you want me to repeat to Leonard?"

"I have sent a parcel and a letter to your buggy. Please hand them to Father and tell him that I am well."

"And what is to become of my conscience in the meantime?"

"Doctor, I might answer in the words of Raphael to the Prefect of Alexandria: 'What will become of it in any case, my most excellent lord?'"

"Humph, child! I am not such a reprobate, after all. But I am thankful I am not as some pharisees I know."

She looked up in his harsh face to read its meaning. He leaned forward, seized her hands, and said hurriedly:

"Do n't look so much like one of your own pigeons might, if you had coaxed it to come to you and then slapped it off. When I say bitter things you may be sure you are the last person in my thoughts. Straighten that bent lip; I did not allude to you, my starry priestess. I meant all that noisy crew down town, who—"

"Let them rest; neither you nor I have any interest in them. I wish, if you please, when you get to Manassas, that you would persuade Father to allow me to come, at least, as far as Richmond. You have some influence with him; will you use it in my favor?"

"You are better off at home; you could possibly do no good."

"Still I want to go. Remember, my father is all I have in this world."

"And what have you elsewhere, Irene?"

"My mother, my Saviour, and my God."

"Are you, then, so very anxious to go to Virginia?" he repeated, after a pause.

"I am. I want to be near Father."

"Well, I will see what I can do with him. If I fail, recollect that he is not proverbial for pliability. Look here—are you nervous? Your fingers twitch, and so do your eyelids occasionally, and your pulse is twenty beats too quick."

"I believe I am rather nervous to-day."

"Why so?"

"I did not sleep last night; that is one cause, I suppose."

"And the reason why you did not sleep? Be honest with me."

"My thoughts, sir, were very painful. Do you wonder at it, in the present state of the country?"

"Irene, answer me one question, dear child; what does the future contain for you? What hope have you?—what do you live for?"

"I have much to be grateful for—much that makes me happy; and I hope to do some good in the world while I live. I want to be useful—to feel that I have gladdened some hearts, strengthened some desponding spirits, carried balm to some hearth-stones, shed some happiness on the paths of those who walk near me through life. There are seasons when I regret my incapacity to accomplish more; but at such times, when disposed to lament the limited sphere of woman's influence, I am reminded of Pascal's grand definition: 'A sphere of which the centre is everywhere, the circumference nowhere;' and I feel encouraged to hope that, after all, woman's circle of action will prove as sublime and extended. Doctor, remember:

> . . . No stream from its source
> Flows seaward, how lonely soever its course
> But what some land is gladdened. No star ever rose
> And set, without influence somewhere. Who knows
> What earth needs from earth's lowest creature? No life
> Can be pure in its purpose and strong in its strife,
> And all life not be purer and stronger thereby."

"But who pointed your aims and taught you these theories?"

"The emptiness of my former life—the insatiable yearning for solid, unalloyed happiness. I enjoy society and cling to many social ties; but these alone could not content me. I love the world better for striving to be of some little use to it, and I should be pained to have anybody believe that I have grown misanthropic or cynical, simply because I sometimes tire of a round of gayety, and endeavor to employ my time usefully and for the benefit of my race. I felt the pressure of the iron signet which the Creator set to his high commissions for life-long human labor, and breaking the spell of inertia that bound me, I have, in part, my reward.

> . . . Get leave to work
> In this world, 't is the best you get at all;
> For God, in cursing, gives us better gifts
> Than men in benediction. God says 'sweat
> For foreheads;' men say 'crowns;' and so we are crowned,
> Ay; gashed by some tormenting circle of steel
> Which snaps with a secret spring. Get work; get work;
> Be sure 't is better than what you work to get.'

"God knows we do little enough for each other in this whirl of selfishness and grasping after gain."

"Have you, then, fully resolved to remain single?"

"Why do you ask me that, Dr. Arnold?"

"Because you are dear to me, Queen; and I should like to see you happily married before I am laid away in my grave."

"You will never see it. Be sure I shall live and die Irene Huntingdon."

"What has induced you to doom yourself to a—"

"Ask me no more, Doctor. If I am content with my lot, who else has the right to question?"

He looked into that fair chiselled face and wondered whether she could be truly "content;" and the purity and peace in her deep calm eyes baffled him sorely. She rose, and laid her hand on his shoulder.

"Dr. Arnold, promise me that, if there is a battle, and Father should be hurt, you will telegraph me at once. Do not hesitate—let me know the truth immediately. Will you?"

"I promise."

"And now, sir, what can I make or have made for you, which will conduce to your comfort?"

"Have you any old linen left about the house, that could be useful among the wounded?"

"I have sent off a good deal, but have some left. In what form do you want it? As lint, or bandages?"

"Neither; pack it just as it is and send it on by express. I can't carry the world on my shoulders."

"Anything else?"

"Write to the overseer's wife to sow all the mustard-seed she can lay her hands on, and save all the sage she can. And, Irene, be sure to send me every drop of honey you can spare. That is all, I believe. If I think of anything else I will write you."

"Will you take Cyrus with you?"

"Of course. What guarantee have I that some villainous stray shell or shot may not ricochet and shave my head off? I shall take him along to drag me off the field in any such emergency; for, if I am not a Christian myself, I want to be buried by Christian people—not by those puritanical golden-calf worshippers, of 'higher-law' notoriety."

"I trust that, in the exercise of your professional duties, you will be in no danger. Surgeons are rarely hurt, I believe."

"Not so sure of that. Spherical-case or grape-shot have very little respect for scientific proficiency or venerable old age. One thing is certain, however—if anything happens to me Cyrus will bring me home; and I want a quiet place near your lot in the cemetery, where your hands, Queen, will sometimes be about my grave. Ah, child, I have lived a lonely, savage sort of life, and spent little love on the world or the people about me. I have had neither wife nor children nor sister in my home to humanize me; but you have always had a large share of my heart, and even Leonard can hardly love you better than I do. Think of me sometimes, Queen, and write to me freely. No eyes but mine will ever see your letters."

He stood with his hands on her shoulders, speaking falteringly; and, unable to reply immediately, she turned her lips to the rough brawny hand which had caressed her for twenty-five years.

Making a great effort, she said pleadingly:

"Dr. Arnold, when I pray for Father I always include you in my petitions. Do you never intend to pray for yourself?"

"I should not know how to begin now, my child."

"Words always come with will. Postpone it no longer. Oh, Doctor! I beg of you to begin at once."

Her lashes were heavy with unshed tears as she looked up in his face.

"I have faith in your prayers, Queen, but not in my own. Pray for me always, dear child. God bless you! my comfort, my light, in a dark, troubled world of sin."

He stooped, kissed her forehead, and hurried out to his buggy.

She could not realize that he would be exposed to such imminent danger as many others—and, having concluded her packing and despatched the box to the depot, she wrote a few lines to a well known book-seller and sent Andrew to the store. An hour after he returned, bringing a package of small, but elegantly bound bibles. From among the number she selected one of beautiful, clear type, and taking it to her room locked herself in to escape all intrusion.

CHAPTER XXIX.

The summer day was near its death, when Colonel Aubrey rode up the stately avenue, whose cool green arches were slowly filling with shadows. Fastening his spirited horse to the iron post, he ascended the marble steps, and John received his card and ushered him into the front parlor. The rich lace curtains were caught back from the wide windows to admit the air, and the whole room was flooded with subtle intoxicating perfume from numerous elegant vases of rare flowers, which crowned mantle, *étagère*, and centre-table. On a small *papier-maché* stand drawn before one of the windows stood an exquisite cut-glass bowl, fringed at the edge with geranium leaves and filled with perfect golden-hearted water-lilies, whose snowy petals spread themselves regally, breathing incense. The proud and moody visitor regarded them a moment, then his piercing eye ran around the room and rested upon a large oval picture on the opposite wall. This portrait of Irene had been painted soon after she left school, and represented only the face and bust rising out of a luminous purplish mist—a face which might have served for Guido's Aurora. Clad in the handsome glittering uniform, which showed his nobly-proportioned and powerful figure so advantageously, the officer stood, hat in hand, the long sable plume drooping toward the floor; and, as he scanned the portrait, his lips moved and these words crept inaudibly, mutteringly, over them:

> "Behold her there,
> As I beheld her ere she knew my heart;
> My first, last love; the idol of my youth,
> The darling of my manhood, and alas!
> Now the most blessed memory of mine age."

The frown on his face deepened almost to a scowl, indescribably stern; he turned abruptly away and looked through the open window out upon the lawn, where flashes of sunshine and dusky shadows struggled for mastery. The next moment Irene stood at the door; he turned his head, and they were face to face once more.

Her dress was of swiss muslin, revealing her dazzling shoulders and every dimple and curve of her arms. The glittering bronze hair was looped and fastened with blue ribbons, and from the heavy folds her favorite clematis bells hung quivering with every motion, and matching, in depth of hue, the violets that clustered on her bosom. The crystal calmness of her countenance was broken at last; a new strange light brimmed the unfathomable eyes and broke in radiant ripples round the matchless mouth. On the white brow, with its marble-like gleam, "pure lilies of eternal peace" seemed resting, as

> "She looked down on him from the whole
> Lonely length of a life. There were sad nights and days,
> There were long months and years, in that heart-searching gaze."

Never had her extraordinary beauty so stirred his heart; a faint flush tinged his cheek, but he bowed frigidly, and haughtily his words broke the silence.

"You sent for me, Miss Huntingdon, and I obeyed your command. Nothing less would have brought me to your presence."

She crossed the room and stood before him, holding out both hands, while her scarlet lips fluttered perceptibly. Instead of receiving the hands he drew back a step and crossed his arms proudly over his chest. She raised her fascinating eyes to his, folded her palms together, and, pressing them to her heart, said slowly and distinctly:

"I heard that you were ordered to Virginia, to the post of danger; and, knowing to what risks you will be exposed, I wished to see you at least once more in this world. Perhaps the step I am taking may be condemned by some, as a deviation from the delicacy of my sex—I trust I am not wanting in proper appreciation of what is due to my own self-respect—but the feelings which I have crushed back so long now demand utterance. Russell, I have determined to break the seal of many years silence—to roll away the stone from the sepulchre—to tell you all. I feel that you and I must understand each other before we part for all time, and, therefore, I sent for you."

She paused, drooping her head, unable to meet his searching steady black eyes riveted upon hers; and, drawing his tall athletic figure to its utmost height, he asked defiantly:

"You sent for me through compassionate compunctions, then—intending, at the close, to be magnanimous, and in lieu of disdain, tell me that you pity me?"

"Pity you? No, Russell; I do not pity you."

"It is well. I neither deserve nor desire it."

"What motive do you suppose prompted me to send for you on the eve of your departure?"

"I am utterly at a loss to conjecture. I once thought you too generous to wish to inflict pain unnecessarily on any one; but God knows this interview is inexpressibly painful to me."

A numbing suspicion crossed her mind, blanching lip and cheek to the hue of death, and hardening her into the old statue-like expression. Had he, indeed, ceased to love her? Had Salome finally won her place in his heart? He saw, without comprehending, the instantaneous change which swept over her features and regarded her with mingled impatience and perplexity.

"If such be the truth, Col. Aubrey, the interview is ended."

He bowed and turned partially away, but paused irresolute, chained by that electrical pale face, which no man, woman, or child ever looked at without emotion.

"Before we part, probably for ever, I should like to know why you sent for me."

"Do you remember that, one year ago to-night, we sat on the steps of the Factory, and you told me of the feeling you had cherished for me from your boyhood?"

"It was a meeting too fraught with pain and mortification to be soon forgotten."

"I believe you thought me cold, heartless, and unfeeling then?"

"There was no room to doubt it. Your haughty coldness carried its own interpretation."

"Because I knew that such was the harsh opinion you had entertained for twelve months, I sought this opportunity to relieve myself of an unjust imputation. If peace had been preserved, and you had always remained quietly here, I should never have undeceived you —for the same imperative reasons, the same stern necessity which kept me silent on the night to which I allude, would have sealed my lips through life. But all things are changed; you are going into the very jaws of death, with what result no human foresight can predict; and now, after long suffering, I feel that I have earned and may claim the right to speak to you of that which I have always expected to bury with me in my grave."

Again her crowned head bowed itself.

Past bitterness and wounded pride were instantly forgotten; hope kindled in his dark, stern face a beauty that rarely dwelt there, and, throwing down his hat, he stepped forward and took her folded hands in his strong grasp.

"Irene, do you intend me to understand— are you willing that I shall believe that, after all, I have an interest in your heart—that I am more to you than you ever before deigned to let me know? If it, indeed, be so, oh! give me the unmistakable assurance."

Her lips moved; he stooped his haughty head to catch the low, fluttering words.

"You said that night: 'I could forgive your father all! all! if I knew that he had not so successfully hardened, closed your heart against me.' Forgive him, Russell. You never can know all that you have been to me from my childhood. Only God, who sees my heart, knows what suffering our long alienation has cost me."

An instant he wavered, his strong frame quivered, and then he caught her exultingly in his arms, resting her head upon his bosom, leaning his swarthy hot cheek on hers, cold and transparent as alabaster.

"At last I realize the one dream of my life! I hold you to my heart, acknowledged all my own! Who shall dare dispute the right your lips have given me? Hatred is powerless now; none shall come between me and my own. Oh, Irene! my beautiful darling! not all my ambitious hopes, not all the future holds, not time, nor eternity, could purchase the proud, inexpressible joy of this assurance. I have toiled and struggled, I have suffered in silence; I have triumphed and risen in a world that sometimes stung my fiery heart almost to madness; and I have exulted, I have gloried, in my hard-earned success. But ambition dims, and my laurels wither, in comparison with the precious, priceless consciousness of your love. I said ambition *shall* content me— shall usurp the pedestal where, long ago, I lifted a fair girlish image; but the old worship followed, haunted me continually. I looked up from MS. speeches to find your incomparable magnetic eyes before me; and now, in the midst of bitterness and loneliness, I have my great reward. God bless you, Irene! for this one hour of perfect happiness in a cold and joyless life. If, when disappointed and baffled by your habitual polished reserve, I have said or done harsh, unjust things, which wounded you, forgive me—remembering only my love and my torturing dread that you would become Bainbridge's wife. Oh! that was the most horrible apprehension that ever possessed me."

"Instead of cherishing your affection for me you struggled against it with all the energy of your character. I have seen, for some time, that you were striving to crush it out— to forget me entirely."

"I do not deny it; and certainly you ought not to blame me. You kept me at a distance with your chilling, yet graceful, fascinating *hauteur*. I had nothing to hope—everything to suffer. I diligently set to work to expel you utterly from my thoughts; and, I tell you candidly, I endeavored to love another, who was brilliant and witty and universally admired. But her fitful, stormy, exacting temperament was too much like my own to suit me. I tried faithfully to become attached to her, intending to make her my wife, but I failed signally. My heart clung stubbornly to its old worship; my restless, fiery spirit could find no repose, no happiness, save in the purity, the profound marvellous calm of your nature. You became the synonyme of peace— rest; and because you gave me no friendly word or glance, locking your passionless face against me, I grew savage toward you. Did you believe that I would marry Salome?"

"No! I had faith that, despite your angry efforts, your heart would be true to me."

"Why did you inflict so much pain on us both, when a word would have explained all? When the assurance you have given me to-day would have sweetened the past years of trial?"

"Because I knew it would not have that effect. I am constitutionally more patient than you, and yet, with all my efforts to be resigned to what could not be remedied and to bear my sorrow with fortitude, I found myself disposed to repine; and, because I was so sure of your affection, to—

"Cry to the winds, oh, God! it might have been."

A belief of my indifference steeled you against me—nerved you to endurance. But a knowledge of the truth would have increased your acrimony of feeling toward him whom you regarded as the chief obstacle, and this, at all hazards, I was resolved to avoid. Russell, I knew that our relations could never be changed; that the barriers, for which neither you nor I are responsible in any degree, were insurmountable; and that, in this world, we must walk widely-diverging paths, exchanging few words of sympathy. Because I realized so fully the necessity of estrangement, I should never have acquainted you with my own feelings, had I not known that a long, and perhaps final, separation now stretches before us. In the painful course which duty imposed on me I have striven to promote your ultimate happiness, rather than my own."

"Irene, how can you persuade yourself that it is your duty to obey an unjust and tyrannical decree, which sacrifices the happiness of two to the unreasonable vindictiveness of one?"

"Remember that you are speaking of my father, and do not make me regret that I have seen you in his house."

"You must not expect of me more forbearance than my nature is capable of. I have lost too much through his injustice to bear my injuries coolly. I was never a meek man, and strife and trial have not sweetened my temper. If you love me, and the belief is too precious to me to be questioned now, I hold it your duty to me and to your own heart to give yourself to me, to gild our future with the happiness of which the past has been cheated. Your father has no right to bind your life a sacrifice upon the altar of his implacable hate; nor have you a right to doom yourself and me to life-long sorrow because of an ancient feud, which neither of us had any agency in effecting."

"Duty, because inflexible and involving great pain, is not therefore less imperative. Russell, have you forgotten Chelonis?"

He tightened his clasping arms, and exclaimed:

"Ah, Irene! I would willingly go into exile, with you for my Chelonis. Perish ambition! I live only such a future. But you remember nothing but Chelonis' filial obligations, forgetting all she owed and all she nobly gave, Cleombrotus. If you would lay your hands in mine and give me his right, oh! what a glory would crown the coming years! Irene, before it is too late, have mercy on us both."

She lifted her head from his shoulder and looked up pleadingly in his flushed, eager face.

"Russell, do not urge me; it is useless. Spare me the pain of repeated refusals and be satisfied with what I have given you. Believe that my heart is, and ever will be, yours entirely, though my hand you can never claim. I know what I owe my father, and I will pay to the last iota; and I know as well what I owe myself, and, therefore, I shall live true to my first and only love and die Irene Huntingdon. More than this you have no right to ask—I no right to grant. Be patient, Russell; be generous."

"Patient! patient! I am but human."

"Rise above the human; remember that, at best, life is short, and that after a little while eternity will stretch its holy circles before our feet. Such is my hope. I look down the lonely, silent vista of my coming years, whose niches are filled, not with joy, but quiet resignation—and I see beyond the calm shores of Rest, where, if faithful here, you and I may clasp hands for ever! To me this is no dim, shadowy, occasional comfort, but a fixed, firm, priceless trust."

She felt the deep, rapid throbbing of his heart as he held her to his bosom; and a dark cloud of sorrow settled on his features while he listened to her low, sweet, steady voice. He kissed her twice, and said huskily:

"Do you intend to send me from you? To meet me henceforth as a stranger?"

"Circumstances, which I can not control, make it necessary."

"At least you will let me hear from you sometimes? You will give me the privilege of writing to you?"

"Impossible, Russell; do not ask that of me."

"Oh, Irene! you are cruel! Why withhold that melancholy comfort from me?"

"Simply for the reason that it would unavoidably prove a source of pain to both. I judge you by myself. A correspondence would keep your mind constantly harassed on a subject which time will inevitably soften, mellow; and the expectation of letters from you would induce a feverish excitement and impatience in my own heart, which I wish to escape. It would feed useless regrets, and be productive only of harm. I want neither your usefulness in life nor mine impaired by continual weak repining. If I can patiently bear a great sea of silence between us henceforth, you certainly should be stronger; should appreciate my motives, without suspecting any diminution of affection on my part. If your life is spared I shall anxiously watch your career, rejoicing in all your honors and your noble use of the talents which God gave you for the benefit of your race and the advancement of truth. No matter how the world may deride, or cynics sneer at the supposition, I tell you solemnly absence has no power over a true woman's heart. Her affection will triumph over separation, over silence, over death! over everything but loss of confidence; over all but discovered unworthiness in its object. It can bid defiance to obstacles, to adverse fate, so long as trust remains intact and respect is possible; that you will ever forfeit either I entertain no fear."

"I am not as noble as you think me; my ambition is not as unselfish as you suppose. Under your influence, other aims and motives might possess me."

"You mistake your nature. Your intellect and temperament stamp you one of the few who receive little impression from extraneous influences; and it is because of this stern, obstinate individuality of character that I hope an extended sphere of usefulness for you, if you survive this war. Our country will demand your services, and I shall be proud and happy in the knowledge that you are faithfully and conscientiously discharging the duties of a statesman."

"Ah! but the wages are hollow. My ambition has already been gratified to some extent, and in the very flush of triumph I sat down to eat its fruit, and smiled grimly over its dust and ashes."

"Because self-aggrandizement was then the sole aim. But a holier, a more disinterested, unselfish ambition to serve only God, Truth, and Country will insure a blessed consciousness of well-spent years and consecrated talents, comforting beyond all else that earth can give."

He shook his head sadly; placing his palm under her chin and tenderly raising the face in order to scan it fully.

"Irene, oblige me in what may seem a trifle; unfasten your hair and let it fall around you as I have seen it once or twice in your life."

She took out her comb, untied the ribbons, and, passing her fingers through the bands, shook them down till they touched the floor.

He passed his hand caressingly over the glossy waves, and smiled proudly.

"How often I have longed to lay my fingers on these rippling folds as they flashed around you so, or were coiled into a crown about your head. With what a glory they invest you! Your picture there upon the wall seems lighted with the golden gleam. Irene, give me a likeness of yourself as you stand now, or, if you prefer it, have a smaller one photographed to-morrow from that portrait and send it to me by express. I shall be detained in Richmond several days, and it will reach me safely. Do not, I beg of you, refuse me this. It is the only consolation I can have, and God knows it is little enough! Oh, Irene! think of my loneliness and grant this last request."

His large brilliant eyes were full of tears, the first she had ever seen dim their light; and, moved by the grief which so transformed his lineaments, she answered hastily:

"Of course, if you desire it so earnestly, though it were much better that you had nothing to remind you of me."

"Will you have it taken to-morrow?"

"Yes."

She covered her face with her hands for some seconds, as if striving to overcome some impulse; then, turning quickly to him, she wound her arms about his neck and drew his face down to hers.

"Oh, Russell! Russell! I want your promise that you will so live and govern yourself that, if your soul is summoned from the battle-field, you can confront Eternity without a single apprehension. If you must yield up your life for freedom, I want the assurance that you have gone to your final home at peace with God; that you wait there for me; and that, when my work is done, and I, too, lay my weary head to rest, we shall meet soul to soul and spend a blessed eternity together where strife and separation are unknown. In the realization of your ambitious dreams, I know that you have given no thought to these things; and it was chiefly my anxiety to impress upon you their importance, their vital necessity, which induced me to send for you. Your hard, bitter heart must be softened; you must try to overcome your vindictiveness; to cherish more charity and forgiveness toward some who have thwarted you. Sometimes, in watching your gloomy, stern face I have almost despaired that you would ever feel otherwise; and many a night I have prayed fervently that you might be influenced to make some preparation for futurity. Oh, Russell! I can be brave and strong and patient; I can bear to see your dear face no more in this world; I can give you up to our country, and not murmur that you died defending her liberties —if I have the conviction that, in that noble death, you found the gate of heaven—that I shall meet you again when my God calls me home. Think of this when you leave me for the temptations of camp-life and go forth to scenes of strife and horror. Think of it by day and night, striving to subdue your heart in accordance with the precepts of Christ; to exert a restraining, purifying influence over your command; and remember, oh, remember, Russell! that this is the only hope I have to cheer me. Will you promise to read the bible I give you now—to pray constantly for yourself? Will you promise to meet me beyond the grave?"

10

His black locks lay upon her forehead as he struggled for composure, and, after a moment, he answered solemnly:

"I will try, my darling."

She put into his hand the bible, which she had carefully marked, and which bore on the blank leaf, in her handwriting: "Colonel Russell Aubrey, with the life-long prayers of his best friend."

The shadow fled from her countenance, which grew radiant as some fleecy vapor suddenly smitten with a blaze of sunlight, and clear and sweeter than chiming bells her voice rang through the room.

"Thank God! for that promise. I shall lean my heart upon it till the last pulsations are stilled in my coffin. And now I will keep you no longer from your regiment. I know that you have many duties there to claim your time. Turn your face toward the window; I want to look at it, to be able to keep its expression always before me."

She put up her waxen hand, brushed the hair from his pale, dome-like brow, and gazed earnestly at the noble features, which even the most fastidious could find no cause to carp at.

"Of old, when Eurystheus threatened Athens, Macaria, in order to save the city and the land from invasion and subjugation, willingly devoted herself a sacrifice upon the altar of the gods. Ah, Russell! that were an easy task, in comparison with the offering I am called upon to make. I can not, like Macaria, by self-immolation, redeem my country; from that great privilege I am debarred; but I yield up more than she ever possessed. I give my all on earth—my father and yourself—to our beloved and suffering country. My God! accept the sacrifice, and crown the South a sovereign, independent nation! Gladly, unshrinkingly, would I meet a death so sublime; but to survive the loss of those dearer far than my life, to live and endure such desolation—oh! my lot, and that of thousands of my countrywomen, is infinitely more bitter than the fate of Macaria!"

She smothered a moan, and her head sank on his shoulder; but lifting it instantly, with her fathomless affection beaming in her face, she added:

"To the mercy and guidance of Almighty God I commit you, dear Russell—trusting all things in His hands. May He shield you from suffering, strengthen you in the hour of trial, and reunite us eternally in His kingdom, is, and ever shall be, my constant prayer. Good-by, Russell! Do your duty nobly; win deathless glory on the battle-field in defence of our sacred cause; and remember that your laurels will be very precious to my lonely heart."

He folded her in his arms and kissed her repeatedly; but, disengaging herself, she put him gently aside; and, snatching up his hat, he left the room. He reached his horse, then paused, and returned to the parlor.

The sun had set, but waves of rich orange light rolled through the window and broke over the white figure kneeling there half-veiled by curling hair. The clasped hands were uplifted and the colorless face was thrown back in silent supplication. He watched the wonderful loveliness of face and form till his pride was utterly melted; and, sinking on his knees, he threw one arm around her waist, exclaiming:

"Oh, Irene! you have conquered! With God's grace I will so spend the residue of my life as to merit your love and the hope of reunion beyond the grave."

She laid her hand lightly on his bowed head as he knelt beside her, and, in a voice that knew no faltering, breathed out a fervent prayer, full of pathos and sublime in faith—invoking blessings upon him—life-long guardianship, and final salvation through Christ. The petition ended, she rose, smiling through the mist that gathered over her eyes, and he said:

"I came back to ask something which I feel that you will not refuse me. Electra will probably soon come home, and she may be left alone in the world. Will you sometimes go to see her, for my sake, and give her your friendship?"

"I will, Russell, for her sake, as well as for yours. She shall be the only sister I have ever known."

She drew his hand to her lips, but he caught it away, and pressed a last kiss upon them.

"Good-by, my own darling! my life-angel!"

She heard his step across the hall; a moment after, the tramp of his horse, as he galloped down the avenue, and she knew that the one happy hour of her life had passed—that the rent sepulchre of Silence must be resealed.

Pressing her hands over her desolate heart, she murmured sadly:

"Thy will, not mine, oh, Father! Give me strength to do my work; enable me to be faithful even to the bitter end."

CHAPTER XXX.

Strange heroic parallelisms startle the grave, reflecting student of history, and propound the inquiry: Is the Buckle theory of immutable cycles correct? Is the throbbing, surging world of human emotions and passions but a mere arithmetical problem, to be solved through the erudition and astuteness of a Quetelet or Hassel, by an infallible statistical rule-of-three? Has the relentless Necessity of Comte erected its huge mill on this continent, to grimly grind out the annual quantity of patriotism, tyranny, noble self-abnegation, or Machiavelism, in the prescribed, invariable ratio of "Sociology?" Is it that times make men and women, through dire necessity of individual or national salvation, or will it be urged that sublime records of the past fire the soul to emulation and duplication of ancient heroism? *Davus sum non Œdipus.* In 1781, when compelled to raise the Siege of Ninety-Six, it became very important that General Greene should communicate with Sumter. The intervening country was, however, so filled with British and Tories, and such dangers attended the mission, that no one could be found willing to undertake it. In this emergency, when even our patriots of the first Revolution shrank back, Emily Geiger, only eighteen years of age, volunteered to make the hazardous attempt, and received from General Greene a letter and verbal messages which he was extremely desirous should reach their destination. Mounting a swift horse, she performed a portion of the journey in safety; but was ultimately arrested by two Tories, who suspected that she might be rendering important, though clandestine, service to "the rebels." Swiftly and unobserved she swallowed the written despatch, and, baffled in their expectation of finding suspicious documents, they allowed her to proceed. Sumter's camp was safely reached, the messages were delivered, General Greene's army was reinforced, and soon became strong enough to assume the offensive. Rawdon was forced to retreat, and Greene subsequently met and vanquished the British army at Eutaw Springs. Was not Emily Geiger's slender womanly hand instrumental in preparing for that battle, the results of which freed the Carolinas?

In July, 1861, when the North, blinded by avarice and hate, rang with the cry of "On to Richmond," our Confederate Army of the Potomac was divided between Manassas and Winchester, watching at both points the glittering coils of the Union boa-constrictor, which writhed in its efforts to crush the last sanctuary of freedom. The stringency evinced along the Federal lines prevented the transmission of despatches by the Secessionists of Maryland, and for a time Generals Beauregard and Johnston were kept in ignorance of the movements of the enemy. Patterson hung dark and lowering around Winchester, threatening daily descent; while the main column of the grand army under McDowell proceeded from Washington, confident in the expectation of overwhelming the small army stationed at Manassas. The friends of liberty who were compelled to remain in the desecrated old capital appreciated the urgent necessity of acquainting General Beauregard with the designs of McDowell and the arch-apostate, Scott; but all channels of egress seemed sealed; all roads leading across the Potomac were vigilantly guarded, to keep the great secret safely; and painful apprehensions were indulged for the fate of the Confederate army. But the Promethean spark of patriotic devotion burned in the hearts of Secession women; and, resolved to dare all things in a cause so holy, a young lady of Washington, strong in heroic faith, offered to encounter any perils, and pledged her life to give Gen. Beauregard the necessary information. Carefully concealing a letter in the twist of her luxuriant hair, which would escape detection even should she be searched, she disguised herself effectually, and, under the mask of a market-woman, drove a cart through Washington, across the Potomac, and deceived the guard by selling vegetables and milk as she proceeded. Once beyond Federal lines, and in friendly neighborhood, it was but a few minutes work to "off ye lendings" and secure a horse and riding-habit. With a courage and rapidity which must ever command the admiration of a brave people, she rode at hard gallop that burning July afternoon to Fairfax Court-house, and telegraphed to Gen. Beauregard, then at Manassas Junction, the intelligence she had risked so much to convey. Availing himself promptly of the facts, he flashed them along electric wires to Richmond and to General Johnston; and thus, through womanly devotion, a timely junction of the two armies was effected ere McDowell's banners flouted the skies of Bull Run.

Carthagenian women gave their black locks to string their country's bows and furnish cordage for its shipping; and the glossy tresses of an American woman veiled a few mystic ciphers more potent in General Beauregard's hands than Talmudish Shemhamphorash.

Her mission accomplished, the dauntless courier turned her horse's head and, doubtless, with an exulting, thankful heart returned in triumph to Washington. When our national jewels are made up, will not a grateful and admiring country set her name between those of Beauregard and Johnston in the revolutionary diadem, and let the three blaze through coming ages, baffling the mists of time—the Constellation of Manassas? The artillery duel of the 18th of July ended disastrously for the advance guard of the Federals—a temporary check was given.

All things seemed in abeyance; dun, sulphurous clouds of smoke lifted themselves from the dewy copse that fringed Bull Run, floating slowly to the distant purple crests of the Blue Ridge, which gazed solemnly down on the wooded Coliseum, where gladiatorial hosts were soon to pour out their blood in the hideous orgies held by loathsome Fanaticism—guarded by Federal bayonets and canopied by the Stars and Stripes. During the silent watches of Saturday night—

"Slowly comes a hungry people, as a lion creeping nigher, Glares at one that nods and winks behind a slowly-dying fire."

A pure Sabbath morning kindled on the distant hill-tops, wearing heavenly credentials of rest and sanctity on its pearly forehead—credentials which the passions of mankind could not pause to recognize; and with the golden glow of summer sunshine came the tramp of infantry, the clatter of cavalry, the sullen growl of artillery. Major Huntingdon had been temporarily assigned to a regiment of infantry after leaving Richmond, and was posted on the right of General Beauregard's lines, commanding one of the lower fords. Two miles higher up the stream, in a different brigade, Colonel Aubrey's regiment guarded another of the numerous crossings. As the day advanced, and the continual roar of cannon toward Stone Bridge and Sudley's Ford indicated that the demonstrations on McLean's, Blackford's, and Mitchell's fords were mere feints to hold our right and centre, the truth flashed on General Beauregard that the main column was hurled against Evans' little band on the extreme left. Hour after hour passed, and the thunder deepened on the Warrenton road; then the general learned, with unutterable chagrin, that his order for an advance on Centreville had miscarried, that a brilliant plan had been frustrated, and that new combinations and dispositions must now be resorted to. The regiment to which Major Huntingdon was attached was ordered to the support of the left wing, and reached the distant position in an almost incredibly short time, while two regiments of the brigade to which Colonel Aubrey belonged were sent forward to the same point as a reserve.

Like incarnations of Victory, Beauregard and Johnston swept to the front, where the conflict was most deadly; everywhere, at sight of them, our thin ranks dashed forward, and were mowed down by the fire of Rickett's and Griffin's batteries, which crowned the position they were so eager to regain. At half-past two o'clock the awful contest was at its height; the rattle of musketry, the ceaseless whistle of rifle-balls, the deafening boom of artillery, the hurtling hail of shot, and explosion of shell, dense volumes of smoke shrouding the combatants, and clouds of dust boiling up on all sides, lent unutterable horror to a scene which, to cold, dispassionate observers, might have seemed sublime. As the vastly superior numbers of the Federals forced our stubborn bands to give back slowly, an order came from General Beauregard for the right of his line, except the reserves, to advance and recover the long and desperately-disputed plateau. With a shout, the shattered lines sprang upon the foe and forced them temporarily back. Major Huntingdon's horse was shot under him; he disengaged himself and marched on foot, waving his sword and uttering words of encouragement. He had proceeded but a few yards when a grape-shot entered his side, tearing its way through his body, and he fell where the dead lay thickest. For a time the enemy retired, but heavy reinforcements pressed in and they returned, reoccupying the old ground. Not a moment was to be lost; General Beauregard ordered forward his reserves for a second effort, and, with magnificent effect, led the charge in person. Then Russell Aubrey first came actively upon the field. At the word of command he dashed forward with his splendid regiment, and, high above all, towered his powerful form, with the long black plume of his hat drifting upon the wind as he led his admiring men.

As he pressed on, with thin nostril dilated and eyes that burned like those of a tiger seizing his prey, he saw, just in his path, leaning on his elbow, covered with blood and smeared with dust, the crushed, writhing form of his bitterest enemy. His horse's hoofs were almost upon him; he reined him back an instant and glared down at his old foe. It was only for an instant; and as Major Huntingdon looked on the stalwart figure and at the advancing regiment, life-long hatred and jealousy were forgotten—patriotism throttled all the past in her grasp—he feebly threw up his hand, cheered faintly, and, with his eyes on Russell's, smiled grimly, saying with evident difficulty:

"Beat them back, Aubrey! Give them the bayonet!"

The shock was awful—beggaring language. On, on they swept, while ceaseless cheers mingled with the cannonade; the ground was recovered, to be captured no more. The Federals were driven back across the turnpike, and now dark masses of reinforcements debouched on the plain and marched toward our left. Was it Grouchy or Blucher? Some moments of painful suspense ensued, while General Beauregard strained his eyes to decipher the advancing banner. Red and white and blue, certainly; but was it the ensign of Despotism or of Liberty? Nearer and nearer came the rushing column, and lo! upon the breeze streamed, triumphant as the Labarum of Constantine, the Stars and Bars. Kirby Smith and Elzey—God be praised! The day was won, and Victory nestled proudly among the folds of our new-born banner. One more charge along our whole line, and the hireling hordes of oppression fled, panic-stricken. Russell had received a painful wound from a minie ball, which entered his shoulder and ranged down toward the elbow, but he maintained his position, and led his regiment a mile in the pursuit. When it became evident that the retreat was a complete rout, he resigned the command to Lieutenant-Colonel Blackwell and rode back to the battle-field. Hideous was the spectacle presented—dead and dying, friend and foe, huddled in indiscriminate ruin, weltering in blood and shivering in the agonies of dissolution; blackened headless trunks and fragments of limbs—ghastly sights and sounds of woe, filling the scene of combat. Such were the first fruits of the bigotry and fanatical hate of New England, aided by the unprincipled demagogism of the West; such were the wages of Abolitionism, guided by Lincoln and Seward—the latter-day Sejanus; such the results of "higher-law," canting, puritanical hypocrisy.

Picking his way to avoid trampling the dead, Russell saw Major Huntingdon at a little distance, trying to drag himself toward a neighboring tree. The memory of his injuries crowded up—the memory of all that he had endured and lost through that man's prejudice—the sorrow that might have been averted from his blind mother—and his vindictive spirit rebelled at the thought of rendering him aid. But as he paused, and struggled against his better nature, Irene's holy face, as he saw it last, lifted in prayer for him, rose, angel-like, above all that mass of death and horrors. The sufferer was Irene's father; she was hundreds of miles away; Russell set his lips firmly, and, riding up to the prostrate figure, dismounted. Exhausted by his efforts, Major Huntingdon had fallen back in the dust, and an expression of intolerable agony distorted his features as Russell stooped over him and asked, in a voice meant to be gentle:

"Can I do anything for you? Could you sit up if I placed you on my horse?"

The wounded man scowled as he recognized the voice and face, and turned his head partially away, muttering:

"What brought you here?"

"There has never been any love between us, Major Huntingdon; but we are fighting in the same cause for the first time in our lives. You are badly wounded, and, as a fellow-soldier, I should be glad to relieve your sufferings if possible. Once more, for humanity's sake, I ask, can you ride my horse to the rear if I assist you to mount?"

"No. But for God's sake give me some water!"

Russell knelt, raised the head, and unbuckling his canteen, put it to his lips, using his own wounded arm with some difficulty. Half of the contents was eagerly swallowed, and the remainder Russell poured slowly on the gaping ghastly wound in his side. The proud man eyed him steadily till the last cool drop was exhausted, and said sullenly:

"You owe me no kindness, Aubrey. I hate you, and you know it. But you have heaped coals of fire on my head. You are more generous than I thought you. Thank you, Aubrey; lay me under that tree yonder and let me die."

"I will try to find a surgeon. Who belongs to your regiment?"

"Somebody whom I never saw till last week. I won't have him hacking about me. Leave me in peace."

"Do you know anything of your servant? I saw him as I came on the field."

"Poor William! he followed me so closely that he was shot through the head. He is lying three hundred yards to the left, yonder. Poor fellow! he was faithful to the last."

A tear dimmed the master's eagle eye as he muttered, rather than spoke, these words.

"Then I will find Dr. Arnold at once, and send him to you."

It was no easy matter, on that crowded, confused Aceldama, and the afternoon was well-nigh spent before Russell, faint and weary, descried Dr. Arnold busily using his instruments in a group of wounded. He rode up, and, having procured a drink of water and refilled his canteen, approached the surgeon.

"Doctor, where is your horse? I want you?"

"Ho, Cyrus! bring him up. What is the matter, Aubrey? You are hurt."

"Nothing serious, I think. But Major Huntingdon is desperately wounded—mortally, I am afraid. See what you can do for him."

"You must be mistaken! I have asked repeatedly for Leonard, and they told me he was in hot pursuit and unhurt. I hope to heaven you are mistaken!"

"Impossible; I tell you I lifted him out of a pool of his own blood. Come; I will show you the way."

At a hard gallop they crossed the intervening woods, and without difficulty Russell found the spot where the mangled form lay still. He had swooned, with his face turned up to the sky, and the ghastliness of death had settled on his strongly-marked, handsome features.

"God pity Irene!" said the doctor, as he bent down and examined the horrid wound, striving to press the red lips together.

The pain caused from handling him roused the brave spirit to consciousness, and, opening his eyes, he looked around wonderingly.

"Well, Hiram! it is all over with me, old fellow."

"I hope not, Leonard; can't you turn a little, and let me feel for the ball?"

"It is of no use; I am torn all to pieces. Take me out of this dirt, on the fresh grass somewhere."

"I must first extract the ball. Aubrey, can you help me raise him a little?"

Administering some chloroform, he soon succeeded in taking out the ball, and, with Russell's assistance, passed a bandage round the body.

"There is no chance for me, Hiram; I know that. I have few minutes to live. Some water."

Russell put a cup to his white lips, and, calling in the assistance of Cyrus, who had followed his master, they carried him several yards farther, and made him comfortable, while orders were despatched for an ambulance.

"It will come after my corpse. Hiram, see that I am sent home at once. I don't want my bones mixed here with other people's; and it will be some comfort to Irene to know that I am buried in sight of home. I could not rest in a ditch here. I want to be laid in my own vault. Will you see to it?"

"Yes."

"Hiram, come nearer, where I can see you better. Break the news gently to Irene. Tell her I did my duty; that will be her only comfort, and best. Tell her I fell in the thickest of the battle, with my face to Washington; that I died gloriously, as a Huntingdon and a soldier should. Tell her I sent her my blessing, my love, and a last kiss."

He paused, and tears glided over his wan cheeks as the picture of his far-off home rose temptingly before him.

"She is a brave child; she will bear it, for the sake of the cause I died in. Take care of her, Arnold; tell Eric I leave her to his guardianship. Harris has my will. My poor lonely child! it is bitter to leave her. My Queen! my golden-haired, beautiful Irene!"

He raised his hand feebly, and covered his face.

"Don't let it trouble you, Leonard. You know how I love her; I promise you I will watch over her as long as I live."

"I believe you. But if I could see her once more, to ask her not to remember my harshness—long ago. You must tell her for me; she will understand. Oh! I—"

A horrible convulsion seized him at this moment, and so intense was the agony that a groan burst through his set teeth and he struggled to rise. Russell knelt down and rested the haughty head against his shoulder, wiping off the cold drops that beaded the pallid brow. After a little while, lifting his eyes to the face bending over him, Major Huntingdon gazed into the melancholy black eyes, and said almost in a whisper:

"I little thought I should ever owe you thanks. Aubrey, forgive me all my hate; you can afford to do so now. I am not a brute; I know magnanimity when I see it. Perhaps I was wrong to visit Amy's sins on you; but I could not forgive her. Aubrey, it was natural that I should hate Amy's son."

Again the spasm shook his lacerated frame, and, twenty minutes after, his fierce, relentless spirit was released from torture; the proud, ambitious, dauntless man was with his God.

Dr. Arnold closed the eyes with trembling fingers, and covered his face with his hands to hide the tears that he could not repress.

"A braver man never died for freedom. He cheered me on, as my regiment charged over the spot where he lay," said Russell, looking down at the stiffening form.

"He had his faults, like the rest of us, and his were stern ones; but, for all that, I was attached to him. He had some princely traits. I would rather take my place there beside him, than have to break this to Irene. Poor desolate child! what an awful shock for her! She loves him with a devotion which I have rarely seen equalled. God only knows how she will bear it. If I were not so needed here I would go to her to-morrow."

"Perhaps you can be spared."

"No; it would not be right to leave so much suffering behind."

He turned to Cyrus and gave directions about bringing the body into camp, to his own tent; and the two mounted and rode slowly back.

For some moments silence reigned; then Dr. Arnold said suddenly:

"I am glad you were kind to him, Aubrey. It will be some consolation to that pure soul in W———, who has mourned over and suffered for his violent animosity. It was very generous, Russell."

"Save your commendation for a better occasion; I do not merit it now. I had, and have, as little magnanimity as my old enemy, and what I did was through no generous oblivion of the past."

Glancing at him as these words were uttered gloomily, the doctor noticed his faint, wearied appearance, and led the way to his temporary hospital.

"Come in and let me see your arm. Your sleeve is full of blood."

An examination discovered a painful flesh wound—the minie ball having glanced from the shoulder and passed out through the upper part of the arm. In removing the coat to dress the wound the doctor exclaimed:

"Here is a bullet-hole in the breast, which must have just missed your heart! Was it a spent-ball?"

A peculiar smile disclosed Russell's faultless teeth an instant, but he merely took his coat, laid it over his uninjured arm, and answered:

"Don't trouble yourself about spent-balls—finish your job. I must look after my wounded."

As soon as the bandages were adjusted he walked away, and took from the inside pocket of the coat a heavy square morocco case containing Irene's ambrotype. When the coat was buttoned, as on that day, it rested over his heart; and during the second desperate charge of General Beauregard's lines Russell felt a sudden thump, and, above all the roar of that scene of carnage, heard the shivering of the glass which covered the likeness. The morocco was torn and indented, but the ball was turned aside harmless, and now, as he touched the spring, the fragments of glass fell at his feet. It was evident that his towering form had rendered him a conspicuous target; some accurate marksman had aimed at his heart, and the ambrotype-case had preserved his life. He looked at the uninjured, radiant face till a mist dimmed his eyes; nobler aspirations, purer aims possessed him, and, bending his knees, he bowed his forehead on the case and reverently thanked God for his deliverance. With a countenance pale from physical suffering, but beaming with triumphant joy for the Nation's first great victory, he went out among the dead and dying, striving to relieve the wounded and to find the members of his own command. Passing from group to group, he heard a feeble, fluttering voice pronounce his name, and saw one of his men sitting against a tree, mortally wounded by a fragment of shell.

"Well, Colonel, I followed that black feather of yours as long as I could. I am glad I had one good chance at the cowardly villains before I got hurt. We've thrashed them awfully, and I am willing to die now."

"I hope you are not so badly hurt. Cheer up, Martin; I will bring a doctor to dress your leg, and we will soon have you on crutches."

"No, Colonel; the doctor has seen it, and says there is nothing to be done for me. I knew it before; everybody feels when death strikes them. Dr. Arnold gave me something that has eased me of my pain, but he can't save me. Colonel, they say my captain is killed; and, as I may not see any of our company boys, I wish you would write to my poor wife, and tell her all about it. I have n't treated her as well as I ought; but a wife forgives everything, and she will grieve for me, though I did act like a brute when I was drinking. She will be proud to know that I fought well for my country, and died a faithful Confederate soldier; and so will my boy, my Philip, who wanted to come with me. Tell Margaret to send him to take my place just as soon as he is old enough. The boy will revenge me; he has a noble spirit. And, Colonel, be sure to tell her to tell Miss Irene that I kept my promise to her—that I have not touched a drop of liquor since the day she talked to me before I went out to build Mr. Huntingdon's gin-house. God bless her sweet, pure soul! I believe she saved me from a drunkard's grave, to fill that of a brave soldier. I know she will never let my Margaret suffer, as long as she lives."

"Is there anything else I can do for you, Martin?"

"Nothing else, unless I could get a blanket, or something, to put under my head. I am getting very weak."

"Leavens, pick up one of those knapsacks scattered about, and bring a blanket. I promise you, Martin, I will write to your wife; and when I go home, if I outlive this war, I will see that she is taken care of. I am sorry to lose you, my brave fellow. You were one of the best sergeants in the regiment. But remember that you have helped to win a great battle, and your country will not forget her faithful sons who fell at Manassas."

"Good-by, Colonel; I should like to follow you to Washington. You have been kind to us all, and I hope you will be spared to our regiment. God bless you, Colonel Aubrey, wherever you go."

Russell changed him from his constrained posture to a more comfortable one, rested his head on a knapsack and blanket, placed his own canteen beside him, and, with a long, hard gripe of hands, and faltering "God bless you!" the soldiers parted. The day of horrors was shuddering to its close; glazing eyes were turned for the last time to the sun which set in the fiery west; the din and roar of the pursuit died away in the distance; lowering clouds draped the sky; the groans and wails of the wounded rose mournfully on the reeking air; and night and a drizzling rain came down on the blanched corpses on the torn, trampled, crimson plain of Manassas.

"I hate the dreadful hollow behind the little wood.
Its lips in the field above are dabbled with blood-red heath,
The red-ribbed ledges drip with a silent horror of blood,
And Echo there, whatever is asked her, answers 'Death!'"

But all of intolerable torture centred not there, awful as was the scene. Throughout the length and breadth of the Confederacy telegraphic despatches told that the battle was raging; and an army of women spent that 21st upon their knees, in agonizing prayer for husbands and sons who wrestled for their birthright on the far-off field of blood. Gray-haired pastors and curly-headed children alike besought the God of Justice to bless the Right, to deliver our gallant band of patriots from the insolent hordes sent to destroy us; and to that vast trembling volume of prayer which ascended from early morning from the altars of the South God lent his ear, and answered.

The people of W—— were subjected to painful suspense as hour after hour crept by, and a dense crowd collected in front of the telegraph-office, whence floated an ominous red flag. Andrew waited on horseback to carry to Irene the latest intelligence, and during the entire afternoon she paced the colonnade, with her eyes fixed on the winding road. At half-past five o'clock the solemn stillness of the sultry day was suddenly broken by a wild, prolonged shout from the town; cheer after cheer was caught up by the hills, echoed among the purple valleys, and finally lost in the roar of the river. Andrew galloped up the avenue with an extra, yet damp from the printing-press, containing the joyful tidings that McDowell's army had been completely routed, and was being pursued toward Alexandria. Meagre was the account—our heroes, Bee and Bartow, had fallen. No other details were given, but the premonition, "Heavy loss on our side," sent a thrill of horror to every womanly heart, dreading to learn the price of victory. Irene's white face flushed as she read the despatch, and, raising her hands, exclaimed:

"Oh, thank God! thank God!"

"Shall I go back to the office?"

"Yes; I shall certainly get a despatch from

Father some time to-night. Go back, and wait for it. Tell Mr. Rogers, the operator, what you came for, and ask him I say please to let you have it as soon as it arrives. And, Andrew, bring me any other news that may come before my despatch."

Tediously time wore on; the shadows on the lawn and terrace grew longer and thinner; the birds deserted the hedges; the pigeons forsook the colonnade and steps; Paragon, tired of walking after Irene, fell asleep on the rug; and the slow, drowsy tinkle of cow-bells died away among the hills.

Far off to the east the blue was hidden by gray thunderous masses of rain-cloud, now and then veined by lightning; and as Irene watched their jagged, grotesque outlines they took the form of battling hosts. Cavalry swept down on the flanks, huge forms heaved along the centre, and the lurid furrows, ploughing the whole from time to time, seemed indeed death-dealing flashes of artillery. She recalled the phantom cloud-battle in the Netherlandish vision, and shuddered involuntarily as, in imagination, she

"Heard the heavens fill with shouting, and there rained a ghastly dew
From the nations airy navies grappling in the central blue."

Gradually the distant storm drifted southward, the retreat passed the horizon, a red sunset faded in the west; rose and amber and orange were quenched, and sober blue, with starry lights, was over all. How the serene regal beauty of that summer night mocked the tumultuous throbbing, the wild joy, and great exultation of the national heart! Mother Earth industriously weaves and hangs about the world her radiant lovely tapestries, pitiless of man's wails and requiems, deaf to his pæans. Irene had earnestly endeavored to commit her father and Russell to the merciful care and protection of God, and to rest in faith, banishing apprehension; but a horrible presentiment, which would not "down" at her bidding, kept her nerves strung to their utmost tension. As the night advanced her face grew haggard and the wan lips fluttered ceaselessly. Russell she regarded as already dead to her in this world, but for her father she wrestled desperately in spirit. Mrs. Campbell joined her, uttering hopeful, encouraging words, and Nellie came out, with a cup of tea on a waiter.

"Please drink your tea, just to please me, Queen. I can't bear to look at you. In all your life I never saw you worry so. Do sit down and rest; you have walked fifty miles since morning."

"Take it away, Nellie. I don't want it."

"But, child, it will be time enough to fret when you know Mass' Leonard is hurt. Don't run to meet trouble; it will face you soon enough. If you won't take the tea, for pity's sake let me get you a glass of wine."

"No; I tell you I can't swallow anything. If you want to help me, pray for Father."

She resumed her walk, with her eyes strained in the direction of the town.

Thus passed three more miserable hours; then the clang of the iron gate at the foot of the avenue fell on her aching ear; the tramp of horses' hoofs and roll of wheels came up the gravelled walk.

"Bad news! they are coming to break it to me!" said she hoarsely, and, pressing her hands together, she leaned heavily against one of the guardian statues which had stood so long before the door, like ancient Hermæ at Athens. Was the image indeed prescient? It tilted from its pedestal and fell with a crash, breaking into fragments. The omen chilled her, and she stood still, with the light from the hall-lamp streaming over her. The carriage stopped; Judge Harris and his wife came up the steps, followed slowly by Andrew, whose hat was slouched over his eyes. As they approached, Irene put out her hands wistfully.

"We have won a glorious victory, Irene, but many of our noble soldiers are wounded. I knew you would be anxious, and we came—"

"Is my father killed?"

"Your father was wounded. He led a splendid charge."

"Wounded! No! he is killed! Andrew, tell me the truth—is Father dead?"

The faithful negro could no longer repress his grief and sobbed convulsively, unable to reply.

"Oh, my God! I knew it! I knew it!" she gasped.

The gleaming arms were thrown up despairingly, and a low, dreary cry wailed through the stately old mansion as the orphan turned her eyes upon Nellie and Andrew—the devoted two who had petted her from childhood.

Judge Harris led her into the library, and his weeping wife endeavored to offer consolation, but she stood rigid and tearless, holding out her hand for the despatch. Finally they gave it to her, and she read:

"CHARLES T. HARRIS:

"Huntingdon was desperately wounded at three o'clock to-day, in making a charge. He died two hours ago. I was with him. The body leaves to-morrow for W———.

"HIRAM ARNOLD."

The paper fell from her fingers; with a dry sob she turned from them and threw herself on the sofa, with her face of woe to the wall. So passed the night.

* * * * *

Four days after, a number of Major Huntingdon's friends waited at the depot to receive the body. The train had been detained; it was nine o'clock at night when the cars arrived, and the coffin was placed in a hearse and escorted to the Hill. By Judge Harris' direction it was carried into the parlor and placed on the table draped for the purpose; and when arrangements had been made for the funeral on the morrow, he dismissed all but a few who were to remain during the night.

Irene sat at her window up stairs, looking out upon the sombre soughing pines that rose like a cloud against the starry sky, while Grace and Salome walked about the room, crying spasmodically and trying to utter something comforting to the still figure, which might have been of ivory or granite, for any visible sign of animation. After a time, when the bustle had ceased, when the carriages had withdrawn, and the hurried tread of many feet had subsided, Irene rose and said:

"Grace, tell your father I wish to see him."

Judge Harris came promptly.

"I am greatly obliged to you for all your kindness. Please take the gentlemen into the dining-room or library, if you will stay, and do not allow any of them to return to the parlor; I shall sit there to-night, and need no one."

"Oh, my child! impossible. It would not be proper. You are not able."

"I know what I am able to do and what I have resolved to do. Be good enough to remove those gentlemen at once."

Something in her face startled him; perhaps its frightful, tearless immobility, and he silently complied.

When all was quiet she crossed the passage, entered the draped room, and, locking the door, was alone with her dead. The coffin stood in the centre of the floor, and upon it lay the sword and plumed hat. She looked down on the lid where the name was inscribed and kissed the characters; and, as all her isolation and orphanage rushed upon her, she laid her head on the table, calling mournfully upon the manly sleeper for comfort and forgiveness.

When morning broke fully, Judge Harris knocked softly at the door. No answer. He rapped loudly, trying the bolt. All within was silent as the grave. He hurried round to the greenhouse, threw up the sash, pushed open the door, and entered, full of undefinable alarm. The wax-candles on the table and mantle had just expired; the smoke from one was still creeping, thread-like, to the ceiling. A white form knelt on the floor, with clasped hands and bowed head, resting against the coffin.

"Irene! Irene!"

She did not stir.

He looped back the curtains to admit the light, and, bending down, lifted the head. The face was chill and colorless as death, the eyes were closed, and a slender stream of blood oozed slowly over the lips and dripped upon the linen shroudings of the table. She had fainted from the hemorrhage, and, taking her in his arms, he carried her up to her own room.

CHAPTER XXXI.

"I intend to trust you with important despatches, Miss Grey—for I have great confidence in female ingenuity, as well as female heroism. The meekest of you women are miniature Granvelles; nature made you a race of schemers. Pardon me if I ask how you propose to conceal the despatches? It is no easy matter now to run the blockade of a Southern port, especially on the Gulf; and you must guard against being picked up by the Philistines."

"I am fully aware of all the risk attending my trip; but if you will give me the papers, prepared as I directed in my note from Paris, I will pledge my life that they shall reach Richmond safely. If I am captured and carried North, I have friends who will assist me in procuring a passport to the South, and little delay will occur. If I am searched, I can bid them defiance. Give me the despatches, and I will show you how I intend to take them."

Electra opened her trunk, took out a large portfolio, and selected from the drawings one in crayons representing the heads of Michael Angelo's Fates. Spreading it out, face downward, on the table, she laid the closely-written tissue paper of despatches smoothly on the back of the thin pasteboard; then fitted a square piece of oil-silk on the tissue missive, and having, with a small brush, coated the silk with paste, covered the whole with a piece of thick drawing-paper, the edges of which were carefully glued to those of the pasteboard. Taking a hot iron from the grate, she passed it repeatedly over the paper, till all was smooth and dry; then in the centre wrote, with a pencil: "Michael Angelo's *Fates*, in the Pitti Palace. Copied May 8th, 1861." From a list of figures in a small note-book she added the dimensions of the picture, and, underneath all, a line from Euripides.

Her eyes sparkled as she bent over her work, and at length, lifting it for inspection, she exclaimed triumphantly:

"There, sir! I can baffle even the Paris detective, much less the lynx-eyed emissaries of Lincoln, Seward, and Co. Are you satisfied? Examine it with your own hands."

"Perfectly satisfied, my dear young lady. But suppose they should seize your trunk? Confiscation is the cry all over the North."

"Finding nothing suspicious or 'contraband' about me, except my Southern birth and sympathies, they would scarcely take possession of the necessary tools of my profession. I have no fear, sir; the paper is fated to reach its destination."

"Are your other despatches sealed up pictorially?"

She laughed heartily.

"Of course not. We women are too shrewd to hazard all upon one die."

"Well—well! You see that we trust important data to your cunning fingers. You leave London to-morrow for Southampton; will arrive just in time for the steamer. Good-by, Miss Grey. When I get back to the Confederacy I shall certainly find you out. I want you to paint the portraits of my wife and children. From the enviable reputation you have already acquired, I am proud to claim you for my countrywoman. God bless you and lead you safely home. Good-by, Mr. Mitchell. Take care of her, and let me hear from you on your arrival."

From the hour when tidings of the fall of Sumter reached Europe, Electra had resolved to cut short the studies which she had pursued so vigorously since her removal to Florence, and return to the South. But the tide of travel set toward, not from, European shores, and it was not until after repeated attempts to find some one homeward-bound, that she learned of Eric Mitchell's presence in Paris, and his intention of soon returning to W———. She wrote at once, requesting his permission to place herself under his care. It was cordially accorded; and, bidding adieu to Italy, she joined him without delay, despite the pleadings of Mr., Mrs. Young, and Louisa, who had recently arrived at Florence, and sincerely mourned a separation under such painful circumstances.

Eric was detained in Paris by a severe attack of the old disease, but finally reached London—whence, having completed their arrangements, they set off for Southampton, and took passage in the Trent, which was destined subsequently to play a prominent part in the tangled *role* of Diplomacy, and to furnish the most utterly humiliating of many chapters of the pusillanimity, sycophancy, and degradation of the Federal government.

The voyage proved pleasant and prosperous; and, once at Havana, Eric anxiously sought an opportunity of testing the vaunted efficiency of the blockade. Unfortunately, two steamers had started the week previous, one to New Orleans, the other to Charleston; only sailing vessels were to be found, and about the movements of these impenetrable mystery seemed wrapped. On the afternoon of the third day after their arrival, Eric, wearied with the morning's fruitless inquiry, was resting on the sofa at the hotel, while Electra watched the tide of passers-by, when Willis, Eric's servant, came in quickly and walked up to the sofa.

"Master, Captain Wright is here. I asked him to come and see you, and he is waiting down stairs."

"Captain Wright?"

"Yes, sir; the captain you liked so much at Smyrna—the one who gave you that pipe, sir."

"Oh, I remember! Yes—yes; and he is here? Well, show him up."

"Master, from the way he watches the clouds, I believe he is about to run out. Maybe he can take us?"

"Willis is invaluable to you, Mr. Mitchell," said Electra, as the negro left the room.

"He is, indeed. He is eyes, ears, crutches, everything to me, and never forgets anything or anybody. He has travelled over half the world with me—could desert me, and be free at any moment he felt inclined to do so—but is as faithful now as the day on which I first left home with him."

"Ah, Captain! this is an unexpected pleasure. I am heartily glad to see you. Miss Grey—Captain Wright. Take a seat."

The captain looked about thirty, possibly older; wore a gray suit and broad straw hat, and, when the latter was tossed on the floor, showed a handsome, frank, beaming face, with large, clear, smiling blue eyes, whose steady light nothing human could dim. His glossy reddish-brown hair was thrust back from a forehead white and smooth as a woman's, but the lower portion of the face was effectually bronzed by exposure to the vicissitudes of climate and weather; and Electra noticed a peculiar nervous restlessness of manner, as though he were habitually on the watch.

"I am astonished to see you in Havana, Mitchell. Where did you come from?"

"Just from Paris, where bad health drove me, after I bade you good-by at Smyrna. What are you doing here?"

"I suppose you have heard of our great victory at Manassas?"

"Yes, and am rejoiced beyond all expression, but feel anxious to see a full list of our loss. I had a brother-in-law in that engagement."

"His name?"

"Huntingdon — Major Huntingdon, of W———, in ———."

"I have seen no mention of his name in the papers, but our loss in officers was very heavy. We can ill afford to spare Bee, Bartow, and Fisher; and I want the war carried on till we burn every public building in Washington and raise a monument to our dead on the site of the Capitol. We owe this debt, and we must pay it."

"Have you a vessel here, Captain?"

"Of course I have! Don't you suppose that I would be in the army if I could not serve my country better by carrying in arms and ammunition? I have already made two successful trips with my schooner—ran in, despite the blockaders. I am negotiating for a steamer, but until I can get one ready I intend to sail on."

"When did you arrive here last?"

"About ten days ago. They chased me for nearly fifteen miles, but I stole out of sight before morning."

"When do you expect to leave here?"

The captain darted a swift, searching glance

at Electra, rose, and closed the door, saying with a light laugh:

"Take care, man! You are not exactly deer-hunting or crab-catching in a free country! Mind that, and talk softly. I am watched here; the Federal agents all know me, and there are several Federal vessels in port. When do I expect to leave? Well, to-night, if the weather thickens up, as I think it will, and there is evident sign of a storm. Most sailors wait for fair weather; we blockade-runners for foul."

"Oh, Captain! do take us with you!" said Electra, eagerly.

"What! In a rickety schooner, in the teeth of a gale? Besides, Miss, I am taking a cargo of powder this trip, and if I am hard pressed I shall blow up vessel and all, rather than suffer it to fall into Yankee clutches. You would not relish going up to heaven after the fashion of a rocket, would you?"

"I am willing, sir, to risk everything you threaten, rather than wait here indefinitely."

"Can't you take us, Wright—Miss Grey, Willis, and myself? We are very impatient to get home."

"But I have no accommodations for passengers. I should be ashamed to ask Miss Grey aboard my little egg-shell—everything is so small and comfortless. I have not lost all my politeness and chivalry, if I am a rough-looking Confederate sailor. I assure you I have every disposition to oblige you, but really it would not be right to subject a lady to such a trip as I may have before me."

"But, Captain, if, with all these facts staring me in the face, I appeal to your chivalry, and beg you to allow me to undergo the hardships incident to the trip in preference to uncertain delay here. If I prefer to run the gauntlet in your schooner, you surely will not refuse me?"

"Really, Miss, I don't know what to say. I thought I would frighten you out of the notion—for, to tell you the truth, I am always so much more anxious when I have ladies' lives in my hands. I pledge you my word I would sooner run afoul of a Federal frigate than see you suffer for want of anything. I can't even set a table half the time."

"But I suppose, sir, we could contrive to live a few days without eating at a regular table. I will take some cheese and crackers and fruit along in a basket, if that will ease your mind. Do waive your scruples, and consent to take charge of us."

"I add my prayers to hers. Wright, do take us. We shall not mind privations or inconvenience."

"Well, then, understand distinctly that, if anything happens, you are not to blame me. If the young lady gets sea-sick, or freckled, or sunburnt, or starved to death, or blown up, or drowned, or, worse than all, if the Yankee thieves by the way-side take her as a prize, it will be no fault of mine whatever, and I tell you now I shall not lay it on my conscience."

"'Rawhead and bloody bones' never frightened me, even when I was a little child, sir; so you may reconcile yourself to the prospect of having us as *compagnons de voyage.*"

"Suppose a small hand-to-hand fight forms a part of the programme?"

"In that case, I have a splendid brace of pistols, which were given to me before I left Europe."

"Do you know how to handle them?"

"Moderately well. I will practice as we go along, by making a target of one of your small ropes."

"I see you are incorrigible; and I suppose I must let you go with me, *bongré malgré.*"

"*Bongré* let it be, by all means. I am inexpressibly impatient to get home."

"Wright, to what port are you bound?"

"Ah! that is more than I can tell you. The winds must decide it. I can't try the Carolinas again this trip; they are watching for me too closely there. New Orleans is rather a longer run than I care to make, and I shall keep my eyes on Apalachicola and Mobile."

"What object have you in starting to-night, particularly in the face of a gale?"

Again the captain's eye swept round the room, to guard against any doors that might be ajar.

"As I told you before, I am watched here. The Federals have a distinguished regard for me, and I have to elude suspicion, as well as run well, when I do get out. Two hours ago a Federal armed steamer, which has been coaling here, weighed anchor, and has probably left the harbor, to cruise between this place and Key West. As they passed, one of the crew yelled out to me that they would wait outside and catch me certainly this time; that I had made my last jaunt to Dixie, etc. I have carefully put out the impression that I need some repairs, which can not be finished this week; and have told one or two, confidentially, that I could not leave until the arrival of a certain cargo from Nassau, which is due to-morrow. That puritanical craft which started off at noon does not expect me for several days, and to-night I shall rub my fingers and sail out right in her wake. Ha! ha! how they will howl! What gnashing of teeth there will be when they hear of me in a Confederate port! And now about your baggage. Have everything ready; I will show Willis the right wharf, and at dark he must bring the trunks down; I will be on the watch, and send a boat ashore. About sunset you and Miss Grey can come aboard, as if for a mere visit. I must go and make what little preparation I can for your comfort."

Nothing occurred to frustrate the plan; Eric and Electra were cordially received, and at dusk Willis and the baggage arrived punctually. The schooner was lying some distance from the wharf, all sails down, and apparently contemplating no movement. With darkness came a brisk, stiffening wind, and clouds shutting out even dim starlight. At ten o'clock, all things being in readiness, the captain went on deck; very soon after the glimmering lights of the city, then the frowning walls of Moro, were left behind, and the "Dixie" took her way silently and swiftly seaward.

About two o'clock, being unable to sleep from the rocking of the vessel, Electra, knowing that Eric was still on deck, crept up the steps in the darkness, for the lights had been extinguished. The captain was passing, but paused, saying in a whisper:

"Is that you, Miss Grey? Come this way, and I will show you something."

He grasped her hand, led her to the bow, where Eric was sitting on a coil of rope, and, pointing straightforward, added in the same suppressed tone:

"Look right ahead—you see a light? The Philistines are upon us! Look well, and you will see a dark, irregular moving mass; that is the steamer of which I told you. They have found out at last that there is going to be all sorts of a gale, and as they can't ride it like my snug, dainty little egg-shell, they are putting back with all possible speed. Twenty minutes ago they were bearing down on me; now you see that they will pass to our left. What a pity they don't know their neighbors!"

"Do you think that they will not see you?"

"Certainly! with sails down, and lights out, there is nothing to be seen on such a night as this. There! don't you hear her paddles?"

"No; I hear nothing but the roar of the wind and water."

"Ah! that is because your ears are not trained like mine. Great Neptune! how she labors already! Now! be silent."

On came the steamer, which Electra's untrained eyes, almost blinded by spray, could barely discern; and her heart beat like a muffled drum as it drew nearer and nearer. Once she heard a low, chuckling laugh of satisfaction escape the captain; then, with startling distinctness, the ringing of a bell was borne from the steamer's deck.

"Four bells—two o'clock. How chagrined they will be to-morrow, when they find out they passed me without paying their respects," whispered the captain.

Gradually the vessel receded, the dark mass grew indistinct, the light flickered, and was soon lost to view, and the sound of the laboring machinery was drowned in the roar of the waves.

"Hurrah! for the 'Dixie!' Strike a light below, Hutchinson, and get some glasses. We must have a little champagne in honor of this performance. Come down, Miss Grey, and you, too, Mitchell; the water is beginning to break very near your feet. Oh! but you must take some wine, Miss Grey. I can't have you looking like a ghost when I land you on Confederate soil. People will swear I starved you, and nothing humiliates me half so much as an imputation on my hospitality. Here's to the Confederacy! and to our Beauregard and Johnston! God bless them both!"

Electra drank the wine; and, before he went back on deck, the captain made a comfortable place for her on the sofa in the little cabin. The storm increased until it blew a perfect hurricane, and the schooner rolled and creaked, now and then shivering in every timber. It was utterly impossible to sleep, and Eric, who was suffering from a headache, passed a miserable night. In the white sickly dawn the captain looked in again, and Electra thought that no ray of sunshine could be more radiant or cheering than his joyous noble face.

"Good-morning. I wonder if I look as much like a drenched lily as you do, Miss Grey? Doubtless, much more like a drenched sunflower, you think. Were you alarmed all night?"

"No, sir; I knew that we were not in the hands of Palinurus."

"Oh! thank you for your confidence! I will tell my wife of that, if I live to see her again. I certainly did not fall overboard, which was lucky—for, though I rather pride myself on my proficiency as a swimmer, I am very sceptical concerning the mythologic three days performance. Mitchell, I hope a good cup of hot coffee will set your head straight."

"How is the storm? Any abatement?" asked Eric.

"Not a whit yet; but the wind has veered a little, and I think that by twelve o'clock it will break away."

"Captain, can I go on deck for a little while?"

"Whew! My dear young lady, you would not be able to catch your breath again for a half-hour. You could not stand a moment; spray and wind would blind you, and the waves would take you overboard—wash you away."

"But I want to see a genuine violent storm at sea. I shall probably never have another opportunity."

"I will answer for the genuineness of this specimen, if you really want to look out. Wrap a shawl round your shoulders; give me your hand; step up; look for yourself. No counterfeit—take my word for that. Squally enough, is n't it?"

A wild howling waste of waters leaped and rolled like leaden mountains against a wan drab sky, where dun smoke-colored clouds trailed sullenly before the wind. Foam-crowned walls towered on either side the schooner, leaned over as if to meet and crush it, and broke in wreaths of spray about the deck, while ghastly sheet-lightning glimmered ceaselessly.

"Old Father Neptune must be in a tearing rage with his pretty Amphitrite, to churn up all this commotion. Don't you think you have seen enough, Miss Grey? You are getting wet."

He saw her face flush and her eyes sparkle strangely.

"If I could only paint this sea! If I could only put that roll and sweep of waves yonder upon canvas! I could afford to die young. Oh! for the brush of Clarkson Stanfield for one hour! to fix that sea—'where it gathers itself into a huge billow, fronting the blast like an angry brow, corrugated in agony and rage.' My father was a sailor, and I think I must have inherited my love of the sea from him."

"Where is he now?"

"Dead—long ago—before I was born. His ship, the 'Electra,' went down with all on board."

"And your mother?"

"Named me for the wreck, and followed my father when I was four months old."

As swirls of spray dashed in her face,

"Her eyes had looks like prisoned birds."

"Captain, I have read somewhere of a Dutch painter who, in his passionate longing to portray accurately such scenes as this, had himself lashed to the deck of a vessel during a terrific gale, where he could study and note the peculiar aspects, so difficult to render correctly. I am tempted to follow his example. Doubtless you could furnish a rope for such a purpose."

"Not even a bit of twine. Come down instantly, Miss Grey. I can't afford the luxury of a physician on board; and if you should be so unfortunate as to catch a catarrh or spell of pneumonia by this piece of imprudence, I should be distressed to death and frightened out of my wits. Come down at once."

About noon the fury of the gale subsided, the sun looked out through rifts in the scudding clouds, and toward night fields of quiet blue were once more visible. By next morning the weather had cleared up, with a brisk westerly wind; but the sea still rolled heavily; and Eric, unable to bear the motion, kept below, loath to trust himself on his feet. Electra strove to while away the tedious time by reading aloud to him; but many a yearning look was cast toward the deck, and finally she left him with a few books, and ran up to the open air.

On the afternoon of the third day after leaving Havana she was sitting on a buffalo-robe stretched near the stern, watching the waves and graceful curls of foam that marked the schooner's path, and forgetful for a season of the fifth volume of "Modern Painters"

which lay open beside her. The wind had blown back her straw hat, and her short black hair fluttered about a face fully exposed to view.

The captain had been tuning a guitar for some moments, and now drew near, throwing himself down on the buffalo-robe.

"What are you staring at so solemnly? Tell me what you are thinking of."

"If you are really curious, you are welcome to know. I was only watching the wake of the vessel and thinking of that beautiful simile of Coleridge in the 'Friend:' 'Human experience, like the stern-lights of a ship at sea, illumines only the path we have passed over.'"

Her clear olive cheeks burned and her great shadowy elfish eyes kindled, as was their wont when her feelings were deeply stirred.

"I believe you are an artist, Miss Grey?"

"I am trying to become one, sir. Before we leave you I want you to examine some of my sketches, and select the one which you like best. It will afford me great pleasure to paint it for you, as a feeble token of my gratitude and appreciation of your kindness."

"Thank you. I hope the day is not distant when I shall have my wife with me once more, and then I shall beg you to paint her portrait for me."

"Where is she?"

"At our home in Maryland."

"Are you a Marylander, Captain."

"Oh, yes! but that is no place for true men now. Nothing can be accomplished there at this juncture, and those who are true to the Constitution and the South have joined the Confederate service in one form or another. We shall have to hang that infamous traitor, Hicks, before we can free the state; and it is because I appreciate the lamentable scarcity of arms and ammunition that I am engaged in my present business. If I arm ten thousand men, it will be better for our glorious cause than if I handled a musket myself. Poor, down-trodden, handcuffed, humiliated Maryland! Miss Grey, you have probably not heard our favorite new song, 'Maryland, my Maryland?' I comfort myself by singing it now and then, while hundreds of miles of stormy sea toss between me and my home. Would you like to hear it?"

"By all means. In Europe I, of course, heard nothing."

He struck a few full rich chords and sang the stirring words, as only a true Marylander can who feels all the wrongs and ignominy of his state.

His fine eyes were full of tears as he began the last prophetic verse; and when it was concluded, he sprang up and repeated triumphantly:

"She breathes—she burns! She'll come! she'll come! Maryland! My Maryland!"

"If such be the feeling of her sons, Captain, she will soon 'gird her beauteous limbs with steel,' and as a state come out proudly from amid the Abomination of Desolation. The music is peculiarly adapted to the burden of the noble thoughts, and invests them with extraordinary power and pathos. The wonderful effect of national lyrics in such stormy times as these exemplifies the truth of the admirable remark, which I have seen very felicitously applied to Béranger, but which was first quoted, I believe, by Fletcher of Saltoun : 'If a man were permitted to make all the ballads, he need not care who should make the laws of a nation.' Oh! what a sunset! I never saw anything from Fiesole comparable to that."

The sun had gone down below the waterline. From the zenith, eastward, the sky was violet-hued; in the west, light cloud-flakes had gathered in fleecy masses and semi-spiral whiffs; some burned like dashes of vermilion in lakes of beryl or chrysoprase; others, in purple pomp, fringed their edges with gold; snowy mountain ranges were tipped with fire, pillared cathedrals with domes of silver; and, beneath all, glared a liquid sea of rippling flame. A sky which only Ruskin could describe or Turner paint.

"The West is an altar where earth daily gathers up her garlanded beauty in sacrificial offering to God. Agamemnon-like, she gives her loveliest."

These words seemed to pass the girl's lips unconsciously as she leaned foward with hands clasped on her lap; and smiling at the breathless eagerness of her face, and the to him incomprehensible enthusiasm she evinced, the captain said :

"If you are so very fond of such things, I wish you could see a midnight sky in the tropics as I have seen it, sailing between Rio Janeiro and Baltimore. I believe I have not much sentiment in my nature, but many a night I have lain awake on deck looking up at the stars that glowed, burned—I hardly know how to express it—like great diamonds clustered on black velvet. There are splendid constellations there, which you have never seen. When we win independence and peace I intend to have a fine steamship of my own, and then I shall ask you to make a voyage with me as far as Uruguay. I will show you scenery in Brazil that will put you on your knees in adoration."

"I shall accept the invitation when peace is made. Captain Wright, have you any children ?"

"Yes—two; a son and daughter; the eldest five years old."

"Then train them up to love sunsets, stars, flowers, clouds of all kinds. We are creatures of education, and I hold it the imperative duty of parents to teach their children to appreciate the beautiful things in this world which God has given to gild life with. There is grief and gloom enough at best; and so much innocent exquisite joy may be extracted from a thousand sources, that it seems philosophic, as well as a sacred duty, to reap the great harvest of happiness which calls to us from a proper appreciation of Beauty. I do not mean learned disquisitions, or tedious, scientific terminology. A child can admire, love an aster or a magnolia, without understanding botany; may watch for and delight in such a sky as that, without classifying the clouds or designating the gorgeous tints in genuine artistic phraseology; may clap its little hands, and shout with joy, in looking at the stars, without knowing Orion from Ursa Major. I have often been laughed at, and requested not to talk nonsense, when I have expressed these views; have been sneered at as an enthusiast; but the longer I live the more earnest becomes my conviction of the truth of my opinion. The useful, the material necessities of life, require little study; our comfort involves attention to them; but the more ideal sources of peace and enjoyment demand care and cultivation. I am an orphan; I had no parental hand to guide my thoughts and aspirations to the Beautiful, in all its protean phases; my life has not been spent in the most flowery paths; but because, as a lonely child, I learned to derive pleasure from communion with Nature and Art, I have seasons of rapturous enjoyment which all California could not purchase. The useful, the practical, and the beautiful are not opposed—are even united—if people would only open their eyes to the truth. I am no morbid sentimentalist or dreaming enthusiast; if nature intended me for such, a cold, matter-of-fact world has cheated me out of my birthright. I live, sustain myself by my art, as you by your sailor's craft; it feeds and clothes my body as well as my mind. But I can't bear to walk through a grand metropolitan cathedral of wonderful and varied loveliness, and see the endless caravan of men and women tramping along its glorious aisles, looking neither to right nor left, oblivious of surrounding splendors, gazing stolidly down at the bag of coins in their hands, or the bales of cotton or hogsheads of sugar or tobacco they are rolling before them. I long to lay my hand on their shoulders, to stay their hurrying steps, and whisper gently : 'Fellow-pilgrims, brothers, sisters, look up at the glories that canopy you. Bend your knees one instant before yonder shrines of Beauty.' Oh! æsthetics is a heavenly ladder, where, like Jacob's angels, pure thoughts and holy aspirations come from and go to God. Whatever tends to elevate and ennoble the soul is surely useful; and love of beauty is a mighty educational engine, which all may handle if they will. Captain, sow the seeds of appreciation early in your children's hearts, and they will thank you when you are an old silver-haired man."

Across that rosy sea tripped magic memories. The sailor's heart found its distant haven in the joyful, tender welcome of his blue-eyed wife—the lisping, birdish tone of his fair-browed, curly-headed children, stretching their little dimpled arms to clasp his neck; and to the artist-woman came melancholy thoughts of by-gone years, shrouded in crumbling garlands—of hopes and feverish aspirations that had found their graves—of her future cheerless life, her lonely destiny.

For some time both were silent; then the captain roused himself from his dream of home, and, passing his hand over his eyes, said:

"Well, Miss Grey, I shall place you on Confederate soil to-morrow, God willing."

"Then you are going to Mobile?"

"Yes; I shall try hard to get in there early in the morning. You will know your fate before many hours."

"Do you regard this trial as particularly hazardous?"

"Of course; the blockading squadrons grow more efficient and expert every day, and some danger necessarily attends every trial. Mobile ought to be pretty well guarded by this time."

The wind was favorable, and the schooner ploughed its way swiftly through the autumn night. The captain did not close his eyes; and just about daylight Electra and Eric, aroused by a sudden running to and fro, rose, and simultaneously made their appearance on deck.

"What is the matter, Wright?"

"Matter! why, look ahead, my dear fellow, and see where we are. Yonder is Sand island and light house, and a little to the right is Fort Morgan. But the fleet to the left is hardly six miles off, and it will be a tight race if I get in."

There was but a glimmering light rimming the East, where two or three stars burned with indescribable brilliance and beauty, and in the gray haze and wreaths of mist which curled up over the white-capped waves Electra could distinguish nothing. The air was chill, and she said with a slight shiver:

"I can't see any light-house."

"There is, of course, no light there, these war-times, but you see that tall white tower, don't you? There, look through my glass. That low dark object yonder is the outline of the fort; you will see it more distinctly after a little. Now, look right where my finger points; that is the flag-staff. Look up over head—I have hoisted our flag, and pretty soon it will be a target for those dogs. Ha! Mitchell! Hutchinson! they see us! There is some movement among them. They are getting ready to cut us off this side of the Swash channel! We shall see."

He had crowded on all sail, and the little vessel dashed through the light fog as if conscious of her danger, and resolved to sustain herself gallantly. Day broke fully, sea and sky took the rich orange tint which only autumn mornings give, and in this glow a Federal frigate and sloop slipped from their moorings and bore down threateningly on the graceful bounding schooner.

"But for the fog, which puzzled me about three o'clock, I should have run by unseen, and they would never have known it till I was safe in Navy cove. We will beat them, though, as it is, by about twenty minutes. An hour ago I was afraid I should have to beach her. Are you getting frightened, Miss Grey?"

"Oh, no! I would not have missed this for any consideration. How rapidly the Federal vessels move. They are gaining on us."

Her curling hair, damp with mist, clustered around her forehead; she had wrapped a scarlet crape shawl about her shoulders, and stood, with her red lips apart and trembling, watching the exciting race.

"Look at the frigate!"

There was a flash at her bow, a curl of white smoke rolled up, then a heavy roar, and a thirty-two pounder round shot fell about a hundred yards to the right of the vessel.

A yell of defiance rent the air from the crew of the "Dixie"—hats were waved—and, snatching off her shawl, Electra shook its bright folds to the stiffening breeze, while her hot cheeks matched them in depth of color.

Another and another shot was fired in quick succession, and so accurate had they become that the last whizzed through the rigging, cutting one of the small ropes.

"Humph! they are getting saucy" said the captain, looking up coolly, when the yells of his crew ceased for a moment—and, with a humorous twinkle in his fine eyes, he added:

"Better go below, Miss Grey; they might clip one of your curls next time. The vandals see you, I dare say, and your red flag stings their Yankee pride a little."

"Do you suppose they can distinguish me?"

"Certainly. Through my glass I can see the gunners at work, and, of course, they see you. Should not be surprised if they aimed specially at you. That is the style of New England chivalry."

Whiz—whiz; both sloop and frigate were firing now in good earnest, and one shell exploded a few yards from the side of the little vessel, tossing the foam and water over the group on deck.

"They think you have hardly washed your face yet, Miss Grey, and are courteously anxious to perform the operation for you. But the game is up. Look yonder! Hurrah for Dixie! and Fort Morgan!"

"From the dim flag-staff battery bellowed a gun."

The boom of a columbiad from the fort shook the air like thunder, and gave to the blockaders the unmistakable assurance, "Thus far, and no farther."

The schooner strained on its way; a few shots fell behind, and soon, under the frowning bastions of the fort, whence the Confederate banner floated so proudly on the balmy Gulf breeze, spreading its free folds like an ægis, the gallant little vessel passed up the channel and came to anchor in Mobile bay, amid the shouts of crew and garrison, and welcomed by a salute of five guns.

CHAPTER XXXII.

Immediately after her arrival in Mobile, Electra prepared to forward her despatches by Captain Wright, whose business called him to Richmond before his return to Cuba; and an examination of them proved that the expedient resorted to was perfectly successful. By moistening the edges of the drawing-paper, the tissue missive was drawn out uninjured, and, to Eric's surprise, she removed the carefully-stitched blue silk which lined the tops of her travelling gauntlets and extracted similar despatches, all of which were at once transmitted to the seat of government. While waiting for a boat, they heard the painful tidings of Major Huntingdon's death, which increased Eric's impatience to reach W———. The remainder of the journey was sad, and four days after leaving the Gulf City the lights of W——— and roar of the Falls simultaneously greeted the spent travellers. Having telegraphed of his safe arrival, the carriage was waiting at the depot, and Andrew handed to Electra a note from his mistress, requesting her to come at once to her house instead of going to the hotel. Eric added earnest persuasion, and, with some reluctance, the artist finally consented. They were prepared for the silent, solemn aspect of the house and for the mourning-dress of the orphan; but not for the profound calm, the melancholy, tearless composure with which she received them. Mental and physical suffering had sadly changed her. The oval face was thinner, and her form had lost its roundness, but the countenance retained its singular loveliness and the mesmeric splendor of the large eyes seemed enhanced. Of her father she did not speak, but gave her uncle a written statement of all the facts which she had been able to gather concerning the circumstances of his death; and thus a tacit compact was formed to make no reference to the painful subject.

As she accompanied Electra to the room prepared for her, on the night of her arrival, the latter asked with ill-concealed emotion:

"Irene, can you tell me anything about Russell? I am very anxious to hear something of him."

Irene placed the silver lamp on the table, and, standing in its glow, answered quietly:

"He was wounded in the arm at Manassas, but retains command of his regiment and is doing very well. Dr. Arnold is the regimental surgeon, and in one of his letters to me he mentioned that your cousin's wound was not serious."

"I am going to him immediately."

"Unfortunately, you will not be allowed to do so. The wounded were removed to Richmond as promptly as possible, but your cousin remained at Manassas, where ladies are not permitted."

"Then I will write to him to meet me in Richmond."

Irene made no reply, and, watching her all the while, Electra asked:

"When did you see him last? How did he look?"

"The day before he started to Richmond. He was very well, I believe; but looked harassed and paler than usual. He is so robust, however, that I think you need entertain no apprehension concerning his health."

The inflexible features, the low, clear, firm voice were puzzling, and Electra's brow thickened and darkened as she thought:

"Her father is dead now; there is no obstacle remaining. She must love him, and yet she gives no sign of interest."

"Good-night, Electra; I hope you will sleep well after your fatiguing journey. Do not get up early. I will send your breakfast to your room whenever you wish it."

She turned away, but the artist stepped before her and caught up both her hands.

"Oh, Irene! it grieves me to see you looking so. Talk to me about your great pent-up sorrows and it will relieve you."

"My sorrows can not be talked away. Graves never give back their dead. Good-night, my dear Electra."

Electra looked at her sadly, wistfully; and, suddenly throwing her arms about the queenly figure, kissed her white cold cheek. Irene returned the caress, withdrew from the embrace, and passed to her own room.

Jealous women are rarely generous toward their rivals, and Electra's exacting, moody character rendered it peculiarly difficult for her to stifle her feelings. She would most certainly have cordially hated any other woman who stood between her and her cousin's heart; but before the nobility, the loftiness, the cool purity of Irene's soul, her own restless spirit bowed down with emotions nearly akin to adoration. The solemn serenity of that pale brow awed and soothed the fevered, tumultuous nature of the artist; and she had schooled herself to look upon her as Russell's future wife—with a pang of pain, it is true, but certainly with no touch of bitterness. She could endure that he should love so devotedly one who ministered at the shrine of Christian charity, and whose hands threw down, wherever she moved, the blessed largess of peace.

contentment, and plenty. They stood in strange relationship, these two women. One ignorant of the absorbing love of the other for the man to whom she had given her heart long years ago; and that other conscious of an undying affection, which she silently inurned in her own bosom.

Two days later they sat together before one of the parlor-windows. Electra was engaged in tearing off and rolling bandages, while Irene slowly scraped lint from a quantity of old linen which filled a basket at her side. Neither had spoken for some time; the sadness of their occupation called up gloomy thoughts; but finally Electra laid down a roll of cloth, and, interlacing her slight fingers, said:

"Irene, as you sit there you remind me of the 'Cameo Bracelet.' You have seen it, of course?"

"Yes; it is one of the finest imaginative creations I have ever read; and I can not divest myself of the apprehension that it adumbrates the fate of New Orleans."

Electra watched the motion of her companion's fingers, and in a rich, musical voice repeated the words, beginning:

"She's sifting lint for the brave who bled.
And I watch her fingers float and flow
Over the linen, as, thread by thread,
It flakes to her lap like snow."

"Irene, the women of the South must exercise an important influence in determining our national destiny; and because I felt this so fully I hurried home to share the perils and privations and trials of my countrywomen. It seems to me that no true son or daughter can linger in Europe now, with the broad ocean surging between them and the bloody soil of their native land. It is not my privilege to enter the army, and wield a sword or musket; but I am going to true womanly work—into the crowded hospitals, to watch faithfully over sick and wounded."

"I approve your plan, think it your duty, and wish that I could start to Richmond with you to-morrow—for I believe that in this way we may save valuable lives. You should, as you have said, go on at once; you have nothing to keep you; your work is waiting for you there. But my position is different; I have many things to arrange here before I can join you. I want to see the looms at work on the plantation; and am going down next week with Uncle Eric, to consult with the overseer about several changes which I desire made concerning the negroes. When all this is accomplished, I, too, shall come into the hospitals."

"About what time may I expect you?"

"Not until you see me; but at the earliest practicable day."

"Your uncle objects very strenuously to such a plan, does he not?"

"He will acquiesce at the proper time. Take care! you are making your bandages too wide."

"A long dark vista stretches before the Confederacy. I can not, like many persons, feel sanguine of a speedy termination of the war."

"Yes—a vista lined with the bloody graves of her best sons; but beyond glimmers Freedom—Independence. In that light we shall walk without stumbling. Deprived of liberty we can not exist, and its price was fixed when the foundations of time were laid. I believe the termination of the war to be contingent only on the method of its prosecution. Agathocles, with thirteen thousand men, established a brilliant precedent, which Scipio followed so successfully in the second Punic war; and when our own able generals are permitted to emulate those illustrious leaders of antiquity, then, and I fear not until then, shall we be able to dictate terms of peace."

"Your devotion, then, is unshaken, even by your sorrows."

"Unshaken! Does the precious blood of a sacrifice unsettle the holy foundations of the altar?"

"But, Irene, if you could have foreseen all that Secession has cost you?"

The mourner raised her eyes from the snowy heap of lint, and answered with impressive earnestness and pathos:

"Could I have foreseen the spirit which actuates the North—the diabolical hate and fiendishness which its people have manifested—and had I known that resistance would have cost the lives of all in the Confederacy, I should have urged Secession as the only door of escape from political bondage. Rather would I have men, women, and children fill one wide, common grave, than live in subjection to, or connection with, a people so depraved, unscrupulous, and Godless. Electra, national, like individual life, which is not noble, free, and honorable, is not worth the living. A people who can survive their liberty are beneath contempt; and to-day, desolate though I am, I would sooner take my place by my father's side than recall him to live a subject of the despotic government at Washington. Even when I believed the friendly professions of thousands at the North—when I believed in the existence of a powerful constitutional and conservative party—I was, from the beginning, a Secessionist; and now that the mask of political cant is stripped from them, I am more than ever convinced of the correctness of my views and the absolute necessity of the step we took. The ultimate result can never affect the question of the right and propriety of Secession, though it may demonstrate the deplorable consequences of our procrastination. In attestation of the necessity of separation stand the countless graves of our dear and gallant dead. I look to a just God to avenge them and deliver us."

"But do you still cling to a belief in the possibility of republican forms of government,"

This is a question which constantly disquiets me."

"My faith in that possibility is unshaken. Entire self-abnegation I certainly expected, hoped for, on the part of our people; and I still feel assured that the great masses are capable of patriotism as sublime as the world ever witnessed, and that our noble armies have had no equal in the history of our race. Nevertheless, it is apparent to those who ponder the aspect of public affairs that demagogism crawls along its customary sinuous path, with serpent-eyes fastened on self-aggrandizement. The pure ore of our country will be found in the ranks of our armies; and the few scheming politicians, plotting for position, for offices of emolument in civil or military departments, will prove the dross in the revolutionary crucible. I have no apprehension for our future as long as demagogism and nepotism can be kept down; for out of these grow innumerable evils—not the least of which is the intrusting of important posts to the hands of men who have none of the requisites, save their relationship to, or possession of the favor of, those in authority. If the nation will but mark the unworthy sons whose grasping, selfish ambition will not even be restrained in hours of direst peril to the cause, and brand them with *Mene, Mene*, we shall yet teach the world that self-government is feasible."

"But in Europe, where the subject is eagerly canvassed, the impression obtains that in the great fundamental principle of our government will be found the germ of its dissolution. This war is waged to establish the right of Secession and the doctrine that 'all just governments rest on the consent of the governed.' With such a precedent, it would be worse than stultification to object to the secession of any state or states now constituting the Confederacy, who at a future day may choose to withdraw from the present compact. Granting our independence, which Europe regards as a foregone conclusion, what assurance have you (say they, gloating, in anticipation, over the prospect) that, so soon as the common dangers of war, which for a time cemented you so closely, are over, entire disintegration will not ensue and all your boasts end in some dozen anarchical pseudo-republics, like those of South America and Mexico? Irene, I confess I have a haunting horror of the influence of demagogues on our future. You know Sir Robert Walpole once said, ' Patriots are very easily raised. You have but to refuse an unreasonable request, and up springs a patriot.' I am afraid that disappointed politicians will sow seeds of dissension among us."

"That is an evil which our legislators must guard against by timely provision. We are now, thank God! a thoroughly homogeneous people, with no antagonistic systems of labor, necessitating conflicting interests. As states, we are completely identified in commerce and agriculture, and no differences need arise. Purified from all connection with the North, and with no vestige of the mischievous element of New England Puritanism, which, like other poisonous Mycelium, springs up pertinaciously where even a shred is permitted, we can be a prosperous and noble people. Rather than witness our national corruption through the thousand influences which have so often degraded people of vast wealth, I would gladly welcome the iron currency and frugal public tables of Lycurgus. One possible source of evil has occurred to me. Unless our planters everywhere become good agricultural chemists, and by a moderate outlay renew their lands every year, the planting interest will gradually drift westward in pursuit of fresh fertile fields, and thus leave such of the more eastern states as possess great advantages in the water line to engage in manufactures of various kinds. That negro labor is by no means so profitable in factory as field seems well established; and if this condition of affairs is allowed and encouraged, contrariety of interests will soon show itself, and demagogues will climb into place by clamoring for ' protection.' Heaven preserve us from following the example of New England and Pennsylvania! But if free-trade is declared, and our ports are thrown open to all the markets of the world, except Lincolndom, the evil will be arrested. True, Europe has no love for the Confederacy, and we certainly have as little for trans-Atlantic nations—but the rigid laws of political economy forge links of amity. If our existence as a Republic depends upon the perpetuity of the institution of slavery, then, it seems to me, that the aim of our legislators should be to render us *par excellence* an agricultural people—and, with the exception of great national arsenals and workshops, to discourage home manufactories. I hope, too, for an amendment of our constitution, which shall render the members of the cabinet, and all our foreign ministers, subject entirely to the appointment of Congress, and the tenure of the latter class of officials for life or good behavior, instead of being selected by the President, as heretofore, for four or six years. To the disgraceful hunt for office is to be attributed much of the acrimony of party-feeling which characterizes presidential campaigns. When our Presidents are selected and supported solely for their intrinsic ability and nobility of soul, instead of for the places they will confer on their party, we shall begin to seek out our Cincinnatus and Aratus, and the premium for demagogism will be lost. But we have statesmen among us who must see all these evils, and doubtless they will arrest them in time. We are paying too high a price for our freedom to have it stolen from us in future by unscrupulous political gamesters, who would sacrifice a valuable principle of government in order to secure a foreign appointment."

"I can not avoid feeling sceptical of the public virtue, when seasons of prosperity and great wealth succeed these years of trial; and of late, in casting the horoscope of our young Confederacy, I have frequently recalled that fine passage in Montagu's 'Reflections on the Rise and Fall of Republics:' 'Greece, once the nurse of arts and sciences, the fruitful mother of philosophers, law-givers, and heroes, now lies prostrate under the iron yoke of ignorance and barbarism. . Carthage, once the mighty sovereign of the ocean, and the centre of universal commerce, which poured the riches of all nations into her lap, now puzzles the inquisitive traveller in his researches after even the vestiges of her ruins. . And Rome, the mistress of the universe, which once contained whatever was esteemed great or brilliant in human nature, is now sunk into the ignoble seat of whatever is esteemed mean and infamous. Should Faction again predominate and succeed in its destructive views, and the dastardly maxims of luxury and effeminacy universally prevail amongst us, such, too, will be the fate of Britain;' and I may add of the Confederacy—for where are the safeguards of its public purity?"

Electra had finished the bandages and was walking slowly before the windows, and, without looking up from the lint, which she was tying into small packages, Irene answered:

"The safeguards will be found in the mothers, wives, and sisters of our land."

"Ah! but their hands are tied; and they walk but a short, narrow path, from hearthstone to threshold, and back again. They have, I know, every inclination to exert a restraining influence, but no power to utilize it. Sometimes I almost fear that the fabled Norse *Ragnarök* is darkening over this continent. The monsters, Midgard Serpent, Fenris, and all, have certainly been unloosed at the North."

"Electra, though we are very properly debarred from the 'tented field,' I have entire confidence that the cause of our country may be advanced, and its good promoted, through the agency of its daughters; for, out of the dim historic past come words of encouragement. Have you forgotten that, when Sparta forsook the stern and sublime simplicity of her ancient manners, King Agis found himself unable to accomplish his scheme of redeeming his degenerate country from avarice and corruption, until the ladies of Sparta gave their consent and support to the plan of reform? Southern women have no desire to usurp legislative reins; their appropriate work consists in moulding the manners and morals of the nation; in checking the wild excesses of fashionable life, and the dangerous spirit of extravagance; of reckless expenditure in dress, furniture, and equipage, which threatened ruinous results before the declaration of hostilities. Noble wives, who properly appreciate the responsibility of their position, should sternly rebuke and frown down the disgraceful idea, which seems to be gaining ground and favor in our cities, that married women may, with impunity, seek attentions and admiration abroad. Married belles and married beaux are not harmless, nor should they be tolerated in really good society. Women who so far forget their duties to their homes and husbands, and the respect due to public opinion, as to habitually seek for happiness in the mad whirl of so-called fashionable life, ignoring household obligations, should be driven from well-bred, refined circles, to hide their degradation at the firesides they have disgraced. That wives should constantly endeavor to cultivate social graces and render themselves as fascinating as possible, I hold their sacred duty; but beauty should be preserved, and accomplishments perfected, to bind their husband's hearts more closely, to make their homes attractive, instead of being constantly paraded before the world for the unholy purpose of securing the attentions and adulation of other gentlemen. I do not desire to see married women recluses; on the contrary, I believe that society has imperative claims upon them, which should be promptly met and faithfully and gracefully discharged. But those degraded wives, who are never seen with their husbands when they can avoid it—who are never happy unless riding or walking with strangers, or receiving their attentions at theatres, concerts, or parties—are a disgrace to the nation which they are gradually demoralizing and corrupting. From the influence of these few deluded weak libels on our sex may God preserve our age and country! They are utterly unworthy the noble work which calls loudly to every true Southern woman. Statesmen are trained up around the mother's armchair, and she can imbue the boy with lofty sentiments, and inspire him with aims which, years hence, shall lead him in congressional halls to adhere to principles, to advance the Truth—though, thereby, votes for the next election fall away, like stricken leaves in autumn. What time has the married belle for this holy hearthstone mission? The conscientious, devoted, and patriotic Christian women of a nation are the safeguards of its liberties and purity."

"All perfectly true, and very encouraging in the abstract; but, Irene, how many women do you suppose sit down and ponder their individual responsibility?"

"Electra, my friend, are you sure that you do? Your profession will give you vast influence in forming public taste, and I hope much from its judicious use. Be careful that you select only the highest, purest types to offer to your countrymen and women, when Peace enables us to turn our attention to the great work of building up a noble school of Southern

Art. We want no feeble, sickly sentimentality, nor yet the sombre austerity which seems to pervade your mind, judging from the works you have shown me."

A slight quiver crossed the mobile features of the artist as she bit her full lip and asked:

"What would you pronounce the distinguishing characteristic of my works? I saw, yesterday, that you were not fully satisfied."

"A morbid melancholy, which you seem to have fostered tenderly, instead of crushing vigorously. A disposition to dwell upon the stern and gloomy aspects of the physical world, and to intensify and reproduce abnormal and unhappy phases of character. Your breezy, sunshiny, joyous moods you have kept under lock and key while in your studio."

"You are right; but I merely dipped my brush in the colors of my own life, and if my work is gray and sad and shadowy, it is no fault of mine. One who sits at her easel, listening ever to

'The low footsteps of each coming ill,'

should be pardoned if her canvas glows not with gala occasions and radiant faces that have never looked beyond the glittering confines of Aladdin's palace. Remember, the 'lines' did not fall to me 'in pleasant places,' and it is not strange that I sometimes paint desert, barren scenes, without grapes of Eshcol or Tokay. Irene,

    '   Long green days,
    Worn bare of grass and sunshine—long calm nights
    From which the silken sleeps were trotted out—
    He witness for me, with no amateur's
    Irreverent haste and busy idleness
    I've set myself to Art!'

I admit the truth of your criticism, and I have struggled against the spirit which hovers with clouding wings over all that I do; but the shadow has not lifted—God knows whether it ever will. Do you recollect, among those fine illustrations of Poe's works which we examined yesterday, the dim spectral head and sable pinions brooding mournfully over 'The City in the Sea?' Ah! its darkening counterpart flits over me. You have finished your work; come to my room for a few minutes."

They went up stairs together; and as Electra unlocked and bent over a large square trunk, her companion noticed a peculiar curl about the lines of the mouth and a heavy scowl on the broad brow.

"I want to show you the only bright, shining face I ever painted."

She unwrapped an oval portrait, placed it on the mantlepiece, and, stepping back, fixed her gaze on Irene. She saw a tremor cross the quiet mouth, and for some seconds the sad eyes dwelt upon the picture as if fascinated.

"It must have been a magnificent portrait of your cousin, years ago; but he has changed materially since it was painted. He looks much older, sterner, now."

"Would you have recognized it under any circumstances?"

"Yes—anywhere; if I had stumbled over it in the dusty crypts of Luxor, or the icy wastes of Siberia. I have never seen but one head that resembled that, or eyes that were in any degree comparable."

"Irene, I value this portrait above everything else save the original; and, as I may be called to pass through various perils, I want you to take care of it for me until I come back to W———. It is a precious trust, which I would be willing to leave in no hands but yours."

"You forget that, before long, I too, shall go to Virginia."

"Then pack it away carefully among your old family pictures, where it will be secure. I left my large and best paintings in Italy, with Aunt Ruth, who promised to preserve and send them to me as soon as the blockade should be raised."

"What are Mr. Young's views concerning this war?"

"He utterly abhors the party who inaugurated it, and the principles upon which it is waged. Says he will not return to America, at least for the present; and as soon as he can convert his property into money, intends to move to the South. He opposed and regretted Secession until he saw the spirit of the Lincoln dynasty, and from that time he acknowledged that all hope of union or reconstruction was lost. Have you heard anything from Harvey since the troubles began?"

"It is more than a year since I received a line from him. He was then still in the West, but made no allusion to the condition of the country."

"Irene, I hope to see Russell soon. You were once dear friends; have you any message for him—any word of kind remembrance?"

One of Irene's hands glided to her side, but she answered composedly:

"He knows that he always has my best wishes; but will expect no message."

On the following day Electra started to Richmond, taking with her a large supply of hospital stores which the ladies of W——— had contributed.

Eric had proposed to his niece the expediency of selling the Hill and becoming an inmate of his snug, tasteful, bachelor home; but she firmly refused to consent to this plan; said that she would spend her life in the house of her birth; and it was finally arranged that her uncle should reserve such of the furniture as he valued particularly, and offer the residue for sale, with the pretty cottage, to which he was warmly attached. During the remainder of autumn Irene was constantly engaged in superintending work for the soldiers, in providing for several poor families in whom she was much interested, and in frequent visits to the plantation, where she found more than enough to occupy her mind; and Eric often wondered at the admirable system and punctuality she displayed—at the grave composure with which she discharged her daily duties, and the invariable reticence she observed with regard to her past life.

CHAPTER XXXIII.

"Did you ring, Mass' Eric?"

"Yes; has Irene come home?"

"Not yet, sir."

"Bring some more wood."

Owing to the scarcity of coal, the grate had been removed and massive brass andirons substituted. John piled them with oak-wood, swept the hearth, and retired. It was a cold evening; there had been sleet the night before; the trees were glittering with icicles; but in the afternoon the sky cleared, and a sharp northwester promised good weather. Eric drew the sofa nearer the blazing fire and laid himself down to rest—waiting impatiently for the return of his niece, who had been absent since dinner. The library looked cheerful, comfortable, luxurious. Irene's pretty work-basket sat on the little mosaic table, close to the hearth; and by its side lay a volume of Tennyson open at "Locksley Hall," with a half-finished glove which she had been knitting that morning resting on the page. Upon the low mantlepiece stood two ruby-colored bulb-glasses containing purple hyacinths in full bloom; between them a fluted crystal vase of perfect white camellias from the greenhouse; and in a rich bohemian goblet three early golden crocuses looked out from a mass of geranium leaves. Bronze busts of Kepler, Herschel, and La Place crowned the heavy carved bookcases; the soft silvery glow of the lamp fell upon the form of the cripple, wrapped in a warm plaid dressing-gown, and showed the thin, sharply-cut visage of Paragon, who had curled himself lazily on the velvet rug. The room was very still, save the sound of the crackling fire and the chirping of the canary, whose cage had been placed on one of the broad window-sills. After a time, the door opened and the mistress came in.

"Irene! you must be nearly frozen. What kept you out so late?"

"I had more than usual to attend to at the Asylum this afternoon."

"What was the matter?"

"We have a new Matron, and I was particularly anxious that she should start right in one or two respects. I waited, too, in order to see the children at supper and satisfy myself about the cooking."

"How many orphans are there in the Asylum?"

"Thirty-four. I admitted two this evening —children of one of our soldiers who died from a wound received at Leesburg."

"Poor little things! I am afraid you will find numbers of similar instances before this war is at an end."

"We will try to find room for all such cases. The building will accommodate one hundred."

"You must be very cold; I will make John bring you a glass of wine."

"No, sir; I do not need it. My shawl was thick and warm."

Resting his elbow on the silken cushions, her uncle leaned forward so as to see her countenance distinctly. She had put out one hand on the shining head of her dog, who now sat close to her chair, gazing solemnly into the red coals; and her posture, as she rested far back against the morocco lining, betokened weariness. By contrast with the thick folds of her bombazine dress the face gleamed singularly white, and the curling brown lashes made fringy shadows on the polished cheeks.

"Irene."

She turned her head slightly and raised her eyes.

"Did you receive a letter which I sent to your room?"

"Yes, sir. It was from Dr. Arnold."

"He has established himself in Richmond."

"Yes, sir; his recent attack of rheumatism unfitted him for service in the field."

"I had a letter from Colonel Aubrey to-day. He wants to buy my house."

She made no comment, and her eyes drooped again to the perusal of the strange shapes which danced and flickered on the burnished andirons.

"What use do you suppose he has for it?"

"I can not imagine, unless he intends it as a home for Electra."

"What a witch you are at guessing; that is exactly it. He says, in this letter, that he may not survive the war, and wishes to have the assurance that his cousin is comfortably provided for before he goes into another battle. His offer is liberal, and I shall accept it."

"Well, I am glad she will own it—for I have often heard her speak of those old poplar-trees in the front-yard. She has always admired the place."

"I trust Aubrey will come back safely, marry some woman worthy of his heart and intellect, and live there happily himself. Do you believe the current report that he is engaged to Salome?"

"No, sir."

"Why not? She is certainly a brilliant girl, and an undoubted beauty."

"Such a temperament as hers would scarcely suit him, I think."

"But people often select their opposites."

"And for that reason I suspect that she would not make him happy. What a glowing beauty she is! As I went to the Asylum I saw her riding with some gentlemen, and I felt as if I could warm my fingers by holding them near her burning cheeks. Such complexions as hers are very rare at the South."

"I should not wonder if Russell married her, after all."

He hoped for some change of countenance implying concern, but no shadow hovered over the fair face. There was no uneasy movement of the dimpled hand which lay on Paragon's head, nor could he detect the faintest indication of interest. At this juncture the tea-bell summoned them to the dining-room, and she allowed her uncle no opportunity of renewing the conversation. When the meal was concluded and they had returned to the library, Irene drew her table and basket near the lamp and resumed her knitting. The invalid frowned, and asked impatiently:

"Can't you buy as many of those coarse things as you want, without toiling night and day?"

"In the first place, I do not toil; knitting is purely mechanical, very easy, and I like it. In the second place, I can not buy them, and our men need them when they are standing guard. It is cold work holding a musket in the open air such weather as this."

He looked annoyed and dived deeper among his cushions.

"Don't you feel as well as usual this evening, Uncle Eric?"

"Oh! I am well enough—but I hate the everlasting motion of those steel needles."

She rolled up the glove, put it in her basket, and rose.

"Shall I read to you? Or, how would you like a game of chess?"

"I do not expect you to humor my whims. Above all things, my child, I dread the thought of becoming troublesome to you."

"You can never be that, Uncle Eric; and I shall always be glad if you will tell me how I can make your time pass more pleasantly. I know this house must seem gloomy enough at best. Let us try a game of chess; we have not played since you came from Europe."

She brought the board and they sat down to the most quiet and absorbing of all games. Both played well, and when Eric was finally vanquished he was surprised to find, from the hands of the clock, that the game had lasted nearly two hours. As she carefully replaced the ivory combatants in their box, Irene said:

"Uncle, you know that I have long desired and intended to go to Richmond, but various circumstances combined to keep me at home. I felt that I had duties here which must first be discharged; now the time has come when I can accomplish my long-cherished plan. Dr. Arnold has taken charge of the hospital in Richmond which was established with the money we sent from W—— for the relief of our regiments. Mrs. Campbell is about to be installed as Matron, and I have to-day decided to join them. In his letter received this afternoon he orders me not to come, but I know that he will give me a ward when he finds me at his elbow. I am aware that you have always opposed this project, but I hope, sir, that you will waive your objections and go on with me next week."

"It is a strange and unreasonable freak, which, I must say, I do not approve of. There are plenty of nurses to be hired, who have more experience and are every way far more suitable for such positions."

"Uncle, the men in our armies are not hired to fight our battles; and the least the women of the land can do is to nurse them when sick or wounded. The call is imperative. Mothers and wives are, in most instances, kept at home; but I have nothing to bind me here. I have no ties to prevent me from giving my services in the only way in which I can aid the cause for which my father died. I feel it a sacred duty; and, Uncle Eric, it is useless to argue the matter. I am determined to go at once. Will you accompany me?"

"You will kill yourself."

"I could not die in a better cause."

"Is life so worthless, that you would rashly throw it away?"

"By no means. I am able to endure what I undertake."

"Does not one querulous invalid cripple sufficiently exercise your patience?"

"No, sir. Beside, I can take care of you in Richmond, as well as of others, who need me much more."

"What do you propose to do with the house, meantime?"

"I shall send the horses to the plantation, and take Andrew with me; he is an admirable nurse. Martha, also, whom I have tested on several occasions, can assist me greatly in the hospital. The other servants I shall leave here. John and Nellie will keep things in order. I have endeavored to foresee and remove all obstacles to my departure."

"Ah! but you have been so delicately nurtured, and the burden you would take upon yourself is so onerous."

"I have counted the cost."

She laid her hand gently on his whitening hair, and added pleadingly:

"Do not oppose me, Uncle Eric. I want your sanction in all that I do. There are only two of us left; go with me as my adviser—protector. I could not be happy if you were not with me."

His eyes filled instantly; and, drawing her close to him, he exclaimed tremulously:

"My dear Irene! there is nothing I would not do to make you happy. Happy, I fear you never will be. Ah! don't smile and contradict me; I know the difference between happiness and resignation. Patience, uncomplaining endurance, never yet stole the garments of joy. I will go with you to Virginia, or anywhere else that you wish."

"Thank you, Uncle Eric. I will try to make you forget the comforts of home, and give you no reason to regret that you sacrificed your wishes and judgment to mine. I must not keep you up any later."

She rang for Willis, and, taking a taper from the stand, proceeded to light the small lamp which had been placed in readiness on the table. With its use her uncle had long been familiar.

"You, surely, are not going up to that icehouse such a night as this? That marble floor will freeze you!"

"I shall not stay long. It is the first clear night we have had for more than a week, and I can not lose such an opportunity. The nebula in Orion will show splendidly, and,

'The Pleiads rising through the mellow shade,
Glitter like a swarm of fire-flies tangled in a silver braid.'

"What a devotee you are! What a bigot you would have been five hundred years ago! What a tireless Rosicrucian you would have made! What an indefatigable traveller after mythic Sangraal! You very often remind me of an aphorism of Emerson: 'No man is quite sane; each has a vein of folly in his composition, a slight determination of blood to the head, to make sure of holding him hard to some one point which Nature has taken to heart.'"

"I am no more insane than Emerson is orthodox or infallible, and a mild form of Sabeism ought to be tolerated even in this age, when it is used as a glittering ladder to God, to purity, and to peace. Here I am continually oppressed with a sense of desolation; as I walk these silent rooms, Father! Father! is the cry of my lonely soul. But yonder I forget my loss. In the observatory my griefs slip from me as did Christian's burden. I remember only the immeasurable heights and depths, the infinitude, the grandeur, and the glory of the universe—and there, as nowhere else, I can bow myself down, and say, humbly and truly, 'Not my will, oh, God! but thine!' Good-night, Uncle Eric. Willis, shut Paragon in his house before you go to sleep."

She wrapped a heavy black shawl around her shoulders, and, taking the lamp, went up to the observatory.

The Army of the Potomac had fallen back to Yorktown when Irene reached Richmond; and the preparations which were being made for the reception of the wounded gave melancholy premonition of impending battles.

Dr. Arnold had been intrusted with the supervision of several hospitals, but gave special attention to one established with the funds contributed by the citizens of W———, and thither Irene repaired on the day of her arrival.

In reply to her inquiries, she was directed to a small room and found the physician seated at a table, examining a bundle of papers. He saw only a form darkening the door-way, and, without looking up, called out gruffly:

"Well, what is it? What do you want?"

"A word of welcome."

He sprang to his feet instantly, holding out both hands.

"Dear child! Queen! God bless you! How are you? Pale as a cloud and thin as a shadow. What the deuce are you doing here? I ordered you to stay at home, did n't I?"

He had caught her hands eagerly to his lips and held them like a vice.

"Home was too dreary. I wanted to see you, to be with you once more, to work here in your sight, by your direction. Don't scold and growl at me for coming. Give me a morsel of affection; oh, Doctor! I am hungry! hungry and desolate."

She lifted her sorrow-stricken face to his and felt his tears fall thick on her silky hair.

"Dear child! I knew how it would be. I wanted to go to you, but I could not. Irene, don't look so dreary and hopeless; it wrings my heart to see that expression on your mouth. You know I am glad to have you, my treasure, my beloved child. You know that you are the very light of my life. Growl at you, Queen! I will see myself hanged first! Sit down here by me. Where is Eric?"

"He was much fatigued, and I left him at the hotel."

"You have been ill a long time, Irene, and have kept it from me. That was not right; you should have been honest in your letters. A pretty figure you will cut nursing sick folks! Work in my sight, indeed! If you say work to me again I will clap you into a lunatic-asylum, and keep you there till the war is over. Turn your face to the light."

"I am well enough in body; it is my mind only that is ill at ease; my heart only that is sick—sorely sick. Here I shall find employment, and, I trust, partial forgetfulness. Put me to work at once; that will be my best medicine."

"And you really missed me, Queen?"

"Yes, inexpressibly; I felt my need of you continually. You must know how I cling to you now."

Again he drew her little hands to his granite mouth and seemed to muse for a moment.

"Doctor, how is Electra?"

"Very well—that is, as well as such an anomalous, volcanic, torrid character ought to be. At first she puzzled me (and that is an insult I find it hard to forgive), but finally I found the clue. She is indefatigable, and astonishingly faithful as a nurse; does all her duty, and more, which is saying a good deal—for I am a hard task-master. Are n't you afraid that I will work you more unmercifully than a Yankee factory-child or a Cornwall miner? See here, Queen; what do you suppose brought Electra to Richmond?"

"A desire to render some service to the sick and suffering, and also to be comparatively near her cousin."

"Precisely; only the last should be first, and the first last. Russell is a perverse, ungrateful dog."

As he expected, she glanced up at him, but refrained from comment.

"Yes, Irene—he is a soulless scamp. Here is his cousin entirely devoted to him, loving him above everything else in this world, and yet he has not even paid her a visit, except in passing through to Yorktown with his command. He might be a happy man, if he would but open his eyes and see what is as plain as the nose on my face—which, you must admit, requires no microscope. She is a gifted woman, and would suit him exactly—even better than my salamander, Salome."

A startled, incredulous expression came into Irene's large eyes, and gradually a look of keen pain settled on her features.

"Aha! did that idea never occur to you before?"

"Never, sir; and you must be mistaken."

"Why, child? The fact is patent. You women profess to be so quick-witted, too, in such matters—I am amazed at your obtuseness. She idolizes Aubrey."

"It is scarcely strange that she should; she has no other relatives near her, and it is natural that she should love her cousin."

"I tell you I know what I say! she will never love anybody else as she loves Aubrey. Beside, what is it to you whether he marries her or not?"

"I feel attached to her and want to see her happy."

"As Russell's wife?"

"No, sir. The marriage of cousins was always revolting to me."

She did not flinch from his glittering gray eye, and her grieved look deepened.

"Is she here? Can I see her?"

"She is not in this building, but I will inform her of your arrival. I have become much interested in her. She is a brilliant, erratic creature, and has a soul! which can not safely be predicated of all the sex, nowaday. Where are you going?"

"Back to Uncle Eric. Will you put me in the same hospital with Electra and Mrs. Campbell?"

"I will put you in a straight-jacket! I promise you that."

Electra was agreeably surprised at the unusual warmth with which Irene received her some hours later; but little suspected why the lips lingered in their pressure of hers, or understood the wistful tenderness of the eyes which dwelt so fondly on her face. The icy wall of reserve had suddenly melted as if in the breath of an August noon, and dripped silently down among things long passed. Russell's name was casually mentioned more than once, and Electra fell asleep that night wholly unconscious that the torn and crumpled pages of her heart had been thoroughly perused by the woman from whom she was most anxious to conceal the truth.

Having engaged a suite of rooms near the hospital, a few days sufficed for preliminary arrangements, and Irene was installed in a ward of the building to which she had requested Dr. Arnold to appoint her.

Thus, by different, by devious thorny paths, two sorrowing women emerged upon the broad highway of Duty, and, clasping hands, pressed forward to the divinely-appointed goal— Womanly Usefulness.

Only those who have faithfully ministered in a hospital can fully appreciate the onerous nature of the burdens thus assumed—can realize the crushing anxiety, the sleepless apprehension, the ceaseless tension of brain and nerve, the gnawing intolerable sickness and aching of heart over sufferings which no human skill can assuage; and the silent blistering tears which are shed over corpses of men whose families kneel in far distant homes, praying God's mercy on dear ones lying at that moment stark and cold on hospital cots with strangers' hands about the loved limbs. Ah! within these mournful penetralia are perpetually recurring scenes of woe, of resignation, and of sublime endurance, transcending in pathos aught that fiction ever painted; and as the Nation's martyrs drop swiftly down into nameless billowy graves, that fret the quiet green surface of our broad and sunny land, the bleeding tendrils of a Nation's sympathy trail athwart the rude head-stones, and from stern lips come the prophecy:

" . . . Let them slumber!
No King of Egypt in a pyramid
Is safer from oblivion, though ho number
Full seventy cerements for a coverlid.
These Dead be seeds of life, and shall encumber
The sad heart of the land until it loose
The clammy clods and let out the spring growth
In beatific green through every bruise.
Each grave our nationality has pieced
By its own majestic breadth, and fortified
And pinned it deeper to the soil. Forlorn
Of thanks be, therefore, no one of these graves!"

Day by day, week after week, these tireless women-watchers walked the painful round from patient to patient, administering food and medicine to diseased bodies, and words of hope and encouragement to souls who shrank not from the glare and roar and carnage of battle—but shivered and cowered before the darling images which deathless memory called from the peaceful, happy Past. It was not wonderful that the homesick sufferers regarded them with emotions which trenched on adoration, or that often, when the pale thin faces lighted with a smile of joy at their approach, Irene and Electra felt that they had a priceless reward.

CHAPTER XXXIV.

"Mother, I did not flinch! They shot the flag out of my hand, and I bathed it with my blood when I fell on it. Here is the staff—I held on to the very last. Don't you see it, Mother, all smeared and clotted with blood?"

Raving with delirium, a light-haired, slender boy of seventeen summers struggled to rise from his cot, and, grasping a corner of the calico quilt, stretched it toward Irene, who sat a few yards off, spreading a blister. Laying aside the ointment, she approached and took the extended hand.

"Yes, Willie, I see it; and I know you did your duty. I will take care of the staff for you; now go to sleep."

"I can't sleep; the din of the cannon wakes me. I want to go home. Mother, why don't you carry me to my own room, my own bed, where I can see Harry and hear Jessie sing? Help me to my feet. Mother; I promised to make a new flag-staff."

His fair smooth cheeks were flushed with fever from the wound received at the Battle of Seven Pines, and his beautiful dilated eyes gleamed unnaturally as he gazed appealingly at the tall form standing at his pillow—an elegant, queenly form, clad in mourning vestments, with spotless linen cuffs and collar and white muslin apron.

She placed her pearly hand on his hot brow and bent tenderly over him.

"Not to-night, Willie. When you are stronger I will carry you to Harry and Jessie. Now you must try to sleep."

"You'll stay by me, Mother, if I shut my eyes?"

"Yes. I will not leave you."

He smiled contentedly; and while her cold fingers wandered soothingly over his forehead the long lashes fell upon his cheeks, and in delirious dreaming he muttered on of the conflict and incidents of carnage. From his entrance into the hospital he had fancied her his mother, and she fostered the only illusion which could gild the fleeting hours of his young life. His deeds of daring had won honorable mention from the brigade commander, and Irene had written to his mother, in a distant state, detailing the circumstances and urging her to hasten to him. But to-night the symptoms showed that, ere the dawning of another day, the brave spirit would desert its boyish prison.

"Give me some water, please."

The feeble voice came from an adjoining cot, where lay an emaciated, wrinkled old man, with gray hair straying over the pillows that propped him into an almost upright posture. She put the glass to his trembling lips, and, as he drained it, tears trickled down the furrowed face.

"What distresses you, Mr. Wheeler? Tell me, won't you?"

"I am about to die, and I long so for the face of my wife. If I could have seen her again it would not seem so hard. It is easy to die on the battle-field, and I expected that when I left home; but to sicken and die in a hospital, away from my family and my comrades—oh! this is bitter! bitter! You have been kind to me—as gentle and good as my own daughter Mary could have been—and, if you please, I would like to send some messages to my people at home. You have written for me once—will you do it again—and for the last time?"

"Certainly; just as often as you like."

She gave him a powerful stimulant; brought her portfolio to the side of the cot, and wrote at his dictation.

"Tell my wife I had hoped and prayed to be spared to get home once more, but it was not the will of God, and I trust she will try to bear up like a Christian. I am not afraid to die; I have done my duty to my God and to my country; and though my heart clings to my dear ones, way down in Mississippi, I know I am going home to rest. Tell her she must not grieve for our brave boy, Joe; he died as a Confederate soldier should. I buried him where he fell, and we will soon meet where battles and separation are unknown. I want Mary and her children to live at home, and if Edward lives through the war, he will provide for all. I want my watch given to my oldest grandson, Calvin, as soon as he is of age. I send my love to all, and especially to my poor sister Emily. I send a kiss to Mary and her children, and to my dear, dear wife, whom I hope to meet soon in heaven. May God bless and preserve them all, for Jesus Christ's sake."

His voice was weak and unsteady, and his breathing rapid, short, labored.

As she folded the letter and closed the portfolio the surgeon entered, and went slowly from patient to patient—speaking gently to some and feeling cautiously at the wrists of others who slept. At the two last cots he lingered long, and his benevolent face saddened as he noted the change that a few hours had wrought.

"Dr. Whitmore, I have been giving Mr. Wheeler strong eggnog this afternoon."

"All perfectly right, and let him have the ammonia as often as his pulse indicates need of it."

He sighed heavily, and she followed him into the passage.

"After all, Miss Huntingdon, we shall lose them both. I had such strong hope of young Walton yesterday; but it is of no use; he will not live till morning. Poor fellow! It is too bad! too bad!"

"Can we do nothing more?"

"Nothing. I have racked my brain, exhausted my remedies. Wheeler, too, is sinking very rapidly, and you must stimulate him constantly. These typhoid-pneumonia cases are disheartening. By the way, you are overtaxing your strength. Let me send Martha down here to relieve you to-night. For forty-eight hours you have not closed your eyes. Take some rest to-night; your presence can do no good now."

"I prefer to remain; how are the cases up stairs?"

"Doing finely, except Moorhouse; and I have strong faith in his constitution. I shall sit up with him to-night, to watch the effect of the veratrum. God bless you, Miss Irene! you have a melancholy watch before you."

As she returned to her post Andrew came in with a pitcher of ice-water; and after creeping across the room several times, arranging the covering on the cots, he unrolled his blankets on the floor and laid himself down to sleep within reach of his mistress' hand.

It was a long, low, rather narrow room, lined with rows of cots, which stretched on either side to the door, now left open to admit free circulation of air. A muffled clock ticked on the mantlepiece. Two soldiers, who had been permitted to visit their sick comrades, slumbered heavily—one with head drooped on his chest, the other with chair tilted against the window-facing, and dark-bearded face thrown back. The quivering flame of the candle gleamed fitfully along the line of features—some youthful, almost childish; others bearing the impress of accumulated years; some crimsoned with fever, others wan and glistening with the dew of exhaustion; here a forehead bent and lowering, as in fancy the sleeper lived over the clash and shock of battle; and there a tremulous smile, lighting the stern manly mouth as the dreamer heard again the welcome bay of watch-dog on the door-step at home, and saw once more the loved forms of wife and children springing joyfully from the cheery fireside to meet his outstretched arms. A few tossed restlessly, and frequent incoherent mutterings wandered, waif-like, up and down the room, sometimes rousing Andrew, who once or twice lifted his head to listen and then sank back to slumber.

Before a small pine table, where stood numerous vials, Irene drew her chair, and, leaning forward, opened her pocket-bible and rested her head on her hand.

She heard the painful breathing of the old man, who had fallen into a heavy stupor, and as she sat reading her hand stole to his feeble pulse, pausing to count its fluttering. Twice she rose, administered the stimulants, and renewed the bottles at his feet, the mustard on his wasted wrists. Taking the skeleton hand in hers she chafed it vigorously; but sixty-three years had worn away the bonds of flesh and the soul was near its exodus. Sorrowfully she watched the sharpening features, which five weeks of nursing had rendered singularly familiar; and as she thought of the aged wife to be widowed, and the daughter orphaned, memories of her own father's kisses stirred the great deeps of her spirit and tears gathered in her calm eyes.

"Ha! ha! ha! They will never get to Richmond! Johnston is down there—and Longstreet is there—and our regiment is there! Johnston is between them and Richmond—ha! ha!"

The wounded boy started up, twirling one arm as if in the act of cheering and then fell back, groaning with pain which the violent effort cost him.

Irene stooped over him, and, softly unbuttoning his shirt-collar, removed the hot bloody cloths from his lacerated shoulder and replaced them with fresh folds of linen, cold and dripping. She poured out a glass of water and lifted his head, but he frowned, and exclaimed:

"I won't have it in a tumbler. Mother, make Harry bring me a gourdful fresh from the spring. I say—send Buddie for some."

She humored the whim, walked out of the room, and paused in the passage. As she did so, a dark form glided unperceived into a dim corner, and when she re-entered the room with the gourd of water the figure passed through the hall-door out into the night.

"Here is your gourd, Willie, fresh and cold."

He swallowed the draught eagerly, and his handsome face wore a touching expression as he smiled and whispered:

"Hush! Jessie is singing under the old magnolia down by the spring. Listen! 'Fairy Belle!' We used to sing that in camp; but nobody sings like Jessie. So sweet! so sweet!"

He set his teeth hard, and shuddered violently; and taking his fingers in hers she found them clenched.

"Andrew!"

"Here I am, Miss Irene."

"Go up stairs and ask the doctor to come here."

The surgeon came promptly.

"I am afraid he is going into convulsions. What shall I do for him?"

"Yes—just what I have been trying to guard against. I fear nothing will do any good; but you might try that mixture which acted like a charm on Leavens."

"Here is the bottle; how much shall I give?"

"A spoonful every half-hour while the convulsions last. If he can swallow it, it can't possibly do any harm and may ease his suffering. Poor fellow! may the vengeance of a righteous God seek out his murderer! I would stay here with you, Miss Huntingdon, if I could render any service. As it is, I am more needed up stairs."

The paroxysms were short, but so severe that occasionally she required Andrew's assistance to hold the sufferer on his cot, and as they grew less frequent she saw that his strength failed rapidly. Finally he fell into a troubled sleep, with one hand clutching her arm.

Nearly an hour passed thus, and the nurse knelt softly beside her charge and prayed long and fervently that the soul of the young martyr might find its home with God, and that his far-off mourning mother might be strengthened to bear this heavy burden of woe. There, in the shadow of Death, the woman's spirit soared far from sin and sorrow, from the stormy shores of Time, and held holy communion with her Maker—pleading for aid, for grace, and resignation through the remaining years of her earthly pilgrimage.

As she knelt with her face upturned a soft warm palm was laid upon her forehead, and a low, sweet, manly voice pronounced in benediction:

"May the Lord bless you, Irene, and abundantly answer all your prayers."

She rose quickly and put out her disengaged hand.

"Oh, Harvey! dear friend! Thank God, I have found you once more."

He lifted the candle and held it near her face, scanning the sculptured features; then stooped and kissed her white cheek.

"I felt that I could not be mistaken. I heard our soldiers blessing a pale woman in black, with large eyes bluer than summer skies, and hair that shone like rays of a setting-sun; and I knew the silent, gentle, tireless watcher before they told her name. For many years I have prayed that you might become an instrument of good to your fellow-creatures, and to-night I rejoice to find you, at last, an earnest coworker."

"Where have you been this long time, Harvey? And how is it that you wear a Confederate uniform?"

"I am chaplain in a Texas regiment, and have been with the army from the beginning of these days of blood. At first it was a painful step for me; my affections, my associations, the hallowed reminiscences of my boyhood, all linked my heart with New York. My relatives and friends were there, and I knew not how many of them I might meet among the war-wolves that hung in hungry herds along the borders of the South. Moreover, I loved and revered the Union—had been taught to regard it as the synonyme of national prosperity. Secession I opposed and regretted at the time as unwise; but to the dogma of consolidated government I could yield no obedience; and when every sacred constitutional barrier had been swept away by Lincoln—when *habeas corpus* was abolished, and freedom of speech and press denied—when the Washington conclave essayed to coerce freemen, to 'crush Secession' through the agency of sword and cannon—then I swore allegiance to the 'Seven States,' where all of republican liberty remained. The fierce and unholy spirit of the North appalled and disgusted me. I felt that I could have no connection with a people who madly plunged into fratricidal war, who goaded their soldiers to rapine, to the massacre of women and children, and who left no means untried to inflict upon the Cotton-States all the unparalleled horrors of a servile insurrection. The billows of innocent blood which their fury shed surged between us as an everlasting gulf. As Ruth to Naomi, so I turned fondly to the fair free land of my adoption and her devoted sons: 'Thy people shall be my people, and thy God my God. Where thou diest I will die, and there will I be buried.' Though I look upon my mother's face no more in this world, and for ever resign the consolation of my father's blessing and my sister's smile, I shall never see New York again. My step has passed away from the homestead—my shadow from the dear old hearthstone. Henceforth my home is with the South; my hopes and destiny hers; her sorrows and struggles mine."

His white scholarly hands were sunburnt now; his bronzed complexion, and long, untrimmed hair and beard gave a grim, grizzled aspect to the noble face; and the worn and faded uniform showed an acquaintance with the positive hardships and exposure of an active campaign.

"I expected nothing less from you, my brother. I felt that our holy cause must claim your sympathy and support; and I am proud, and inexpressibly happy, to find you in our matchless and devoted army. You were dear to me before; but, ah, Harvey! how much dearer now in these dark days of trial, which you have voluntarily chosen to share with a young, brave, struggling Nation!"

His eyes dwelt upon her face as she looked gladly at him, and over her waving hair his hands passed tenderly, as they had done long years before, when she was an invalid in his father's house.

"You have found your work and learned contentment in usefulness, since that Spring day on which we talked together in the shadow of the wild-cherry tree. Irene, the peaceful look of your childhood has come back to your face."

"Yes, thanks to your guidance, I have found employment for head and hands; but my heart is not conquered. I have yet to learn patient, perfect resignation."

"You ought to be grateful and happy for the good you are accomplishing every day. I hear much of the influence you exert here; your name is constantly on the lips of many a convalescent; and in the dead of night, in the deep hush of camp, I have listened to a fervent, tearful petition ascending to the Throne of Grace from an elderly man, who told me he had not prayed since his childhood till you knelt beside his cot here and asked God to spare his life to his country and his family. Does not such blessed fruitage content you?"

"You overrate my services. I try to do my duty; but such cases as these two before us discourage me—bow down my heart."

"I accept the estimate of those of your countrymen over whom you have watched and prayed and toiled. True, it is very melancholy to lose any; but, in such a mass, we must not expect to save all. With my face pressed against the window-pane, I have been watching you for more than an hour—ever since Col. Aubrey came out—and I know all the sadness of the circumstances that surround you; how painful it is for you to see those two men die."

"Col. Aubrey? He has not been here."

"Yes; I passed him on the steps; we rode up together from camp. He came on special business, and returns at daylight; but I shall remain several days, and hope to be with you as much as the nature of your engagements will permit. Aubrey is from W———; you know him, of course?"

"Yes, I know him."

He saw a shade of regret drift over her countenance, and added:

"I have many things to say to you, and much to learn concerning your past; but this is not the time or place for such interchange of thought and feeling. To-morrow we will talk; to-night I could not repress my impatience to see you, though but for a few moments."

They had conversed in low, smothered tones, and now, gently unclasping young Walton's fingers, which still grasped her arms, Irene went back to the old man's pillow and bent over the ghastly face, where the chill of death had already settled.

"Feel how thready and feeble the pulse is; a few more throbs, and the heart will be stilled. It is hard, hard to see him die, after all my care and watching. Five long weeks I have nursed him, and now this is the end. Harvey, pray for the departing soul, that, through Christ, his salvation may be sure."

The chaplain bowed his head, but no sound broke the sad silence; and, some moments after, Irene laid her ivory fingers on the lids and pressed them down over the glazed eyes.

"He is at rest. 'Whosoever believeth in Me shall never die,' saith the Lord. He believed, and read much to him during his illness, and found that he had no fear of eternity. Another patriot gone—another soul to bear witness before God against our oppressors and murderers."

She drew the sheet over the face of the dead, and beckoning to the two soldiers who now stood near, silent and awe-struck, they took up the cot and bore it into a small room adjoining.

"Ah, Irene! how harrowing such frequent spectacles must be. I should think this position would be almost intolerable to one of your keen sympathies."

"How harrowing, only God knows."

She drew a chair near young Walton, and, seating herself, continued:

"It would be intolerable, but for the conviction that I sometimes save lives—lives precious to friends and country. Hard as that case may seem, this is sadder still. That old man had but few years left at best; this boy stands on the verge of manhood, with the fair green meadows of life stretching dewy and untrodden before him, enamelled with hope and bounded by shining peaks which his brave, ambitious spirit panted to scale. A mother's pride and solace, a sister's joy, one of a Nation's treasured guardians, stricken down in his first battle—bathing his country's riddled banner in his warm young blood. How long—how long will Almighty God withhold his vengeance from the wolfish hordes who are battening upon the blood of freemen? Harvey, if there be not a long and awful retribution for that Cain-cursed race of New England, there is neither justice nor truth in high heaven. I have become strangely attached to this boy. He mistakes me for his mother, follows me eagerly with his eyes, clings to my dress, fondles my hands. Around his neck is suspended a locket containing her miniature; and yesterday, when I dressed his wound, he felt for it—showed me how he kissed it before going into battle—believing that it would prove a talisman. What harm could befall, with his mother's face over his heart? Only a private in the ranks! No stars and bars to deck his homespun jacket—no official pomp and glittering paraphernalia to please his youthful fancy—none of the gorgeous accessories which gild the 'stern profession' like jewels on a corpse—no badge of distinction, save his ghastly death-wound. The tenderly nurtured darling of Southern parents, cheerful in the midst of unparalleled hardships, content with meagre rations which his negroes at home would scornfully reject, standing dreary watch in snow and sleet and rain, with memories of luxury and fireside joys tempting him from his gloomy, solitary post—springing to meet the columns of the foe as though the Nation's fate depended upon his individual valor, and asking but a grave on the soil he died defending. Only a private in the ranks! Oh, to this consecrated legion, stretching like a wall of flesh along the borders of our land, what a measureless debt we owe! When Independence is obtained, and white-robed Peace spreads her stainless hands in blessing over us, let history proclaim, and let our people reverently remember, that to the uncomplaining fortitude and sublime devotion of the private soldiers of the Confederacy, not less than to the genius of our generals and the heroism of our subordinate officers, we are indebted for Freedom.

She laid her head close to the boy's mouth to listen to his low breathing, and the minister saw her tears fall on his pillow and gleam on his auburn locks. The delirium seemed to have given place to the dreamless sleep of exhaustion, and folding one of her hands around his fingers, with the other she softly stroked the silky hair from his fair smooth forehead.

"Irene, will my presence here aid or comfort you? If so, I will remain till morning."

"No; you can do no good. It is midnight now, and you must be wearied with your long ride. You can not help me here, but to-morrow I shall want you to go with me to the cemetery. I wish his family to have the sad consolation of knowing that a minister knelt at his grave when we laid the young patriot in his last resting-place. Good-by, my brother, till then. Electra is in the next room; will you go in and speak to her?"

"No; I will see her early in the morning."

He left her to keep alone her solemn vigil; and through the remaining hours of that starry June night she stirred not from the narrow cot—kept her fingers on the sufferer's fleeting pulse—her eyes on his whitening face. About three o'clock he moaned, struggled slightly, and looked intently at her. She gave him some brandy, and found that he swallowed with great difficulty.

"Willie, are you in pain?"

"Is it you, Mother—and are we at home?" he asked indistinctly.

"You are going home, Willie; you will soon be there."

"I have not said my prayers to-night. Mother, hold my musket a minute."

He put out his arm as if to consign it to her care and folded his hands together.

"Our Father, who art in heaven, hallowed be thy name——." His voice sank to a whisper, inaudible for some seconds; then he paused, as if confused; a troubled look crossed his features, the hazel eyes filled, and the hands fell powerless on his chest. Laying her hand on his brow, Irene slowly repeated a favorite psalm which had seemed to haunt his mind two days before—that psalm of promise: "The Lord is my Shepherd; I shall not want." Whether he understood it now she never knew, but his fingers crept caressingly to her face, feebly stroking her cheek while she spoke, and when she concluded he seemed trying to recall something.

"Jessie knows it all; I don't——." Then came, indistinctly, snatches of the infant prayer which had been taught him at his truckle-bed in the nursery.

After a short silence he shivered, and murmured:

"Corporal of the guard! post number nine! Mother, it is cold standing guard to-night, but the relief will soon be round. Standing guard——Mother——."

His eyes wandered around the dim room then slowly closed, as he fell into the sleep that knew no earthly waking.

A sick man a few yards off asked for some water, and as Irene received the tumbler from his hand he said, under his breath:

"He is worse to-night, is n't he, Ma'm?"

"Yes. How is that pain in your side? I must put a blister on it if it grows more severe."

"It does not trouble me as much as it did about dark. How is my fever?"

"Not so high by fifteen beats. You will be able to take quinine at seven o'clock."

She snuffed the candle and resumed her seat, and again silence reigned—silence broken only by the deep breathing of the patients and the sudden jingle of the vials on the table as a hungry mouse ran among them to nibble at the open jar of simple cerate.

The air grew chilly as a light mist gathered along the James, and finally the rumble of wheels on the paved streets told that people were beginning to stir in the sleeping city. Slowly a half-hour rolled away; Irene could barely feel the faint pulsations at Willie Walton's wrist, and as she put her ear to his lips a long, last shuddering sigh escaped him—the battle of life was ended. Willie's Relief had come. The young sentinel passed to his Eternal Rest.

"The picket 's off duty for ever."

Tears dropped on the still face as the nurse cut several locks of curling hair that clustered around the boyish temples and took from the motionless heart the loved picture which had been so often and so tenderly kissed in the fitful light of camp-fires. Irene covered the noble head, the fair, handsome features, with her handkerchief, and, waking Andrew, pointed to the body—left her own ward and entered one beyond the passage.

It was smaller, but similar in arrangement to the room where she had passed the night. A candle was sputtering in its socket, and the cold, misty, white dawn stared in at the eastern window upon rows of cots and unquiet, muttering sleepers. There, in the centre of the room, with her head bowed on the table, sat, or rather leaned, Electra, slumbering soundly, with her scarlet shawl gathered about her shoulders—her watch grasped in one hand and the other holding a volume open at "Hesperid-Æglé."

Irene lifted the black curls that partially veiled the flushed cheek, and whispered:

"Electra, wake up! I am going home."

"Is it light yet, out of doors? Ah, yes—I see! I have been asleep exactly fifteen minutes—gave the last dose of medicine at four o'clock. How are those two men? I am almost afraid to ask."

"Dead. Willie lived till daylight. Both dead."

"Oh! how sad! how discouraging! I went to your door twice and looked in, but once you were praying, and the last time you had your face down on Willie's pillow, and as I could do nothing, I came back. Dr. Whitmore told me they would die, and it only made me suffer to look at what I could not relieve. I am thankful my cases are all doing well; that new prescription has acted magically on Mr. Hadly yonder, who has pneumonia. Just feel his skin—soft and pleasant as a child's."

"I have some directions to leave with Martha, about giving quinine before the doctor comes down, and then I shall go home. Are you ready?"

"Yes. I have a singular feeling about my temples and an oppression when I talk—should not wonder if I have caught cold."

"Electra, did you see Harvey last night?"

"No. Where did he come from?"

"He is chaplain in a regiment near Richmond, and said he would see us both this morning. Was Russell here last night?"

"Russell? No. Why do you ask? Is he in the city? Have you seen him?"

She rose quickly, laid her hand on Irene's, and looked searchingly at her.

"I have not seen him, but your cousin Harvey mentioned that Col. Aubrey came up with him, on some very important errand, and had but a few hours to remain. I will get my shawl and join you in five minutes. Electra, you must stay at home and rest for a day or two; you are feverish, and worn-out with constant watching."

CHAPTER XXXV

"It is a mercy that she is delirious; otherwise her unavoidable excitement and anxiety would probably prove fatal. She is very ill, of course; but, with careful nursing, I think you have little to apprehend. Above all things, Irene, suffer nobody to bolt into that room with the news—keep her as quiet as possible. I have perfect confidence in Whitmore's skill; he will do all that I could, though I would not leave her if I did not feel it my duty to hurry to the battle-field. Queen, you look weary; but it is not strange, after all that you have passed through."

"Doctor, when will you start?"

"In twenty minutes."

"Has any intelligence been received this morning?"

"Nothing but confirmation of last night's news. Hill holds Mechanicsville, and the enemy have fallen back in the direction of Powhite Swamp. A general advance all along our lines will be made to-day, and I must be off. What is the matter? Surely you are not getting frightened."

"Frightened—Dr. Arnold? No. I have no fears about the safety of Richmond; defeat is not written in Lee's lexicon; but I shudder in view of the precious human hecatombs to be immolated on yonder hills before McClellan is driven back. No doubt of victory disquiets me, but the thought of its awful price."

She shaded her face and shuddered.

"Cheer up, child. We may make quicker work of it than you seem to imagine. But suppose reverses should overtake us, what would you do?"

"I shall remain here as long as a man or woman is left to attend to the wounded; and if—which God forbid!—our army should be forced back by overwhelming numbers, I rejoice to know that the spirit of 'Edinburg After Flodden' will be found in Richmond. Northern banners shall never flaunt over our capital, tainting the atmosphere we breathe; in such dire emergency the people are resolved, and we will chant the grand words of Aytoun, as we gather round our magnificent national pyre:

'T were better that in fiery flame the roofs should thunder down,
Than that the foot of foreign foe should trample in the town!
* * * * * *
Though the ramparts rock beneath us, and the walls go crashing down,
Though the roar of conflagration bellow o'er the sinking town;
There is yet one place of shelter, where the foeman can not come,
Where the summons never sounded, of the trumpet or the drum.
There shall we find rest and refuge, with our dear departed brave;
And the ashes of the city be our universal grave.'

I repeat it, Doctor—not the fate of Richmond troubles me—for I have not a shadow of doubt that God will give us victory—but the thought of the lives to be yielded up in its defence. As a nation, we shall rejoice; but, ah! the desolation hovering over thousands of happy home-circles, ready to swoop down, darkening peaceful hearthstones for all time. What a burden of wailing woe this day will bear to the ears of a pitying God."

"True, it is an awful reflection; but we have counted the cost and it will not do to repine. Extermination, rather than submission to their infamous tyranny. Hampden's immortal motto has become our own: '*Vestigia nulla retrorsum!*' But I must go, Queen. I wish you were safely back in W———, away from these horrors that so sicken your soul. Child, take care of yourself. Have you anything more to say? Talk fast."

"I directed Andrew to give Cyrus a small box of cordials, which I received yesterday from home. You may find use for it."

She paused, and her whole face quivered as she laid her clasped hands on his arm.

"Well—what is it? Dear child, what moves you so?"

"Doctor, promise me that if Colonel Aubrey is mortally wounded you will send instantly for me. I must see him once more."

Her head went down on her hands, and she trembled as white asters do in an early autumn gale. Compassionately the old man drew one arm around her.

"After all, then, you do care for him—despite your life-long reserve and apparent indifference? I have expected as much, several times, but that imperturbable sphinx-face of yours always baffled me. My child, you need not droop your head; he is worthy of your love; he is the only man I know whom I would gladly see you marry. Irene, look up—tell me—did Leonard know this? Conscious of your affection for Aubrey, did he doom you to your lonely lot?"

"No. My father died in ignorance of what would have pained and mortified him beyond measure. Knowing him as well as you do, can you suppose that I would ever have allowed him to suspect the truth? I realized my duty, and fulfilled it; that is the only consolation I have left. It never caused him one throb of regret, or furnished food for bitter reflection; and the debt of respect I owe to his memory shall be as faithfully discharged. If Colonel Aubrey lives to enjoy the independence for which he is fighting—if he should be spared to become a useful, valued member of society—one of the pure and able statesmen whom his country will require when these dark days of strife are ended—I can be content; though separated from him and watching his brilliant career afar off. But if he must give his life for that which he holds dearer still, I ask the privilege of seeing him again, of being with him in his last moments. This consolation the brave spirit of my father would not withhold from me, were communion allowed between living and dead; this none can have the right to deny me."

"If such be your stern and melancholy resolution, what happiness can the future contain?"

"My future holds the hope of promoting God's glory, and of contributing, as far as one feeble woman can, to the happiness and weal of her fellow-creatures. I cheat myself with no delusive dreams; I know that my way is, and ever must be, lonely; but, putting my trust in Him who never yet withheld strength and guidance in the hour of need, I say to myself:

'O, pusillanimous Heart, be comforted—
And, like a cheerful traveller, take the road,
Singing beside the hedge.'"

The doctor gathered up her hands in his, and said coaxingly:

"May I tell Aubrey all this? it will, at least, comfort him in some degree."

"No; you must tell him nothing. I know what is best for him and for me."

"Oh, child! what harm could come of it?"

"Ask me no more; but give me the promise to send a messenger, if he should be severely, dangerously wounded."

"I promise that you shall know all as early as possible. If you receive no tidings, believe that he is uninjured. As yet, his regiment has not moved forward, but I know not how soon it may. Heaven preserve you! my precious child."

He pressed a kiss on the drooped head and left her to resume her watch in the darkened room where Electra had been ill with typhoid-fever for nearly three weeks. It was thought that she contracted the disease in the crowded hospital; and when delirium ensued, Irene temporarily relinquished her ward to other nurses and remained at the boarding-house, in attendance on her friend. It was a season of unexampled anxiety, yet all was singularly quiet in the beleaguered city. Throughout the Confederacy hushed expectancy reigned. Gallant Vicksburg's batteries barred the Mississippi; Beauregard and Price, lion-hearted idols of the West, held the Federal army in Corinth at bay; Stonewall Jackson—synonyme of victory—after sweeping like a whirlwind through the Valley, and scattering the columns that stealthily crept southward, had arrived at Richmond at the appointed time. A greater than Serrurier, at a grander than Castiglione, he gave the signal to begin; and as a sheet of flame flashed along the sombre forests of Chickahominy the nation held its breath and watched the death-grapple of bannered armies around its proud young capital. Thank God! we had no cravens there to jeopardize our cause; the historic cycle had revolved and heroic ages dawned again. Neither ancient, mediæval, nor modern lore can furnish a parallel for the appalling panorama of blood and fire which stretched from Mechanicsville to Westover—for the brilliant Seven Days conflict, which converted twenty-six miles of swamp and forest into a vast necropolis.

During Friday the wounded came slowly in, and at four in the afternoon the roar of artillery told that the Battle of Gaines' Mill was raging; that the enemy were fighting desperately, behind entrenchments which none but Confederate soldiers could successfully have assaulted. Until eight at night the houses trembled at every report of cannon, and then McClellan's grand army, crippled and bleeding, dragged itself away, under cover of darkness, to the south bank of the Chickahominy. Saturday saw a temporary lull in the iron storm; but the wounded continued to arrive, and the devoted women of the city rose from their knees to minister to the needs of these numerous sufferers. Sunday found our troops feeling about the swamps for the retreating foe; and once more, late in the afternoon, distant thunder resounded from the severely-contested field of Savage's Station, whence the enemy again retreated.

On Sabbath morning Irene learned that Russell's command had joined in the pursuit; and during that day and night, as the conflict drifted farther southward and details became necessarily more meagre, her anxiety increased. Continually her lips moved in prayer, as she glided from Electra's silent room to aid in dressing the wounds of those who had been disabled for further participation in the strife; and, as Monday passed without the receipt of tidings from Dr. Arnold, she indulged the hope that this day would end the series of butcheries and that Russell would escape uninjured. During Tuesday morning Electra seemed to have recovered her consciousness, but in the afternoon she relapsed into incoherent muttering of "Cuyp," "Correggio," "Titian's Bella," and "my best, great picture left in Florence."

Irene was sitting at her bedside, rolling bandages, when the sudden, far-distant, dull boom of cannon, followed by the quick rattling of the window-panes, gave intimation that the long contest was fiercely renewed. Prophetic dread seized her; the hideous To-Come scowled at her in the distance; and, as the roll of cloth dropped from her fingers, she covered her eyes to shut out the vision of horror. The long evening hours crept by in mournful procession—trooping phantom-shadows filled the room—night fell at last, an unheeded flag of truce—and people stood in their doors, at their windows, many clustered on the pavements, listening in solemn silence to the fiend-like roar of the fifty pieces of artillery that, like a fiery crescent, crowned Malvern Hill. A courier had arrived with intelligence that here the enemy's forces were very strongly posted, were making desperate resistance; and, though no doubt of the result was entertained, human nature groaned over the carnage.

At ten o'clock, having given a potion and renewed the folds of wet linen on Electra's head, Irene stole back to the window, and, turning the shutters, looked down the street. Here and there an anxious group huddled on the corners, with ears strained to catch every sound, and, while she watched, a horseman clattered at hard gallop over the paving-stones, reined up at the door of the boarding-house, swung himself to the sidewalk, and, an instant after, the sharp clang of the bell rang startlingly through the still mansion.

"Oh, my God! It has come at last!"

Irene groaned, and leaned heavily against the window-facing; and quick steps came up the stairway—Martha entered, and held out a slip of paper.

"Miss Irene, Cyrus has just brought this."

Her mistress' icy fingers clutched it, and she read:

"Come at once. Aubrey is badly wounded. Cyrus will show the way.
"HIRAM ARNOLD."

"You are going to faint, Miss Irene! Drink some of this cordial!"

"No. Tell Andrew to go after the carriage as quick as possible, and have it brought here immediately; and ask Uncle Eric to come to my room at once."

Irene went to her own apartment, which adjoined Electra's, put on her bonnet and veil, and, though the night was warm, wrapped a shawl about her.

Mr. Mitchell entered soon after, and started at sight of his niece's face.

"Irene, what does this mean? Where are you going at this hour?"

"To the battle-field!—to Malvern Hill. Colonel Aubrey is mortally wounded, and I must see him. Will you go with me? Oh, Uncle Eric! if you have any mercy in your soul, ask me no questions now! only go with me."

"Of course, my dear child, I will go with you, if it is possible to procure a carriage of any kind. I will see—"

"I have had one engaged for three days. Martha, stay with Electra till I come back; leave her on no account. If you notice any change, send for Dr. Whitmore. Here is my watch; count her pulse carefully, and as long as it is over one hundred give her, every two hours, a spoonful of the medicine in that square vial on the table. I trust to you, Martha, to take care of her. If she should be rational and ask for me, tell her nothing about the battles, and say I have gone to see a sick man and will be back soon. Come, Uncle Eric."

They entered the close-carriage which she had ordered reserved for her, and she called Cyrus to the door.

"Did you see Colonel Aubrey after he was wounded?"

"I only had a glimpse of him, as they brought him in. Miss Irene, he was shot in the breast."

"You know the way; ride outside; and, Cyrus, drive as fast as possible."

The night was gloomy and spectral as Sheol, and the wind sobbed a *miserere* through the sombre forests that bordered the road, which was now crowded with vehicles of all descriptions hastening to and returning from the field of action. Under ordinary circumstances, with no obstacles intervening, it was a long ride; and to Irene the way seemed interminable. During the first hour utter silence reigned within the carriage, and then, as the driver paused to allow an ambulance to pass, Eric put his hand on his niece's arm and said tenderly:

"Irene, why did you deceive me so long? Why could you not trust your uncle's love?"

She shrank farther back in one corner, and answered with a voice which he could scarcely recognize as hers.

"If you love me spare me all questions now."

By the glimmer of the carriage-lamps she could see the wagons going to and fro—some filled with empty coffins, some with mangled sufferers. Now and then weary, spent soldiers sat on the roadside, or struggled on toward the city which they had saved, with their arms in slings, or hands bound up, or bloody bandages across their stern faces. After another hour, when the increasing number of men showed proximity to the scene of danger, Cyrus turned away from the beaten track, and soon the flash of lights and hum of voices told that they were near the place of destination. The carriage stopped and Cyrus came to the door.

"We are at the lines and I can't drive any nearer. If you will wait, I will go and find Master."

It was one o'clock; and as they waited, men passed and repassed with blazing torches, some bearing wounded men, whose groans rose above the confusion. The cannonading had long since ceased, and Eric called to a group of soldiers belonging to the Infirmary corps.

"What is the last news from the front? Have the enemy fallen back?"

"Not yet; but they are getting ready to run again, as usual. By daylight they will be out of sight, and we shall be all day to-morrow hunting them up. Their style is to fight about three hours and run the balance of the twenty-four. They take to the swamps like all other such miserable varments."

The delay seemed intolerably long, and for the first time an audible moan escaped Irene just as Cyrus came back accompanied by a muffled figure.

"Irene, my child."

She leaned out till her face nearly touched Dr. Arnold's.

"Only tell me that he is alive and I can bear all else."

"He is alive, and sleeping just now. Can you control yourself if I take you to him?"

"Yes; you need not fear that I will disturb him. Let me go to him."

He gave her his arm and led her through the drizzling rain for some distance—avoiding, as much as possible, the groups of wounded, where surgeons were at their sad work. Finally, before a small tent, he paused, and whispered:

"Nerve yourself, dear child."

"Is there no hope?"

She swept aside her long mourning-veil and gazed imploringly into his face.

Tears filled his eyes, and, hastily averting his head, he raised the curtain of the tent and drew her inside.

A candle burned dimly in one corner, and here, on a pallet of straw, over which a blanket had been thrown, lay the powerful form of the dauntless leader, whose deeds of desperate daring had so electrified his worshipping command but a few hours before. The noble head was pillowed on a knapsack; one hand pressed his heart, while the other drooped nerveless at his side, and the breast of his coat was saturated with the blood which at intervals oozed through the bandages and dripped upon the straw. The tent was silent as a cemetery, and not a sound passed Irene's white fixed lips as she bent down and looked upon the loved face, strangely beautiful in its pallid repose. The shadowy wings of the bitter By-Gone hovered no longer over the features, darkening their chiselled perfection; a tranquil half-smile parted the lips and unbent the lines between the finely-arched black brows.

Sinking softly on the floor of the tent, Irene rested her chin on her folded hands and calmly watched the deep sleep. So passed three-quarters of an hour; then, as Dr. Arnold cautiously put his fingers on the pulse, the sufferer opened his eyes.

Irene was partially in the shade, but, as she leaned forward, a sudden, bewildered smile lighted his countenance; he started up and extended one arm.

"Irene! My darling! Do I dream, or are you indeed with me?"

"I have come to nurse you, Russell; but if you do not calm yourself the doctor will send me away."

She took the outstretched hand in both hers, and pressed her lips repeatedly upon it.

"Come close to me. I am helpless now, and can not go to you."

She seated herself on the edge of the straw, laid her shawl in her lap, and lifting his head, rested it on the soft woollen folds. Dr. Arnold removed the warm cloth soaked with blood, placed a cold, dripping towel on the gaping wound, and, after tightening the bandages to check the hemorrhage, passed out of the tent, leaving the two alone.

"Oh, Irene! this is a joy I never hoped for. I went at night to the hospital in Richmond, just to get a glimpse of you—to feast my eyes with another sight of your dear, dear face! I watched you ministering like an angel to sick and wounded soldiers, and I envied them the touch of your hand—the sound of your voice. I little expected to die in your arms. This reconciles me to my fate; this compensates for all!"

Her fingers tenderly smoothed the black locks that clung to his temples, and, bending down, she kissed his forehead. His uninjured arm stole up around her neck, drew her face to his, and his lips pressed hers again and again.

"Dear Russell, you must be quiet, or you will exhaust yourself. Try to sleep—it will refresh, strengthen you."

"Nothing will strengthen me. I have but a short time to live; shall I sleep away the opportunity of my last earthly communion with you, my life-long idol? Oh, Irene! my beautiful treasure! this proof of your love sweetens death itself. There have been hours (even since we parted a year ago) when I reproached you for the sorrow and pain you sternly meted out to me and to yourself. When I said bitterly, *if* she loved me as she should, she would level all barriers—she would lay her hands in mine—glorify my name by taking it as my wife, and thus defy and cancel the past. I was selfish in my love; I wanted you in my home; I longed for the soft touch of your fingers, for your proud, dazzling smile of welcome when the day's work was ended; for the privilege of drawing you to my heart and listening to your whispered words of encouragement and fond congratulation on my successes. I knew that this could never be; that your veneration for your father's memory would separate us in future as in the past; that my pleadings would not shake your unfortunate and erroneous resolution; and it was hard to give up the dearest hope that ever brightened a lonely man's life. Now I know, I feel, that your love is strong, deathless as my own, though long locked deep in your heart. I know it by the anguish in your face, by the quiver of your mouth, by your presence in this place of horrors. God comfort and bless you, my own darling!—my brave, patient, faithful Irene!"

He smiled triumphantly and drew her hand caressingly across his cheek.

"Russell, it is useless now to dwell upon our sorrowful past; what suffering our separation has cost me none but my God can ever know. To His hands I commit my destiny, and 'He doeth all things well.' In a little while you will leave me, and then—oh! then I shall be utterly desolate indeed! But I can bear loneliness—I can walk my dreary earthly path uncomplainingly; I can give you up for the sake of my country, if I have the blessed assurance that you have only hastened home before me, waiting for me there—that, saved through Christ, we shall soon meet in Heaven and spend Eternity together. Oh, Russell! can you give me this consolation, without which my future will be dark indeed? Have you kept your promise, to live so that you could at last meet the eyes of your God in peace?"

"I have. I have struggled against the faults of my character; I have earnestly endeavored to crush the vindictive feelings of my heart; and I have conscientiously tried to do my duty to my fellow-creatures, to my command, and my country. I have read the bible you gave me; and, dearest, in praying for you I have learned to pray for myself. Through Jesus, I have a sure hope of happiness beyond the grave. There, though separated in life, you and I shall be united by death. Oh, Irene! but for your earnest piety this precious anticipation might never have been mine. But for you, I would have forgotten my mother's precepts and my mother's prayers. Through your influence I shall soon join her where the fierce waves of earthly trial can lash my proud soul no more."

"Thank God! Oh, Russell! this takes away the intolerable bitterness of parting; this will support me in coming years. I can brave all things in future."

She saw that a paroxysm of pain had seized him. His brow wrinkled, and he bit his lips hard, to suppress a groan. Just at this moment Dr. Arnold re-entered, and immediately gave him another potion of morphine.

"Aubrey, you must be quiet, if you would not shorten your life."

He silently endured his suffering for some moments, and, raising his eyes again to Irene's, said in a tone of exhaustion:

"It is selfish to make you witness my torture; but I could not bear to have you leave me. There is something I want to say while I have strength left. How is Electra?"

"Partially delirious still, but the doctor thinks she will recover. What shall I tell her for you?"

"That I loved and remembered her in my dying hour. Kiss her for me, and tell her I fell where the dead lay thickest, in a desperate charge on the enemy's batteries—that none can claim a nobler, prouder death than mine—that the name of Aubrey is once more glorified—rebaptized with my blood upon the battle-field. Irene, she is alone in the world; watch over and love her for my sake. Doctor, give me some water."

As the hemorrhage increased despite their efforts to staunch it, he became rapidly weaker, and soon after, with one hand locked in Irene's, he fell asleep.

She sat motionless, supporting his head, uttering no sound, keeping her eyes fixed on his upturned countenance. Dr. Arnold went noiselessly in and out on various errands of mercy; occasionally anxious, weather-beaten soldiers softly lifted the curtain of the tent, gazed sadly, fondly, on the prostrate figure of the beloved commander, and turned away silently, with tears trickling down their bronzed faces. Slowly the night waned, and the shrill tones of *reveille* told that another day had risen before the murky sky brightened. Hundreds, who had sprung up at that call twenty-four hours ago, now lay stiffening in their gore, sleeping their last sleep, where neither the sound of fife and drum, nor the battle-cry of comrades, would ever rouse them from their final rest before Malvern Hill— over which winds wailed a requiem, and trailing, dripping clouds settled like a pall.

The bustle and stir of camp increased as preparations were made to follow the foe, who had again taken up the line of retreat; but within the tent unbroken silence reigned. It was apparent that Russell was sinking fast, and at eight o'clock he awoke, looked uneasily around him, and said feebly:

"What is going on in front?"

"McClellan has evacuated Malvern Hill and is in full retreat toward his gunboats," answered the doctor.

"Then there will be no more fighting. My shattered regiment will rest for a season. Poor fellows! they did their duty nobly yesterday. Tell my men for me that I am inexpressibly proud of their bravery and their daring, and that, though my heart clings fondly to my gallant regiment, I glory in the death I die—knowing that my soldiers will avenge me. Give my love to one and all, and tell them, when next they go into battle, to remember him who led their last charge. I should like to have seen the end of the struggle—but Thy will, oh, my God! not mine."

He lifted his eyes toward heaven, and for some moments his lips moved inaudibly in prayer. Gradually a tranquil expression settled on his features, and as his eyes closed again he murmured faintly:

"Irene—darling—raise me a little."

They lifted him and rested his head against her shoulder.

"Irene!"

"I am here, Russell; my arms are around you."

She laid her cheek on his and listened to catch the words; but none came. The lips parted once, and a soft fluttering breath swept across them. Dr. Arnold put his hand over the heart—no pulsation greeted him; and, turning away, the old man covered his face with his handkerchief.

"Russell, speak to me once more."

There was no sound—no motion. She knew then that the soldier's spirit had soared to the shores of Everlasting Peace, and that not until she joined him there would the loved tones again make music in her heart. She tightened her arms around the still form and nestled her cheek closer to his, now growing cold. No burst of grief escaped her, to tell of agony and despair:

"But like a statue solid set,
And moulded in colossal calm,"

she sat, mute and resigned, at the foot of the Red Dripping Altar of Patriotism, where lay, in hallowed Sacrifice, her noble, darling Dead. In the morning-light her face looked rigid, pallid as his, and the tearless but indescribably mournful eyes were riveted on his placid, handsome features. Eric and Harvey Young stood in one corner of the tent, wiping away tears which would not be restrained; and finally Dr Arnold stooped, and said falteringly:

"My dear child, come with me now."

She did not seem to hear him, and he repeated his words, trying, at the same time, to unwind her arms.

She yielded, and with her own hands smoothed out and cut a lock of hair that waved over his gleaming forehead.

Leaning over him, she kissed the icy lips; then rose, and clasping her hands, murmured:

"Farewell, my own brave Russell!"

The minister approached and stood before her. She lifted her wan dry face, and, as she put out her arms to him, a wintry smile flitted over the mouth that had seemed frozen.

"Harvey! Harvey! he was my all! He was the idol of my childhood! and girlhood! and womanhood! Oh! pray for me—that I may be patient and strong in my great desolation."

* * * * *

Electra's speedy convalescence repaid the care bestowed upon her; and one afternoon, ten days after quiet had again settled around the Confederate capital, she insisted on being allowed to sit up later than usual, protesting that she would no longer be regarded as an invalid.

"Irene, stand in the light where I can see you fully. How worn and weary you look! I suspect I am regaining my health at the expense of yours."

"No; I am as well in body as I could desire; but, no doubt, my anxiety has left its traces on my countenance."

She leaned over Electra's chair and stroked back the artist's shining hair.

"I wish you would let me see the papers. My eyes are strong enough now, and I want to know exactly what has taken place everywhere during my sickness. It seems to me impossible that General Lee's army can face McClellan's much longer without bringing on a battle, and I am so anxious about Russell. If he should be hurt, of course I must go to him. It is very strange that he has not written. Are you sure no letters came for me?"

"There are no letters, I am sure; but I have a message for you. I have seen him once since you were taken sick."

"Ah! what is it? He heard that I was ill, and came to see me, I suppose. When was he here?"

Irene bent down and kissed her companion tremulously, saying slowly:

"He desired me to kiss you for him. Electra, I have not told you before, because I feared the effect upon you in your weak state; but there have been desperate battles around Richmond during your illness, and the Federals have been defeated—driven back to James river."

"Was Russell wounded? Yes—I understand it all now! Where is he? Oh! tell me! that I may go to him."

She sprang up, but a death-like pallor overspread her face and she tottered to the open window.

Irene followed the thin figure, and, putting her arms about her, made her lean against her.

"He was wounded on the last day, and I went to see him; you were then delirious."

"Let me go at once! I will not disturb him; I will control myself! Only let me see him to-day!"

"Electra, you can not see him. He has gone to his God; but in his dying hour he spoke of you fondly, sent love, and—"

The form reeled, drooped, shivered, and fell back insensible in Irene's arms.

So heavy was the swoon that it seemed as if her spirit had fled to join her cousin's in endless union; but at length consciousness returned, and with it came the woful realization of her loss. A long, low wail rose and fell upon the air like the cry from lips of feeble, suffering, helpless children, and her head sank upon the shoulder of the sad-faced nurse, whose grief could find no expression in sobs, or moans, or tears.

"Dead! dead! and I shall see his dear face no more! Oh! why did you not let me die, too? What is my wretched life worth now? One grave might have held us both! My noble, peerless Russell! the light of my solitary life! Oh, God! be merciful! take me with my idol! Take me now!"

Very tenderly and caressingly Irene endeavored to soothe her—detailed the circumstances of her cousin's death, and pointed her despairing soul to a final reunion.

But no rift appeared in the artist's black sky of sorrow; she had not yet learned that, in drawing near the hand that holds the rod, the blow is lightened; and she bitterly demanded of her Maker to be released from the burden of life.

"Electra, hush your passionate cries! crush back your rebellious words. Your heart knows no depth of agony which mine has not sounded; and yet, in this season of anguish, when Russell is taken from us both, I look upon his grave and feel that,

". . . . . I am strong,
Knowing ye are not lost for aye among
The hills, with last year's thrush. God keeps a niche
In Heaven, to hold our idols: and albeit
He brake them to our faces, and denied
That our close kisses should impair their white,
I know we shall behold them raised, complete,
The dust swept from their beauty—glorified
New Memnons, singing in the great God-light!'"

CHAPTER XXXVI.

The sunlight of a warm spring day flashed through the open window, and made golden arabesque tracery on the walls and portraits of the parlor at Huntingdon Hill. The costly crimson damask curtains had long since been cut into shirts for the soldiers and transported to the Army of Tennessee, and air and sunshine entered unimpeded. Electra sat before her canvas in this room, absorbed in the design which now engaged every thought. The witchery of her profession had woven its spell about her, banishing for a time the spectral Past.

The extension of the Conscription statute had, several months before, deprived Irene of a valued and trusty overseer; and to satisfy herself concerning the character of his successor, and the condition of affairs at home, she and her uncle had returned to W———, bringing Electra with them.

Irene stood on the colonnade, leaning over the back of Eric Mitchell's arm-chair, dropping crumbs for the pigeons that cooed and scrambled at her feet, and looking dreamily down the avenue at the band of orphans who had just paid her a visit, and were returning to the asylum, convoyed by the matron.

"What contented-looking, merry little children those are," said her uncle, watching the small figures diminish as they threaded the avenue.

"Yes; they are as happy as orphans possibly can be. I love to look into their smiling rosy faces and feel their dimpled hands steal timidly into mine. But, Uncle, Dr. Arnold has finished his nap and is waiting for you."

She gave him her arm to the library-door, saw him seated comfortably at the table where the doctor was examining a mass of papers, then joined Electra in the parlor.

"What progress are you making, Electra?"

"Very little. I can't work well to-day. Ruskin says that no artist has fully grasped or matured his subject who can not quit one portion of it at any moment and proceed to the completion of some other part. Doubtless he is correct; but I am so haunted by those blue eyes that I can paint nothing else this afternoon. Do you recognize them? Yours, Irene. Forgive me; but I can find no others, in imagination or in life, that so fully express serenity. My work has taken marvellous hold upon me; sleeping or waking, it follows, possesses me, I shall not hurry myself; I intend that the execution shall be equal to my ideal—and that ideal entirely worthy of the theme. I want to lay my 'Modern Macaria,' as the first offering of Southern Art, upon my country's altar, as a nucleus around which nobler and grander pictures, from the hands of my countrymen and women, shall cluster. In sunny climes like ours, my glorious Art had its birth, its novitiate, its apotheosis; and who dare say that future ages shall not find Art-students from all nations pressing, like pilgrims, to the Perfected School of the Southern States? Ancient republics offered premiums, and saw the acme of the arts; why not our Confederate republic, when days of national prosperity dawn upon us? If the legislature of each state would annually purchase, for the embellishment of the galleries and grounds of its capital, the best picture or statue produced within its borders during the twelvemonths, a generous emulation would be encouraged. Our marble-hearted land will furnish materials, which Southern genius can mould into monuments of imperishable beauty. This war furnishes instances of heroism before which all other records pale, and our Poets, Sculptors, and Painters have only to look around them for subjects which Greek or Italian Art would glorify and immortalize.

"'I do distrust the poet who discerns
No character or glory in his times,
And trundles back his soul five hundred years.'

"Our resources are inexhaustible, our capabilities as a people unlimited, and we require only the fostering influences which Cosmo De Medici and Niccolo Niccoli exerted in Florence, to call into action energies and latent talents of which we are, as yet, scarcely conscious. Such patrons of Art and Literature I hope to find in the planters of the Confederacy. They have wealth, leisure, and every requisite adjunct, and upon them, as a class, must devolve this labor of love—the accomplishment of an American Renaissance—the development of the slumbering genius of our land. Burke has remarked: 'Nobility is a graceful ornament to the civil order; it is the Corinthian capital of polished society.' Certainly Southern planters possess all the elements of this highest order of social architecture, and upon their correct appreciation of the grave responsibility attending their wealth and influence depends, in great degree, our emancipation from the gross utilitarianism which has hitherto characterized us, and our progress in refinement and æsthetic culture. As we are distinct, socially and politically, from other nations, so let us be intellectually and artistically. The world has turned its back upon us in our grapple with tyranny; and, in the hour of our triumph, let us not forget that, as we won Independence without aid or sympathy, so we can maintain it in all departments."

"Electra, in order to effect this 'consummation devoutly to be wished,' it is necessary that the primary branches of Art should be popularized and thrown open to the masses. Mill contends, in his Political Economy, that the remuneration of the peculiar employments of women is always far below that of employments of equal skill carried on by men, and he finds an explanation in the fact that they are overstocked. Hence, in improving the condition of women, it is advisable to give them the readiest access to independent industrial pursuits and extend the circle of their appropriate occupations. Our Revolution has beggard thousands and deprived many of their natural providers; numbers of women in the Confederacy will be thrown entirely upon their own resources for maintenance. All can not be mantua-makers, milliners, or school-teachers; and, in order to open for them new avenues of support, I have determined to establish in W—— a School of Design for women—similar in plan, though more extensive, than that founded some years ago by Mrs. Peter, of Philadelphia. The upper portion of the building will be arranged for drawing-classes, wood-engraving, and the various branches of Design; and the lower, corresponding in size and general appearance, I intend for a circulating-library for our county. Over that School of Design I want you to preside; your talents, your education, your devotion to your Art fit you peculiarly for the position. The salary shall be such as to compensate you for your services; and, when calmer days dawn upon us, we may be able to secure some very valuable lecturers among our gentlemen-artists. I have a large lot on the corner of Pine street and Huntingdon avenue, opposite the courthouse, which will be a fine location for it, and I wish to appropriate it to this purpose. While you are adorning the interior of the building, the walls of which are to contain frescos of some of the most impressive scenes of our Revolution, I will embellish the grounds in front, and make them my special charge. I understand the cultivation of flowers, though the gift of painting them is denied me. Yesterday I sold my diamonds for a much larger amount than I supposed they would command, and this sum, added to other funds now at my disposal, will enable me to accomplish the scheme. Dr. Arnold and Uncle Eric cordially approve my plan, will aid me very liberally, and as soon as tranquillity is restored I shall succeed in erecting the building without applying to any one else for assistance. When your picture is finished, I wish you to make me a copy to be hung up in our School of Design, that the students may be constantly reminded of the debt of gratitude we owe our armies. How life-like your figures grow; I can almost see the quiver of that wife's white lips and hear the dismal howling of the dead man's dog."

The canvas, which she leaned forward to inspect more closely, contained an allegorical design representing, in the foreground, two female figures. One stern, yet noble-featured, crowned with stars—triumph and exultation flashing in the luminous eyes; Independence, crimson-mantled, grasping the Confederate Banner of the Cross, whose victorious folds streamed above a captured battery, where a Federal flag trailed in the dust. At her side stood white-robed, angelic Peace, with one hand over the touchhole of the cannon against which she leaned, and the other extended in benediction. Vividly the faces contrasted—one all athrob with national pride, beaming with brilliant destiny, the other wonderfully serene and holy. In the distance, gleaming in the evening light which streamed from the west, tents dotted a hill-side; and intermediate between Peace and the glittering tents stretched a torn, stained battle-field, over which the roar and rush of conflict had just swept, leaving mangled heaps of dead in attestation of its fury. Among the trampled, bloody sheaves of wheat, an aged, infirm Niobe-mother bent in tearless anguish, pressing her hand upon the pulseless heart of a handsome boy of sixteen summers, whose yellow locks were dabbled from his death-wound. A few steps farther, a lovely young Wife, kneeling beside the stalwart, rigid form of her Husband, whose icy fingers still clutched his broken sword, lifted her woful, ashen face to heaven in mute despair, while the fair-browed infant on the ground beside her dipped its little snowy, dimpled feet in a pool of its father's blood, and, with tears of terror still glistening on its cheeks, laughed at the scarlet coloring. Just beyond these mourners, a girl of surpassing beauty, whose black hair floated like a sable banner on the breeze, clasped her rounded arms about her dead patriot-Lover, and kept her sad vigil in voiceless agony—with all of Sparta's stern stoicism in her blanched, stony countenance. And, last of the stricken groups, a faithful dog, crouching close to the corpse of an old silver-haired man, threw back his head and howled in desolation. Neither blue shadows, nor wreathing, rosy mists, nor golden haze of sunset glory, softened the sacrificial scene, which showed its grim features strangely solemn in the weird, fading, crepuscular light.

"How many months do you suppose it will require to complete it?" asked Irene, whose interest in the picture was scarcely inferior to that of its creator.

"If I work steadily upon it, I can soon finish it; but if I go with you to a Tennessee hospital, I must, of course, leave it here until the war ends. After all, Irene, the joy of success does not equal that which attends the patient working. Perhaps it is because 'anticipation is the purest part of pleasure.' I love my work; no man or woman ever loved it better; and yet there is a painful feeling of isolation, of loneliness, which steals over me sometimes and chills all my enthusiasm. It is so mournful to know that, when the labor is ended and a new chaplet encircles my brow, I shall have no one but you to whom I can turn for sympathy in my triumph. If I feel this so keenly now, how shall I bear it when the glow of life fades into sober twilight shadows and age creeps upon me?

"'O my God! my God!
O supreme Artist, who, as sole return
For all the cosmic wonder of Thy work,
Demandest of us just a word—a name.
"My Father"—thou hast knowledge—only thou,
How dreary 't is for women to sit still
On winter nights by solitary fires,
And hear the nations praising them far off,
Too far!'"

She threw down her brush and palette, and, turning toward her companion, leaned her purplish head against her.

"Electra, it is very true that single women have trials for which a thoughtless, happy world has little sympathy. But lonely lives are not necessarily joyless; they should be, of all others, most useful. The head of a household, a wife and mother, is occupied with family cares and affections—can find little time for considering the comfort or contributing to the enjoyment of any beyond the home-circle. Doubtless she is happier, far happier than the unmarried woman; but to the last belongs the privilege of carrying light and blessings to many firesides—of being the friend and helper of hundreds; and because she belongs exclusively to no one, her heart expands to all her suffering fellow-creatures. In my childhood I always thought of Old-Maids with a sensation of contempt and repulsion; now I regard those among them who preserve their natures from cynicism and querulousness, and prove themselves social evangels of mercy, as an uncrowned host of martyrs. Electra, remember other words of the same vigorous, gifted woman whom you so often quote:

"'And since we needs must hunger—better, for man's love,
Than God's truth! better, for companion sweet,
Than great convictions! let us bear our weights,
Preferring dreary hearths to desert souls!'

"Remember that the woman who dares to live alone, and be sneered at, is braver and nobler and better than she who escapes both in a loveless marriage. It is true that you and I are very lonely, and yet our future holds much that is bright. You have the profession you love so well and our new School of Design to engage your thoughts; and I a thousand claims on my time and attention. I have Uncle Eric to take care of and to love; and Dr. Arnold, who is growing quite infirm, has promised me that, as soon as he can be spared from the hospitals, he will make his home with us. When this storm of war has spent itself, your uncle's family will return from Europe and reside here with you. Harvey, too, will come to W—— to live—will probably take charge of Mr. Campbell's church—and we shall have the pleasure and benefit of his constant counsel. If I could see you a member of that church I should be better satisfied—and you would be happier."

"I would join to-morrow, if thereby I could acquire your sublime faith and strength and resignation. Oh, Irene! my friend and comforter! I want to live differently in future. Once I was wedded to life and my Art—pre-eminence in my profession, fame, was all that I cared to attain; now I desire to spend my remaining years so that I may meet Russell beyond the grave. His death broke the ties that bound me to this world; I live now in hope of reunion in God's eternal kingdom. I have been selfish and careless and complaining; but, oh! I want to do my whole duty henceforth. Irene, my calm, sweet, patient guide, teach me to be more like you."

"Electra, take Christ for your model, instead of an erring human being like yourself, constantly falling short of her own duty. With Harvey to direct us, we ought to accomplish a world of good, here in sight of Russell's grave. Cheer up! God's great vineyard stretches before us, calling for laborers. Hand in hand we will go in and work till evening shades close over us; then lift up, in token of our faithfulness, rich ripe clusters of purple fruitage. You and I have much to do during these days of gloom and national trial—for upon the purity, the devotion, and the patriotism of the women of our land, not less than upon the heroism of our armies, depends our national salvation. To jealously guard our homes and social circles from the inroads of corruption, to keep the fires of patriotism burning upon the altars of the South, to sustain and encourage those who are wrestling along the border for our birthright of freedom, is the consecrated work to which we are called; and beyond this bloody baptism open vistas of lifelong usefulness, when the reign of wrong and tyranny is ended, when the roar of battle, the blast of bugle, and beat of drum is hushed among our hills, and Peace! blessed Peace! again makes her abode in our smiling, flowery valleys. Hasten the hour, oh! my God! when her white wings shall hover over us once more!"

The eyes of the artist went back to the stainless robes and seraphic face of her pictured Peace in the loved "Modern Macaria," and, as she resumed her work, her brow cleared, the countenance kindled as in days of yore, bitter memories hushed their moans and fell asleep at the wizard-touch of her profession, and the stormy, stricken soul found balm and rest in Heaven-appointed Labor.

Standing at the back of Electra's chair, with one hand resting on her shoulder, Irene raised her holy violet eyes and looked through the window toward the cemetery, where glittered a tall marble shaft which the citizens of W—— had erected over the last quiet resting-place of Russell Aubrey. Sands of Time were drifting stealthily around the crumbling idols of the morning of life, levelling and tenderly shrouding the Past, but sorrow left its softening shadow on the orphan's countenance and laid its chastening finger about the lips which meekly murmured, "Thy will be done." The rays of the setting sun gilded her mourning-dress, gleamed in the white roses that breathed their perfume in her rippling hair, and lingered like a benediction on the placid, pure face of the lonely woman who had survived every earthly hope; and who, calmly fronting her Altars of Sacrifice, here dedicated herself anew to the hallowed work of promoting the happiness and gladdening the paths of all who journeyed with her down the chequered aisles of Time.

"Rise, woman, rise!
To thy peculiar and best altitudes
Of doing good and of enduring ill,
Of comforting for ill, and teaching good,
And reconciling all that ill and good
Unto the patience of a constant hope.
. . . Henceforward, rise, aspire,
To all the calms and magnanimities,
The lofty uses and the noble ends,
The sanctified devotion and full work,
To which thou art elect for evermore!"

www.ingramcontent.com/pod-product-compliance
Lightning Source LLC
Chambersburg PA
CBHW031443160426
43195CB00010BB/827